The Church Bells of Warwickshire

Their Founders, Inscriptions, Traditions and Uses

By

The late Rev H T Tilley, M A

(Sometime Vicar of Claverdon)

and

H B. Walters, M A , F S.A

With 26 Plates and 20 Illustrations in the Text

Birmingham

Cornish Brothers Ltd

Publishers to the University

37 New Street

1910

Oswestry
Woodall, Minshall Thomas & Co,
Caxton Press

DEDICATED TO

THE VEN. WILLIAM WALTERS, M.A.

ARCHDEACON OF WORCESTER.

PREFACE.

THE CHURCH BELLS OF WARWICKSHIRE, like some other books of the same kind, has been long in process of compilation. But my satisfaction at its final completion and publication can only be tempered with regret that the original compiler of the work has not lived to issue it under his own name alone.

Henry Timothy Tilley was an enthusiastic "bell-hunter" from his undergraduate days, and though I do not know what first attracted him to this pursuit, his notes shew that he began to visit Warwickshire belfries and collect bell-inscriptions in 1874, when he was only about twenty years of age. In the two or three succeeding years before his ordination he visited from his home at Edgbaston a large number (about 120) of the Warwickshire churches, chiefly in his own neighbourhood and round Nuneaton and Kineton. The results of his labours up to 1877 were admirably summarised in a short paper read before the Birmingham and Midland Institute in that year. Parochial duties naturally had the first claim on his time thenceforward, but in 1892 he had visited nearly every church steeple in the county, and a second paper read before the same Society in that year not only formed a useful supplement to the first, but in conjunction with it gave an interesting survey of the campanological treasures of Warwickshire.

It was then his intention to work up and enlarge his notes into book form, but devotion to parochial work and intermittent breakdowns in health frustrated his hopes, and although during his last years beneficed almost in the centre of the county, the care of an extensive parish demanded all his time and energies. Thus when he was called to his rest in December 1905 he left behind him no more than a carefully compiled list of the bell-inscriptions with occasional interesting notes, the two published papers summarising the more valuable results of his labours, and such rubbings and casts of stamps as he had been able to collect from time to time.

It was the earnest wish of his widow and family that these notes should not suffer neglect, but should be published in such a form as he had meditated, and when the work of editing and completing them was offered to the present writer, it was with the greatest satisfaction and gratitude that he undertook to pay this tribute to the memory of his friend and fellow-worker. Though the Introduction is necessarily my own work throughout, as well as the actual text of the second part, and though in the necessary process of revising and bringing up to date I have personally visited over sixty of the towers in the county, I could not but feel that my predecessor's careful and patient labours (if only embodied in my own) justified the appearance of his name in the chief position on the title-page.

My warmest thanks in the first place are due to Mrs. Tilley for the great interest she has shewn in the work, and the generous assistance she has rendered with a view to its completion and publication. I have also to express my gratitude to a long list of helpers in my own labours, first and foremost to Mr. W. E. Falkner of Stratford-on-Avon, a most diligent and painstaking worker, who has most kindly devoted the greater part of his hard-earned leisure for over a year to examining bells in his own neighbourhood and elsewhere, which I was unable to visit myself Mr Falkner has been most enthusiastic and persevering, and his work has been done with the utmost care and accuracy The bell-founding firms of Messrs. Mears and Stainbank, Taylor Barwell, and Carr have shewn their usual courtesy and readiness to give information, and to the first-named I am specially indebted for the illustrations of the old bells at Exhall and Combrooke

To name the numerous helpers among the clergy and laity who have sent information about customs or extracts from documents, or have given personal assistance in various ways would be impossible here, but I trust justice has been done to all in the body of the work I should like, however to single out by name Rev J J Agar-Ellis of Offchurch, Rev H. Hanmer of Grendon, Rev W Finch of Shustoke, Rev E K Graham of Barston Rev J H Bloom of Whitchurch Mr Adams of St Mary, Warwick Mr A J Brookes of Coventry, and Mr W Salt Brassington The Rev Preb Deedes of Chichester kindly visited Fenny Compton, Shotteswell, and Warmington for me, and copied the Churchwardens' Accounts of the first-named place Mr A H Cocks has been good enough to supply casts for Plate XIV and numerous text-blocks and also many useful hints and suggestions, and for two other blocks (Figs 5 and 7) I am indebted to Dr A D Tyssen

Though I have personally visited many belfries in different parts of the county, I can only regret that I have failed to complete my predecessor s deficient notes in a few difficult cases, viz Combrooke Copston, Walton, and Weethley My only apology can be that enough information has been acquired in each case to shew that further efforts would hardly have been repaid The same applies to the modern churches To include all these would have meant much time spent in the grime of some fifty Birmingham belfries, with little or no result to shew and I trust future antiquaries will pardon the omission

The plates accompanying the text are all photographs from casts of the original marks or letters, and if not always perfect in detail, give the general appearance better than any process which involves drawing, and the consequent introduction of the personal equation The special types and ornaments used in the printing of the inscriptions represent as far as possible the general appearance of the original stamps, but a certain amount of convention is unavoidable My best thanks are due to the printers, Messrs Woodall, Minshall and Thomas of Oswestry for all the trouble they have taken in the matter

It only remains to say that I feel the dedication of this work to have a peculiar appropriateness, apart from the ties of filial affection Archdeacon Walters not only gave H T Tilley his first title as Curate, but also presented and inducted him to his last incumbency Moreover, nearly one-third of the bells described in this volume were for twenty years under the jurisdiction of my Father who has visited all but one of the churches, and inspected all the more accessible bells in person He has always been zealous for the welfare and preservation of the bells, and one of his earliest charges after his appointment dealt with this very subject

H B WALTERS

London, May, 1910

CONTENTS.

LIST OF PLATES.

LIST OF ILLUSTRATIONS IN TEXT.

BIBLIOGRAPHICAL NOTE

1 MANUSCRIPT RECORDS OF WARWICKSHIRE BELLS

(1) Practically the earliest written record of bells in the county is to be found in the Inventories of Church Goods compiled for the Commissioners of Edward VI in 1552. These have been transcribed at the Record Office, and published in the *Warwickshire Antiquarian Magazine* (1859—1877), pp. 154ff., 241ff. They are remarkably complete as far as this county is concerned, and we are able to ascertain from them virtually the total number of bells existing in the county at that time. The only ancient parishes for which there are no inventories existing, or where the number of bells is not stated, are Alcester, Anstey, Astley, Atherstone, Baddesley Ensor, Barton-on-Heath, Castle Bromwich, Charlcote, Compton Verney, Compton Wynyates, Copston, Coventry, Deritend, Exhall (Coventry), Foleshill, Gaydon, Henley, Honily, Knowle, Merevale, Newton Regis, Norton Lindsey, Lower Shuckburgh, Stivichall, Stoke, Temple Balsall, Water Orton, Weethley, Nether Whitacre, Wilnecote, Wolford, and Wyken—a total of thirty-two. References to these inventories are made under the heading '1552' for each parish in Part II.

(2) About 1750 a list of parishes in the various English and Welsh dioceses with the dedications of the churches and number of bells in each, was drawn up by the famous antiquary Browne Willis. These lists are now with his collections in the Bodleian, and transcripts of them are included in the MS. collections of the Cambridgeshire antiquary, William Cole, now in the Department of MSS., British Museum (Add. 5827, 5828). They are on the whole very accurate, and are practically complete for the two dioceses Worcester, and Lichfield and Coventry, in which the county then lay. References to them are made under the heading '1750.'

(3) MS. notes made by the late Dr. Raven (Brit. Mus. Add. MSS. 37432—37439) and Rev. W. D. Sweeting (*ibid.* 37180) giving inscriptions of a few parishes. Humphrey Wanley's MS. notes on the bells of St. Michael, Coventry, are in Harl. MSS. 6030. Rubbings collected by the late Canon Ellacombe (*ibid.* Add. 33203) and Rev. J. H. Bloom (*ibid.* 36819).

2 PRINTED BOOKS (a) *General Works*

DUGDALE (Sir William). The Antiquities of Warwickshire. Second edition printed from a copy corrected by the author himself and with the original copper plates. The whole revised, augmented and continued down to this present time by W. Thomas. 2 vols. London 1730. Fol. [The original edition appeared in 1656.]

This well-known and model county history is invaluable for all students of Warwickshire history or antiquities. The church bells are not often described or even mentioned, but there are some valuable notes, *e.g.* under Hatton and Kenilworth, and for historical and genealogical records Dugdale's work with Thomas's additions must frequently be laid under contribution. Some MS. notes collected with a view to a third edition will be found in the Brit. Mus. Add. MSS. 29264.

Notices of Warwickshire Churches. 2 vols. Warwick, 1844—1858. 8vo. Comprising the Deanery of Warwick and part of Alcester. To full and well illustrated descriptions of the churches are added in most cases the inscriptions on the bells, but not always accurately reported. This work was partly compiled by the well-known antiquary Matthew H. Bloxam

Warwickshire Antiquarian Magazine Parts 1—8 1859—1877 Warwick 4° Useful for heraldry and pedigrees also some valuable notes on Solihull bells The Inventories of Church Goods for the county are here published (see above) as are also the Heraldic Visitations in Part 2

(b) Special parishes and districts

BARTLET (B.) Manduessedum Romanorum, being the history and antiquities of the parish of Mancetter and also of the adjacent parish of Ansley in the County of Warwick Included in J Nichols Miscellaneous Antiquities (in continuation of the Bibliotheca Topographica Britannica), Vol I No 1 1791

BROOKES (A J) St Michael's Church Coventry Past and Present 3rd edn Coventry N D

BUNCE (J T) History of Old St Martin's Birmingham Birmingham, 1875 Fol.

HALLIWELL (J O afterwards Halliwell-Phillipps) Extracts taken from the Vestry-Book of the Church of the Holy Trinity, Stratford-on-Avon 1865 4°

——— The Accounts of the Chamberlains of the Borough of Stratford on-Avon for the year 1590 to 1597 1866 4°

——— Extracts from the same from the year 1585 to 1608 London 1866 4°.

——— Do do from the year 1609 to 1619 London, 1866 4°

[These three were privately printed and only ten copies of each are now in existence]

——— A Descriptive Calendar of the ancient manuscripts and records in the possession of the Corporation of Stratford-on-Avon London, 1863 Fol (75 copies printed)

HANNETT (J) The Forest of Arden its towns villages and hamlets A topographical account of the district between and round Henley and Hampton London and Birmingham 1863 8°

Kenilworth Illustrated, or the History of the Castle, Priory and Church of Kenilworth Chiswick, 1821 4° (Chiefly extracted from Dugdale)

MILLER (Rev G) Rambles Round the Edge Hills and in the Vale of the Red Horse London, E Stock, 1900 8°

[Gives inscriptions on the bells of several churches, mostly inaccurate]

PEMBERTON (Rev Robert) Solihull and its Church Exeter, 1905 4°

SAVAGE (R) The Churchwardens' Accounts of the Parish of St Nicholas, Warwick 1547—1621 transcribed and edited by Richard Savage (Reprinted from the Parish Magazine Warwick, H T Cooke and Son, 1890

SHARP (T) Illustrative Papers on the History and Antiquities of the City of Coventry Edited by W G Fretton Birmingham, 1871 4°

WAIT (Rev W O) Rugby Past and Present, with an historical account of neighbouring parishes Rugby, 1893 4°

[Good and accurate notes on the bells of Rugby and other places]

(c) Campanological works

Transactions of the Birmingham and Midland Institute, Vol ix (1878), p 10ff, Vol. xviii (1892), p 14ff Papers by H T Tilley on the Church Bells of Warwickshire summarising the chief points of interest, with some useful and original contributions to comparative campanology These results are incorporated in the Introduction to the present work

[The books on the bells of the various English counties by Cocks, Ellacombe, North Stahlschmidt, and others, need not be given in detail here, and it will suffice to note that they are generally referred to in the course of the work by the name of the author and county, *e g* 'Cocks, *Bucks*,' *etc* See for a detailed list Deedes and Walters, *Church Bells of Essex*, p xiii]

ADDENDA ET CORRIGENDA.

Page 1 foot-note 2 The reference number should be attached to the figure 1051 in the table above

„ 5, line 4 For Plate II 9 read Plate II 14

„ 5, line 5 „ „ „ 10-14 read Plate II 15-18

„ 5, line 10 „ „ „ 17 „ „ „ 10

„ 5, line 14 „ „ „ 18 19 „ „ „ 11, 12

„ 6 Add to list under heading (2) Lea, Hereford, 2nd Under heading (3) *dele* Gretton, Glouc , which is a doubtful example

„ 7, line 19 Formerly five bells of this type in Wiltshire now only two

„ 8, line 30 For 1353 read 1350

„ 13, foot-note 1, page 19 foot-note 1, and page 61 foot-note 1 The volumes of the *Victoria History* referred to have not yet been published (May, 1910)

„ 21 note 10 For p 28 read p. 29

„ 27, line 10 For Pl XVI 1 read Pl XV 1

„ 33, line 4 *Dele* ' a rubbing 33203 and insert ' a note by the late Dr Raven '

„ 37 Under Baginton for LORDE read LORD

„ 48 The occurrence of the name Richard at Brailes instead of Roger has been unfortunately overlooked, but the discrepancy has been adjusted under that heading in Part II (p 124)

„ 56, line 12 from bottom A Gawin Baker of Henley cast a bell for Solihull about 1600, and is possibly identical with this Godwin See p 219

„ 59, line 29 *Dele* ' and just over Shipston-on-Stour ' The bells here are by Matthew Bagley I cannot now trace my authority for stating that they were by Keene

„ 61, bottom line Paul Hutton cast a bell for Solihull in 1619 (see p 219)

„ 66 To list of existing Bagley bells add ' Rutland 1 '

„ 71, line 12 from bottom For ' four ' read ' three '

„ 72 Add to list ' 1752 Brailes, old 3rd '

„ 80, line 10 For ' dimutive ' read diminutive

In the following list for Wormington read Wormleighton

„ 82, foot-note Add 'p 133ff

„ 84, line 2 For 1717 read 1787

„ „ line 30 *Dele* ' as at Warwick St Nicholas '

„ 88, line 3 *Dele* ' such as Shropshire

„ 101 Arrow The border is Pl XXII , Fig 10 Add ' Thanks to Mr Falkner '

„ 102, last line but two. For 1760 read 1750

„ 107, line 5 from bottom For 1753 read 1750

„ 111, Head-line For Bedworth read Beaudesert

Page 115 — Binton Add 'Thanks to Mr Falkner

125 Head-line — For Brownsover read Bromwich

128 — Burmington See Appendix, p 273

„ 141 — Coughton See Appendix

215 Head-line — For Shottery read Shotteswell

215 — Lower Shuckburgh It may be worth mentioning that Canon Ellacombe had the inscription-band cut from a bell said to have been formerly at the Hall here It was inscribed AVE MARIA in the type used by Robert Norton of Exeter (c 1380) But there is some doubt as to whether a bell from this foundry would have found its way into Warwickshire See H T Tilley in *Trans Birm and Mid Inst* 1878, p 18

„ 232-233 — Under Sutton Coldfield add the new church of All Saints, Streetly, which has one bell by Barwell, put up 27 May, 1909 weighing 2 cwt, diam 21¼ in

„ 242 line 2 (6th bell) For Fig 14 read Fig 15

„ 256, line 14 For Add 37180 read Add 36819

PART I

INTRODUCTION

I. THE FOUNDERS OF WARWICKSHIRE BELLS

THE County of Warwick contains 220 ancient parish churches (*i e*, of Pre-Reformation origin) and about 90 of more modern foundation including three or four rebuilt on the site of ancient edifices fallen into ruin, but not including chapels-of-ease. In these 310 churches[1] there are roughly about 1,050 bells, which may be classified as follows —

Rings of twelve bells	1	=	12
Rings of ten bells	5	=	50
Rings of eight bells	17	=	136
Rings of six bells	39	=	234
Rings of five bells	42	=	210
Rings of four bells	20	=	80
Rings of three bells	49	=	147
Rings of two bells	22	=	44
Single bells	116	=	116
Sanctus bells, clock bells, etc	22	=	22
		Total	1051

Modern churches are credited with one bell where no information of a larger number has been received. Among these, two (St Agatha, Sparkbrook, and Christ Church, Leamington), contain the old bells from Christ Church, Birmingham, and Leamington Parish Church respectively; St Margaret, Ward End, Birmingham, has a second-hand bell from Greenwich Hospital, and an old bell from Ullenhall is said to be at a Mission Church in Sparkbrook, Birmingham[3]. The churches of St Bartholomew, St Mary, and St Paul, Birmingham, were founded in the eighteenth century, as was also St James, Aston. At Luddington, Nuthurst, and elsewhere new churches have been erected on the sites of old ones fallen into ruin, but the churches of Newnham Regis, Pillerton Priors, and others have partially or wholly disappeared. In some cases, as at Baddesley Ensor and Ettington, the bells have been placed in a new church built on a different site from the old one, but at Ullenhall one old bell remains in the old church, while the modern church contains a new ring. Included in the above category are the Guild Chapel at Stratford-on-Avon and the chapel of Leicester Hospital at Warwick, which though not parochial, may be considered as churches. Of these churches, that of Rugby is unique in the possession of two distinct rings of bells.

---

[1] This number includes Sutton under Brailes, formerly in Gloucestershire, but not Little Compton or Wibtoft, the bells of which churches are described in the books on Gloucestershire and Leicestershire respectively. Among modern churches, those of Amington and Bolehall cum Glascote in the ancient parish of Tamworth, are excluded.

[2] Not including the chimes at Foleshill St Thomas or the tubulars at Saltley St Saviour.

[3] In the parish of Yardley, and therefore in Worcestershire, not Warwick.

It is possible to classify these 1,050 bells in another manner, according to age, as follows —

Pre-Reformation (anterior to 1550)	46 } 58
Other ancient bells but uninscribed	12 }
"Transitional period" (1550—1600)	37
Seventeenth century	255
Eighteenth century	272
Nineteenth century and later	416
Bells of uncertain date or uninscribed	13
Total	1051

The number of Pre-Reformation bells is therefore 58,[1] a surprisingly small proportion, even when compared with neighbouring counties such as Worcestershire (about the same number out of 910) or Staffordshire (40 ancient out of 1,200) The percentage is almost exactly $5\frac{1}{2}$ per cent, as against 8 per cent in Leicestershire and 6 per cent in Worcestershire, Northants has rather over 5 per cent of old bells, and Staffordshire only about $3\frac{1}{3}$ per cent If, however we reckon in the 37 "Transitional bells, this percentage is largely increased rising to about 9 per cent In the adjoining counties of Leicester and Northants the same conditions obtain due there as here to the remarkable activity of the founders at Leicester and Nottingham during the reign of Queen Elizabeth Moreover, many of the bells cast during this period have all the characteristics of mediaeval bells, and few of them are dated We may further note here that eleven mediaeval bells in the county have been recast during the last fifty years (see below)

Of the 58 Pre-Reformation bells 32 are inscribed in Gothic capitals throughout, 14 in black letter minuscules or "mixed Gothic", twelve are devoid of inscription or only recognisable as ancient from their shape The tenor at Meriden has only impressions of mediaeval coins stamped upon it There are no complete mediaeval rings in the county, except pairs" at Hunningham and Morton Bagot, but there are three ancient bells at Bilton, and two each at Coventry St John, Mancetter, Atherstone-on-Stour, Beaudesert, and Offchurch Uninscribed ancient bells are at Barston, Brailes (sanctus), Gaydon, Haseley Merevale (2), Norton Lindsey, Over Whitacre, Wixford, and Wolverton of these Barston dates from the fourteenth century There was formerly also another at Willenhall, which from its shape may have belonged to the 13th or even 12th century, this bell is now at Birmingham (see above)

The chief interest of Warwickshire bells is derived from the fact that owing to its geographical position in the centre of England, and the absence of any local foundry between 1400 and 1700, the number of foreign foundries represented is remarkably large Besides the great foundries of London, Leicester, Nottingham, and Worcester, we find bells from such distant places as Wellington (Salop), Bridgwater, Aldbourne (Wilts), and Stamford, during the 17th and 18th centuries, but the majority of the bells during that period are successively from the Wattses of Leicester and the Bagleys of Chacomb The mediaeval bells are chiefly from London (nine), Leicester (ten), and Worcester (seven), but one or two groups may have been cast in the county Not until the eighteenth century did any local star appear on the horizon, and then we shall see that Joseph Smith of Edgbaston acquired a reputation sufficient to keep at bay even such powerful rivals as the Rudhalls of Gloucester, to say nothing of the Bagleys of Chacomb, who had previously held the field

At the present day the old bells are disappearing fast Mr Tilley has recorded[2] the fate of three or four mediaevals which succumbed to the furnace just at the time when he began his labours in the county, including the great tenor at Brailes, and since that time we have to

[1] I exclude from this reckoning all bells cast by the Newcombes of Leicester, some of which are at least mediaeval in style, though evidence points to their being of later date See below, p 16

[2] *Birm and Mid Inst Trans* 1878, p 18

regret the disappearance of interesting bells at Allesley, Halford, and Stoke by Coventry. The total list of mediaeval bells recast within the last fifty years[1] is as follows —

Allesley	1901
Baxterley	1875
Bearley	1875
Brailes (tenor)	1877
Combrooke	1867
Exhall by Alcester (two)	1864
Halford	1883
Ladbroke	1875
Ryton-on-Dunsmore	1864
Stoke by Coventry	1902

To which may be added interesting "transitional" bells at Grendon and Withybrook

I MEDIAEVAL PERIOD

It is well known to campanists that in most parts of England—more particularly the east and south east—the use of Gothic capitals for bell inscriptions was superseded about the year 1400 by that of "mixed Gothic" or black-letter minuscules with capitals for initials But in the Midlands we have ample evidence that this was not the case The important foundries at Gloucester, Worcester, and Leicester, for some unknown reason, appear to have avoided the use of minuscules altogether and continued to use capitals only down to the end of the fifteenth century at least Of this evidence will be given in succeeding pages But for the present this fact concerns us in that it increases the difficulty of dating those Warwickshire bells, the founders of which are unknown, and the dates of which are not determinable from other evidence There are, moreover, no dated mediaeval bells in the county—none, in fact, earlier than 1580 Taken in conjunction with the number of contemporaneous mediaeval foundries represented in the county, these considerations render it difficult to treat of the pre-Reformation bells in anything like chronological order As, however, the indeterminable bells are mainly of fourteenth-century character, if not actually of that period, it will be more convenient to treat of them first before discussing the known foundries.

I therefore begin by describing two or three groups of bells which on geographical or other grounds I think were probably cast within the county itself, though we have at present little evidence of a local foundry at Warwick, Coventry, or elsewhere

BELLS OF LOCAL MANUFACTURE

First we have to deal with a group of eight bells, four of which are in Warwickshire and which from their geographical distribution I am inclined to attribute to a founder either at Coventry or (more probably) Warwick First of all we have in the county itself (1) the treble at **Halford**, inscribed

✠ AGIOS IN HONORE SANCTI IOHANNIS BAPTISTE SUM RENOUATA

of which Mr Tilley, with perhaps unnecessary caution, says —"I certainly think it must belong to the fourteenth century"[2] He is, however, undoubtedly right in regarding it as the oldest inscribed bell in the county, and I should be inclined to say positively that it belongs to the earlier years of that century. That being the case, it is interesting to note that the word

---

1 Other ancient bells, long since gone, are recorded by Dugdale and other writers as existing at Coventry, Hatton, Kenilworth Stoneleigh and Warwick

2 *Trans Birm and Mid Inst*, 1878, p 13

RENOVATA implies that it had a predecessor The shape of the bell, the use of the two-dot stop and the formula IN HONORE (occurring on the 13th century bell at Caversfield, Oxon), all point to an early date The use of the word AGIOS (Greek ἅγιος = *sanctus*) is, so far as I know unique in bell inscriptions, it is a pity that the founder spoiled the effect by a false concord [1] The chief points to be noted in the lettering (see Plate I.) are the elongated A, which is larger than the rest, the reversed N, the square Roman T, and the U form of V [1] The cross is a plain Maltese one, about an inch high, with diagonal bars between the arms

A slightly enlarged and more ornate version of this cross (Plate II., Fig. 1) occurs with a more developed set of lettering (but in some respects of similar character) on the following bells —

(2) **Beaudesert** 1st

✠ AVE MARIA GRATIA PELNA

(3) **Beaudesert** 2nd

✠ IHESUS NAZSARINUS RCX IUDEORUM [2]

(4) **Whitchurch** bell

✠ I N R I ✠ A E M A G A

(5) *Dalby Parva*, Leicestershire, 2nd

✠ ISTA ❀ CĀPANA ❀ EST ❀ CŌPOSITA ❀ IN ❀ HONORE ❀ B̄TE ❀ MARIE ❀ VIRḠIS

(the mark of contraction used over four of the words is formed of three lozenges ⋄⋄⋄ *Leics*, fig 66)

(6) *Wadenhoe*, Northants, 2nd ·

✠ AVE MARIA GRATIA · PLENA DOMINUS TECUM

(7) *Broughton Hackett*, Worcestershire, 1st

✠ AVE MARIA GRATIA

(8) *Broughton Hackett* 2nd, an exact duplicate of Beaudesert 2nd

All of these bells bear the cross, Plate II , Fig 1, and at Whitchurch there is also a plain floriated cross (Plate II , Fig 2) in the middle of the inscription At Dalby a sort of wheel or star occurs as stop (*Leics* fig 57), which is also found on the sanctus at Preston, Rutland , but it is doubtful whether the latter bell can be added to our list It will be noted that this founder only employs two inscriptions (except at Dalby), and further that at Whitchurch he has combined these two in an abbreviated form, the last six letters representing A(*v*)E M(*ari*)A G(*raci*)A The lettering on Broughton Hackett 1st differs from that on the Warwickshire trio, which is given in Plate II , Figs 3-8 It is slightly smaller, and the M is of a peculiar narrow form It is not likely that the Halford bell is by the same founder , but I should be inclined to regard it as the work of a predecessor, about 1320, placing the other group some thirty years later

Next come a pair of bells, the larger one at **Hunningham,** and the bell in the turret of the old church at **Ullenhall,** both inscribed

✠ AVE MARIA GRACIA PLENA

---

[1] This is also found on early bells from the Lynn foundry (*Church Bells of Essex*, pl XVI)

[2] The popularity of this inscription with Midland founders, especially those of Leicester, is worth noting

With these we may group, from the identity of the initial cross, the 3rd at *Willoughby Waterless*, Leicestershire, inscribed

✠ SANCTE LAVRENCI ORA PRO NOBIS

This cross (Plate II, 9) is of peculiar type, being plain, with small St Andrew's crosses between the arms The lettering (Plate II, 10-14) is about one inch in height, plain in character, and the bells may be dated about 1350 They were probably cast in the county, but that is all we can say about them

The single bell at **Wyken** bears the inscription

✠ IHC NAZERENUS REX IUDEORU ●[1]

with an initial cross crosslet something like that at Whitchurch (Plate II, 17) So far as I know it stands alone, but there was formerly a similar bell at **Baxterley** inscribed

+ AVE MARIA

(with a cross which is only vaguely indicated in the rubbing), which was recast in 1875 Mr Tilley considered the letters (Plate II, 18-19) to resemble those used by Johannes de Stafford (p 14), but I do not myself regard the similarity as very marked, except in one or two cases, such as the M and U, they are smaller than his, about one inch high But whether these two bells came from a local or from some better known foundry it is hard to say

Recently my attention has been called to a discovery by the Rev J H Bloom[2] of the name of *John Kingston*, bellyeter, living in Northgate, Warwick, in 1401 It may perhaps be justifiable to assign to this man the bells at Hunningham and Ullenhall just described, they suit the date and locality better than the others discussed in this section

THE GLOUCESTER FOUNDRY.

Of the various non local mediaeval foundries represented in the county I propose to take first that at Gloucester, as not only can it be traced back to the beginning of the fourteenth century, but its earliest representatives in the county may be of that date. These are the 1st and 2nd bells at **Atherstone-on-Stour**, which, though differing in character and probably also in date, must yet be from the same foundry

They are inscribed respectively

✠ MARIA MATER DEI MISERERE MEI

and

✠ IHESU · CAMPANAM : TIBI . SEMPER PROTEGE . SANAM

Now the initial crosses on these two bells (Plate II, 15-16) are to be found on a fairly large group in the Western Midlands, accompanied by two corresponding varieties of lettering, one smaller and apparently earlier than the other Curiously enough, the lettering on the Atherstone bells does not belong to either alphabet, that on the 1st (Plate III) being somewhat intermediate in size, that on the 2nd larger than the latter set (Plate IV and upper line, Plate III) Still in each case it is of similar character. It may be worth while to give a complete list of those known, distinguishing the two groups by the crosses used —

(1) Smaller cross (Ellacombe, *Gloucs*, No 52)

Gloucestershire	Sapperton	1st
	Turkdean	2nd
Hereford	Credenhill	Recast 2nd
	Thruxton	1st
Somerset	Clapton-in Gordano	Sanctus
Warwick	Atherstone on-Stour	1st
Worcester	Besford	1st

[1] The M has been cut out and a plain circle is left here

[2] *Stratford Herald*, 5 June, 1908, from the accounts of John Sherman, Bailiff (Greville Charter 4821

(2) Larger cross (Ellacombe, *Gloucs.*, No. 105).

Gloucestershire	Brookthorpe	1st
	Leonard Stanley	1st
	Notgrove	1st
	Winstone	2nd
Hereford	Dorstone	2nd
	Stoke Lacy	1st and 2nd
Shropshire	Clungunford	2nd
	Neen Sollars	1st
Warwick	Atherstone-on-Stour	2nd
Worcester	Broadwas	4th
	Great Malvern	Service Bell
	Little Malvern	Bell
Glamorgan	Llantwit Major	Town Hall Bell

(3) The same lettering appears with a *plain* cross (*Gloucs.* 78) on the following:—

Gloucester	Gretton	Old bell (inscription reproduced)
Shropshire	Acton Scott	1st and 2nd
	Broughton	1st
	Onibury	2nd and 3rd

In view of the localities in which these bells are found, it seems a fair conclusion that they were cast at Gloucester; and it will be noticed that they are commonest in that county. Now, we know that there was an important foundry in that city in the fourteenth century, and we have on record the names of several founders of that period. Of these, the earliest are "Hugh the bell founder" and Christina "la belyutare," his daughter, whose dates are 1260—1300.[1] But though the names are of interest as showing the early existence of the foundry we cannot assign any known bells to so distant period. Next we have a seal found in the river Thames about 1850,[2] bearing the legend S' (*sigillum*) SANDRE-DE-GLOVCETRE (Fig. 1), which has been assigned to the year 1300 or thereabouts. The centre of the device is occupied by a laver-pot, surmounted by a bell; and, as we know that laver-pots often occur on bell-founders' trade-marks (see pp. 23, 25), we need have no hesitation in regarding this as the seal of a bell-founder. Thirdly, we have in 1346[3] the name of "John the bell-founder," who is evidently identical with a "Master John of Gloucester," whose name occurs in the Sacrists' Rolls of Ely Cathedral.[4] In that very year, 1346, a ring of four new bells by this founder was placed in the lantern of the Cathedral, having been brought by water from Northampton, by way of the Nene and Ouse rivers. "Master John" was, doubtless, the son of Sandre, or at any rate, his successor, and, the fact that his fame had reached as far as Ely, shows that it was considerable.

Fig. 1.

The first group of bells, with the small lettering and cross, may then be assigned to Sandre of Gloucester, and therewith, on the strength of the cross, we may place the Atherstone treble, though the lettering, as I have said, does not occur elsewhere. The lettering on the Besford (Worcs.) bell also differs from the others, and, having regard to its more archaic character and to the early form of the inscription,[5] I am almost inclined to refer it back to

The second group will then fit in with Master John, at all events, those bells included in the heading (2), with the possible exception of Atherstone, where there are some differences in the lettering, the bells in heading (3) are even more doubtful, but on these the lettering, at least, is of the usual type

For about 100 years we lose sight of any bell-founding at Gloucester, but between the middle of the next century and the middle of the sixteenth, we have four names Of these one, **Robert Hendley,** occurs on the 4th at *St Nicholas, Gloucester*, with the words TEMPORE CLEMENTIS LICHFILD SACRISTA, the others *William Henshaw*, who was Mayor in 1508-9, and whose brass is to be seen in St Michael's Church there, *Richard Atkyns*, whose will exists, dated 1529 and *Thomas Loveday*, who made the chimes for Gloucester Cathedral in 1527,[1] have not left their names on any bells The name of Clement Lichfield may throw some light on the date of Hendley, as the last Abbot of Evesham, who built the magnificent bell-tower of that abbey in 1534, bore that name So far it has not proved possible to connect the two names, but it is not at all unlikely that they were the same person If that is the case, Robert Hendley's bell may be dated about 1500, or perhaps a few years earlier

The cross and lettering on this bell (Plate V, Figs 1—9) are found on a fairly large group, comprising no less than eighteen in Gloucestershire, nearly all of which are in the northern half of the county, there are also several in Herefordshire, one each in Monmouth, Shropshire, Wiltshire, Worcester, and Montgomery, and three in Warwickshire[2] These last are the 3rd at **Butler's Marston,** inscribed

✠ ANCTA KATHERINA . ORA PRO NOBIS

and the 1st and 3rd at **Offchurch,** respectively inscribed

✠ SANCTE MICHAEL ORA PRO NOBIS

and

✠ VIRGINIS ♔ EGREGIE ♔ VOCOR ♔ CAMPANA ♔ MARIE

All these bells bear the same peculiar cross, with one plain and three floriated arms, some, as Offchurch 3rd, have a crown (Pl V, 10) by way of stop others a stop of a star between two circles, and others merely three dots They are thus sufficiently homogeneous to forbid their being distributed into groups, otherwise it might be tempting to assign some to Henshaw or Atkyns[3]

THE WORCESTER FOUNDRY

As we have now discussed all the bells that can with any certainty be attributed to the fourteenth century, and the Gloucester foundry has brought us down into the fifteenth, we will next turn to what appears to have been one of the most important centres of this industry in the Midlands during the latter period This is the city of Worcester, in which we can find evidence of the duration of a foundry from about 1400 down to the end of the seventeenth century, almost without a break

In point of fact there is evidence that bell-founding was practised in Worcester at a much earlier date than 1400 The Rev J H Bloom has extracted from the Diocesan Records notices of one *Simon, Campanarius*, living in Sidbury, between 1226 and 1266 In 1294 we hear of *Simon le Bellyeter*, who died in 1306, and probably succeeded him The name of *Richard*

---

[1] See *Glouc Cathedral Records* (ed Bazeley), I, p 129

[2] I am not sure whether the 3rd at Priston, Somerset, and the tenor at Horton, Gloucs, should be included with these They have the Hendley lettering and crown, but the cross is one used by Robert Norton, of Exeter There were formerly two similar bells at Crudwell, Wilts

[3] It is worth noting that the tenor at Aston Ingham, Herefordshire, has the initials I S, which also occur (in different lettering) at Charlton Abbots, Gloucs

Bellyeter occurs frequently between 1305 and 1318, and he was several times Bailiff A lease of lands in Timberdine dated 1305 has his seal affixed, a wide-mouthed bell, with the legend SIGILLVM RICARDI LE BELYETERE But we cannot assign existing bells to them, unless the treble at Hill Croome, Worcs, is the work of Richard it certainly dates from his time For the present, however, I must confine myself to the later history of the foundry, between 1400 and 1550.

Among the various stamps used by English bell-founders none are more familiar to campanists than the heads of Kings and Queens, usually known as the "Royal Heads" Of these there are three known varieties, two of a King and Queen which are closely connected, and from their resemblance to one another have been thought to represent the same pair, viz, Edward III and Philippa These I will call for convenience Sets A and B (Plate V Figs 13-14, Plate X Fig 3) noting *en passant* that some have identified set A as Edward I and Queen Eleanor Of set C, which represent Henry VI Queen Margaret, and Prince Edward, and are quite distinct from the others, I shall have something to say later (p 10)

Meanwhile, two facts are clear, firstly that set B (and probably also A) cannot be earlier than 1327 secondly, that they were probably first in use during the reign of Edward III Now we find both sets of heads on a group of bells in the south-east midlands, which have been attributed with some probability to one *John Rufford*, who was living about 1367 [1] Two or three of these bells are to be found in the adjoining counties of Leicester and Northants, and one at Slapton in the latter county bears the set (B), one at Grafton Regis the set (A) These heads are found in connection with more than one group In the first instance they appear in East Anglia on a group of bells centring round King's Lynn,[2] one or two of which bear the name of a founder Derby, who probably lived about 1350, and was thus contemporaneous with John Rufford Next we find them on a group which covers almost the same territory as the John Rufford group but with the cross and lettering used by Derby (Pl V, 12) One bell in this group (at Westmill, Herts), bears the name of *William Roffořde* as founder Assuming then that the earlier group of bells is John Rufford's we arrive at the following conclusions

(1) John and William Rufford (probably father and son) were successive owners of a foundry which had the privilege of using Royal effigies on their bells, for some reason not now known Their date is about 1353—1400

(2) The distribution of the bells in both groups clearly points to the neighbourhood of Bedford as their place of abode, and Mr Cocks has lately proved that this was Toddington [3]

(3) William Rufford discarded his father's stamps, and introduced new ones derived from Derby of Lynn The B set of heads went to Nottingham about 1400 with John Rufford's lettering, as we shall see later (p 19)

We next find the Derby-Rufford lettering, or rather an almost identical alphabet, on four bells in the Midlands, none of which, however, bear the Royal Heads These are found at Beachampton, Bucks,[4] Sherborne Gloucestershire, Alkerton, Oxfordshire, and Radstone, Northants, each with a plain Maltese cross and a three-dot stop In this connection we must deal with the 3rd at **Monk's Kirby** in this county, which is of a somewhat different type. It is inscribed

✠ ECCE S AGNVS S CII S ET PVRE S PROFETA

[1] North, *Northants*, p 64, Cocks, *Bucks*, p 10

[2] The King from the A set appears at Chippenham, Cambs, the other King at Ampton, Suffolk

[3] William Rufford de Tudyngton, belmaker, is mentioned in a license dated S Oct, 1390 He is probably identical with William belmaker of Toddington mentioned in a Patent Roll of 1395 See *Victoria County Hist of Bucks*, II p 118 These dates are important as showing that Rufford's stamps did not migrate to Worcester before 1400

[4] The cross, stop, and lettering are illustrated by Mr Cocks, *Bucks*, Pl V He points out (in a letter to me) that the Monk's Kirby lettering is not the same, but it is similar in character, and the cross unquestionably connects it with this group The Alkerton cross is more ornate than that at Beachampton, and there is a fleur de lys stop like that at Morton Bagot (see later), which may suggest a connection with the group to which that bell belongs

the cross being the Derby-Rufford one (Pl V 12), with which we are already familiar, while the stop (Pl VII, 2) is in the form of a reversed S with floral terminations, unknown elsewhere The lettering (Pl VII, 1), however, occurs on the late tenor at *Brewood*, Staffordshire, with a fleur-de-lys (Plate V, 11) also occurring at Alkerton, of which more anon [1]

It is not easy to "place" these six bells They form indeed a connecting link between the Rufford group and that which we are about to describe, but we cannot say certainly whether they are the work of a distinct founder residing at Buckingham, Banbury, or elsewhere in the neighbourhood It is at least extremely probable Mr Cocks, in assigning the group to Leicester or Nottingham, was not then aware that the migration of William Rufford's stamps was at first in another direction

We must then follow the fortunes of these stamps, with the (A) set of Royal Heads, in a westerly direction Here we find another and larger group of bells with the Derby-Rufford cross (Pl V, 12), the (A) set of Heads, and lettering which in many respects so closely resembles the other set, that there must have been some succession of stamps These bells are found in the counties of Gloucester (8), Monmouth (1), Montgomery (1), Oxford (2), Radnor (2), Salop (6), Warwick (3), Wilts (1), and Hereford and Worcester, each of the latter containing not less than ten Apart from other evidence it is pretty clear that the geographical distribution points to Worcester as their centre, and we shall see not only that other evidence points in the same direction but that the date of these bells accords with the theory that the stamps came from William Rufford

The key to the situation is a bell at *Bitterley* in Shropshire, which I have discussed fully elsewhere,[2] and need only now mention that it bears (in conjunction with the Royal Heads and other stamps) a prayer to Jesus and St Anne for the soul of Alice Stury This lady died in 1415, making a bequest to the Rector of Hampton Lovett, near Worcester, of which living she was patroness and benefactress It may fairly be assumed that the bell which she gave to Bitterley was cast in the locality, and Worcester naturally seems the most likely place The date of this bell may be put at about 1415—1420, at all events, shortly after her death

The whole group of bells is one of considerable interest, more particularly from the variety and originality of the inscriptions, of which Warwickshire yields one good specimen, the treble at **Ipsley**, inscribed

✠ DVM [K] TONAT [Q] HOC [K] SIGNVM [Q] PRECE [K] PELLE [Q] ROBERTE [K] MALIGNVM

Of this there is a variant at *Hallow*, Worcestershire

✠ DVM [K] SONAT [Q] HOC [K] SIGNVM [Q] HOSTEM [K] FVGAT [Q] ANNA [K] MALIGNVM

The other examples in the county are **Aston Cantlow** 4th

✠ AD [K] LAVDEM [Q] CLARE [K] MICHAELIS [Q] DO [K] RESONARE

and **Lighthorne** 3rd

✠ IOHANNIS [K] PRECE [Q] DVLCE [K] SONET [Q] ET [K] AMENE

All these bells are remarkably good specimens of casting, Mr Tilley describes that at Lighthorne as "one of the cleanest castings I have ever seen Peculiarities of lettering that

[1] See for the Brewood bell Lynam, *Staffs* pls 16, 17 The inference seems to be that the Monk's Kirby and Alkerton bells have more in common with the Worcestershire group than with the Bucks bell The fleur-de lys is also found at Hinton-in Hedges, Northants, but not having seen the lettering I can only hazard a guess that this bell belongs to the same group

[2] See *Assoc Archit Socs Reports*, xxv (1901), p 362ff, *Arch Journal*, lxiii, p 67

may be noted are ᴅ for D, the Roman Γ and the almost invariably reversed S See generally Plate V, 15 24

Once located at Worcester the Royal Heads seem to have remained there for many years We find them associated (though not in any Warwickshire examples) with our next group, a group which like the last, extends over the western Midlands, but concentrates in considerable numbers round Worcester [1] Out of some 35 bells, no less than 16 are or were in that county Here again the stamps employed have a curious history

In the year 1403 a Salisbury bell-founder, by name *John Barber*, was gathered to his fathers, leaving one *Peter Brasier* as the inheritor of his stock-in trade, and further traces of his identity on a bell at *Chittern* in Wiltshire inscribed

✠ IHON ❀ BARXBVR ❀ ME ❀ MADE

His will, which is of considerable interest, has lately been unearthed and transcribed by Dr A D Tyssen for the Wilts Archaeological Society [2] Of the stamps which he used, the wheel-stop at Chittern became the property of a later Bristol foundry, but the cross and the small, somewhat plain capitals which he affected appear on the above-mentioned Worcester group (see Pl VII, 5-9) The Worcester founder, however discards the crowns over the letters (except in the case of initials) and also a rectangular stop which Barber himself often used In view of the date to be given to the Bitterley-Ipsley group, which must belong to the period 1410—1420, we must allow for the lapse of some time before these stamps came to Worcester, and probably the founder acquired them from Peter le Brasier It is to be noted that the letters often show decided signs of wear, especially the A On the other hand, we know that they were in the possession of a London founder about 1478 (see below, p 25), and therefore they cannot have been at Worcester later than about 1475 Their sojourn there must be dated between the years 1425 and 1475 Mr Bloom finds the name of *Richard le Belyetere* again occurring in 1464 Very likely he was the founder of this group of bells, and a descendant of the earlier Richard (see p 8)

In Warwickshire there remains now only one bell of this group, the 3rd at **Lapworth,** inscribed

✠ SANCTA KATERINA ORA PRO NOBIS

but there was formerly another at **Allesley** (the old 2nd) which was exactly similar We shall, however, meet with the lettering again in this county in somewhat unexpected company, as already noted

I have said that the Royal Heads are found on bells belonging to this group, this is the case at *Spetchley* and *Stanford-on-Teme* in Worcestershire,[3] and also on one or two bells in Herefordshire It is interesting to note that at *Pembridge* in the latter county there is a bell with John Barber's cross in conjunction with the Ipsley lettering, a further instance of the connection between these two groups

We now take leave of the set (A) of Royal Heads for a time and come to speak of another Worcester group, which, in my opinion, is quite the most interesting to be found in the Midlands and which further has the merit of including two dated examples It is on this group that we find the third or (C) set of Royal Heads It includes in all thirteen examples of which nine are or were in Worcestershire, two in Salop, one in Hereford, and one in

[1] See *Assoc Archit Socs Reports*, xxv (1901), p 561

[2] *Wilts Arch Mag* xxxv p 351 ff

[3] They also occurred on a bell at Shelsley Walsh, Worcestershire, now recast, on this bell all the letters were crowned

Warwickshire Before touching on the last-named, I must say something of this group in general[1]

In 1879 Mr Tilley lighted on a very remarkable bell at *Grimley*, near Worcester, of which he has given some account in his second paper on Warwickshire bells,[2] with the Royal Heads and sundry other stamps, and the date 1482 in small Roman numerals This discovery the present writer supplemented in 1901 by the investigation of a similar but much more inaccessible bell at *St Michael's, Worcester*, bearing the date 1480 Further evidence, if such were needed, as to the date of this group, is afforded by the 2nd at *Wichenford* in the same county, which bears in small Gothic capitals on its crown the name of the Vicar, Thomas Field, who died in 1489

These small capitals are found on two small sanctus bells, which in each case are of interest as the only relic of the original church at *Lindridge* in Worcestershire, and at **Great Packington** in this county The latter is inscribed

✠ AVE MARIA GRACIA PLENA S I D

with a plain initial cross (Pl VI, 6-7) The initials S I D, which cannot represent any personal name, I entirely fail to interpret But we may safely attribute this bell to the unknown Worcester founder, and place its date between 1475 and 1490[1]

It is a matter for great regret that in none of these cases has any certain evidence come to light as to the names of the founders of these Worcester bells Mr Tilley had a suspicion, and personally I am inclined to agree with him, that some may have been cast under ecclesiastical supervision We know that monastic communities did reckon bell-founding among the arts which they practised, and the use of scholarly "leonines" on two of these groups, the names of Worcester ecclesiastics occurring on the Grimley bell and others of that group, and other details may point to this explanation, and account for silence as to the names of bell-founders at this period

But we have now reached a time when an actual Worcester bell-founder appears on the scene This is **Nicholas Grene**, whose will, proved 28 April, 1542, and now in the Worcester Registry (No 64) I have given at length elsewhere[3] He was of the parish of St Nicholas, and among certain parishes the wardens of which owed him money, he mentions that of Lapynton, which may be meant for Lapworth There is, as we have seen, a bell from the Worcester foundry at that church, but it must be at least a century older than Nicholas Grene's time

The question then confronts us Are there any bells that we can identify as his? I cannot trace any in Worcestershire, but I think that the clue may be afforded us by three Warwickshire bells, one of which is no longer in existence They are all near the western border of the county the pair at **Morton Bagot** and the former bell at **Bearley**, of which a rubbing is preserved in the Ellacombe collection in the British Museum (Add MSS 33,203) as well as Mr Tilley's notes This bell and the larger one at Morton Bagot were very similar, and unquestionably by the same founder, but as to the smaller at Morton Bagot I am not so certain, as the stamps thereon do not occur elsewhere Still it is of the same character as the others, so I give it here The bell has the inscription

✠ Snjtar trinitas

headed by a Maltese cross, the letters being ill-formed and of a late type, they are set on well-marked *paterae*, rather far apart, and the two S's and C are reversed See Pl VI, Fig 4-5

The larger bell here is inscribed

✠ [K] ✤ maria ✠ [K] maria [K] ✤ maria ✤ ✠ maria

---

[1] See also *Assoc Archit Socs Reports*, xxv (1901), p 565

[2] *Trans Birm and Mid Inst*, 1892, p 24

[3] *Arch Journal*, lxiii, p 189

the cross being like that on the 1st, but larger and plainer (Pl VI 4) the fleur-de-lys is one we have already met with on some earlier bells (see pp 8-9) See for these stamps Pl VI, Figs 1-3 The other stop is also an old friend, the head of King Edward III, which we have seen already in the possession of two Worcester founders Later in the sixteen century —but not before 1530—we find this stamp being used by the Oldfields of Nottingham, and unless any other instance of its use can be traced in the intervening period it may be assumed to have remained at Worcester until Nicholas Grene's death in 1541, and then have been transferred to Nottingham (see below, p 20) This being the case, we may regard the Morton Bagot and Bearley bells as Grene's handiwork, and perhaps also the smaller bell at the former church The Bearley bell was inscribed

✠ airam ✠ [K] ⚜ airam [K] ✠ airam ⚜ [K]

being thus very similar to the other The King's head again appears with the cross and fleur-de-lys, the word **maria** is placed backwards each time The lettering is poor and late both here and at Morton Bagot The Bearley inscription has been reproduced on the new bell, but not very accurately, the black-letter being replaced by capitals

These three bells stand quite by themselves, but if the King's head on the one hand connects them with Worcester, on the other the fleur-de-lys connects them with another group of bells whose location is not quite certain Among these is the tenor at **Curdworth** with the unusual inscription in capitals

✠ SANCTA MARIA VIRGO INTERSEDE PRO TOTO MVNDO

found in a more extended form at *Hartlebury*, Worcs, where the 6th has following this the words

QVEYA GENVISTI REGEM ORBIS

The cross (Pl VII, 10) is something like that on Morton Bagot 2nd but the connecting link of the fleur-de-lys is still wanting That however, we meet with on a third bell, the 3rd at *St Martin's Worcester* and it is also found on bells of this type in Staffordshire The lettering is illustrated on Pl VII, Figs 11-15 The complete list, besides those already given is made up by four bells in Staffordshire Baswich 2nd, High Offley 1st and Weston-under-Lyziard 1st and 2nd, two in Salop Wrockwardine 3rd and 6th an old bell in the destroyed church of St Hilary Denbigh, and possibly also the 3rd at Barkby, Leicestershire

It should also be noted that there are four or five bells in Shropshire (at Adderley, Middle, Hope Bowdler, Hordley and Shrawardine), and one in Staffordshire (Keele[1]), with very similar lettering but a different cross, the Adderley bell has the same inscription as at Curdworth These have evidently some connection with the other group but must be by an earlier—or later—founder, probably residing at Shrewsbury

As to the locality of the Curdworth group, I was at one time inclined to place them at Worcester, where they would fill in a convenient gap previous to Nicholas Grene, but we have to reckon with the fact that several are to be found in Staffordshire and four others very near its borders, a fact which in my opinion points to Wolverhampton or Stafford as the founder's home Next as to date In spite of the occurence of the fleur-de-lys on the two later bells, I am not disposed to put the Curdworth group much later—if at all—than the fourteenth century They are, so far as I have observed, somewhat archaic in shape, in fact those at Weston-under-Lyziard and Wrockwardine are markedly so, and resemble, in the squareness of their shoulders and long-waisted sides, bells known to date from the early part of the fourteenth century. There was a *Michael de Lichfield* founding in the fourteenth century in Staffordshire, who may possibly be the man of whom we are in search

[1] The Keele bell has the Royal Heads, which implies a connection with the Worcester foundry

THE LEICESTER FOUNDRY[1]

With three exceptions, all the remaining mediaeval Warwickshire bells with inscriptions in capitals may be shewn with more or less probability to have been cast at Leicester, and though we have not much information to go upon, we cannot doubt the importance of that foundry in the fourteenth and fifteenth centuries as well as in later times. In each case with which we have to deal, I shall hope to shew that there is good reason for the suggested attribution.

Meanwhile our first duty is obviously to investigate the records of Leicester during the period, and see what is known of bell-founders from that source. Since the publication of North's books, which hardly attempted to trace the foundry earlier than the sixteenth century, the late Miss Mary Bateson's three sumptuous volumes of *Records of the Borough of Leicester*[2] have considerably increased our available sources of information.

The earliest bell-founder of whom I can find mention—and in fact the earliest with whom we need be concerned—is

STEPHEN LE BELLEYETER (1328-1348),[3]

who became a member of the Merchants' Gild in 1328-9 and whose name also appears in a Tallage Roll of 1336. In 1337 he pays 1s. rent for a chamber near the North gate. In 1346 and 1348 there are records of grants of land, one from Stephen to John of Stafford (see below) and others, another to the same Stephen. Next comes

JOHN HOSE (1352-1366),[4]

whose cottage near All Saint's Church is mentioned in 1352, and in the Merchant Gild entries of 1366: "John Hose belleyeter, heres patris sui petit libertates ville Leycestrie tanquam heres et filius primogenitus et iuratus est secundum usum Leycestrie."

To one of the above I am inclined to attribute a group including two Warwickshire bells, in regard to which we have no clue to the founder's name. While, however, geographical evidence clearly points to Leicester, the fact that the stamps and lettering on these bells were afterwards (about 1560-1600) in the hands of Leicester founders is also in favour of the attribution. But as evidence points to these bells having been cast in the middle of the fourteenth century, it is curious that for two hundred years there should be no signs that the stamps were in use.

The group is a small one numbering not more than ten bells; they all have the same initial cross and stop, and are inscribed in a set of fine and very richly-ornamented capitals (Plate VIII.). The letters are double-lined, and the surfaces are covered with a sort of diapering of various patterns. Among these bells we have in Warwickshire the 3rd at **Coventry St. John**:

C ⁝ SCI ⁝ IOHIS
✠ HENRIC ⁝ DODENHALE ⁝ ME ⁝
FIERI ⁝ FECIT

and the 4th at **Mancetter**:

✠ HEC ⁝ IN ⁝ HONORE ⁝ PIE ⁝
CONSTAT ⁝ CAMPANA ⁝ MARIE

---

[1] See Miss Hewitt's excellent epitome of the history of this foundry in the second volume of the *Victoria County Hist. of Leics.*

[2] Published in 1901–1905. Vols. II. and III. cover the period 1327–1603.

[3] *Records*, II., pp. 4, 27, 36, 391, 392.

[4] *Records*, II., pp. 143, 396.

The other examples are at Ashby-de-la-Zouch, Fenny Drayton, and Syston in Leicestershire, Deene, Northants, Newton Solney 2nd, Derbyshire and three now recast, at Bretby and Taddington (2nd) in Derbyshire, and Beverley St Mary, Yorkshire One or two of the later Leicester bells with these stamps (*e g* Cranoe 1st and 2nd, Leics) might possibly be included but the brevity of the inscriptions points to their being of a later date The evidence for the date of this group is afforded by the Coventry bell, whose donor, Henry Doddenhale, was Mayor of that City in 1350 and though we have no record of Stephen le Bellyeter after 1348, the inference is that they were his work, rather than John Hose's, as the latter's activity probably began later

JOHANNES DE STAFFORD (1338-1354)

Contemporary with the two last named is a founder of this name who was admitted to the Merchant's Gild in 1338-9, and is described as a "Bellyetere" in a Tallage Roll of 1354[1] The name occurs again frequently in the Records of Leicester between 1360 and 1390,[2] and one John de Stafford was Mayor in 1366 and 1370-72, and Burgess of Parliament for the town in 1384 But in none of these cases is he described as a "Bellyetere" We cannot therefore be certain of his identity with the bell-founder, though it is, to say the least, quite probable Further we learn from the Fabric Rolls of York Minster that Johannes de Stafford cast a bell there in 1371[3] and again we cannot be certain that this is the Leicester man

North records the existence of bells bearing the name of Johannes de Stafford as founder at *All Saints' Leicester*, and at *Scawby*, Lincolnshire, and many similar bells are found in neighbouring counties The fact that out of nearly thirty bells in this group no less than nine are found in Leicestershire, while no other county has more than five, clearly points to their being cast in that county We should therefore naturally assume that they may be assigned to the "bellyetere" of 1338-1354 But as regards the date there is some conflicting evidence which must not be overlooked,

At *Aylestone* in Leicestershire there is a bell of this type given by William Resevour, whose date is about 1412, and more significant still two more of these bells, at *Morley* in Derbyshire, are known to have been given by one John Statham whose brass in that church is dated 1454 On these grounds Mr Tilley (without the documentary evidence before him) placed the date of Johannes de Stafford about 1420-1460 declining to accept his identity with the Mayor of Leicester[4] It is of course clear that on the evidence of the Morley brass the bells there must be assigned to the fifteenth century and even if we extend the career of John de Stafford to the latest recorded date of 1392, it is still too early for the Morley bells if not for that at Aylestone A career which began in 1338 can hardly be prolonged beyond 1400, if so late

The difficulty therefore remains, and though the preponderating evidence is in favour of the earlier date for these bells, it can only be accepted by discovering an alternative explanation for the date of those at Morley Meanwhile we must be content with considering the existing bells which can be attributed to Johannes de Stafford There are, as already noted nine of these in Leicestershire, five each in Derbyshire and Warwickshire, three in Lincolnshire, three (and perhaps more) in Yorkshire and one in Staffordshire They are all very similar in character, having the same initial cross (Plate VII, Fig, 16) and a stop of three dots between the words, but no other ornaments, the T is of Roman form, and the S invariably reversed See Plate VII, Figs 17-19

The Warwickshire five include **Atherstone** single bell

✠ IH NAZARENUS REX IUDEORVM

---

[1] *Records*, II, pp 43, 96

[2] See Index to *op cit*, Vol II

[3] North, *Leics*, p 37

[4] *Trans Birm and Mid Inst*, 1892, p 19

Leek Wootton 5th

✠ IHS · NASARINUS REX IUDEORUM

Berkswell 4th

✠ AUE MARIA GRA PLENA

Coventry St. John 4th

✠ IOHES MALLERI AND ALISANDER YO UICA OF KYRKBY

and **Wolston** 2nd, with the unique and interesting inscription

✠ MARCUS MATHUS LUCAS IOHES

Emblems of the Evangelists are found on London-cast bells, as at Impington in Cambridgeshire, but nowhere else do their names occur. The order of the names should be noted, with Mark first (as if anticipating the Higher Criticism!) It may be noted that the Coventry bell appears to afford additional confirmation of the earlier date for John de Stafford, as there was a John Mallory of Winwick, Northants, who married Alice Revel of Newbold Revel about 1360.[1] But the name may be that of his son John who became owner of Fenny Newbold in 1382 and Commissioner for the Peace in 1391.

THOMAS DE MELTON (1368-1392)

Somewhat later in date than John de Stafford is Thomas de Melton, bellmaker, mentioned in the Merchant Gild Rolls of 1368-69, and subsequently in 1377 and 1392.[2] Nothing more is known of him or of his works.

WILLIAM NOBLE (1417-1427)

Our next name is that of a man twice described as "bellyettere," viz. in 1417 and 1423, his name occuring in those years in connection with grants of land;[3] in 1427 he witnesses another grant. One of the grants of 1423 is sealed with several seals, one of which is William Noble's; it is described by the editor of the *Records* as a bell-founder's seal, and appears to bear the mark of a bell, but the reproduction is not very clear.[4]

THOMAS INNOCENT (1458-1469)

This man, mentioned as a "potter" in 1458,[5] is also described as a "bellyetere" in 1469.[6] I am inclined to assign to him or to William Noble a group of bells described below (p. 17).

WILLIAM MELLORS (1497-1508)

North mentions a William Millers, Alderman of Leicester as the earliest founder known to him from records,[7] but it would seem that the name is more correctly spelled as above. If so, it is an additional support to his suggestion that this William was connected with the Mellers or Mellour family of Nottingham (see p. 21). He is first mentioned in a Subsidy Roll of 1497, and in 1500-1, in the Merchant Gild entries occurs the name of "Will Mellers bellheyteras."

---

1 See Dugdale, I., p. 82.
2 *Records*, II., pp. 143, 404, 409.
3 *Records*, II., pp. 415—417.
4 *Ibid.*, pl. 2, fig. 7.
5 *Ibid.*, p. 266.
6 *Cal. Pat. Rolls*, 9 Ed. IV., pt. 1, No. 23, p. 144. I owe the reference to Miss E. M. Hewitt.
7 *Leics.*, p. 39.

In 1504 he was chamberlain of the borough, and is also mentioned in that capacity in 1505 and 1508 The latter year gives an entry under date April 5 to this effect —

> 'Memorandum that their was founden dewe to Thomas Newcombe for the fote of this accompte of William Mellors chamburleyn by the town of Leycestre the sum of iiij^{li} vij^{d} . And for the makeynge of the dener (*dinner*) by William Mellers and his wif and hymselff the some of xliij^{s} iij^{d} [1]

The Thomas Newcombe herein mentioned was also a bell-founder, but of him more anon William Mellors, according to North, died in 1506

THOMAS BETT (1524-1538)

The next bell-founder is Thomas Bett, who held several civic offices, being Auditor in 1524 and 1526, Steward in 1525 1527, and 1531, Coroner in 1526-27, and finally Mayor in 1529-30 [2] He is not in any case described as a bell-founder, but his Will is in existence, dated 19 December 1538, in which he makes various bequests to his son-in law Robert Newcombe (see below) Other details about him are given by North

Neither Mellors nor Bett have been definitely recognised as the makers of any existing bells, and it is curious that there are very few in this district of England which can be assigned to the period 1450 1550 But there are a few bells in the North of England which bear a shield with the letters T B, with black-letter inscriptions, and this shield has been thought to be Thomas Bett's These bells are at Cubley and Monyash, Derbyshire, Halton and formerly Broughton, Lancashire Appleby, Lincolnshire, Blithfield, Staffordshire, and Braithwell, Yorkshire Mr Cocks also assigns to Bett a bell at Hardmead, Bucks,[3] but on somewhat conjectural grounds

THOMAS NEWCOMBE I (1506-1520), ROBERT NEWCOMBE I (1520-1561)

The last of the mediaeval Leicester founders known to us is Thomas Newcombe, the founder of a successful dynasty, lasting over a hundred years, the history of which must however, be detailed on a later page, as belonging to the post mediaeval period This Thomas we have already seen mentioned in connection with William Mellors, whom he succeeded, he died in 1520, and is described in his will as *fusor campanarius* [4] His name occurs in the Merchant Gild Entries of 1508-09 as "Tho Newcome yeoman," and he was Chamberlain in 1509-10 and also Auditor [5]

It has not been possible to identify any existing bell as his work, but there is a group to be dealt with subsequently (p 28) which as will be noted might be the work of this Thomas,[6] though we have no evidence It is at all events clear that any bells he cast would have been purely pre-Reformation in character, which is not the case with those with which we have to deal He was buried in All Saints Church, and mentions in his will his son Robert, who, as we have already seen, married Thomas Bett's daughter Robert Newcombe succeeded to his business and kept it on until his death in 1560-61 [7] He was Mayor in 1550, held other civic offices [8] and seems to have been generally a prosperous man But though he was undoubtedly a bell-founder we cannot trace his work anywhere at present, all the known Newcombe bells being apparently of later date North suggests that the cross (Pl XVI, 2) used by his son Thomas (see

---

1 *Records*, II, pp 352, 365, 375, 378, 466

2 *Records*, III, pp 28, 29, 458ff see also North, *Leics*, p 44

3 See *Bucks*, p 143

4 *Leics*, p 41

5 See *Records*, II, pp 378, 445 407, III, p 462

6 Cf Owen, *Hunts*, p 8

7 *Leics* p 41

8 *Records*, III, pp 55, 57, etc On p 90 is given "thaccounpte of Rich Pratte one of the executoures of the tastament of Roberte Newecomme of Leicester bellfounder deceased," dated April, 1561 He is also recorded as purchasing various bells at the Dissolution

below, p 28) was originally his, and that he also used the crown (Pl XVII, 3). But bells with these two marks are of the same character as those bearing Thomas' special trade-mark, and I do not see how any distinction can be drawn, which would enable us to assign any to the earlier founder. If any Warwickshire bells may be regarded as his, the treble at Little Packington (see p 34) has perhaps the strongest claim.

JOHANNES DE YORKE

A group of bells which on the ground of geographical distribution must apparently be associated with Leicester is that to which the tenor at **Wolvey** belongs. It is inscribed

✠ GLORIA ⁝ IN ⁝ EXCELSIS ⁝ DEO

in large Gothic capitals (Pl X, 1), with a handsome initial cross and an oblong stop of three floral designs in squares one above the other. The founder of this group is revealed on the 2nd at *Sproxton*, Leicestershire, with the inscription

✠ IHOANNES ✠ DE ✠ YORKE ✠ ME ✠ FECIT ✠ IN ✠ HONORE ✠ BEATE ✠ MARIE ✠

✠ IHESVS ⁝ NAZARENVS ⁝ REX ⁝ IVDEORVM

Here the second line only is in the Wolvey type, the upper line has a reduced version of the cross, a small quatrefoil stop, and smaller letters. Of these bells there are no less than ten in Leicestershire, while outside the limits of the county there are two in Notts (Edingley 1st and Rolleston 3rd), one in Northants (Great Billing 3rd), and there was formerly also one at St Mary-the Great Cambridge. All have inscriptions in capitals except the 2nd at Wanlip, Leicestershire, which is in black-letter, and therefore forbids us dating the group much earlier than 1400, it may even be later.

Nothing is known of this John of York, no similar bells are found in Yorkshire or neighbourhood, but that there was an important foundry at York in the fourteenth century is well-known, and John may have learned his business there, and migrated to Leicester. The fact that two thirds of his bells are found in that county seems to be conclusive evidence that he resided there, and doubtless there were once more. But we cannot be certain whether he preceded or succeeded Johannes de Stafford, and it is certainly singular that his name does not occur in the local records.

Another group of bells, of which Warwickshire claims one representative, is probably also to be referred to the Leicester foundry, though we have no evidence to go upon beyond geographical distribution. The treble at **Mancetter** bears in large ornamental capitals (Pl IX, 2-5) the inscription

✠ GABRIEL

preceded by a handsome cross (Pl IX, 1), which is found on four other bells in the Midlands. Of these the treble at *Preston*, Rutland, is exactly similar to the Mancetter bell, the treble at *Fradswell*, Staffordshire, has the inscription + IESVS in the same capitals. But at *Frowlesworth* in Leicestershire we find the cross accompanied by a black-letter inscription, and the same appears to be the case with the 2nd at *Water Newton*, Hunts, though Mr Owen's description reads rather as if capitals were used throughout. To this list may be added the 3rd at *Stowe* Staffordshire, inscribed

Nos A Ruina Salvet Virgo Katerina

The cross does not appear in Mr Lynam's book, but the capital letters seem to be the same as at Mancetter.

All these bells being clearly from the same founder, the use of black-letter forbids our dating them earlier than 1400, though the first three here named would, if regarded by themselves, certainly appear to be much earlier. They have nothing in common with any other known bells, but we may hazard the conjecture that they fill in a gap in the history of the Leicester foundry somewhere about the middle of the fifteenth century, and may perhaps be the work of William Noble or Thomas Innocent, who belong to that time (p. 15). The capitals are not indeed unlike those used by an early Nottingham founder on bells in Notts and Leicestershire (p. 20), but they are clearly a different alphabet.

JOHANNES DE COLSALE

I now come to a founder whose date is the first decade of the fifteenth century, but whom I have placed at this point because I have not yet satisfied myself whether he hailed from Leicester or Nottingham (the next foundry with which I propose to deal). There are about twenty bells which may be grouped together by means of the initial cross they bear (Pl. IX., 6), and by the use of one or both of two alphabets, but as far as geographical distribution goes, one centre would suit almost as well as the other. The balance is perhaps slightly in favour of Nottingham, but against this must be urged the fact that so far only one of these bells has turned up in that county.

The founder's name we know from a remarkable bell at *Milwich* Staffordshire, which bears (in two different alphabets) the inscription

+ IHOANNES DE COLSALE ME FECIT ANNO DOM·NI M CCCC IX

+ IHESVS :: NAZARENVS :: REX :: IUDEORVM

It is thus also a rare instance of a dated mediaeval bell, and it is curious that there was not only a very similar bell at *Beckingham*, Notts, also dated 1409, recast in 1848, but that we can date the group almost as certainly by means of another undated bell, the sanctus at *Harringworth*, Northants, which bears the name of Philip de Repyngdon, Bishop of Lincoln, 1405—1420. This multiplicity of chronological evidence is only paralleled by the Worcester group discussed on p. 11. In reference to the position of the foundry, the name of the owner is worth noting, as Colsale seems more likely to stand for Cossall (a village near Nottingham) than any other place in the Midlands, but in view of what has been said about the Johns of Stafford and York, we must not lay too much stress on that point.

As they have not been previously collected, I give here a full list of Johannes de Colsale's bells, followed by a description of the two or rather three specimens in Warwickshire —

Derbyshire	Sutton-on-Hill	3rd
Leicestershire	Barleston	2nd
	Foxton	3rd
	Gumley	3rd
	Hungarton	2nd
	Rotherby	2nd
	Walton Isley	1st
Lincolnshire	Grayingham	2nd
	Lincoln, St Mary Magdalen	Bell
Northants	Harringworth	Sanctus
	Walgrave	Sanctus
Nottingham	Beckingham	Recast bell. Similar to that at Milwich. See L'Estrange, *Norfolk*, p. 84[1]

[1] L'Estrange confused this group with one in East Norfolk, having somewhat similar but larger lettering, with a quite distinct cross.

Rutland	Whitwell	2nd
Shropshire	Stirchley	1st
Stafford	Milwich	3rd
	Weston-on-Trent	2nd
Yorkshire	Kellington	2nd

and in Warwickshire

Corley .. .. 3rd, inscribed

GLORIA TIBI DOMINE

and **Stoke-by-Coventry** 6th, inscribed

SIT NOMEN DOMINI BENEDICTUM

The old 2nd at Stoke, now represented by the 5th, was exactly similar to this All three are inscribed in the same small neat Gothic letters (Pl IX, Fig 7, 8), which occur on the upper line of inscription at Milwich (Lynam, *Staffs* pls 6-8), but elsewhere, as at Kellington, Stirchley, and Grayingham, we find the other Milwich set

THE NOTTINGHAM FOUNDRY[1]

Four Warwickshire bells though all different in type, may be assigned to this important mediaeval foundry, of which unfortunately we know little at present, though we may hope that Mr W P W Phillimore, when his labours on Nottinghamshire bells are given to the world, will do something by way of further elucidation

I take first the 2nd at **Stoneleigh**, a bell which has long been known to campanists, though it has never yet been properly considered in relation to others The inscription in small neat Gothic capitals runs

MICHAELE TE PVLSANTE WYNCHELCVMBAM A PETENTE DEMONE TV LIBRA

R  K

The lettering (Pl X 4) appears to be that used by John Rufford (see p 8), and the heads of King and Queen (Pl X 3) at the end are also his stamps On the other hand the R K (Pl X 7) are in a larger type, and seem to belong to an alphabet peculiar to Nottingham The same capitals occur with this shield (*Lincs* 137) at *Muston* and *Kegworth* in Leicestershire, on bells cast at Nottingham The smaller or Rufford lettering is found on a Nottingham bell at *Ledsham* in the West Riding of Yorkshire[2]

As was long ago pointed out by Ellacombe,[3] the bell must obviously have come from Winchcombe Abbey in Gloucestershire, as the inscription shews This is further borne out by the inscription on the old 4th at Stoneleigh, recast by Briant in 1792[4] which was dedicated to Winchcombe's patron saint, St Kenelm

O KENELME NOS DEFENDE NE MALIGNI SENTIAMVS FOCVLA

Ellacombe supposed that R K were the initials of Richard Kidderminster, the last abbot, but this, says Mr Cocks,[5] is an anachronism At all events the bell may well be of earlier date than 1488—1531, the time of Kidderminster's office Mr Cocks (without having seen the lettering) pronounced it "late fourteenth century" But I am not sure whether it goes quite so far back The initial W of WYNCHELCVMBAM (Pl X, 5) is of a late type (it is a

---

[1] For a useful *resumé* of this foundry s history, see Miss Hewitt's article in *Victoria County Hist of Notts*, vol ii

[2] *Ex inform* J E Poppleton

[3] *Church Bells of Gloucs* p 132

[4] So Colvile, *Stoneleigh Abbey*, p 39 but Ellacombe, *loc cit*, says it was the treble, recast by Layre in 1752

[5] *Bucks*, p 191

minuscule or "lower case" letter), and the shield with saltire cross *incuse* (Pl X 2) at the beginning of the inscription is found on many bells in the north Midlands, which from their black-letter inscriptions cannot be earlier than the fifteenth century Further, the shield which Ellacombe took to be the Abbot's arms is found without the crown and initials on bells in Leicestershire (as noted above) and Lincolnshire, one of the latter, formerly at *Grasby*, is said to have been dated 1500 It is then obvious that if we may accept the Grasby bell as evidence, the Stoneleigh bell might have been cast in Kidderminster's time, and the initials might be his

The next question is, at what foundry this bell (and probably the other also) was cast? The bells on which these two shields (*Lincs* 124 and 137) occur, are found principally in the counties of Derby, Leicester, Lincoln, Northants, Notts, Stafford, and Yorkshire, the majority being found in Yorkshire and Lincoln[1] This fact points to Nottingham as their centre. Secondly, we know that the Royal Heads which appear on the Stoneleigh bell were in the hands of Nottingham founders for many years, from the 15th century at least[2] They are not found anywhere else after their original use by the Ruffords in the fourteenth century, and we may presume that they went to Nottingham about 1400, when the other stamps went to Worcester We thus get, in addition to the probability that this group was cast at Nottingham, a *terminus post quem* for its date On the other hand, the evidence of bells at *Conway* in North Wales and *Bolton-by-Bowland* in Yorkshire seems to place it much later than 1400 The former bears the name of John Byrchynshaw, Abbot of Chester 1493—1537, and the latter can also be dated about 1510[3] But the cross, or rather shield (Pl X 2), may have been in use for some years

There is or rather was, another Warwickshire bell which belongs to this class, the old treble at **Ryton-on-Dunsmore,** recast by George Mears in 1864 Fortunately a drawing of the inscription was made at the time by Mr W T Kimber, which is preserved at Mears and Stainbank's foundry[4] The inscription was

Sca maria mater dei

the shield being as at Stoneleigh, the other stamp the Virgin and Child, which occurs on other bells of this class at Stanion, Northants, and elsewhere

We have, however at present no absolute proof that these bells were cast at Nottingham, and in the present state of our knowledge it can only be assumed, though North was quite satisfied on this point, and there seems no reason for doubt But towards the middle of the fifteenth century we begin to tread on firmer ground in reference to this foundry, for documentary evidence comes to our aid Whether we can regard John de Colsale (see p 18) as a Nottingham man or not, it yet seems extremely likely that the Nottingham foundry was flourishing for at least a hundred years before the documents begin There are bells at Thorpe in Notts and Croxton Kerrial and Melton Mowbray in Leicestershire which seem to have been cast in Nottingham, and date from the fourteenth century. But we can hardly accept as a Nottingham founder the "William Brasyer of Nottingham" who appears at Norwich in 1376[5]

There is, however a *William Belyetere* of Nottingham, who is mentioned in 1437, and is probably identical with *William Langton*, mentioned in 1437-38[6] Closely connected with the

---

[1] Examples also occur in Cheshire, Rutland, Westmoreland, and North Wales

[2] They are, as already noted, the second or B set used by the Ruffords (see above, p 8) The other set, as we know, were at Worcester down to the Reformation Ten other Nottingham mediaevals have the Stoneleigh heads

[3] See Poppleton in *Yorks Arch Soc Journ*, xvii, p 198

[4] I am indebted to Mr A Hughes for the loan of the volume containing this and many other interesting records

[5] See Raven, *Cambs*, p 13

[6] *Records of the Borough*, ii pp 160, 162, 166, 172

latter is *Richard Redeswell*, who was founding in 1433-37 [1] Mr Phillimore also mentions a family named Selyoke as casting bells at Nottingham in 1499, and *Richard Selyoke* occurs 1536-1548, also a John Selioke is frequently mentioned, but not as a bell-founder [2] Another name of the same period is *John Wolley* (1536) A much more important family was that of the *Mellours* or Mellerses, father and son, about whom much information has been collected by Phillimore and North The father, Richard, described as "Ric'us Mellour de Notyngham Belyetter" was living in 1488,[3] and was first Alderman, then Mayor in 1499 and 1506 [4] He died about 1508, his widow, "Dame Agnes Mellers" being executrix of his will.

He was succeeded by his son *Robert Mellour*, also an Alderman, who cast bells for Louth in 1510, and whose will is dated 1525 Robert's daughter Elizabeth married *Humphrey Quarnbie*, Alderman, Mayor in 1543, and M P for the town, who in due course succeeded to the foundry The only record that we have of him as a bell-founder is that he recast the bells of Worksop in 1560 [5] In the Borough Records he is only once spoken of in this capacity, under date 1547 [6] Humphrey Quarnbie was succeeded by his son Robert, born about 1540,[7] who is mentioned in the Churchwardens' Accounts of St Mary's, Nottingham, as doing repairs to the bells in 1589 [8]

But before we proceed with the history of this foundry under Robert Quarnbie and his contemporaries, which belong rather to a later page, we may pause to enquire whether any bells can be traced to the Mellours, who were evidently persons of civic importance, and therefore successful craftsmen, or to any other of the known names

In the first place it is not impossible that we may be able to attribute to Richard Redeswell and his contemporary William Langton the group of bells of which those at Stoneleigh and Ryton are examples They vary sufficiently in character to admit of classifying them in earlier and later groups,[9] and it is probable, as the Conway and Bolton bells seem to shew, that the stamps were still in use about 1500 The earliest group, with inscriptions in Gothic capitals, of which the Stoneleigh bell is a striking example, may be assigned to Redeswell or Langton, and consequently dated about 1435 Later bells with inscriptions in black-letter smalls, or such as that at Conway, may possibly be the work of Richard Selyoke

There are also in Nottinghamshire and the adjoining counties a number of bells marked by the use of a foundry-shield of the "Merchant-mark" type, on which appears the letter R with a bell (Pl X 8) [10] The majority of these bear the inscription in black-letter (with a Tudor rose, Pl X 6, by way of a cross)

Celorum xte placeat tibi rex sonus iste

The initial C, the only capital used, is of decidedly late, sixteenth-century type, and I should be disposed to date the whole group about 1520-1540 They may then be the work of the younger

---

[1] *Ibid*, pp 142, 145, 158, 162

[2] See Briscoe's *Old Nottinghamshire*, 1st ser p 112, fuller information in *Records of the Borough*, vol II, p 198, etc., and see the index, *s vv*

[3] *Records*, III, p 200

[4] *Reliquary*, XIII p 81, North, *Lincs* p 103, see also *Records*, index to vol III for refs

[5] R White, *Worksop*, p 329

[6] *Records*, IV, p 395, see also vol III, pp 194, 214, 214, 443, 458, and IV *passim* (see Index)

[7] *Op cit* IV pp 111, 156, 166, 243, 398, 399

[8] *Ibid* p 232

[9] The earlier group seems to be that with the shield *Lincs*, 137 as at Stoneleigh and inscriptions in capitals, the later has the shield, Pl X 2, (as at Ryton) and inscriptions in black letter, usually without initial capitals But the shield 137 is used on a bell of quite late date at Thurcaston, Leicestershire

[10] This shield occurs at Morcott in Rutland in company with the stamps of Newcombe of Leicester (p 25) It would seem therefore to have migrated to that town in the course of the sixteenth century The Morcott bell must be later than 1560 I have to thank Mr V B Crowther Beynon for a rubbing

Mellour, Robert for there is no doubt that they were cast at Nottingham, and it seems probable that the R in the shield may represent his Christian name We have one of this class in Warwickshire, the second at **Wormleighton,** with the rose, shield, and inscription as above

The same stamps occur on a group of bells of which there are several in Lincolnshire and Notts, merely inscribed in Gothic capitals (Pl X 10 11)

S S S

with the initial cross Pl X 9 North calls them "Bells of S S" This cross we find on the treble at **Seckington,** with the inscription

✠ I E S V S

These brief inscriptions are thoroughly characteristic of the earlier Nottingham founders Though not an "S S" bell, the Seckington one clearly ranks with the group Similar bells occur at Kirklington in Notts and (formerly) Hunmanby in the East Riding of Yorkshire, the latter with a full inscription I am inclined to think that these bells may be the work of *Richard Mellour* (1488-1506), as the others are to be attributed to his son

LONDON FIFTEENTH CENTURY FOUNDERS

In the fifteenth century there were in London two main lines of founders, working contemporaneously, of which the less important and shorter-lived is represented by three examples in Warwickshire, the other by nine Their history has been fully told elsewhere (*vide Church Bells of Essex*, and Stahlschmidt's works), and I do not propose to enter into much detail here, but merely to give a brief outline in order to shew the places occupied by the Warwickshire examples [1] I begin with three from the less important foundry

The stamps employed by two fourteenth century founders, *Robert Burford* of London and *Stephen Norton* of (probably Maidstone in) Kent fell into the hands of one *Richard Hille* about 1420 This Hille's widow by name Joanna, after carrying on his business herself for a short time, married one *John Sturdy* about 1444 Again left a widow, she for a second time kept on business on her own account, and on her death the foundry passed into the hands of a founder named John Kebyll, with whom it appears to have come to an end, about 1485

Of the three Warwickshire bells attributable to the founders of this line we may take first the larger bell at **Wolfhamcote** a fine bell weighing nearly a ton It is inscribed

✠ ⊕ ✤ In Multis Annis Resonet Campana Iohannis

and, while the first cross (Pl XI 2) is an old Londoner dating from the fourteenth century, the second one, a cross of four fleurs-de-lys in an octagon (Pl XI 3) appears to have been first introduced by John Sturdy The capital letters (Pl XI 6-14) belong to an alphabet originally used by Stephen Norton, with the crowns over them which are found elsewhere This bell being certainly John Sturdy's, in spite of the absence of initials as elsewhere, may be dated about 1445

Next we have the old treble at **Ladbroke,** inscribed

Sancta Katerina Ora Pro Nobis ✠ I ◊ S

The initials here (Pl XI 4-5) might at first sight be taken for those of John Sturdy, were it not for a small detail which renders it certain that they are those of his *widow*, Joanna This is the lozenge, the heraldic mark of womanhood, which is placed over the coin between the initials The cross is the same as the first on the Wolfhamcote bell, and the capital letters are

[1] For a specimen of fourteenth century London founding in Warwickshire, see below, p 27

also the same, but without the usual crowns over them About thirteen bells by *Joanna Sturdy* (marked by the lozenge) are or were recently in existence

About the third bell, the 2nd at **Bilton,** there is some room for doubt It is inscribed

✠ Sancta Katerina Ora Pro Nobis ✠

with the same crowned capitals as at Wolfhamcote The initial cross is the same as the second, on the Wolfhamcote bell (Plate XI, Fig 3) here repeated twice But there is a small though important difference to be noted The frame of the cross is not octagonal as before, but *lozenge-shaped* Now this alteration appears to be due to Joanna Sturdy's successor *John Kebyll,* who usually employs this form of the stamp, and though his almost invariable trade-mark—a shield with a chevron between three stars and a crescent—is absent, yet this small detail is enough to justify the attribution of the bell to Kebyll It will therefore rank later in date than the two Sturdy bells, and later than its two mediaeval companions in the tower described below (p 24)

I turn now to the longer or main line of London founders, established in Aldgate from 1370 to about 1530, to which belong the great majority of London-made mediaeval bells now existing First of this line was *John Langhorne,* who died in 1405 He used small Gothic capitals with a wheel-stop between the words, and his foundry-stamp was a shield with three laver pots (Pl XII 1), which however only occurs on one or two of his bells There are also two or three bells with "mixed Gothic" inscriptions, which may be assigned to the later part of his career, when the new style of lettering was coming into favour He was succeeded by a founder named *William Dawe* or William Founder (1385—1418), whose bells are distinguished by the use of a medallion as a stop between the words, on which are two birds on a plant surrounded by the words **William ffounder me fecit.** His bells are nearly all inscribed in "Mixed Gothic," the minuscules being somewhat larger than the capitals, which are an enlarged version of Langhorne's One of these bells has capitals throughout, and there are a few others entirely in these capitals, but without the founder's mark, which may be his earliest productions He also uses the "laver shield," and a characteristic initial cross Contemporary with him (and possibly in partnership with him) was *William Wodewarde* (1395—1420), who uses another type of initial cross and a still more enlarged set of the Langhorne-Dawe capitals

Dawe in his will left his business to one John Walgrave and his plant to one John Bird, the former of whom we shall come to presently Meanwhile there is a large group of bells on which we find the stamps used by Dawe and Wodewarde, clearly by a later founder, which I think there are very good grounds for attributing to John Bird And with one of these bells, the most remarkable of all, we have now to deal

JOHN BIRD

The old tenor at **Brailes** was remarkable as being almost the largest mediaeval bell existing to our time in England, it is only surpassed in size by Great Peter of Gloucester, and even attracted the notice of Dugdale or his later editor Dr Thomas, who gives the inscription in the 1730 edition of the *Antiquities of Warwickshire* (II p 555) For many years this bell hung in the tower cracked and useless, but when it was finally recast in 1877 by Blews of Birmingham, it is a matter for gratitude to be able to record that the old inscription was reproduced in fac-simile with perfect accuracy It was as follows

✠ Gaude Quod Post Ipm Scandis Et Est Honor Tibi Grandis In Celi Palacio

The exceedingly beautiful letters (Pl XII 5-8) are a combination of Wodewarde's large capitals with Dawe's large and elaborate minuscules (which fit these capitals better than his own) At the conclusion of the inscription we find the laver-shield in company with another bearing a chevron between three trefoils slipped (Pl XII 3) and preceding them seven crowns (Pl XII 2) The initial cross of peculiar form (Pl XII. 4) and the second shield are both introductions of this founder, who is clearly the successor of Dawe and Wodewarde and whom I therefore identify as John Bird The shield, it may be remarked, bears the arms of the Underhill family, as observed by Dr Thomas but we do not know why it was adopted by Bird The very beautiful inscription is said to be from an old Ascension Day hymn it also appears on a later bell at Eton College, dated 1777, where the founder doubtless reproduced it from his predecessor [1]

JOHN WALGRAVE

Dawe's business being left to a founder of this name in 1418 it has been generally agreed that he may be credited with bells bearing a trade-mark on which are the initials I W, combined with a cross in the form of a merchant's mark (Plate XII 10) Of these a considerable number still exist, [2]all inscribed in "Mixed Gothic," with a new cross *fleurie* (Plate XIII, Fig 1) and the aforesaid trade-mark, the capitals are either the large ones used by John Bird or a smaller set introduced by Walgrave himself and used (together with his cross and the larger set) by four successive founders (Pl XIII, Figs 2-6) There are now no bells by Walgrave in Warwickshire, but there was formerly one at **Halford**, the 2nd, inscribed

✠ Sancta Katerina Ora Pro Nobis

It was cracked in 1876, and has since been recast by Taylor

Walgrave was succeeded by one *Robert Crowch*, whose bells are not found in Warwickshire, though they occur in the adjoining counties of Northants and Worcester His date is about 1440, and he was succeeded by two founders who appear to have been more or less contemporary, so far as we have evidence

JOHN DANYELL

Of these two John Danyell is slightly the earlier He has been identified as the founder who cast a ring of bells for King's College, Cambridge, in 1460, placing on the treble his initials I D His bells are very numerous, about 90 in all existing, and are found in many counties from Durham to Cornwall They fall into several distinct groups, according to the stamps he employs all of which are not found together Besides the initial cross introduced by Walgrave, he employs a distinctive one of his own which in fact also occurs on one or two of Walgrave's bells, though it was not regularly employed by him (Plate XIII, Fig 12) This cross, curiously enough, is never found in conjunction with the initials I D, but as the other marks are common to both we may divide the bells into two main heads those with the initials and those with the new cross This is not to say that the two groups are by different founders, for which supposition we have no apparent grounds, but it does raise a point which deserves some consideration, supposing that we knew of another London founder of the time We might then dissociate from Danyell all the bells without his initials, but as the new founder would then have no distinctive mark of his own, it seems safer to ignore the combinations of stamps and assign the whole group to Danyell

The 3rd and 4th bells at **Bilton** belong to the second group of Danyell's bells, without the initials, they are not identical in respect of marks, the 3rd being inscribed

✠ Wox Augustini Sonet In Aure Dei

[1] See Ellacombe, *Ch Bells of Somerset*, Suppl p 135, and Cocks, *Bucks*, p 384

[2] To those already described in various books should be added the 2nd at Cold Overton Leicestershire, overlooked by North

with the two crosses Plate XIII., Fig. 1, 12, and the Royal Arms of the period; the 4th

Beata Katerina   Ora  Pro Nobis

with a beautiful cross in a medallion (Pl. XI. 16) in place of the older London cross, round which are the words ihu merci ladi helpe.

The use of the Royal Arms (Pl. XIII. 11) is peculiar to Danyell, and they appear on almost all his bells; they were in fact his trade-mark, and their use may have been granted to him in virtue of his having cast bells for the Royal College at Cambridge. If these bells were cast at the beginning of his career (and we do not know its exact limits), this might account for the few on which they do not occur, as being his earliest productions; all these bells, it should be noted have the initials.

HENRY JORDAN.

Danyell's contemporary, Henry Jordan or Jurden, was an even more successful founder, and of his beautiful bells over 100 still remain, covering England from Yorkshire to Cornwall. As with Danyell, the limits of his career are not known, only the fact of his being commissioned to recast some of the former's bells at King's College in 1466.[1] From the fact that they use two stamps in common it must be supposed that they were more or less in partnership. These two stamps are the cross Plate XIII., Fig. 1, derived from Walgrave, and the beautiful "Jesu Mercy" medallion (Pl. XI. 16.) Jordan had also two trade-marks of his own in the form of a somewhat unheraldic shield and a merchant's mark, in which may lie concealed a subtle rebus (Pl. XI. 15, 17.) On the majority of his bells he employs the medallion between the two shields, but in other cases he replaces it by the cross aforesaid.

In Warwickshire the shields and medallion occur on two bells, the 2nd at **Brailes**

In Multis Annis Resonet Campana Iohannis

and the 3rd at **Milverton**

Sancta Katerina Ora Pro Nobis   

in the first case with the large capitals used by Bird on the tenor in the same tower, but here *uncrowned*; at Milverton we have a smaller set of plain flat capitals (Pl. XIII. 7-9), known as "Powdrell's," from their original use by a founder of that name.

THOMAS HARRYS.

In the year 1478 one Thomas Harrys, a London bell-founder, was employed to mark another stage in the chequered career of the King's College bells, one of which he then re-cast A small but widely-scattered group of bells with the initials T. H. has been recognised as this founder's work, including one in Bucks, two in Essex, one in Middlesex, two in Northants, one each in Surrey and Sussex, and one in Warwickshire. He uses none of the well-known London marks, but has two sets of capitals, one of his own invention, the other acquired from other sources and already familiar to us, as will be seen. With both sets he uses a large Maltese cross, a rose, and the impression of a coin; the new set of letters is found at Nettleden, Bucks, Hampton Court, Middlesex, and Limpsfield, Surrey. But on his other bells the capitals are no others than the crowned initials employed by the Worcester founder of the bells at Allesley,

[1] For further details of Henry Jordan see *Surrey Bells*, p. 56ff., and other works.

Lapworth, and elsewhere (Pl XIII 16-17 see p 10 and Pl VII) Thus they appear on the treble at **Lillington**, inscribed

✠ Sancta Katerina Ora Pro Nobis ⊕ T H

Here as elsewhere they are much worn from long usage, and it is difficult to get good rubbings or "squeezes," while they have the additional disadvantage of being too small for the accompanying black-letter So far as I know this is the only instance earlier than the end of the sixteenth century of a London founder acquiring stamps from the provinces

THOMAS BULLISDON

About 1500—1510 a founder of the name of Bullisdon was working in London, apparently reviving the business of the Aldgate line which after Jordan had suffered temporary misfortune He cast bells for the Church of St Mary-at-Hill, London, in 1509 He has been identified with the founder of bells bearing a shield with a bell and the initials T B (Pl XIII 17), some of which can be dated about this time and though there is no mention of his Christian name in any records, we may assume from the shield that it was Thomas

In Warwickshire this shield is found on a very beautiful bell the tenor at **Wroxhall**, inscribed

Assit Principio Sca Maria Meo

The capitals are those used by Wodewarde and Bird, and the initial medallion of six fleurs-de-lys (Pl XIII 14) was also used by those two founders The inscription is of interest as seeming to imply that it was his first effort[1] it is generally supposed that this bell was one of the ring of seven at the old Abbey

Another bell that we may attribute to Bullisdon, though contrary to the almost invariable rule of these founders it bears no trade-mark is the smaller at **Hunningham**, inscribed

✠ In ⁘ Nomine ✠ Ihesu ✠ Vocor ✠ Sancte ✠ Margareta

The cross is Plate XIII, Fig 1, and the stop (Pl XIII 15) occurs on undoubted Bullisdon bells at St Bartholomew-the-Great, London, East Dean, Sussex, and Hoddesdon, Herts With him we take our leave of the London founders, as his contemporary William Culverden is unfortunately not represented in our county

THE READING FOUNDRY.

There is only one bell in Warwickshire which can be attributed to this somewhat distant foundry, the treble at **Baddesley Clinton**, inscribed

Sacte Nicolae Ora ⛨ Pro W Nobis H

The initals W H enable us to identify this bell as the work of *William Hasylwood*, who succeeded to the good will of the important fifteenth-century foundry at Wokingham about the year 1495, but transferred the business to Reading and introduced new stamps and lettering of his own[2] Mr Cocks tells how two men from Thame in Oxfordshire journeyed to Wokingham in 1495 to see about the casting of a bell, but found no one there to do it, and a further journey to Reading was entailed Hasylwood died in 1509, his will being dated 8 March 1507-8, and his parish church was that of St Lawrence Mr Cocks enumerates five bells by him, at Chearsley and Ilmer in Bucks, and at Compton, Farley Chamberlayne and St Michael,

[1] Cf a bell at Takeley, Essex, by his contemporary William Culverden, and see Raven, *Suffolk*, p 38

[2] *Bucks*, p 58

Winchester in Hants; to which may be added the tenor at Whatley, Somerset, a bell at Broadwell, Oxon., and our Warwickshire example. Possibly the bell at Caldecote, Cambs., is also his work, though Mr. Cocks attributes it to his successor John White (see *Bucks.*, p. 67.)

William Hasylwood uses a fine set of well-formed capitals and initials (Pl. XIV., 1—5), but his W is of a plain Roman type; his only ornaments are a plain cross patée and a shield with the cross of St. George (Pl. XIV., 6) as here, though his successor revived some of the old Wokingham marks. All that we know of him is due to Mr. Cocks' extensive researches, as set forth in his *Bucks.* book.

Our list of existing mediaeval bells closes with the sanctus at **Long Compton**, which now no longer hangs in its original cot. It bears an unintelligible inscription (Pl. XVI., 1) of six letters in minuscules, with a fleur-de-lys as stop:

a ? o a ? ? ⚜

The date may be assumed to be the sixteenth century; possibly as late as Queen Mary's reign; but in any case the inscription is quite unintelligible. The sanctus bells at *Keynsham*, Somerset, and *Westcote*, Gloucestershire (not given in Ellacombe's books) have similar inscriptions, and may be by the same founder.

A few words may be added on some of the bells no longer existing, of which a list has been given above (p. 3). Of these the most interesting was the old 2nd at **Exhall**, near Alcester, inscribed

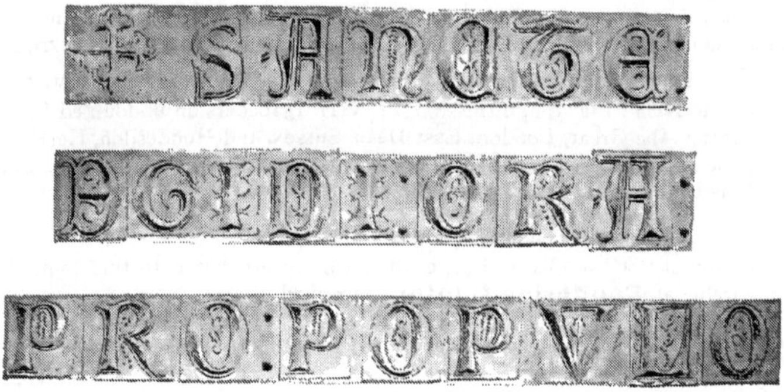

Fig. 2.

The cross and lettering are identical with those on bells at *Iwerne Minster*, Dorset, and *Magdalen Laver*, Essex, and the bell must have been cast in London early in the fourteenth century, perhaps by one of the well-known family of Wymbish.[1] The other old bell at Exhall was more of the Midland type, with an elaborate cross and handsome floral capitals:

[1] See Deedes and Walters, *Church Bells of Essex*, p. 6.

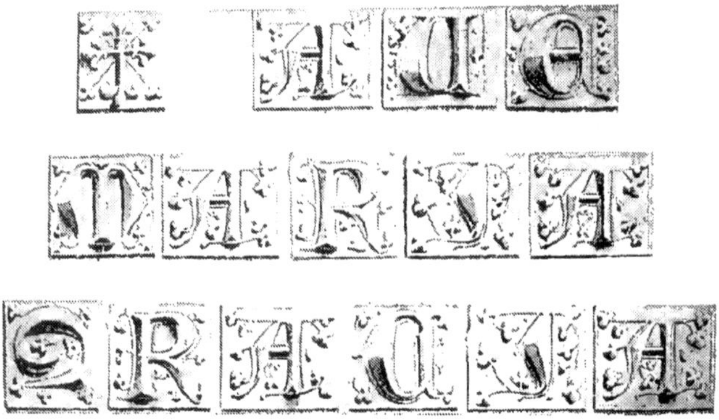

Fig. 3.

I cannot identify these with any known founder or group of bells.

The old bell at **Combrooke** had merely three medallions, one with ihc, the other two with

Fig. 4. COMBROOKE.

a four-petalled flower and a double intersecting triangle respectively (see Fig. 4). It probably dated from the sixteenth century.[1]

I can only note here the three foreign bells formerly at Hatton, of which Dr. Thomas has preserved a record, and the bells at Warwick St. Mary, Kenilworth, and elsewhere, of all of which some description will be found in Part II.

II. POST-REFORMATION FOUNDERS.

THE LATER LEICESTER FOUNDRY.[2]

I. THE NEWCOMBES.

Warwickshire is extremely rich in bells from the Leicester foundry during the period 1560–1640, which are found, to the total of 126, all over the county, and are especially plentiful, as is natural, in the north and east. They fall into two groups, overlapping in date, but more or less clearly defined as the work of two different families during this period, the Newcombes

[1] For the illustrations of these three bells I am indebted to Mr. Kimber's drawings, kindly lent by Mr. Hughes, of [illegible]

and the Wattses Both families enjoyed a great reputation, especially the latter, but it may be noted that their bells are much commoner to the south of Leicester than the north, where the great Nottingham foundry blocked their path They are comparatively rare in Derbyshire, Notts, and Lincoln as also in Staffordshire

We have already traced the earlier history of the Newcombe family down to 1561 (p 16), and have seen that no traces of their work seem to remain But after the death of Robert Newcombe the foundry appears to have had a new lease of life He left three sons, Thomas, Robert, and Edward, all of whom certainly practised the bell founders' craft, and of whom the eldest first claims our attention

THOMAS NEWCOMBE II (1562-1580)

In 1562 the 5th bell at *Melton Mowbray*, Leicestershire was cast by **Thomas Newcombe**,[1] and as this bell still exists, though it does not bear his name, it is obviously an important piece of evidence as to the style of his work It is inscribed in black letter smalls

be at a ma ri a

and bears in addition three stamps, a kind of cross *fleurie* and a crown (Pl XVII, 2, 3), and a shield or trade-mark on which are a bell and the letters T N (Pl XVI, 3 Of these, the crown is common on all Leicester bells down to about 1600 (see below, p 36), the cross will be discussed later on (p 35) with reference to the dozen or so of bells on which it occurs, and for the present we will content ourselves with the consideration of the shield which is obviously to be regarded as Thomas Newcombe s trade mark In passing, it may be noted that there is a bell (the 4th) at *Elvaston*, Derbyshire, dated 1564 and bearing a stamp of a wyvern (*Leics* 62) which is also found in conjunction with the crown This appears to be the earliest existing *dated* Newcombe bell, and is presumably the work of Thomas

But we may take the bells with the T N shield as representing the normal type of Thomas Newcombe II 's bells They usually have in addition a cross with ornaments between the arms (Pl XVI, 2), which is often found in such an abraded condition that it has been taken for a plainer variety The inscription almost invariably consists of the name of a saint, with or without a preceding S in widely-spaced Gothic capitals, some of which, in particular the A, are late in character (see Pl XVI, Figs 7-10) Mr Owen in his *Hunts* book appears to regard these bells as genuine mediaevals, and assigns them to Thomas Newcombe I (1506-1520), but in spite of the style of the inscriptions they are, to my mind, distinctly 'transitional' rather than pre-Reformation in character,[2] as indeed are all the Leicester bells of this century Moreover the stamps occur on many other bells with non-religious inscriptions or bearing dates in Elizabeth's reign and even though it is conceivable that Thomas I could have used the stamps and handed them on all evidence seems to point the other way We cannot definitely distinguish an earlier and a later group, and even in Elizabethan times the mere name of a saint, often without a prefix, might have passed muster in an inscription It is unfortunate that the few dated bells, such as Elvaston, and Haddon, Hunts (1568), do not yield more evidence

In considering the bells of the normal Thomas Newcombe type it will be sufficient to discuss the Warwickshire examples as representative of the whole, and I will take first the four

---

[1] *Leics* p 48 He is mentioned in the Borough Records as Bailiff, Steward, Coroner, and in other capacities between 1566 and 1578

[2] The *Ora Pro Nobis* being invariably omitted, such inscriptions could not greatly offend Puritan susceptibilities and it may be that Newcombe had Papist leanings, to which he gave as much scope as he dared

bells on which we find both the cross and the shield These are

Ansley 1st.

✠ M A R G A R E T A

Bourton-on-Dunsmore 1st.

✠ S A N N A L 

Priors Hardwick 2nd

✠  S A N C T A M A R E A

Sheldon 3rd

✠ S M A R I A 

The shield without the cross is found on **Baddesley Clinton** 3rd

S T O M A 

On the other hand **Wappenbury** 2nd has only the cross

✠ S G E O R G E

And **Allesley** 2nd merely S A N N A, without cross or shield

With these we must group three bells bearing portions of the alphabet, together with the cross, Pl XVI, 2, but no shield

Bourton-on-Dunsmore 2nd

✠ A B C D E F G H I K L M N O P Q R S T ✠

Bubbenhall 1st

✠ A ✠ A B D C B D B D C E F G

Lower Shuckburgh 2nd

✠ A B C D E F G H I

None of the five last-named can be definitely attributed to Thomas Newcombe, and some or all may be by his successor, or even predecessor, but they are conveniently placed here as being of the same character as those which are certainly his

ROBERT NEWCOMBE (1580--1598)

Thomas Newcombe died in 1580,[1] and was succeeded by **Robert Newcombe II**, who has left his name on several bells, others again are dated during the period of his activity, and consequently afford additional evidence of his work I note first the bells bearing his name, which are as follows —

---

[1] *Lees*, p 53 His name does not occur in the Borough Records On the other hand, according to the Registers of All Saints, a Thomas Newcombe bell founder, was buried in 1594 (*Mid Count Hist Collector*, ii, p 229) I suspect this to be a mistake, afterwards corrected by North

In 1585 we have the 4th at *Catworth*, Hunts, inscribed

♔
✠ ROBARTE [K] NEWCOMBE [K] MADE [K] ME
O 1585

The marks on this bell are interesting, besides the crown (Pl XVII 3), we have the head of Edward III (Plate X, Fig 3), which occurs on other Newcombe bells, and seems to have been used at Leicester and Nottingham contemporaneously [1] The initial cross (*Leics* 42, see Pl VIII) is familiar as one used in Pre-Reformation times at Mancetter and St John, Coventry (p 13), and we shall meet with it yet again

In 1586, the 4th at *All Saints, Leicester*

✠ ROBARTE NEWCOMBE MAD ME 1586

Here again we have an unexpected cross (Pl XVIII, 6), which was originally in the possession of the Brasyers of Norwich, and which when found on Leicester bells is invariably associated with the Watts stamps, as at Wootton Wawen (see below, p 40); but towards the end of the sixteenth century, and even later, there is evidence that the two firms worked at times in partnership, or at all events had certain stamps in common

Of undated bells there are three inscribed alike, in the ordinary Newcombe lettering, with the cross, Pl. XVI, 2

✠ ROBART ✠ NEWCOMB

These are the treble at **Arley** in this county, and the 1st at *Little Bowden* and 3rd at *Pytchley* Northants There also several dated bells of this period, which are presumably to be assigned to Robert Newcombe, one of the most interesting being the former treble at **Withybrook** in this county

✠ ✠ CHRISTOPHER [K] WRGHT [K] OF [K] HAPPISFORD [K] ESQVIER Below —1585.

With the cross, Pl XVI, 2, is here associated the head of Edward III which we have already met at Catworth (a bell of the same year) The other bells are

1585	Desborough, Northants,	5th.	Stamps *Leics* 71 and 62
1588	Stanground, Hunts,	4th.	Stamps and lettering as Little Packington 1st (see below)
1589	Higham, Leicestershire,	3rd	Cross, Pl XVI, 2
	Clipston Northants,	4th	Cross, Pl XVI, 2
1592	Keystone, Hunts,	1st	Cross, Pl XVI, 2, other stamps as Stanground
1593	Gretford, Lincolnshire,	2nd	Cross, Pl XVI, 2
	Tong, Shropshire,	3rd	Cross, Pl XVI, 2
	Bushbury, Staffordshire,	7th	Cross, Pl XVI, 2

We must also include for consideration here a group of bells linked by the use of a small cross *fleurie* (Pl XVI, 4), which may be assigned to Robert Newcombe from the appearance of his name on one of them the treble at *Gloucester Cathedral*, dated 1598 The lettering is plain Roman, small and thin like that on Edward Newcombe's bells at Ettington (see below) Six other dated bells occur in this group, ranging from 1586 (or 1589) to 1596, the earliest of which is a bell formerly existing at **Baxterley**, inscribed

✠ A B Ɔ H Ɔ Ǝ E D Λ ⊥ S ꓤ ✤ λ X 1986

The date is probably intended for 1586, but may be 1589 Of the same type is the single bell at **Burmington**, inscribed

✠ PRAISE ✤ THE ✤ LORDE 1592

[1] Messrs North and Owen in all cases give the head *Leics*, fig 28 (Plate X, Fig 13), as used on Newcombe's bells, but on all those I have seen it is certainly the other type as at Stoneleigh Both were at one time or another in use at Nottingham, and I think Newcombe must have got a duplicate of the Stoneleigh variety from the Nottingham foundry

Other bells of this class are: Ashby Parva, Leics., 1st (1591), Orton, Leics., 3rd, and Fotheringhay, Northants, 1st (1595), Aston Flamville, Leics., 1st (1596), and Tong, Salop, sanctus, undated. The fleur-de-lys at Burmington (Pl. XVI., 5), also occurs at Tong, and the cross is found on a later Newcombe bell at Upton Magna, Salop, dated 1604.

Mr. Cocks also notes that Robert Newcombe's name occurs in 1590 on a bell at Hardwick Bucks., with modified copies of the cross, Pl. XVIII., 6, and the Brasyer-Watts shield (p. 34), but with the lettering used by Bartholomew Atton (see below). He evidently cast the bell during a temporary partnership with the latter at Buckingham; but the treble at Tidmington, Worcestershire, is interesting for comparison, as it bears Atton's name with Newcombe's lettering and stamps (Pl. XVII., 2, 3). Atton learned his business at Leicester, and the Tidmington bell probably comes from that foundry.

EDWARD NEWCOMBE (1570-1616).

The name of the third brother, **Edward,** is found on seven or eight bells in all, and he appears to have been working intermittently between 1570 and 1616, contemporaneously with his brother. We shall see that certain conjunctions of marks seem to indicate that he was the one who entered into partnership with the Wattses. His name frequently occurs in the Borough Records,[1] though not as a bell-founder. He was the fourth representative of the craft to become Mayor of Leicester (in 1599).

Of the bells with his name three are dated:

1595. **Ettington,** Warwickshire, 1st:

✠ MR GEORG VNDEREHILL 1595 

1595. **Ettington,** Warwickshire, 2nd:

✠ MR VMPHERY VNDERHILL 1595 

1602. **Warmington,** Warwickshire, 3rd:

 EDWARDE NEWCOME MADE MEE 1602

Fig. 5.

The first two are in plain small Roman letters, the only mark being a circular stamp with E N and a bell; but the Warmington bell is in a new type, the large Gothic capitals acquired by the Wattses from the Brasyers of Norwich, and frequently used by them.[2] The cross is Fig. 5=Pl. XV., 8, a typical Watts mark (see below, p. 40). This is one instance of the partnership already alluded to.

The other bells with his name are:

Covington, Hunts.	... ...	2nd	Cross, Pl. XVI., 2.
Haddon, Hunts.	... ...	3rd	Pl. XVI., 2.
Ilston-on-Hill, Leicestershire	...	1st	Pl. XVI., 2, and *Leics.* 70: crown, Pl. XVII., 3.

[1] See Vol. III., pp. 172, 256, 347, 361, 383, 409, 459 ff.

[2] See p. 38 and Plate XVIII. Note the use of the minuscule ꝛ for W. The Wattses did not possess the capital W, as it had never been used by the Brasyers.

Holcott Northants	3rd	Pl XVI 2, and fleur-de-lys *Leics* 86
Stanion, Northants	2nd	Pl XVI 2 and fleur-de-lys.
Winwick, Northants	1st	Brasyer Shield (see p 35) and fleur-de-lys

and, *teste* a rubbing in Ellacombe's collection (Brit Mus Add 33203) the old 2nd at Kingsbury, Warwickshire, dated 1602

So far the subject has been comparatively plain sailing, and the bells discussed may be assigned to their respective founders with a fair degree of probability But we now have to deal with various bells which were unquestionably cast at Leicester in or about the reign of Queen Elizabeth, but which from the stamps or combinations of stamps employed it is difficult to assign to any particular founder They may be said to fall into two classes bells which from stamps or lettering were clearly cast by one of the Newcombes, and bells which combine with the Newcombe stamps those otherwise found on bells by the Wattses The latter, I think, clearly imply some kind of partnership, such as has already been suggested and in view of the fact that most of the known Watts bells are dated subsequently to 1600, whereas most of the Newcombe bells are earlier, we may perhaps assign the period of that partnership to the closing years of the sixteenth century

Dealing first with the bells which bear only Newcombe stamps, the first which claims our attention in Warwickshire is the 2nd at **Haseley,** with a somewhat puzzling and partly illegible inscription

✠ *(dog)* W 3 5 *(dog)* K I *(dog)* H G *(dog)* F *(dog)* E *(dog)* C C B A

The initial cross appears to be the ordinary Pl XVI, 2 and the inscription is obviously intended for the first ten letters of the alphabet (to K), but the third fourth and fifth stamps, which I read as W 3 5, are very uncertain[1] The most interesting feature is the stamp of a dog (Pl XV, 9), which occurs no less than six times, and by its presence affords a clue to the date and founder It is found on three other bells, the 1st at *Hannington*, Northants, the old 4th at *Brewood*, Staffordshire,[2] and the 2nd at *Haddon*, Hunts, which is dated 1568 and bears the Leicester cross (Pl XVI 2) We have therefore good grounds for supposing these four bells to be the work of Thomas Newcombe II

The lettering on the Haseley bell is also found on the 2nd at **Little Packington,** inscribed

DOG FO EMAN EHT nI

The words, though not the letters, are reversed throughout, there are no marks of any kind, but the lettering is of a mixed type, the E, H and I being from the Haseley alphabet, while the rest are decidedly smaller The latter appear to be from an alphabet which occurs on the

Fig 6

2nd at *Olney* Bucks (Fig 6=Cocks p 153) Mr Cocks reads the date 1599 on this bell

[1] I regret that I cannot accept Mr Tilley's reading as 1531 (see *Birm and Mid Inst Trans* 1878, p 12)

[2] The Brewood bell is important for its combination of stamps The lettering is partly Newcombe's ordinary Gothic, partly the "Mancetter" type as on Little Packington 1st (see below, and p 13 above) The stamps are the Brasyer shield, the dog, the crown (Pl XVII, 3), and the stops *Leics* 43 and 86

(with some hesitation); it may at all events afford a clue to the date of Little Packington 2nd.[1] It is possible that, as he suggests, this may be the alphabet used by Norwich founders at Eaton and Witton, Norfolk, and at Frostenden, Suffolk. The Olney bell appears to bear also the Brasyer cross (Fig. 5) and lion's head (Fig. 7), the former of which is a Watts stamp (see below, p. 41; used at Warmington and Lapworth with Watts' lettering), the other, a Newcombe mark. Mr. Cocks therefore draws the conclusion that the Olney bell was cast at Bedford (see *Bucks*, p. 154) by a Newcombe and Watts in partnership.

Fig. 7.

He is obviously on the right lines: but in view of the distance of the Packington and other similar bells from Bedford, I hesitate to say that they were cast there, rather than at Leicester, where these stamps were certainly in use. The Warmington bell (p. 32) is evidence that there was a partnership at this time, and if we may date these bells about 1595—1600, it is probable that they are the work of Edward Newcombe. Additional confirmation of the partnership between this founder and the Wattses comes from Stratford-on-Avon, where Edward Newcombe and Francis Watts cast the Guild Chapel bell together in 1591.[2] The other bells of the Little Packington type are at *Thurlaston*, Leicestershire (part of alphabet in the Haseley lettering with stamps *Leics.* 71 and 62); *Kingstone*, Staffordshire, dated 1595, with mixed lettering as at Packington; and *Great Oakley* and *Duddington*, Northants, both with mixed lettering and a variety of stamps.

The Olney bell introduces us to another group, linked by the use of certain stamps, of which we may instance first the 4th at **Churchover,** inscribed:

✠ S I O K A N N E S

As far as the cross (Pl. XVI., 2), lettering, and style of inscription are concerned, this bell ranks with the group described on p. 30, and assigned to Thomas Newcombe. But at the end of the inscription we find not only the stop *Leics.* 43 twice repeated, but the lion's face stamp (Fig. 7), which as noted above occurs at Olney. The stop 43 is the same that accompanies the cross *Leics.* 42 on the Mancetter and Coventry fourteenth-century bells (p. 13), and links this bell to the next, the treble at **Little Packington,** inscribed:

S A N N A

Here the cross, stop, and lettering are all of the Mancetter-Coventry type (Pl. VIII), though the stamps are very much worn from use. But it is interesting to note the presence of the T. N. shield, which enables us to assign the bell to Thomas Newcombe, and date it previous to 1580.[3] Similar lettering is found on the tenor at **Budbrooke,** inscribed:

A C S I O H I

The letters here also are much worn and difficult to read: the stamps are the head of Edward

[1] Another clue to the date of this bell may be given by the fact that the Olney lettering occurs on a bell by Hugh Watts at South Luffenham, Rutland, dated 1593 (see p. 39). This is additional evidence of a partnership at the time.

[2] See under that heading in Part II

[3] There are similar bells at Higham-on-Hill, Houghton-on-Hill, and Theddingworth, Leicestershire, the last-named with the T. N. shield; also Brampton, Hunts., 3rd (cross *Leics.* 42). On the other hand the Stanground bell (p. 31) is by Robert Newcombe, dated 1588

III as at Stoneleigh (p 19) and a shield or trade-mark with which we have not met so far in the county but which is destined to become the typical stamp of the Leicester foundry [1] This is the shield with three bells and a crown on a sprigged ground (Plate XVIII Fig 11),[2] which came with other stamps from the Brasyers of Norwich, and was apparently used first by the Newcombes, and subsequently appropriated by the Wattses as their trade mark

The Brasyer-Watts shield introduces us to the next group, of which there are two examples in Warwickshire the 5th at **Butler's Marston,** inscribed

Uox dni ihu xpi vox exultacionis ⁊ salutis

and the 4th at **Bulkington**

Uox dni ihu xpi vox exultacionis ⁊ salutis

The shield, it will be noticed, only occurs on the former, the lettering is illustrated on Plate XVII, Figs 4, 5 In neighbouring counties there are six similar bells

Derbyshire	Repton	5th	Pl X 3, Pl XVIII 11, Fig 7, *Leics* 86
Leicestershire	Lockington	1st	Pl X 3, Pl XVI 3, Fig 7, *Leics* 42
	Market Bosworth	2nd	Pl XVI 2, Pl XVII 3
		5th	Pl XVII 2, 3, *Leics* 43
	Peatling Magna	3rd	Pl X 3, Pl XVII 3
Northants	Paulerspury	4th	Pl XVI 3, Fig 7

The Paulerspury and Repton bells present a curious parallel to the Little Packington treble and Budbrooke tenor, the former having the T N shield, the latter the Brasyer-Watts shield Other Newcombe marks are also found at Paulerspury (Fig 7), Market Bosworth, and Peatling, and thus the connection of this group with the Newcombes seems attested

The initial cross at Repton and on Market Bosworth 5th is a new one, Pl XVII 2, which we have noticed as used by Thomas Newcombe II at Melton Mowbray Further the 4th at Repton has the Watts-Brasyer shield together with the large Brasyer cross (Pl XVIII 6) used by Robert Newcombe at Leicester All Saints (p 31), the crown (Pl XVII 3) and the lion's face (Fig 7) The inscription on this bell and the cross on the 5th assist in connecting this group with the next, of which Warwickshire claims three examples

Of these the most important is the 5th at **Berkswell,** inscribed

Nomen Magdelene Gerit Melodie

The initials are plain medium-sized capitals, which I have not been able to identify Of the two crosses, the one at the end is Pl XVII 2, that at the beginning apparently *Northants* 17, a small cross *botonnée* which occurs at *Heyford*, Northants, on a bell of 1601, probably by Watts It is followed by the lion's face (Fig 7) and the Brasyer-Watts shield (Pl XVIII 11) The other bells are less instructive They are the old 3rd and the 4th at **Grendon,** inscribed respectively

A B ✠ D C F E

and ✠ M E L E D E ✠ G E R I T

[1] It occurs at Hardwick, Bucks, in 1590, see above, p 32

[2] The Brasyers themselves more commonly used a shield, with the same charges on a field *ermine*, see L'Estrange, *Norfolk*, p 31

The former has the cross XVII 2 and a small fleur de-lys stop (*Leics* 86), the latter the crown XVII 3 and the same stop, the lettering in both cases being the ordinary Newcombe alphabet

There are ten other bells with the cross Pl XVII 2

Leics	Houghton-on-Hill	2nd	Pl XVII 3 Pl XVIII 11
	Kegworth	2nd	Pl XVII 3, *Leics* 70
	Market Bosworth	5th	See above
	Peatling Parva	1st	Pl XVI 3, *Leics* 70
Northants	Geddington	3rd	Pl XVII 3, *Leics* 42 43
	Tansor	1st	Pl XVI 2 Pl XVII 3
Rutland	Barrowden	4th	
Hunts	Upwood	2nd	Pl XVI 2 Pl XVII 3
Derbyshire	Repton	5th	See above
Worcestershire	Tidmington	3rd	Pl XVII 3 Bartholomew Atton s name in Newcombe's lettering see below p 46

At Peatling we find the T N shield, and elsewhere the cross Pl XVI 2 The same form of inscription as at Berkswell also occurs at Wanlip, Leics (1st), Apethorpe (4th) and Great Billing (2nd), Northants, Bitchfield, Lincs North Luffenham, Rutland, and as already noted, at Repton and Leicester The occurrence of Thomas Newcombe's own marks again compels us to connect the group with that family, and on the evidence of the Melton Mowbray bell and of the use of the T N shield, it may be possible to assign both groups to Thomas Newcombe The evidence of the Repton bells further suggests the contemporaneity of the two groups

In a class by itself so far as Warwickshire is concerned, stands the tenor at **Little Packington**, inscribed

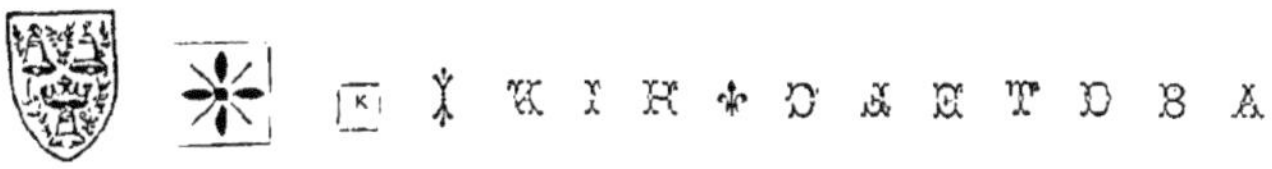

Of the stamps, the Royal Head has been noted at Budbrooke, and the fleur-de-lys stop at Grendon the other stop is *Leics* 43 as at Churchover, and there is also the now familiar Brasyer shield So far the bell may seem to fall into line with those previously described but the initial cross and lettering are quite of a new type The former, a large and elaborate floriated cross (Pl XV 2=*Northants*, fig 77) is only to my knowledge found on three other bells *Higham Ferrers* old 4th, *Old Weston* Hunts, 1st, *Overbury*, Worcestershire 3rd In all cases the inscriptions are of similar character, portions of the alphabet or meaningless collocations of letters, in large capitals of a florid quasi-Gothic type (Pl XV 3-7) At Higham Ferrers we find the Brasyer shield, but no other stamps at Old Weston or Overbury[1] Thus it is clear that all four bells are from the Leicester foundry and in view of the evidence from Little Packington they must be assigned to the Newcombes rather than the Wattses

It may be further noted here that the Brasyer-Watts shield is found in conjunction with Newcombe stamps on several other bells besides those already mentioned Narborough 4th, Leics, Isham 3rd Mears Ashby 3rd, and Winwick 1st (by Edward Newcombe) Northants· North Witham, Lincolnshire 2nd The same combination occurs on bells at Houghton-on Hill and Wanlip, Leics, already noted above

The combination of stamps on these bells is at first sight very puzzling but I think two solutions are possible Either the Brasyer stamps (the shield and the lion s face, Figs 5, 7

[1] Mr Owen in *Hunts*, p 11, has not done justice to the Old Weston bell He describes it first as "of early date, then as "probably of the Marian period" and finally as "Pre Reformation"

and the large cross Pl XVIII 6) were at first in the Newcombes' possession, *i e* down to about 1590, or there was for a time a partnership between the two firms The former may be a simpler solution, but the evidence seems to favour the latter We shall see later that there is not much evidence of the Watts' activity at Leicester previous to 1600 and it is probable that they did not start an independent business there much before 1595, it was not much later that the Newcombes discontinued the use of their old stamps and lettering (see below) In any case it should be noted that the Brasyer lettering, which the Wattses so frequently used, is hardly ever found except on undoubted Watts bells [1] The earliest known bell with the name of a Watts is dated 1590 but there are none dated earlier than 1591 which we can unhesitatingly claim as cast at Leicester (see p 40) On the whole I incline to attribute all the bells described in the preceding section to *Thomas or Robert Newcombe* (for which in some cases we have definite evidence), though it is impossible to attain to more accuracy in classification or chronology in the present state of our knowledge

There now remains for consideration a group with similar inscriptions which there is some reason for assigning to *Edward Newcombe* Two of these are of distinctly "transitional" character, and are probably not later than 1600 but others are dated 1615-16 and indicate a revival of the old style of lettering discarded about 1600 (as we shall presently see) for a simpler style, more in accordance with seventeenth-century feeling We have first the 2nd at **Wroxhall** inscribed

✠ PRAES ✢ THE ✢ LORDE ✢ ALWAEIS ♔

in the usual Newcombe lettering with the ordinary Newcombe cross (Pl XVI 2) and the crown (Pl XVII 3) which occurs on many other bells [2] Very similar is the 3rd at **Burton Hastings**

✠ PRASE ⚜ GOD ⚜ ONLI ♔

with the same cross and crown, and the stop *Leics* 86, as at Grendon Of similar type again is the 2nd at **Baginton** inscribed

PRES ⚲ THE ⚲ LORDE

the only mark being the stop *Leics* 43 (see Plate VIII)

After an interval of some years there is a curious revival of this lettering on the latest bells cast by the Newcombes in 1615-16, of which there are four examples in Warwickshire —

Birdingbury bell

✠ ABC CEFG HIK 1615

Warmington 2nd inscribed

✠ PRAISE THE LORD 1616

and the 1st and 2nd at **Morton Morrell** both inscribed

PRASE THE LORDE 1616

Two similar bells, dated in the same year, are the 2nd and 4th at *Church Brampton* Northants

These conclude the list of Newcombe bells of what we may call "transitional" character But there remain nineteen more with dates ranging between 1602 and 1612 with inscriptions in Roman type, altogether in a severer style than any of the others The only marks are a plain initial Maltese cross, and a scroll or plait-band following the date except in a few cases to be duly noted The inscription in all but four cases follows the same formula

✢ BE YT KNOWNE TO ALL THAT DOTH ME SEE THAT NEWCOMBE OF LEICESTER MADE MEE

---

1 Warmington 2nd (p 32) seems to be the only exception

2 There is a similar bell at Hignam on hill Leicestershire

which occurs on the following bells

1602	Pillerton	3rd (with various running borders)
1603	Shilton	3rd
1605	Bulkington	2nd (with plait-band after date)
	Offchurch	2nd (with running borders, and rose and crown on waist)
1607	Astley	1st—4th (with running borders)
	Frankton	2nd
1608	Stockton	1st
1609	Ansley	3rd
1610	Allesley	5th (with Oldfield's running border)
	Haselor	2nd (with plait-band after date)
1612	Kingsbury	old 4th
	Withybrook	old 2nd

At Offchurch there is a crowned rose (Pl XVI 1) on the waist of the bell at Allesley a running scroll-border (Pl XVI 6), afterwards used by the Oldfields of Nottingham (see p 61), at Bulkington and Haselor, a narrow plait-band (Pl XX 4) At Offchurch and Pillerton are running borders of a type subsequently found on most of Hugh Watts' bells (see below, p 44)

On the 3rd at Morton Morrell, the 3rd at Rowington (both 1609), and the 2nd at Nether Whitacre (1612) we find only a portion of the formula

NEWCOMBE OF LEICESTER MADE MEE

and at **Newton Regis** (1st bell, dated 1602) is the inscription in the same type

✠ RAPHE WOOLLEY CHARLES HOLDEN HARRE SPENCER CHURCH-WARDENS 1602

with the crowned rose as at Offchurch four times on the waist The running borders on this bell are the same as at Pillerton

It will be noted that no Christian name of the founder appears, but we know that Edward Newcombe was still alive in 1616 (in which year his wife died) We also know that his three sons Robert Thomas, and William were working with him [1] Robert's name appears at St Martin's Leicester, in 1611 Thomas at Hoby, Leics, in 1604 and Sapcot in 1611, and William cast Great Tom of Lincoln with Oldfield of Nottingham in 1610 The name 'Newcombe' in these cases therefore represents a joint-stock company of the father and three sons With them in 1612, or rather in 1616, ends this important foundry, and hands on its lamp to its former partner's son and present rival Hugh Watts, whose career we must now follow [2]

2 THE WATTSES (1) 1587—1615

The first mention we have of this famous bell-founding family is in the person of **Francis Watts,** who cast bells for St Peter's, Leicester, in 1564-65, and the tenor at Loughborough in 1585 He was Alderman in 1599, and also filled the offices of Chamberlain, Coroner, and Steward [3] His daughter Helen married Robert Newcombe II (p 30), and this may bear out the view already expressed that there was for a time (*sc* 1590—1602) some sort of partnership between the two families He died in 1600, and his will is given by North [4] It has already been noted that he cast the bell at Stratford-on-Avon Guild Chapel together with Edward Newcombe in 1591

[1] North, *Leics*, p 55

[2] For Newcombe pedigree and extracts from the Leicester registers see *Leics*, p 58

[3] *Records of the Borough*, iii, p 361 ff

[4] *Leics*, p 59

His name occurs on one existing bell, the 2nd at *Bingham* in Nottinghamshire which is undated, but inscribed in the fine ornamented capitals derived from the Brasyers of Norwich (Plate XVIII), which were almost invariably used by this firm from 1587 down to about 1615, but only occasionally afterwards. As noted (p 37), they practically never occur on the Newcombe bells. It would be natural to attribute to Francis Watts all bells of this type earlier than 1600, but two circumstances stand in our way. One is the contemporaneous existence of a founder William Watts, of whom more anon; the other, the fact of a **Hugh Watts** being at work between 1593 and 1605. That this Hugh is not the famous founder of the name, whom we shall discuss in due course is certain from the fact that he was only born in 1582, and probably as I shall shew, did not do much till after the extinction of the Newcombe dynasty in 1616. The only clues we have to the existence of an earlier Hugh Watts are two in number. Firstly, there is—or rather was—a bell at *South Luffenham*, Rutland, the old treble, recast in 1886 by Taylor, the original inscription being reproduced:

3951 EM  EDAM  S11AW  WEH 

North read this date as 1563, but it is clearly intended for 1593, which, if it does not dispose of difficulties, at least lightens them, as it lessens by thirty years the period of the earlier Hugh's career. The interesting feature of this bell is that the lettering is clearly the same as used at Olney and on Little Packington 2nd (see p 33), additional confirmation of a partnership with the Newcombes at the time (see p 37). Moreover the stop is the lion's head (Fig 7), which we have seen to be common to both founders.

The second piece of evidence is an entry in the Churchwardens' Accounts of St Martin's Leicester for 1617-18.[2]

Item for the bells for old Mr Watts and burvall in the church xij

The importance of this entry is that it shews that "old Mr Watts," whom we may assume to be this Hugh, may have been working as late as 1615 or 1616, and that this was the time when the younger Hugh came on the scene. I suggest on the ground that it is just then that we find a great change in the style of inscriptions and use of stamps, new lettering and new inscription-formulae introduced, and used consistently thenceforward. If it is considered necessary to assume an earlier date for the beginning of the younger Hugh's career, it is amply accounted for by supposing that he succeeded William Watts at Bedford (see below). He is described as the second son of Francis Watts and Mr Cocks assumes that William was the elder son.[3] But having regard to their known dates it seems to me much more probable that William and Hugh I were younger brothers of Francis.

We may also assign to Hugh Watts I bells bearing the name at *Burrow-on-the-Hill* (dated 1600), and *Evington* (dated 1605), both in Leicestershire. The former has long been recast, but the latter is of the ordinary Watts type with "Brasyer" lettering.

WILLIAM WATTS AND THE BEDFORD FOUNDRY

We have next to consider the nameless and undated bells of the period 1587—1615, during which the Brasyer lettering was in use. We cannot say definitely whether these bells down to 1600 are the work of any one of the three, but **William Watts** was certainly founding at

---

1 I suspect a similar error in regard to the 1st and 4th at St John the Baptist, Stamford, said by North to be dated 1561. I have to thank Mr Crowther Beynon for a rubbing of the Luffenham bell.

2 North, *C B of Rutl*, p 54

3 See pedigree *Bucks* p 140

Bedford between 1587 and 1597, and we must by preference assign to him bells of that period which are found nearer to that centre than to Leicester, as well as three or four which actually bear his name It may be convenient to dispose of him first

One of the most interesting of this group is a Warwickshire bell the 2nd at **Ryton-on-Dunsmore**, inscribed

WILLAM WATTES aabcdefghiklmnopqu [illegible]

It closely resembles the 4th at *Sherington* Bucks, which is dated 1591.[1] and it may therefore be assigned to the same time But the Bucks bell does not bear the founder's name, which here appears in the Brasyer lettering,[2] accompanied by the familiar shield (Pl XVIII. 11) with the bottom cut off the alphabet, which is incomplete, is in very rough black-letter, and several letters, such as the *r*, are repeated in varying forms The name occurs again on the 3rd at *Eletton*, Hunts inscribed in 'enriched' (presumably Brasyer) capitals[3]

WILLIAM ☐ WATES ☐ MADE ME 1590

with the cross, Plate XVIII 6, which is consistently used by William Watts I assume that these three bells were cast at Bedford, round which most of the others concentrate more closely There are in that county not only two more bells bearing William Watts name but also a group of half-a-dozen, dating about 1589—1597, all of similar character, with Brasyer capitals, the shield, and the cross Pl XVIII 6 The name occurs on the 5th at Harlington, and on the 7th at Clifton (1590), where the 6th also has the initials w w[4] Other bells are Clifton 8th, Harlington old 1st, Northill 2nd (1589), Thurleigh 2nd (1593), Farndish 3rd (1597)[5]

The Bedford foundry was apparently revived between 1599 and 1603, and again in 1610 11[6] and in 1603 we find bells of this type (at Dean and Kempston, Beds) with the name of Hugh Watts upon them, which I think are quite likely to have been cast by the younger Hugh, who succeeded his uncle William there about 1600, learning the trade which he afterwards brought to such perfection at Leicester

As to bells of this period in other counties than Beds and Bucks, it is difficult to say whether they were cast at Bedford or Leicester, especially as the bells from both centres are similar in ornamentation and inscriptions It is however worth noting that we have definite evidence in the parish accounts of a bell at Shillington, Beds, having been cast in 1602 at Leicester, not Bedford Generally speaking, geographical position is the safest guide, and on this ground, if on no other, I would attribute to Hugh Watts I, working at Leicester, two Warwickshire bells, which are the earliest we can assign to his foundry

The 2nd at **Wootton Wawen** is inscribed

1591 ✠

ABCDE FGHIK LMNOPQRS

the cross being Pl XVIII 6, as on William Watts' bells, and this, though already met with on some by the Newcombes (p 31), we must regard as a typical Watts stamp The capitals

[1] See *Bucks*, p 149

[2] The minuscule w should be noted, see note on p 32

[3] Owen, *Hunts*, p 20 He gives a Gothic capital W here, but I am not sure it should not be a minuscule

[4] North (*Beds*, p 68) says the old 4th and 5th were also by Watts But one of these was recast by James Keene in 1637, as I learn from Kimber's drawings

[5] For further details see North's *Bedfordshire*, p 58, and Cocks's *Bucks*, p 147

[6] There are twenty five bells of this period in Bedfordshire

here are from the larger Brasyer alphabet (Plate XVIII 1—5), of which this is the only example in the county Another "alphabet bell" of this date is the 5th at *Sherington*, Bucks, which is obviously by William (see above), but in view of the distance from Bedford I hesitate to deprive Hugh or Francis of the credit of the Wootton Wawen bell At **Weston-under-Weatherley** the 2nd has

THOMAS MORGAN S SQUIER 1592

the cross here being Fig 5, which we may style the "smaller Brasyer" cross, in contradistinction to the large one, Pl XVIII 6, with the exception of the "partnership" bell at Warmington (p 32) it is never found on Newcombe's bells, the other marks are the lion's face (Fig 7), and the Brasyer shield, which for some reason here (as also at Ryton) has the bottom cut off[1] The lion's face is on the whole more used by Newcombe than by Watts The shield, which we here meet with first on a genuine Watts bell, now becomes his mark *par excellence* appearing almost universally on all later bells

During the period 1592—1615 the Wattses are scantily represented in Warwickshire, though they appear in most of the intervening years in other counties[2] Nor do any of the latter call for special remark at present We may, however, note that between 1593 and 1599 the Watts favourite inscription is "Cum Cum and Pray," from 1599 to 1603 almost invariably "Praise the Lord" while from 1607 to 1613 we seldom find anything but portions of the alphabet, usually from A to O, though sometimes it runs as far as T After 1614 a new set of inscriptions is adopted by Hugh Watts II on his promotion to the head of the foundry From 1590 to 1615, and even later, "God save the Queen," or "King," is found intermittently in almost every year

Two Warwickshire bells belong to the period 1599—1603, the 4th at **Lapworth** dated 1600, and the 3rd at **Lower Shuckburgh,** dated 1601, both being inscribed

PRAISE THE LORDE

with the smaller Brasyer cross (Fig 5) Both, I think, were clearly cast at Leicester, and as this "Praise the Lord" group only begins in 1599, it must with equal probability be assigned to Hugh Watts I, so far as concerns the Leicester-cast bells[3] Similar bells occur at *Brampton*, Hunts, *Frisby-on-Wreake*, Leicestershire, and *Helpringham*, Lincolnshire From this time onwards the foundry is unrepresented until 1615, when we find the younger Hugh in sole possession

In summing up the earlier Watts bells a few points may be noted

(1) The Bedford bells form two distinct groups (*a*) 1589—1597, by William Watts, (*b*) 1600—1603 and 1609—1610, by Hugh Watts II

(2) The cross, Pl XVIII 6 is characteristic of William Watts though not used by him exclusively

(3) Bells before 1600 may be attributed to Francis Watts or Hugh Watts I., except those in Beds. and Bucks, and others obviously from the Bedford foundry

(4) Francis Watts consistently uses the Brasyer lettering, as does Hugh Watts I except in the one instance noted (p 38)

[1] Query, is this small detail a reason for assigning the Weston bell also to William Watts?

[2] They are not represented by any bells in 1594, 1604, 1606, or 1608

[3] After 1599 the foundry at Bedford appears to have been worked only intermittently I suspect that William Watts died in 1598, and that old Hugh Watts worked it through his nephew's agency after that date

(5) The "alphabet bells" belong only to the years 1591 and 1607—1613

(6) The "Praise the Lord" bells with the cross Fig 5, belong only to the years 1599 to 1603

(7) Bells between 1600 and 1615 were either cast by Hugh Watts I at Leicester or by Hugh Watts II at Bedford

(2) HUGH WATTS II FROM 1615 TO 1643

We may now pass to consider the work of **Hugh Watts II**, who as we have seen took sole charge of the Leicester foundry about 1615 By the final retirement of the Newcombe family in the following year he was left in possession of the field, and he signalises his new position by gradually discarding the old lettering and stamps (with the exception of the Brasyer shield) and introducing new letters and ornaments and new styles of inscriptions, as will be duly noted hereafter

North has collected many interesting details about his life,[1] which need not be repeated here, and we need only note that he was Chamberlain in 1620-21 and Mayor in 1633-34, being the fifth Leicester bell founder to fill the latter office He died in 1643 and was buried in St Mary's Church where his epitaph was put up, giving his age as 61[2] North gives the text of his will[3] in which his business and plant are left to his son Hugh who does not, however appear to have availed himself of his opportunities, and in fact with the death of Hugh Watts II the foundry came practically to an end for many years

We have seen that 1615 is to be regarded as his opening year at Leicester, at least so far as Warwickshire is concerned There are in point of fact a few bells of the preceding years, 1613-14, which are of the same character as those of the later period and which point to the probability of his having been actually at work earlier, but they are isolated instances, and it must have been in 1615 that he began regular work

In that year we have the 5th at **Leamington Hastings**, a fine and richly-ornamented bell inscribed

 GOD SAVE THE KING 1615

with the Brasyer shield and ornamental borders between the words. These borders are double, a row of narrow scrolls above and an acorn-pattern below (Plate XVII, Fig 8), the latter being generally used alone in this position In the following year there are two similar bells the old 3rd at **Chilvers Coton** and the 2nd at **Foleshill**, only differing in the date from the one just described Henceforward he drops the Gothic capitals, which are not revived till about 1633 and adopts a small heavy Roman type He also reduces his stock of inscriptions to four, from which he rarely afterwards departs The first of these

CELORVM CHRSTE PLATIAT TIBI REX SONVS ISTE

only remains in fashion for the two years with which we are dealing, it occurs on the following bells

1615 Southam 4th
1616 Chilvers Coton old 1st
Foleshill 3rd
Frankton 4th
Marton 3rd
Over Whitacre 2nd

---

[1] *Leics*, p 65n

[2] It is given by Nichols, *Hist of Leicestershire*, i p 316

[3] *Leics*, p 70

The second word always has the I omitted, and there are never any borders between the words

In Roman type his original favourite

GOD SAVE THE KING

still remains in favour and is found (with the shield, and ornamental borders between the words) on the following ten bells

1617 Willey 3rd
1622 Churchover 1st
1625 Wolvey 1st
1632 Austrey 1st
1636 Radford Semele 1st
1637 Budbrooke 1st
1641 Corley 1st
Maxstoke 2nd
1646 Cubbington 1st

There are no borders at Willey or Austrey. at Corley the old lion's head stamp is revived, but it is very rare to find any stamp except the shield on Hugh Watts' bells The date at Cubbington is somewhat startling, seeing that Watts died in 1643! Either it is an error, or else the bell was cast by his son Hugh, to whom he left his business, but we do not know that the latter ever cast any other bells

Eight bells bear the inscription

CVM SONO SI NON VIS VENIRE NVNQVAM AD PRECES CVPIES IRE

1623 Long Itchington 2nd
1625 Lillington 2nd
1631 Brownsover Former bell
Leamington Hastings 4th
1632 Austrey 5th
Sherborne 4th
1633 Rowington 5th (inscription in Brasyer capitals)
1636 Radford Semele 4th

Borders between the words occur in four instances

We now come to Watts' typical inscription one indeed which was specially favoured by the Leicester foundry (cf pp 14 17) and rarely occurs elsewhere

IHS NAZARENVS REX IVDEORVM FILI DEI MISERERE MEI

It was from his frequent use of it that his bells came to be known as Watts Nazarenes The S of the first word is always reversed There are thirty-seven bells in Warwickshire with this inscription (with or without borders between the words[1])

1617 Wormleighton 3rd
1618 Monks Kirby 6th
1620 Fillongley 5th
Leamington Hastings 3rd
Rowington 4th
Stretton-on Dunsmore 3rd
Stockton 3rd
1622 Churchover 2nd
Stockton 2nd
1623 Frankton 3rd
1623 Grendon 5th
Monks Kirby 4th
Marton 2nd
1624 Clifton 2nd
Marton 1st
Stoke 5th
Weston 1st
1625 Arley 2nd
Stoneleigh 3rd and 5th
1625 Shotteswell 5th

[1] There are no borders at Wormleighton, Churchover, Frankton, Grendon Marton and Bedworth, arabesques at Shotteswell, Brownsover, Chilvers Coton, Cubbington (4th), and Mancetter, elsewhere, "acorn border

1626	Cubbington 3rd	1635	Foleshill 1st
1627	Bedworth old 1st	1636	Brownsover bell
1628	Leamington Christ Ch. bell		Frankton 1st
	Lower Shuckburgh 1st		Long Itchington 4th
1629	Bedworth 6th	1639	Chilvers Coton old 2nd
	Wappenbury 3rd	1640	Cubbington 4th
1632	Austrey 4th	1641	Mancetter 3rd
	Loxley 2nd	1646	Cubbington 2nd

The only one of these which calls for remark is the 2nd at Cubbington with the impossible date already noted as occurring on the treble in the same tower.

It may be noted here that Watts uses on most of these bells two ornamental borders, one which may be called the "Acorn" border (Pl. XVII. Fig. 7) only between the words of the inscriptions; the other an effective arabesque pattern (Pl. XVII. Fig. 9), sometimes between the words, but usually as a band of ornament above or below the inscription.

Other inscriptions in the same Roman type occur in three instances:

Church Lawford 1st

MARKE BREWSTER GAVE THE GREAT BELL OF THIS RINGE 1621

Bedworth old tenor

CVM CVM AND PRAIE 1639

and **Austrey** 2nd 1632, with churchwardens' names. The Bedworth inscription occurs on other Watts bells.

About the year 1638 Hugh Watts suddenly introduced a new type of Roman lettering, thin, square, and somewhat ornate. With this he entirely drops the stock inscriptions, and we find either names of churchwardens and donors, as on four interesting bells in Worcestershire (*Worcester St. Martin* 4th and 6th, *Yardley* 1st and 5th, all dated 1638, except the St. Martin's tenor, which is 1640), or else the alphabet arranged in a somewhat peculiar fashion. The latter style is exemplified by three bells in Warwickshire:—

Clifton 3rd

MLKIHG *(Acorn-border)* FEDCBA *(border)* XWVTS *(border)*
RQPON *(border)* 1640 *(border)*

Newton Regis 2nd

FEDCBA MLKIHG XWVTS RQPON FEDCBA MLKIHG
1642 XW *(bits of arabesque pattern between words)*.

Seckington 3rd

MLKIHG *(border)* FEDCBA *(border)* XWVTS *(border)*
RQPON 1640 *(border)*.

All these bear the Brasyer shield, and have the usual "acorn" border between the words. The N is always reversed. There are similar bells at *Barrow-on-Soar*, Leicestershire (2nd and 3rd, 1642), *Lutterworth* (3rd and 4th, 1640), and *Norton* Northants (2nd, 3rd,

4th, 1640). It will be noted that this type was not used in 1641, in which year he reverted to his old style, as at Corley, Mancetter, and Maxstoke. Setting aside the Cubbington eccentricities of 1646, we may assume that the Newton Regis and Barrow-on-Soar bells represent his latest efforts, as he died early in 1643.

Alphabet inscriptions were no new thing with the Wattses, as we have already met with one in the Brasyer type at Wootton Wawen in 1591. I am not certain whether three Shropshire bells of uncertain date should also be ascribed to Hugh Watts. They have no mark or date, but only the letters M to S in various combinations, the alphabet resembling the larger set of Brasyer letters (Pl. XXIII. 1-5). They are found at Child's Ercall, Kinnersley, and Norton-in-Hales in that county. As however none of these bells bear Watts' marks and the lettering also occurs on a later bell by William Clibury at Clunbury, Salop (1620), I am inclined to think that these bells are the work of John Clibury, who was casting at Wellington about 1595 (see p. 49) and may have learned his business at Leicester.

Other inscriptions in Gothic type are found at **Rowington**, where there are three dated 1633, the old treble having only churchwardens' names; the inscription has been reproduced in facsimile. The tenor has the CVM SONO inscription (see p. 43), and on the 2nd is a new form of injunction:—

CREDE RESIPISCE MORI MEMENTO 1633

Still more noteworthy is the bell of the **Guild Chapel, Stratford-on-Avon**, cast in the same year, which has an inscription in two lines, each headed with the Brasyer shield. Part of the inscription is concealed by an iron band, and as the reading of the whole is somewhat doubtful I will not repeat it here, but refer the reader to Part II., where the bell is fully discussed. It gives the initials and names of sundry Stratford burgesses.

In concluding here the history of the Leicester foundry, I am conscious of many deficiencies in my account, of possibly unjustifiable hypotheses and unwarrantable assumptions. But, chiefly owing to the confusing interchanges and long-continued use of stamps and the somewhat archaic style of the Newcombe inscriptions, there are many difficulties in the classification and dating of the bells. One can only endeavour to evolve a working hypothesis, and wait for more light from records or comparison of inscriptions. Meanwhile I think there are two main questions which specially demand consideration: (1) What bells, if any, can we attribute to Thomas Newcombe I. and Robert Newcombe I. (covering the period 1506-1560), (2) What was the exact relation of the Newcombes and Wattses between 1590 and 1600. Lastly we greatly need more information about the elder Hugh Watts.

THE BUCKINGHAM FOUNDRY

I. THE APPOWELLS (1550-1578)

For our knowledge of this foundry we are entirely indebted to the industrious historian of the Buckingham bells, Mr. A. H. Cocks, and I can only give here a *résumé* of his researches on the subject, adding from my own investigations a few more specimens of its productions to his list.

Mr. Cocks (*Bucks*, p. 174) quotes various documents to show that one *John Appowell* was carrying on the trade of a bell founder in Buckingham between 1550 and 1577, the year in which his death is recorded in the parish registers. He cast a bell for Wing, Bucks, in 1556, another for Thame, Oxon, in 1567, and a third for Shillington, Beds, in 1575. He was succeeded by his son George, who died in the following year. The wills of both men are given *in extenso* by Mr. Cocks. The same writer goes on to point out that there are no *existing* bells which bear direct evidence of being the work of the Appowells; and he mentions eight bells in the more or less immediate neighbourhood of Buckingham[1] which evidently date from this period, but bear no founder's name One or two of the more distant ones may equally well be from the contemporary Reading foundry, but they are mostly nearer to Buckingham The bells in question are mostly inscribed with portions of the alphabet in curious semi-Gothic, semi-Roman capitals and some of them as at *Croughton*, Northants and *Bloxham* Oxon, bear an initial cross (Pl XVII, Fig 1) which we find on two bells of the same type in Warwickshire. We may then accept Mr Cocks' conclusions and attribute these two bells to Appowell of Buckingham

The 2nd at **Fenny Compton** is inscribed —

✠ F G H I Z

the letters and cross being those given on Plate XXVII of Mr Cocks' book Somewhat different in type but with the same cross is the smaller bell at **Loxley**

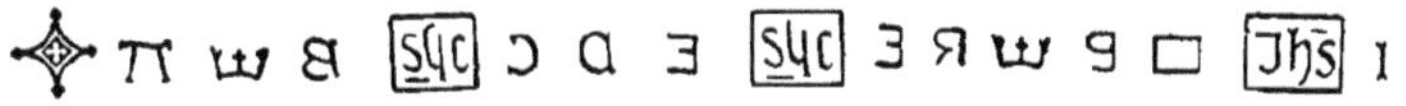

the inscription being here reproduced in exact facsimile

BARTHOLOMEW ATTON (1582—1610)

A few years after George Appowell's death the foundry at Buckingham was occupied by a man who, as we shall see had learned his business under the Newcombes at Leicester This was one **Bartholomew Atton**, whose name occurs on a bell at *Tidmington* in Worcestershire, just over the border of (and in fact geographically in) Warwickshire, as

BARTELMEW ATON

The lettering is undoubtedly that employed by the Newcombes and I regard this particular bell as cast by Atton at Leicester, while he was working for the Newcombes before his migration[2] But this is not the only evidence of his Leicester connection. The peculiar large florid letters which he afterwards affects (*Bucks*, Pls XXVIII, XXIX) appear not only on a bell at *Hardwick*, Bucks,[3] with Robert Newcombe's name, but also on bells by one Richard Bentley (1585) who appears to have lived and worked at Leicester Further, the bell at Hardwick bears a modified version of the familiar Brasyer-Watts shield, together with the large florid Brasyer cross (Pl XVIII. 12), which we have seen so often used both by Newcombe and Watts Mr Cocks therefore thinks that for a time, down to 1592, Robert Newcombe was in partnership with Atton at Buckingham

He enumerates fourteen bells in Bucks with the florid lettering, some of which bear Atton's name, the dates ranging from 1590 to 1609 There are also two or three in Northants, and doubtless more will turn up some day in Oxfordshire In 1605 Bartholomew took his son Robert into partnership and after making some changes of stamps retired in 1613, finally dying in 1630

In Warwickshire he has left us one bell, the tenor at **Barcheston,** which it is interesting to compare with its neighbour across the Stour at Tidmington It is inscribed in the florid letters (Pl XIV 7—12)

BARTHOLOMEW ATTYN MADE ME 1596

with a sort of scroll between the two words The date figures are very small

[1] To this list may be added bells at South Hinksey, Berks, and Wendlebury Oxfordshire

[2] The cross is Pl XVII 2, as at Berkswell, and the crown is Pl XVII 3 See above, p 36

[3] See above, pp 32, 35

GEOFFREY GILES

Except for those from the Leicester foundry there are very few bells in Warwickshire which can be assigned to the period 1550–1600 only some half-dozen in fact. Of these, three are by a founder who does not occur in any other county, and who therefore may be fairly assumed to be a local man. His most probable *habitat* is Coventry. These bells are the 3rd at **Berkswell,** inscribed

GALFRIDVS ◆ GILES ◆ ME ◆ FESIT ANNO ◆ DM ◆ 1584

and the 2nd and 3rd at **Weston-under-Weatherley,** both now hopelessly cracked, which are inscribed in much more elaborate fashion

2nd **GALFRIDVS ◆ GILES ◆ FECIT ◆ ME ◆ ANNO ◆ DM 1583 ◆**

⚜ Cantate Dono Canticum Nouum Laus Eius In Ecclesia Sanctorum

3rd Morgan *(coat of arms)* Sanders Anno Dni **1585**

⚜ Laudate Domn Quia Bonus Donus Psallite Noie Eius quoniam suaue

The three were thus cast in successive years 1583-84-85. The lettering at Berkswell and on Weston 2nd (top line) is Roman, of a broad flat kind very common about 1600 and used in particular by the Purdues (see below). The rest of the lettering at Weston is large coarse black-letter with large 'rustic' capitals of a quasi-Roman type the quotations from the Psalms being placed round the middle of the waist, with a fleur-de-lys before them in each case.

THE GLOUCESTER FOUNDRY

HENRY FARMER (1602–1622)

In the post-Reformation period the foundry at Gloucester seems to have continued intermittently from about 1580 down to about 1670, and then again from 1684 on to 1836 it rose to the greatest height of its popularity and importance under the famous Rudhalls. In the first period it appears to have been in three successive hands. Between 1580 and 1608 there was a founder whose initials I B are found on bells in Gloucester Hereford Salop and Worcester. He was overlapped by one **Henry Farmer,** whose bells range between 1602 and 1622 and who was succeeded by *John Palmer* (1621–1662). With the latter was apparently associated a certain T S of whom we know little beyond finding his initials on bells in Gloucester and Pembroke but Palmer's bells are fairly common in Gloucestershire and adjoining counties.

Of the above the only one represented in Warwickshire is Henry Farmer who cast the 2nd at **Alveston** in 1616. It is inscribed

THOMAS ⚜ WELLS THOMAS ⚜ HIGGINS 1616 ⚜ GOD ⚜ SAVE ⚜ NOBEL ⚜ KINGE ⚜ IAMES ⚜ ANO THOMAS ⚜ TOVNSEND

in very neat regular letters with a fleur-de-lys stop[1]. These stamps were afterwards in the possession of Thomas Hancox (p. 53), and I think also the Keenes of Woodstock (see p 59). He also cast the bell in the gatehouse at **Warwick Castle,** which is inscribed

THIS BELL ⚜ WAS ⚜ FOVNDED ⚜ ANNODOMINI ⚜ FOR ⚜ WEDGNOCK 1605

[1] Cf Pl XIX, Figs 7, 9, 10

Farmer's name only occurs on one bell the tenor at *Throckmorton* in Worcestershire, his chief characteristic is his fondness for giving the day of the month as well as the year on his bells I have failed to find his will in the extant list of Gloucester wills

THE PURDUES OF BRISTOL

In the seventeenth century there was a famous family of bell-founders working in the West of England, where their bells remain in large numbers These were the Purdues, of whom no less than six can be traced working successively at Taunton, Bristol, Salisbury, and Closworth in Somerset This family has not hitherto been investigated with the care that its importance demands, and much still remains to be done But from an examination of the existing bells in conjunction with documentary evidence and other published records, I have been able to draw up a brief summary of their respective careers More than this I do not propose to give as only one is represented in Warwickshire, and it belongs more properly to the second editor of Wiltshire or Somerset bells (both are badly needed) to discuss them in full detail

1 GEORGE PURDUE OF TAUNTON (1584—1632)

The founder of the dynasty first appears in 1584 at Penselwood, Somerset His bells are fairly frequent in that county, Dorset Devon, and Wilts and there are three in Worcestershire just a few yards from the Warwickshire border at *Tredington* He is frequently associated with the next member of the family, Roger I, who was probably his younger brother That he lived at Taunton we know from the parish accounts of Nettlecombe in Somerset His latest bell is at Cothelston, Somerset (1632)

2 ROGER PURDUE OF BRISTOL (1600—1640)

Roger Purdue set up his foundry at Bristol apparently assisted by another brother William whose initials occur at Winkfield, Wilts (1607) and elsewhere His earliest bell (1600) is at Horsington, his latest (1640) at Chiselborough both in Somerset His bells are both more numerous and more widely distributed than George's (with whom as at Tredington) he is often associated I have traced him in the following counties Cornwall, Dorset, Gloucester, Northants, Oxford, Somerset Warwick and Wilts, and there may be others

The Warwickshire examples are two in number, the treble at **Brailes**

✠ I ◆ AM ◆ HEE ◆ FOR ◆ RICHARD ◆ PVRDI ◆ MADE ◆ MEE ✠ ANNO ◆ DOMINI
1624
R P

and the 3rd at **Ettington**

✠ ANNO ◆ DO MI ◆ NI ◆ 1624 ◆ R P

On the waist of each bell is a large representation of the arms of Charles I when Prince of Wales, with the motto ICH DIEN These are also found at Fovant and Boyton Wilts The lettering used by him and the two other earlier Purdues is very thick and clumsy but flat and in very low relief, and Mr A D Tyssen suggests that it was reproduced not from moulds made in the ordinary way, but from flat pieces of metal which were impressed into the cope of the bell to make the mould for the letters to be cast Geoffrey Giles lettering (see above) is of this type

The existence of a group of the Purdues bells within a somewhat confined area and all about the same date, one in South Northants (1624) four in North Oxfordshire (1618—1624[1]), the three in Worcestershire (1622-24) and the two of 1624 in South Warwickshire, seems

---

[1] These are at Alkerton, Chipping Norton, Lower Heyford, and Tadmarton

to imply that at that time they made a temporary sojourn at Banbury or at some place in the neighbourhood It is hardly easy otherwise to account for this synchronous and much localised group

3 ROGER PURDUE II (1649-1687) AND WILLIAM PURDUE II (1637-1669)

These two founders, probably sons of Roger I, worked together at Bristol for the greatest part of their career, and most bells of the time bear the initials of both They cast many bells for the six South-Western counties especially Wilts and Somerset, and William is also found in Berks William's earliest bell is at Stocklinch Ottersay, Somerset (1637), his latest at Brislington and Keynsham in the same county (1669) Roger's earliest, Bristol St John (1649, with William), his latest Mangotsfield (1687) Between 1655 and 1664 we have evidence that William was at Salisbury, where he was assisted by Nathaniel Bolter and Francis Foster, after this he spent the year 1665 at Chichester, supplying several bells to Sussex He finally migrated to Ireland, and died in 1673 at Limerick, where his tomb is or was to be seen in the Cathedral (see Ellacombe's *Church Bells of Gloucestershire*, p 200)

4 THOMAS PURDUE OF CLOSWORTH (1656-1697)

The last of the line was Thomas Purdue, who set up a new foundry at Closworth near Chard about 1656 His bells are chiefly confined to Somerset and Dorset He died at Closworth in 1711, aged 90, and was commemorated on his tomb by an epitaph similar to that on William s

THE WELLINGTON (SALOP) FOUNDRY

WILLIAM CLIBURY (1605-1642)

This foundry, of considerable local importance, lasted from the end of the sixteenth century down to about 1700 The earliest representative, John Clibury, Clebery, or Clibberie (from Cleobury in Shropshire), cast bells for Condover and Cheswardine in Shropshire in the years 1591 and 1592 respectively, So much we learn from the accounts of those two parishes, but neither these nor any other bells certainly traceable to this John remain[1] Next we find one **William Clibury** casting between 1605 and 1642, whose bells can be identified not only by shield with the initials W C, but in two cases by a large foundry-stamp on the waist, with a bell surrounded by the words WILLIAM CLEBRY MADE ME, these are at *Clunbury* and *Kemberton*, Salop It should be noted that at Clunbury he uses the large Brasyer capitals then in the hands of Hugh Watts, but his are not quite identical with Watts' and must be a duplicate set (see p 45) Of William Clibury, curiously enough, no traces can be found in the Wellington Registers, but they only begin in 1626, which would explain the absence of his birth and marriage He died about 1642, possibly in some other parish During the seventeenth century we find a John and at least three Thomas Cliburys mentioned in the Registers, and of the latter two can be traced as bell founders, one contemporary with William, who died in 1637, and another who carried on the business until 1673 These two also use shields with their initials Finally, Henry Clibury, born to the second Thomas in 1645, carried on the foundry until 1682, when it passed into the hands of a founder whose initials are I B, and with whom it came to an end about 1700

The evidence yielded by the Wellington Registers is somewhat confusing and it is difficult to connect the various individuals mentioned, still more so to draw up a proper pedigree but as I shall have to treat of the Cliburys more fully in my *Church Bells of Shropshire*, I do not propose to do more in the present instance than to note their connection with Warwickshire

---

[1] See, however, p 45 for a suggestion

In this county we have two bells which must be assigned to William Clibury, though they bear neither initials nor trade-mark the 2nd at **Grendon** inscribed

GLORIA IN EXCELSVS DEO 1615

and the 3rd at **Wolston**, the inscription and cross on which are similar

GLORIA DEO IN EXCELSVS 1620 *(with Churchwardens' names below)*

The inscription is a very favourite one with William Clibury, and he almost invariably makes the mistake EXCELSVS for EXCELSIS, elsewhere he uses IESVS BE OVR SPEED, GOD SAVE HIS CHVRCH, or CANTATE DOMINO CANTICVM NOVVM The initial cross (Plate XXI Fig 11) is found on many of his bells, but he possessed a large assortment of these, as also of ornamented borders, employed between the words as here (Plate XXI Figs 8, 12, 13) or above and below the inscription His letters are thin, but well-formed, with slight elaborations, and with sprigged ornamentation within them, there appear to be two sizes employed

THE HANCOXES OF WALSALL (1622—1640)

From the researches of Dr Wilmore, of Walsall,[1] we know that in the seventeenth century there was a foundry in that town, owned first by **Thomas Hancox**, who was Mayor in 1620, it was located at the 'Pot-house" in Park Street This Hancox died in 1631, as we know from the entry in the registers of St Matthew's Church

Burials Oct 25 Thomas Hancox, Alderman

But there are many bells of the same type as his, with dates covering the following ten years, and these must be attributed to his son, **Thomas Hancox II.**, who married Anne Wollaston in 1630 There is no record of his death, but as "Widow Hancox' died in 1641, and his latest bell is dated 1640, it must have been in one of those two years

Some thirty-four bells by the two Hancoxes are known, of which eight are in their own county of Staffordshire, eight also in Warwickshire and in Worcestershire, Derbyshire has four, Herefordshire and Leicestershire each two, Gloucestershire and Shropshire one apiece They were founders of decided originality and taste, more particularly the younger one, and not only reproduced mediaeval inscriptions, but adorned their bells with elaborate medallions, borders and impressions of mediaeval seals. The trade-mark of the elder was a shield with an anchor and his initials (Plate XIX Fig 4) the younger uses the same device, but within a heart-shaped frame (Plate XIX Fig 2) Besides the bells mentioned above, Thomas Hancox I cast the ring for the old parish church of Liverpool, and his son cast the great bell at St Mary's, Lichfield, in 1634, together with Thomas Clibury of Wellington[2]

As the Hancoxes have not so far had full justice done to them by any previous writer, even by the historian of Staffordshire bells, I propose to treat them in fuller detail than I have done with other founders of this period who are represented in Warwickshire I will therefore go through their bells in chronological order, including the examples from this county

I THOMAS HANCOX I (1622-1631)

1622 The only bell of this year, Hancox's earliest example, is the priest's bell at *St Mary, Stafford*, inscribed in plain flat, rather small, letters —

THOMS HANOOX ME FISET 1622

[1] *History of Walsall*, p 275 *Registers of St Mary's, Walsall*, pp 230, 245
[2] Harwood, *Hist of Lichfield*, p 466

The stops are a fleur-de-lys and the crossed keys of St Peter, the latter of which was also used by Godwin Baker of Worcester (see p 56), with whom Hancox must have had some connection Of the device below the date I shall have more to say later on (p 55) The plait-band (Pl XX 4) after the date is the same as used by the Newcombes (p 38)

1626 In this year there are four bells the 4th and 5th at *Holmer*, Herefordshire, and the 2nd and 3rd at **Aston Cantlow** in this county —

Holmer 4th

THO ✠ HANCOX ME EESCIT ✤ ☐ 1626 (*arabesques*) ✤ GLORIA DEO IN EXCESIS ✠ ✤ ✤

5th

MY ROARING SOVND DOTH WARNING GIVE THAT MEN CANNOT HERE 1626 *Below* —T ✤ H ALWAYES LIVE

Aston Cantlow 2nd

✠ IOZIAH FVLLWOOD GENTLEMAN THOMAS ADKINS CHVRCHWARDEN ; *Below* —*Shield with* T H *and* 1626; *above and below, arabesques*

3rd

✠ (*Rosette*) SANA MANET CHRISTI PLEBISQVE RELIGIO VANA 🔔 1626 🔔 (*Vine-pattern*) *Below* — *Heart-shaped mark with* T H

Of these, the two Holmer bells have plain lettering like that at Stafford, but on the 2nd at Aston Cantlow he introduces a new set, apparently identical with Henry Farmer's (see p 47), which he may possibly have acquired The lettering on the 3rd is of a narrow "spindly" type The stop at Holmer is a fleur de-lys (also Farmer's, see Pl XIX 7), which only occurs once on the 5th, he also introduces on the 4th a crown and arabesques The N is reversed throughout We find the last-named pattern (Pl XX 7) on Aston Cantlow 2nd, with a peculiar kind of cross *moline* (Pl XIX 8), and the shield trade-mark (Pl XIX 4), but on the 3rd the ornaments are a bell (Pl XIX 5), a running vine pattern (Pl. XXII 3), and the heart-shaped trade-mark (Pl XIX 2) usually associated with his son (see below)

1628 The only bell of this year is *South Littleton*, Worcestershire, old 2nd —

IESVS BEE OVR SPEED 1628

with type as Aston Cantlow 2nd, fleur-de-lys stop, and a border of ornament in which are set five medallions (Pl XX 1-3, see below)

1629 The treble at **Aston Cantlow**

IOHN ✤ GIBBES ✤ WIL ✤ BARDSHA (*Medallion Border*) C ✤ W (*border* Pl XX 5) 1629 (*border*)

1630 Four bells belong to this year *Swindon*, Gloucestershire, 4th —

✤ GLORIA ✤ DEO ✤ IZ ✤ ✤ EXCELSIS ✤ 1630 T ✤ H (*Vine-pattern*).

Acton Trussel, Staffordshire, 3rd

SOM ROSA POLSATA MONDE MARIA VOCATA

the letters as Aston Cantlow 3rd, with vine and medallion borders, and the heart-shaped mark.

Whittington, Staffordshire, 1st Type and marks as Aston Cantlow 2nd
Birtsmorton, Worcestershire, 4th

GLORIA DEO IN EXCELSIS IOHN ZANFAN ESQVYER EDWARD ✤ COWPER *(vine)* **PARSON 1630**

Fleur-de lys, vine-border, and lettering as before, the shield with T H (Pl XIX 6) is not the same as at Aston Cantlow

2 BELLS OF THE YEAR 1631

These may be either by Thomas Hancox I or II It does not seem possible to differentiate their stamps, or to say that particular marks were used by one or the other The bells, five in number are —

Corley 5th **IESVS BEE OVR SPEED** *(narrow border)* **WILLIAM HALLEY FRANCIS MILLER** *(border)* **WARDENS**) ✤ **1631** *(plait band)*
On waist ♡

Elmdon 1st IESVS *(floral border)* BE *(vine pattern)* OVR SPED *(floral border)* 1681 *(medallion border)* ✤ ☐

Maxstoke 1st GLORIA DEO IN EXCELSIS 1631

On waist 

All these being in Warwickshire, also *Droitwich, St Andrew*, Worcestershire 4th and 6th with inscriptions as Elmdon and Maxstoke respectively, type as Aston Cantlow 1st, fleur-de lys stop and vine borders, on one is an oval medallion on the other a circular one, and on both is the shield-shaped trade-mark (Pl XIX 4) as Aston Cantlow 2nd The border at Corley (Fig 8= Pl XX 6 see below) is a narrow variety of the usual vine, at Elmdon two new floral borders are introduced[1] The type at Corley is a small variety of the usual thick type, that at Maxstoke is thinner The Maxstoke medallion is discussed below, p 54.

3 THOMAS HANCOX II (1632—1640)

1632 *Ibstock*, Leicestershire, 1st

SOLI ✤ DEO ✤ GLORIA ✤ PAX ✤ HOMINIBVS 1632 *(medallion and vine borders)*
(with arabesques and cable-borders above and below the inscription)
Do do 3rd

✠ SOMROSA *(vine)* POLSATA *(vine)* MONDE *(vine)* MARIA *(vine)* VOCATA ✤ 1632 ✤ H ✤ W ✤ *(medallion border), trade-mark and seal as at Maxstoke.*

Shareshill, Staffordshire 4th lettering as Aston Cantlow 1st, fleur-de-lys stop, heart-shaped trade-mark, inscription as Maxstoke

Stafford, St Chad, 1st inscribed as Acton Trussel, with floral border as Elmdon, stop and trade-mark as last

---

[1] One is Pl XX Fig 5, the other, like others of Hancox's stamps, is derived from Henry Farmer (p 47), see for this, *Reliquary*, Vol xxi, Fig 182

Stowe, Staffordshire, 1st lettering as Shareshill, with fleur-de-lys and floral border

1633 In this year we have the 2nd at **Mancetter** in this county

✣ SOLI *(floral border)* DEO *(vine)* GLORIA *(floral border)* PAX *(medallion border)* ✣ O HOMINIBVS ꕥꕥꕥ 1633 C V *(border Pl XX 5) Below heart-shaped mark, above and below, arabesques*

The medallion here is discussed below, p 54, the border before the date (Pl XX 8) occurs on a bell at Bulkington by John Greene of Worcester (p 55)

Abbot s Morton, Worcestershire, 2nd inscription as Elmdon, with heart-shaped mark and initial cross

Doveridge, Derbyshire, tenor, the most elaborately-ornamented of all his bells [1]

✠ SOMROSA *(vine border)* POLSATA *(vine)* MONDE *(vine)* MARIA *(vine)* VOCATA ☐ 1633 ✣ *(medallion border)* ☐

Below heart-mark and two seals See below, p 54

1634 *Harlaston*, Staffordshire, 1st small type as at Maxstoke, no marks

1636. **Bickenhill**, Warwickshire, 3rd

☒ IESVS BE OVR SPED ♡ 1636 *(vine and medallion borders)*

The cross here and on Ibstock 1st *supra* (Pl XXI 7), was afterwards used by John Martin (p. 57)

Derby, St Peter, three remaining from the original ring (the 1st, 2nd, and 4th),[2] all with fleur-de-lys stop and borders between words, the 1st inscribed as Elmdon, the fourth as Maxstoke, the second GOD SAVE OVR KING

1638 *Wolverhampton, St. Peter*, Sanctus, small letters as Maxstoke, fleur de-lys stop

✣ ALL ✣ PRAISE ✣ AND ✣ GLORY ✣ BE ✣ TO ✣ GOD ✣ FOR EVER 1638

1640 *Hartlebury*, Worcestershire, 5th and 7th, the latter inscribed

MASTER EYRE THE CORONER GAVE TO THIS BELL THIRTIE POVNDES 1640

The 5th has fleur-de-lys stop and scroll-border, and both have arabesques above and below, lettering as Aston Cantlow 1st

In addition there are two undated bells, the 3rd at *Hampton Lovett*, Worcestershire, inscribed as Acton Trussel, with cross as Aston Cantlow 2nd, and the 3rd at *Ashford Carbonell*, Shropshire, which has simply the inscription

IHESVS BE OVRE SPEDE

in the Maxstoke lettering, without any ornaments

The numerous stamps employed by the Hancoxes demand more detailed description, at least as regards those found in Warwickshire It will be seen that there is little distinction between those employed by the elder and the younger In all they use six varieties of lettering, but only one is at all common On the majority of the bells we find a type (Pl XIX Figs 9, 10) previously used by Henry Farmer (p 47), subsequently passing into the hands of Richard

[1] See for an account of this bell, *Reliquary*, xxi p 66

[2] See for these *Trans Derbyshire Arch and N H Soc*, xxi p 90

Keene (p 59), as did also a smaller variety of the same used by Hancox at Corley On others, as at Elmdon and Aston Cantlow (3rd) is a set of thin narrow letters, and at Maxstoke a smaller set of similar type The bells at St Mary Stafford, Holmer, and Ibstock are inscribed in plain thick letters of two sizes The fleur-de-lys stop Pl XIX 7, (also used by Farmer and Keene) appears on most of the bells from first to last, with a smaller and plainer version at St Mary, Stafford, and at Wolverhampton Of initial crosses we find three varieties a plain one on Aston Cantlow 3rd (Pl XX 9) a double-lined cross moline (Pl XIX 8) on Aston Cantlow 2nd, and an elaborate form at Bickenhill and Ibstock (Pl XXI Fig 7) afterwards used by John Martin (p 57) There are also some half-dozen varieties of ornamental borders used in the inscriptions (1) Arabesques like Watts' (Pl XX 7), on Aston Cantlow 2nd above the inscription (2) A running 'vine" pattern also used at Leicester and Nottingham (pp 38, 62), (3) A narrow version of the same (at Corley, Fig 8=Pl XX 6) [1] (4) A border (Pl XX 8) also

Fig 8

used by John Greene at Bulkington (p. 55), which occurs at Mancetter, (5) an elegant floral scroll derived from Farmer found at Elmdon, Mancetter and Doveridge (see p 52), (6) a remarkable type of scroll-border with busts in medallions at intervals (Pl XX Figs 1-3), occurring at Aston Cantlow, Bickenhill, and Mancetter, (7) a variety of type (3) found at Elmdon (Pl XX 5) The foundry-marks have already been noted, as have other marks where they occur, with some exceptions presently to be discussed Meanwhile, it is interesting to see how many of the above stamps were also used by other founders, both earlier and later, as noted in most instances

But of all their stamps the most remarkable are the three impressions of seals which occur in several instances, sometimes also in a mutilated form At Mancetter, and also at Doveridge and Droitwich St Andrew, we find thus impressed the seal of the Guild of Corpus Christi and St Nicholas of Coventry, which was founded in 1348 [2] The design (Pl XIX Fig 3) is thus described by Llewellyn Jewitt[3] "A full length figure of St Nicholas, habited as a bishop, with mitre, standing with hands outstretched in an attitude of adoration before an altar, on which stands a chal ce with paten In front of his upturned face, over the altar, is the usual emblem of the Deity—a hand in the act of benediction, issuing from clouds, and surrounded by rays of heavenly light The entire field is diapered with foliage The surrounding legion is Sigillu fraternitatis Gilde Corp is Xpi & s'c'i nich'i de Cove't' ✠ '

At Maxstoke and Doveridge the bells have similar seals on the waist, in this case the seal of the Premonstratensian Abbey of the B V M and St Thomas at West Langdon, Kent, founded in 1212 The obverse, as here given (Pl XIX Fig 1) represents 'within a richly-decorated and gabled Gothic tabernacle or shrine, elaborately arcaded, a seated figure crowned of the B V M, her right arm supporting the Infant Saviour, her left supporting one of her breasts" The legend is SIGILL' COMMUNE MONASTERII ECCE BE MARIA V DE LANGDON The reverse of the seal, not given on the bell, represents the murder of Thomas-à-Becket [4]

---

[1] Also used by James Keene (*Bucks*, fig 60)

[2] See Fretton in *Reliquary*, XXI p 68

[3] *Ibid*, p 66

[4] *Ibid*, see also *Brit Mus Cat of Seals*, No 3396

Thirdly, we find at St Mary, Stafford, and St Andrew, Droitwich, a vesica-shaped seal, recognisable as that of Edmund Scambler, a not very reputable Bishop of Peterborough (1560-1585) The impression is indistinct, but the arms of the see impaling the Bishop's own may be seen in the exergue The two central figures, cut out from this seal (Pl. XIX Fig. 7), are found on the bell at Elmdon

THE WORCESTER FOUNDRY (1609—1693)

We have already seen (p 11) that one Nicholas Grene was founding at Worcester in the first half of the sixteenth century, and the name was not destined to die out for more than 100 years As we gather from his will, his business passed into the hands of his son Henry, whose works, if any still exist cannot now be traced, but as early as 1599 we find bells in Worcestershire bearing the initials I G These, with one in Gloucestershire, form a group of five, and the clue to the meaning of these initials must be sought in a later group, of which the earliest is dated 1609, the latest 1633 Of these several bear a shield with three bells and the initials I G (Pl XXI Fig. 4), from which we may deduce that the founder was the son and successor of the earlier I G On one bell, however, the sanctus at *St John's, Worcester*, the founder fortunately reveals his full name as John Greene, and thus we may now consider the family succession of Grenes from Nicholas to be established Before I was aware of the existence of the Worcester bell, I had arrived at this conclusion from external evidence, and am glad that my theories have thus been proved correct

This **John Greene**, with whom I deal more fully than the other members of the family, because he was working in Warwickshire, occurs twice in public documents, in one case in a more or less discreditable fashion In the records of Stratford-on-Avon, under date 26 July, 1627, is the entry, "John Greene, bell-founder, was presented by the minister and churchwardens for working on Sabbath-day July 13, in ye time of divine service,' and probably fined [1] And in those of Ludlow there is a payment in 1623-24

to Greene the Bell founder towards his chardges by the appoyntmt of Mr Bayliffs iijs iijd

Although the same accounts for the following year give a most interesting description of the casting of bells for Ludlow Church, it is doubtful if Greene's tender was accepted, as we read of a subsequent payment to a founder named Oldfield, and the facts that the casting took place on the spot, and that Oldfield was an itinerating worker point to his being the successful man.

There are however, a fair number of bells remaining, which from the presence of the shield above mentioned, or the similarity of lettering and initial cross, may be assigned to this John Greene Two of these are in Warwickshire, curiously enough, on the far side of the county

Bulkington 1st IESVS ✠✠✠✠ BE ✠✠✠✠ OVR ✠✠✠✠ SPEEDE ✠✠✠✠ [shield] 1614

with a border between the words also used by Hancox at Mancetter (p 53), and

Shilton 4th ✠ IESVS BE OVR SPEED 1614 R W [shield]

Both bells bear the foundry-shield, and the latter a plain initial cross the lettering is neat and well-formed, about one inch high I have elsewhere given a list of John Greene's bells then

---

[1] North and Stahlschmidt, *Herts*, p 33, Halliwell, *Churchwardens' Papers*, p 25

known to me,[1] but as I can now give a fuller list I may be pardoned for doing so here In chronological order they are —

1609	Herefordshire	Holmer 1st
1614	Warwick	Bulkington 1st
,,	,,	Shilton 4th
1618	Worcester	Upton Warren 3rd
1620	,	Stoke Prior 7th
1625	Hereford	Stoke Lacy 3rd
1626	Worcester	Grimley 5th
,	,,	Worcester St John small bell inscribed ✠ IHON CREN 1626
1627	,,	Bockleton 1st
1628	Hereford	Little Hereford 2nd
1632	Worcester	Holt 3rd
1633	,,	Cotheridge 2nd and 3rd
,	,,	Pirton 1st and 2nd
1674[2]	,,	Naunton Beauchamp old tenor

Of these it may be noted that the Upton Warren bell also bears the initials B G perhaps denoting another member of the family who acted as John's foreman Mention should also be made of a later bell, the 3rd at *Lugwardine* near Hereford, cast by "John G of Wostar,' in 1651 This is probably a later John, and the existence of yet a fourth is implied by an entry in the registers of St Helen s, Worcester, of the baptism of a John Greene in 1650-51 But we can trace no further efforts of the Greene family in the bell-founding line, and they doubtless suffered eclipse by a star which appeared in the horizon in 1644 in the person of one John Martin

Before we come to John Martin however, it should be mentioned that in the interesting accounts of St Nicholas, Warwick, for 1619 there are two entries which appear to relate to Worcester founders

> In primis p^{d} to Richard Dawkes in Ernest when he undertooke the Casting of the fourth Bell — xij^{d}
> Given to Symon Baker the Belfounder over and above — v^{s}

This bell, apparently the joint production of the two men named, was recast by Richard Keene in 1695 The accounts imply that it was actually cast at Stratford, but the existence of Worcestershire bells dated 1613—1633 with the initials R D, and of another of 1615 at *Worcester St Peter* with the name of *Godwin Baker*, seems to imply that they were Worcester founders[3] On the other hand, when the great bell of Stratford Guild Chapel was recast by *Richard Dawkes* in 1606 he is spoken of as "the bell-founder at Evesham"[4] Possibly he was there temporarily, but the distribution of his bells points to his foundry being at Worcester

JOHN MARTIN (1644-1693)

This founder, who enjoyed for some fifty years a long and prosperous business career, would seem to have been born about the year 1620, and to have set up his foundry in Silver Street in the parish of St Martin, Worcester, on a site still known as Bell-founder's yard The well-known practice of giving foundlings a surname from their adopted parish may possibly explain the identity of his surname with that of his locality, it is at all events significant that the registers do not record his baptism, or any earlier Martins If, however he appeared in Worcester without even the traditional half-crown, he appears to have risen rapidly, as he must

---

[1] *Archaeol Journal*, lxiii, p 190

[2] Date probably intended for 1624 The bell was certainly John Greene's

[3] See *Arch Journal*, lxiii p 191

[4] See the extracts from the Chamberlains' Accounts, quoted *s v* in Part II

have been under thirty when he cast his first bell and by the time that the troubles of the Civil War were over he was evidently in a prosperous position, with an extended *clientele*. His marriage took place under the strictly civil conditions of the Commonwealth in 1655, as the parish registers set forth —

> Memor[d] that John Martin of y[e] pish of Martins in y[e] Cittie of Worcester & Anne Knight of y[e] pish of Sweathin's [Swithin's] in y[e] Cittie aforesayd were maried by Mr John Nash on of y[e] Justic' of y[e] peace of y[e] Cittie of Worcester y[e] 8th daye of December 1555 being publickely proclaimed 3 several Lord dayes in y[e] pish Church of Martins in y[e] Cittie of Worcester. Witnesses John Martin & Maria Gallowaye and John Roberts Register.

The presence of a John Martin as witness may perhaps run counter to the theory I have put forward above, as one would naturally suppose him to be our founder's father. I have also sometimes thought that a career of fifty years is too long for one man, and that there may have been two John Martins; but at all events there is no evidence to this effect to be derived from the bells themselves, on which the same stamps are employed throughout. However, if he began his career in 1644 at the age of twenty-five, he would only be 71 when he cast his last bell, and 78 at his death, which is recorded in the registers as follows —

> 1697 John Martin was buried April y[e] 18

His wife Anne only preceded him by a few days, being buried on the 15th of the same month.

We have very few bells from John Martin between 1644 and 1650, which need not be a matter for surprise, and very few again after 1685; but between 1650 and 1670 he was in the heyday of his career, and out of 135 Worcestershire bells cast during the whole fifty years no less than 80 are his work. He is also found in the counties of Gloucester, Montgomery, Radnor, Shropshire, Stafford, Hereford and Leicester,[1] and there are fifteen of his bells in Warwickshire, as follows —

1650	Bickenhill 4th.	1655	Clifton 5th
	Sheldon 4th	1661	Temple Grafton bell
	Wishaw 1st and 2nd	1663	Curdworth 2nd
1653	Ryton 3rd	1664	Ipsley 1st and 2nd
	Tachbrook 1st	1670	Gt. Alne bell
1654	Fillongley old 2nd	1672	Wixford 2nd
	Withybrook old 3rd		

It will be noted that these only cover a period of some twenty years. Their distribution is also worth noting. Those of 1650 are all near Birmingham; those of 1653—55 are all on the far side of Warwickshire, while those of 1661—72 are nearly all close to the Worcestershire border. In connection herewith it is curious that John Martin's bells are very rare in East Worcestershire, where the Bagleys proved too strong for him.

John Martin used two sets of lettering, one thick, the other thin, and a foundry-stamp of which there are three varieties (Pl. XXI. Figs. 2, 3, 10). He either employs a large oblong shield[2] surrounded by mantling, on which are three bells and the initials I. M., or a heart-shaped mark like Hancox's, with the initials and only one bell. A smaller variety of the latter appears on his smaller bells, accompanied by a correspondingly small variety of the thin lettering (as at Temple Grafton, etc.). He sometimes (as at Bickenhill) uses an effective initial cross (Pl. XXI. Fig. 7; derived from Hancox, see p. 54), and is fond of ornament between the words, usually a series of "palmettes" (Pl. XXI. 6) as at Ipsley, and sometimes a narrow running border (Pl. XXI. 8) as at Great Alne. In addition he is fond of arabesques like those used by Watts and Hancox (Pl. XX. 7) as a lower border to the inscriptions.

---

1 At Asnby Magna and Thurlaston, not identified by North.

2 This shield appears to have come from Buckingham. It is used (without the initials) by R. Atton in 1631 on the 4th at Olney, Bucks (see Cocks, p. 207).

His inscriptions do not call for much comment, at least so far as concerns Warwickshire By far the commonest is the

SOLI DEO GLORIA PAX HOMINIBVS

which is found at Bickenhill, Sheldon, etc, but frequently he merely gives the names of churchwardens

BRYAN ELDRIDGE OF CHERTSEY (1640—1661)

The Eldridges, first of Wokingham, Berks, then of Chertsey, Surrey, had a flourishing foundry lasting through four generations, from 1565 to 1715 Their history is fully detailed in Stahlschmidt's *Surrey*, p 109ff (see also *Bucks* p 242) As a rule their bells are not found far north of the Thames Valley, but the fourth of the name, Bryan Eldridge II, who succeeded his father, Bryan I, in 1640, probably found his business during the period of the Civil War and early Commonwealth in a very unsatisfactory condition Whether this was so or not, he appears to have attempted a new departure about 1656, in which year we find him settled at Coventry, and casting bells for Warwickshire and adjoining counties He did not however give up his Chertsey foundry, as he was casting bells there for Wraysbury, Bucks, in 1657, and probably he paid intermittent visits to Coventry, leaving a foreman in charge In 1658 he left the neighbourhood

Of his bells in the Midlands there are eleven now existing, others have disappeared more or less recently There is one at Tamworth (the 5th) two in Leicestershire (Shawell and Stoke Golding trebles), and the old 2nd at Crick, Northants, all dated 1656 He is also to be found at Standish in Gloucestershire (1656) but we cannot be certain that these last-named bells were not cast at Chertsey In Warwickshire we have

1656	Kenilworth	6th	1657	Harborough Magna	2nd and 3rd
	Lapworth	2nd		Wappenbury	1st
	Withybrook	old 2nd	1658	Fillongley	1st
1657	Burton Hastings	1st		Willey	1st

all inscribed alike

BRYANVS ELDRIDGE ME FECIT

with the date Stahlschmidt notes that he always used the English version of this formula up to 1648, afterwards always the Latin There were formerly three of these bells at Kenilworth, each having the initials O P I D after the date, but now only the tenor, a fine bell, remains In 1656 we read that he cast a bell for St Mary's, Warwick which must have perished in the fire of 1693, and it is from the Churchwarden s accounts of that parish that we learn the place of his foundry during these two years The entries run [1]

Paid to Mr Eldridge for casting three new Bells and making the rest tunable .	£28
Paid for going to Coventry to seal the articles with the bell-founder	3s

It might also be gathered from the geographical position of these bells that Coventry was the natural centre whence they emanated

WILLIAM ELDRIDGE (1661—1715)

Bryan Eldridge was succeeded by his younger brother William, who had a fairly prosperous career of some fifty years, finally relinquishing the foundry at Chertsey in 1714, when he retired to West Drayton in Middlesex, and died in 1716, after becoming churchwarden and recasting the bells there His bells are very like his brother's as regards the style of the inscriptions only one has penetrated so far as Warwickshire, the single bell at **Temple Balsall**, which is inscribed

WILLIAM ELDRIDGE MADE MEE 1670 ◆ ◆ ◆ ◆ ◆

in plain but good Roman lettering

[1] *Notices of Warwickshire Churches*, i, p 29

THE KEENES OF WOODSTOCK

In 1612 a founder named **James Keene,** in conjunction with Edward Newcombe (see p 38) was carrying on a branch of the Leicester foundry at Bedford He worked here for at least ten years, but some time after the death or retirement of Newcombe in 1622 probably between that year and 1631, migrated to Woodstock in Oxfordshire He is the maker of a considerable number of bells still existing in Beds, Bucks, and Northants, and of others in Oxfordshire and neighbouring counties, which may be presumed to have been cast at Woodstock They date between the years 1626 and 1654, the year of his death, while the bells cast at Bedford go down to 1641 Mr Cocks notes that there are none to be traced in the years 1642—1647, the cause of which is undoubtedly the Civil War [1]

James Keene is only represented in Warwickshire by one bell—and that only just within the border—the second at **Long Compton,** which was cast by him in 1652 It has merely the names of churchwardens in neat narrow letters, remarkably like those used by Thomas Hancox (p 51) on the Aston Cantlow treble, with a similar fleur-de-lys as stop (*Bucks*, pl 26, fig 5) I rather suspect that he inherited or bought up some of that founder s plant

It is interesting to note that the treble in the same tower of Long Compton is very similar to the 2nd, having the same lettering, stop, and date, but the churchwardens' names are different, and the founder's initials are not I K, but R K, letters which obviously stand for **Richard Keene,** the successor and probably the son of James His birth does not occur in the Woodstock Registers, and he was probably born at Bedford The initials on this bell are followed by a sort of double scroll border (*Bucks* Fig 62) which seems to have come from Godwin Baker of Worcester (see p 56)

Richard Keene carried on the foundry at Woodstock from James' death in 1654 until 1698, when he removed to Royston in Cambridgeshire, and set up his foundry there for four or five years [2] A list of his bells in Bucks, Oxon, and elsewhere is given by Mr. Cocks but his celebrity was more than purely local, and he occurs as far away as Martley in West Worcestershire, where he cast a ring of six in 1673, going down there specially for the purpose, as local records shew. In Warwickshire we can reckon, besides the Long Compton treble, thirteen of his bells, and five others now departed; and just over the border is a ring of six at Shipston-on-Stour The first that comes under our notice is the old 4th at **Brailes**, with its boastful jingle, which has been thoughtfully preserved on its successor of 1900 (by Mears and Stainbank) —

IME NOT THE BELL I WAS BUT QUITE ANOTHER
IME NOW AS RITE AS MERRY GEORGE MY BROTHER 1668
RICH KEENE ME FECIT

Three years later Keene tried his hand once more at Brailes, and to the same poetical effect, on the existing 5th

ILE CRACK NO MORE NOW RING YOVR FILL
MERRY GEORGE I WAS AND WILL BE STILL ◆ JOHN OKELY
RIC CAPELL C W
R 1671 K

Here at all event his prophecy has been justified.

In 1669 we have the inner four of the six at **Chadshunt**, to which he added a treble and tenor in 1693 The inscriptions on the 2nd, 4th, and 5th are Latin, and all worth quoting:

NVMEN INEST NVMERIS, *etc*
IN MEDIO TVTISSIMVS IBIS
AMICI MVSARVM MEI GENITORES

[1] See generally, *Bucks*, p 162ff

[2] See Raven, *Cambs* p 97, Deedes and Walters, *Essex*, p 118

the 3rd has only churchwardens' names. On the two bells of 1693 he indulges in further flights of ingenuity, as follows —

1st PROCAROLO NEWSHAM HANC RESVNO MVSAM

6th VITAM EXHILARO MORTEM CONDOLEO, *etc*

We also find him at **Aston Cantlow**, where he gives his name on the tenor RICH KEENE MEDE MEE 1681, and at Leamington Hastings, where he supplied a small sanctus bell in 1677 In 1689-90 he cast the ring of six at **Great Wolford**, of which the 1st, 2nd, and 4th remain, giving in various forms the name of their donor, Major Thomas Kyte, whose "canting" coat-of-arms (a chevron between three kite's heads erased), occurs on each, as also on bells by Keene at Chipping Campden in Gloucestershire The inscriptions are as follows

1st MAIOR THOMAS KYTE CAST MEE LEADER OF THIS RING TO BE 1690

2nd CAPTAIN THOMAS KEYTE CAST MEE 1689

4th MAYGOR KEYTE CAST THIS RINGE 1690

Finally in 1695 he cast a ring of six for **St. Nicholas, Warwick**, of which the 2nd and 4th remain (as the present 4th and 6th), inscribed

LAVDATE DOMINVM IN EXCELSIS M D CXCV

RICHARD KEENE CAST THIS RING M D CXCV

The 3rd of the ring, recast by Charles and George Mears about 1850, had merely the date 1695.

On most of these bells the lettering is of the same type as at Long Compton (cf Pl XXII Figs 5, 8), but the 3rd, 4th and 5th at Chadshunt and the treble and 2nd at Great Wolford are inscribed in a similar but smaller alphabet,[1] with the larger date-figures on the last-named bell Keene seems to have dropped all the crosses and ornaments used by his father

Mr Cocks[2] thinks James Keene s bells were superior to his son's, and both far inferior to 'their trade-parents,' Newcombe and Watts He has collected some interesting details about their foundry at Woodstock,[3] in which town remains of bell-metal have been dug up in a garden in Oxford Street[4] We know from an existing deed that Richard Keene at one time lived in that very street In the Registers of Woodstock there is an entry of the burial of one Richard Keene in 1704, and as his Royston cast bells do not go later than 1703, it is possible that he returned to his native town to end his days

TOBY NORRIS OF STAMFORD (1662—1698)

The Stamford foundry covered the whole of the seventeenth century, lasting just over 100 years (1607—1708) Its first representative was *Tobias Norris*[5] I (1607—1626), its second *Thomas Norris*, whose name occurs on Northants bells between 1629 and 1671, but neither is represented in Warwickshire Tobias or **Toby Norris II** born in 1634, appears to have begun casting during his father s life-time, as he occurs in Northants as early as 1662 He died in 1698, and was succeeded by *Alexander Rigby*, with whom the foundry came to an end ten years later

---

[1] Also used by Hancox at Corley (see p 52)

[2] *Bucks*, p 171

[3] *Ibid* p 167

[4] *Ibid* p 170

[5] The late Dr Raven informed me that in 1900 he had met with a schoolmaster named Tobias Norris, to his great satisfaction

The only Warwickshire bell from this foundry is the 2nd at **Wolvey**, supplied by Toby Norris II in 1680 and inscribed —

✠ **I ASTLEY ESQ C FITCH GENT T FRASER GENT E PHIPPES GENT**
(*Scroll between words*)

I TOONE C W TOBY NORRIS CAST ME 1680 (*Plait-band between words*).

The initial cross (Pl XXII Fig 5) was used by his predecessors, but the arabesque ornaments between the words in the first line are his own, the plait-border in the second line (Pl XX Fig 4) apparently came originally from Newcombe and Hancox, but it was also used by James Keene His lettering is of a thick type, something like Hugh Watts'

THE NOTTINGHAM FOUNDRY (1550—1741).[1]

We have seen on an earlier page (p. 21) that previous to 1560 the Nottingham foundry was in the hands of one Humphry Quarnbie, from whom it descended to his son Robert The latter associated himself with a family of Oldfields in whose hands it remained for many years As, however, there are no Nottingham bells in Warwickshire between 1510 (or thereabouts) and 1647, I propose to give only a brief outline of their career down to the period when they are again represented in the county

The first Oldfield of whom we hear is one Thomas who cast the sanctus bell at Melton Mowbray, Leicestershire, in 1553, but nothing more is known of him It may be noted in passing that the earliest dated Nottingham bell known to me is the 4th at *North Muskham*, Notts, which has an inscription in small Gothic capitals with the Mellour rose and "R" shield (Pl X Figs 6, 8), and the date MDLVI (1556) But this is more likely to be Humphrey Quarnbie's work, in view of the use of Mellour's stamps I may also note here that in 1567 four bells were cast for Worksop by Thomas and Michael Reve[2], but there is nothing to indicate that they were Nottingham men Their names are not otherwise known; nor do we know more than the name of William Wood, living in 1573[3]

Next we have *Henry Oldfield I*, working about 1545—1580,[4] to whom North assigns certain bells of 'transitional" character bearing the A set of Royal Heads (p 8) and William Rufford's cross (Pl. V 12-14) These stamps, derived from the Worcester founders (p 12), seem to have come from Nicholas Grene of Worcester about 1540 to Nottingham They are found with Nottingham lettering at *Kemberton*, Salop, in 1594, and the cross with the corresponding lettering, on bells at *Tattenhall*, Cheshire, dated 1595 But as the earliest dated Nottingham bell with these stamps is one of 1585, they are clearly too late for Henry Oldfield I, and must be the work of his successor

We know more about the third holder of the name, *Henry Oldfield II* (1582—1619),[5] whose bells in Notts. and adjoining counties are very numerous, being recognised by the use of a foundry-stamp with his initials h o, a cross, a crescent, and a star (Pl XXII Fig 1) He had assistants at different times (1) *Robert Quarnbie*, whose name appears with his on a circular foundry-stamp at Nottingham St Mary (9th, 1595), Lincoln Cathedral tenor (1593), and at Ruskington, Lincs, with Mellour's rose and shield (2) *Henry Dand*,[6] whose bells are mostly undated, but marked by the use of Pre-Reformation inscriptions and stamps, and by his initials in very fine large Gothic capitals (3) *Paul Hutton*, whose initials occur on a shield at Cromwell,

---

1 See *Vict County Hist of Notts*, Vol ii

2 R White, *Worksop*, p 331, Eddison, *Hist of Worksop*, p 70

3 *Records of the Borough of Nottingham*, iv, p 155

4 See *op cit*, iii, p 445, iv, p 232 He died in 1589—90

5 See *op cit*, iv, pp 205 232, 264, 334, 343

6 He assisted Oldfield to recast one of the Shrewsbury Abbey bells in 1591 (North, *Lincs*, p 124), and in 1587—88 was "presented that he comes not to the churche" (*Records of the Borough* iv, p 218)

Notts and elsewhere, and who was also employed by his successor (as was also William Wragg in 1628[1])

George Oldfield I., born about 1600, succeeded his father in 1620 and enjoyed a long prosperous career of sixty years. His name rarely occurs on his bells, but he either used his father's h o stamp with a g fixed over the h so as to obliterate it or a similar one made with his own initials. For the most part he drops all the old Nottingham stamps and the only other ornaments used by him are running borders of vine-pattern (Pl XXII Fig 3) between the words, a stamp apparently derived from the Newcombes (cf the 5th at Allesley). He had three sons, all of whom died in his life-time, but his daughter married a Hugh Oldfield, and had a son George born in 1671 who eventually carried on his grandfather's business.

George Oldfield's bells are very numerous in Notts, Derbyshire, and Lincolnshire but in Warwickshire they number no more than half-a-dozen, all in the north of the county near Atherstone. The earliest is the tenor at **Mancetter**, dated 1647, with an inscription in a favourite Nottingham style, a verse in black letter followed by churchwardens' names in Roman

my | roaring sound | doth warning · | give that

men cannot | heare always | lyve

RT GOVLD W GOODWEINE R BENTLEY 1647

The same is found at *Whatton*, Notts, on a bell by Henry Oldfield (1618), and other favourites, more usually found on Henry's bells, are —

I sweetly toling men do call to taste on meate that feeds the soule

as at *North Collingham* and *Rolleston*, Notts, and *Tong*, Shropshire,

all men that heare my mournful sound repent before you lie in ground

as at *Caunton*, *Kelham*, and elsewhere in the former county

More typical of George are such inscriptions as GOD SAVE HIS CHVRCH and others occurring as noted below —

Shuttington bell, dated 1664, has

IESVS BEE OVR SPEED 1664 (*vine-pattern between words*)

The G O stamp is here inverted

Polesworth 5th, dated 1654, has churchwarden's names the G O stamp, and arabesques (Pl XXII 4) above and below the inscription, the 6th (1664)

ALL GLORY BEE TO GOD ON HIGH 1664

 (*vine-pattern between words*)

and the 4th (1667)

FEARE GOD HONOR THE KING 1667

(*vine-pattern between words*).

---

[1] Brown *Annals of Newark* (1904), i, p 325.

Ansley 2nd (1667) is similar, with the G O stamp but no arabesques

At George Oldfield's death in 1680 there must have been an interregnum in the foundry, as his grandson was then only ten years old, at all events there is a drop in the Nottingham bells for ten or twelve years, and it is not certain whether it was kept open at all **George Oldfield II.**, when he succeeded, does not appear to have had so good a business His name is not found on bells, nor does he continue the G O stamp, but he alone can be the founder of many bells in Notts and adjoining counties cast between 1690 and 1740 He revived the old ornamental lettering and inscriptions employed by Henry Dand over a hundred years previously, and there are not a few bells of this period on which we find the inscription (peculiar to the Nottingham founders)

Trinitate Sacra Fiat Hec Campana Beata

in good black letter with large handsome Gothic capitals, and churchwardens' names in humbler Roman type Examples are *North Collingham* 4th (1715) and *Flintham* 3rd (1718) in Notts The 2nd at *Alstonfield*, Staffs, (1677) seems to be an attempt in this line by his grandfather We may probably attribute to him the bell at **Weddington**,[1] inscribed

GILBERTVS ADDERLEY ARMIGER HV ECCL PATRONVS 1703

In 1741 George Oldfield II died, and the dynasty came to an end The business was acquired by a family named Hedderley, who also came into possession of their predecessors' stamps It is not known quite certainly where they were residing previously, they are variously described as of Bawtry (1722) and of Derby (1732), and they do not usually give the place of their residence on their earlier bells, which are fairly common in Derbyshire and Lincolnshire We know however that **Thomas Hedderley** worked at Nottingham between 1744 and 1778, the year of his death, and he was succeeded by his sons Thomas, who died in 1785, and George, who emigrated to America in 1800 Up to 1743 Thomas I had been in partnership with one Daniel Hedderley.

From this foundry we have three bells in Warwickshire the single bell at **Wilnecote**, inscribed

THOMAS HEDDERLY FOUNDER NOTT 1763

and the 1st and 3rd at **Nether Whitacre**, dated 1783 and 1785 with

THOS HEDDERLY NOTTM FECIT (and churchwardens' names)

To these may also be added the bell at *Wibtoft*, which is described in North's *Leicestershire*, but now ranks as an inhabitant of Warwickshire, it is dated 1758

THE BAGLEYS OF CHACOMB, NORTHANTS

In 1631 a foundry was opened at Chacomb in Northants, near Banbury, which throughout its long life of 150 years was presided over by various members of a family named Bagley Few bell-founding families have hitherto presented to the enquirer such genealogical difficulties as this, owing to the fact that their Christian nomenclature was very limited, and Henrys succeed to Henrys, Matthews to Matthews, with bewildering rapidity [1] Mr Cocks did much to elucidate them in working at Bucks bells, and where he has failed, lesser men can hardly hope to succeed, still I am able to add a few facts which perhaps only serve to provide a fresh puzzle, and like him, leave it to the future chronicler of Oxfordshire to avail himself of his opportunities of best unravelling the tangle

The first of the line, whom we will call **Henry Bagley I.**, seems to have learned his business with the Attons of Buckingham,[2] from whom he derived some of his stamps,[3] and it

[1] The 2nd at Thurcaston, Leicestershire, dated 1701, is in the same lettering

[2] *Bucks* p 209

[3] *E g*, the border of linked fleur de lys (Fig 9), cf *Bucks*, fig 09

will be noticed that the Chacomb foundry opens just two years before that at Buckingham ended The earliest Bagley bell which I have been able to trace is at *Souldern*, Oxon , dated 1631 A Henry Bagley, probably our man s grandfather, was buried at Chacomb in 1609 The later Henrys are, as Mr Cocks says, very puzzling, as also the localities in which they lived. But I cannot discover any traces of bells cast away from Chacomb before 1685 or thereabouts, and it is only in the eighteenth century that the geographical difficulties arise By way of preliminary I will note the names that occur, in a chronological sequence, with dates and localities so far as they can be ascertained

1631—1674 For the first forty-four years we find only the name of Henry Bagley , and it must be assumed that only one man is indicated, as we know that the first Henry Bagley died in 1684 (aged 76) All the bells of this period are of a very similar character, though they fall into two distinctly-marked periods, divided by the Civil War, during which he was practically idle The differences between his bells of 1631-42 and those of 1649-74 will be duly noted hereafter

1674—1679 In 1674 Henry Bagley took into partnership his son Henry, at least this is the first record we have of the second of the name The ring of six bells at St Michael's, Coventry, was cast by "Henry Bagley sen and Henry Bagley jun," in 1674 5 (see Part II) But the single name still appears on bells down to 1679

1679—1687 During this period we find the name of **Matthew Bagley** associated with that of Henry , he was the son of John Bagley, a younger brother of Henry Bagley I , baptised at Chacomb 6 April 1653 My impression is that Henry Bagley I retired from business in or about 1679, and that the Henry whose name appears during the eight years is the son **Henry II.** Some of the larger rings of this date bear both names but on separate bells

1687—1712 In 1687 there seems to have been a split in the firm The Chacomb foundry was left in the hands of **William Bagley,** the younger son of Henry I , born 29 June, 1663 whose name occurs as early as 1681 on a bell at Clipstone, Northants, as of Northampton He remained in charge down to 1712, the year of his death Meanwhile Matthew Bagley migrated to Evesham, where he died and was buried in 1690,[1] having cast there a few bells still remaining in the neighbourhood

1687—1703 The third member of the firm, Henry II , migrated to Ecton in Northants, between Northampton and Wellingborough, and there set up a foundry which lasted until his death in 1703 On bells at Castor, Northants dated 1700, he describes himself as "of Ecton" He may, however, also have been at Chacomb from time to time

1693—1716 A curious complication is produced by the appearance at this time of a *Matthew Bagley* in London He cannot be connected genealogically with the known members of the Chacomb family, still less can he be any of the known Matthews That he was settled in London in 1693 is shewn by his casting bells for Chigwell, Essex, in that year He remained there till 1716, when he, and his son Matthew were killed in an accident, and his son *James* (see below, p 72) succeeded him. He seems to have taken on the business of William and Philip Wightman of Cripplegate That he was a relation of the Chacomb Bagleys seems implied by the fact that James Bagley subsequently joined one of that firm for a time (see below) Mr Cocks[2] accounted for this Matthew by supposing that the original one (born in 1653) migrated to London about 1690 But the evidence of the foundry at Evesham from 1687—1690 and death of Matthew in the latter year was not of course before him

1703—1746 We now have to deal with a long period of over forty years, in which after 1712 a Henry is the sole representative of the firm William, as already noted, kept on the

[1] See *Arch Journal*, lxiii , 1906, p 192
[2] *Bucks*, p 213

Chacomb foundry until 1712, but we find his initials associated with those of Henry Bagley at Horley, Oxon., in 1706, at Eynsham, Oxon., in 1708, and at Wolvercot, Oxon., in 1710. The same H B occurs alone at Greatworth, Northants, in 1707. Who then is this Henry? Henry II., "of Ecton," is dead, and there are two possible alternatives. Either he is a younger brother of Matthew Bagley, or much more likely, a son of William. In the Chacomb registers the birth of a son Matthew to William is recorded in 1700, but from the evidence of dates we shall see that Henry must be older, born not later than 1686, when his father was twenty-three.

Henry Bagley III was a restless individual, and between 1710 and 1746, the year of his latest bell, we find him at work in four different places. In 1710 he was at Witney in Oxfordshire, where he cast bells for Appleton, Berks., in 1714 at Northampton (bells at Thornby, Northants), in 1721 at Buckingham (bells at Priors Marston, Warwickshire), in 1723 at Reading (bells at Tilehurst, Berks.), and in 1731-32 he was once more at Witney, where he may have spent the rest of his days.[1] We have no evidence that the Chacomb foundry was kept going between 1712 and 1726, when it was re-opened by Matthew, Henry's younger brother. In 1732 Henry Bagley published at Witney a printed fly-sheet[2] on which he gives a list of the bells cast by him and his predecessors down to that year. He apparently takes to himself the full credit for the whole number.

1726—1782 The name of **Matthew Bagley II**, as already noted, appears again on bells in 1726, when William's younger son, now aged 26, re-started the Chacomb foundry. He kept it on with apparently continuous success for no less than fifty six years, dying in 1785, at the age of 85. His latest bell is dated 1782, at Tysoe, Warwickshire. It is probable that Henry Bagley III was also at Chacomb during his latest years (1743-46), (see below, p 71). Matthew's only migration was in 1747-48, when we find him casting bells in Staffordshire, apparently in partnership with a James Bagley, who *may* be the Londoner already mentioned. But as James Bagley's London bells only date from 1710 to 1719 the interval is difficult to account for unless this is a younger James. However Matthew and James together cast a bell for Woolvercot, Oxon., in 1747,[3] and another for Cannock in Staffordshire. At Gayton in the latter county is a bell of 1748 by "Matthew Bagley of Wolverhampton."

The accompanying pedigree is a suggestion worked out on lines of the family history as above given, with the necessary deviations from that drawn up by Mr Cocks, it puts forth no pretensions to finality.

1 Henry Bagley of Witney cast a bell for Hurstbourne Prior, Hants., in 1741

2 Printed in Supplt to Ellacombe's *Gloucestershire*, p 120, a copy by Browne Willis in the Bodleian Library, Oxford (xliii fol 21)

3 James Bagley also occurs at East Hendred, Berks, in 1746

PEDIGREE OF THE BAGLEY FAMILY

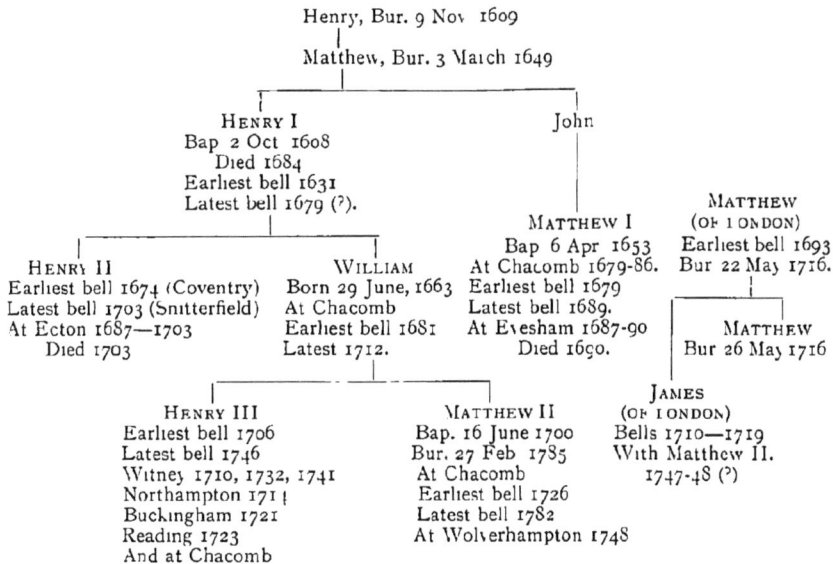

Henry, Bur. 9 Nov 1609

Matthew, Bur. 3 March 1649

Henry I
Bap 2 Oct 1608
Died 1684
Earliest bell 1631
Latest bell 1679 (?).

John

Henry II
Earliest bell 1674 (Coventry)
Latest bell 1703 (Snitterfield)
At Ecton 1687—1703
Died 1703

William
Born 29 June, 1663
At Chacomb
Earliest bell 1681
Latest 1712.

Matthew I
Bap 6 Apr 1653
At Chacomb 1679-86.
Earliest bell 1679
Latest bell 1689.
At Evesham 1687-90
Died 1690.

Matthew
(of London)
Earliest bell 1693
Bur 22 May 1716.

Matthew
Bur 26 May 1716

James
(of London)
Bells 1710—1719
With Matthew II.
1747-48 (?)

Henry III
Earliest bell 1706
Latest bell 1746
Witney 1710, 1732, 1741
Northampton 1714
Buckingham 1721
Reading 1723
And at Chacomb

Matthew II
Bap. 16 June 1700
Bur. 27 Feb 1785
At Chacomb
Earliest bell 1726
Latest bell 1782
At Wolverhampton 1748

NOTE —One explanation of the London Matthew seems not impossible The Matthew founding at Chacomb from 1679 onwards *may* have been a younger brother of Henry I, who assisted him in his business, and only used his own name at Henry I's partial retirement in 1679 Then the Matthew, son of John, born in 1653, would be the one who worked in London

Bells by the Bagleys are very numerous all over the Midlands The list published by Henry of Witney in 1732 gives the following numbers —

Berkshire	8	Stafford	16
Buckingham	31	Warwick	61
Gloucester	29	Wiltshire	8
Northants	129	Worcester	51
Oxfordshire	101	York	13

At the present day the numbers are roughly as follows —

Bedford	8	Lancashire*	12
Berkshire*	20	Leicester	9
Buckingham	30	Northants	192
Carmarthen*	1	Oxford*	140 (*approx*)
Cheshire*	2	Stafford	49
Derbyshire	1	Warwick	152 (20 re-cast)
Gloucester	35	Wiltshire*	6
Hampshire*	1	Worcester	65

* The investigation of these counties is not as yet complete

It will be thus seen that Warwickshire ranks second to Northants, though it will probably drop to third place when Oxfordshire has been completely explored We may now proceed to discuss these 152 bells[1] in chronological order, noting by the way the various methods of ornamentation employed

I HENRY BAGLEY I (1631—1679)

By far the greater majority of the bells belong to this founder, who seems to have been more successful and prosperous than the rest of the family His first work in the county is at **Shotteswell** almost the nearest parish to his Northamptonshire home Here the priest's bell is dated 1634, without any other inscription or mark except an ornamental floral scroll (Pl XXII Fig 10=*Bucks*, Pl XXXII Fig 2) filling up the rest of the band With this we may combine the smaller bell at **Wasperton**, which has merely the date 1638 Next comes a group of sixteen bells covering the period 1636—1642, *ie*, down to the break caused by the Civil Wars, distinguished from all the rest by the use of a foundry-mark in the form of an inverted shield charged with three bells. This never occurs in later years The list is as follows —

1636	Fenny Compton	1st	
	Idlicote	bell	Date uncertain, may be 1656, no shield.
1639	Barford	2nd	
	Grandborough	5th	
	Halford	3rd	
1640	Upper Shuckburgh	3rd	No shield.
1641	Grandborough	1st and 3rd	
	Ilmington	Ring of five	No shield on 1st and 3rd
	Monk's Kirby	1st	No shield
	Radford Semele	3rd	
1642	Wormleighton	1st	No shield

Fenny Compton, Grandborough, and Wormleighton trebles have a very favourite Bagley inscription (from *Ps* 98, 1)[2] —

CANTATE DOMINO CANTICVM NOVVM

The bells at Fenny Compton Shuckburgh, Grandborough (3rd), Ilmington (2nd) and Radford Semele bear the founder's name, in his usual formula —

HENRY BAGLEY MADE MEE

Two inscriptions characteristic only of his earlier years occur, one at Barford and Halford —

PRAYSE THE LORD YE PEOPLE

the other on Grandborough 5th (also at Feckenham, Worcestershire) —

BY MY VOYCE THE PEOPLE MAY KNOWE TO COME TO HEARE THE WORDE OF GOD

The treble at Monk's Kirby is somewhat unique bearing (with other ornaments) a shield with three swords in pale, and an inscription, part of which is to the following effect —

MY NOBLE FOVNDERS THEY HAVE BENE SO MANY BECAVSE NOT AL I WILL NOT HERE NAME ANY

The lettering used is throughout the same, a small thin type, about ⅜ in high, between the words are various ornamental borders, of which the commonest is a band of linked fleur-de-lys alternately upright and inverted, as at Wormleighton (Fig 9=*Bucks* fig 69) a single member of which sometimes occurs as a stop. Above and below the inscription a very effective floral scroll (as at Shotteswell and Grandborough) frequently occurs, of this there is more than one variety [3]

---

[1] I have not included in this total the old rings at St Martin's, Birmingham, and St Michael, Coventry

[2] Where there are several bells by Bagley this usually occurs on the treble

[3] See *Bucks*, Pl XXXII, Nos 1, 2 Fig 10 (=*Bucks* fig 73) is another variety used between the words

Fig. 9.

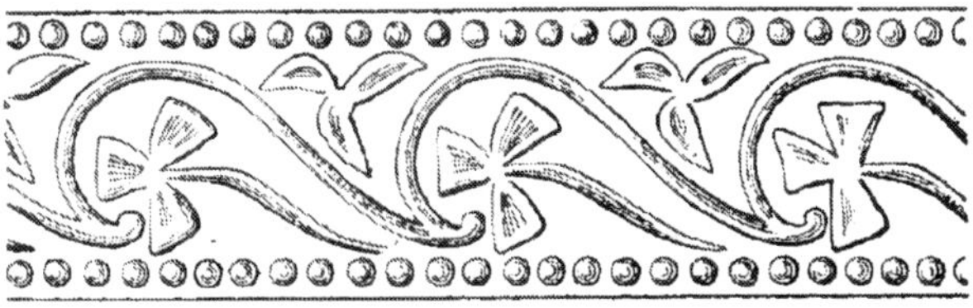

Fig. 10.

From 1649 to 1669, after the complete break caused by the Wars, the bells call for little additional comment; the inscriptions are almost confined to the two first given above, and the ornamentation is of the same character. Any special features will be found noted on the following list:

1649.	Long Itchington	3rd	Founder's name only; letters widely spaced.
1651.	Upper Shuckburgh	4th	
1652.	Whatcote	old 1st	
1656.	Ladbroke	old 2nd—4th	
1657.	Arrow	bell	
1658.	Alveston	1st	
1661.	Barford	3rd	
1662.	Bilton	5th	
	Butlers Marston	1st, 3rd, 4th	
	Haselor	old 1st	
1663.	Fenny Compton	3rd	
1664.	Wroxhall	1st	
1665.	Snitterfield	old 3rd	
1668.	Pillerton	1st	(With an unusual but uncertain stamp).
1669.	Binton	bell	

Our next group covers the period 1670—1679. It is marked by the fact that Henry Bagley now tries his hand at Latin, and substitutes HENRICVS BAGLEY ME FECIT for his previous formula. The list of bells is:—

1670.	Bubbenhall	2nd	
	Clifton	old 3rd	
	Long Itchington	1st	
	Prior's Hardwick	1st and 3rd	
	Warwick St. Mary	fire bell	
1672.	Pillerton	2nd	(With initial cross and two new stamps; see Pl. XXII., Figs. 6, 7, 9).

1674	Shotteswell	2nd	
1675	Coventry St John	5th[1]	
	Elmdon	2nd	
	Lillington	3rd	(With cross, Pl XXII 7)
1676	Bulkington	3rd	(With cross)
	Coventry St John	1st	
	Southam	6th	
1677	Ratley	2nd	
1678.	Badaesley Clinton	2nd	
1679	Lighthorne	3rd	

II MATTHEW BAGLEY I AND HENRY BAGLEY II (1679—1690)

The year 1680 is marked by the (probable) retirement of Henry Bagley I and the succession to his business of his son Henry II. and his nephew Matthew I as partners The joint occupation of the foundry lasted for eight years, and about 1687 the partners migrated, Henry to Ecton and Matthew to Evesham, leaving the Chacomb business in the hands of Henry's younger brother William, who had probably already been working with them for a few years, as his name occurs on bells in 1681

The bells of this period are as follows[2] —

1680	Whitnash	3rd and 4th	Matthew
1681	Offchurch	4th	Do
	Wellesbourne	1st-6th	Henry
1682	Birmingham St Martin old ring of six		Henry (?)
1683	Barston	5th	Matthew
	Solihull	3rd and 4th	Do
	Stratford on-Avon	4th, 7th & former 4th	Do
1685	Edgbaston	3rd—6th	Henry and Matthew
	Solihull	6th, 9th, 10th	Henry
1686	Burton Dasset	1st-6th	Henry and Matthew
	Coughton	1st-6th	Do.
	Packwood	2nd-6th	Do (original ring of five)
	Solihull	8th	Henry
1687	Burton Hastings	2nd	Do

This group of bells introduces us to some more or less pleasing varieties of inscriptions, such as the orthodox

FEARE GOD AND HONOVR THE KING

of which one example occurs in each of the larger rings here given At **Coughton** the tenor has a somewhat coarse jest to the effect that

CAMPANA GRAVIDA PEPERIT FILIAS

Apparently with an allusion to an increase in the number of bells, perhaps by re-casting the old tenor into two trebles The same is to be found at *Dodford*, Northants, but there the tenor only is Bagley's, and the joke seems to lose its point More characteristic of the period is the adoption of the formula beloved of the later Newcombes and John Martin, on the 5th at **Burton Dassett**

BE IT KNOWNE TO ALL THAT DO MEE SEE THAT BAGLY OF CHARCOM MADE MEE 1686

---

[1] This bell and the treble of 1676 are the remains of a ring of eight cast by Henry Bagley sen and jun for St Michael's Church, of which these two were subsequently transferred to St John's See Part II for further details

[2] Where the bells are by Matthew and Henry the fact is usually indicated by giving their names separately on different bells, as at Edgbaston and Packwood

The methods of ornamentation remain the same, except for the introduction of the characteristic 17th century arabesque borders above and below the inscriptions, which are

Fig. 11.

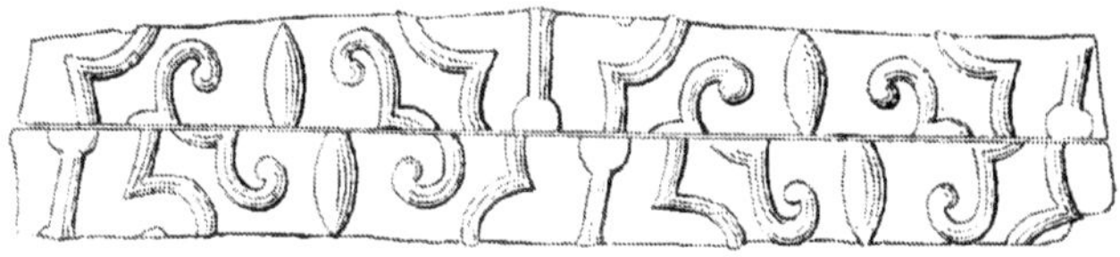

Fig. 12.

often cut up into bits and placed between the words (see Pl. XXII. Figs. 8, 11=Figs. 11, 12). Matthew Bagley also introduced a curious form of **A** with a hook at the top.

The following bells were cast by Matthew alone:—

1687.	Honington	2nd, 3rd, 5th, 6th.
	Knowle	old 1st-3rd.
1688.	Studley	1st-5th.

The Honington bells, as he definitely tells us, were cast by "Matthew Bagley of Chacomb"; but as we have already seen, he probably migrated to Evesham in that year, where he died in 1690, having left the foundry at Chacomb in the hands of William Bagley, the younger son of Henry I. The 2nd bell at **Barston**, dated 1689, bears the names of both Matthew and William, but I think it is more likely to have been cast by William at Chacomb, as was the treble of that ring in 1691. On the other hand, the rings at Knowle and Studley were probably cast at Evesham.

3. WILLIAM BAGLEY (1689—1706).

William Bagley's bells in Warwickshire are as follows:—

1689-91.	Barston	2nd and 1st.	
1695.	Whichford	4th (also old 1st-3rd).	
1697.	Charlcote	1st and 2nd.	
1698.	Shustoke	2nd and 3rd.	(Originally five).
1701.	Oxhill	1st and 3rd (also old 2nd).	
1702.	Walsgrave	4th and 5th.	
1703.	Snitterfield	old 2nd.	
1706.	Whichford	Priest's bell.	

His bells are much the same in character as his predecessors', but not marked by the same love of ornament. He introduced a new type of inter-twining scroll-pattern (Fig. 13=*Bucks.*,

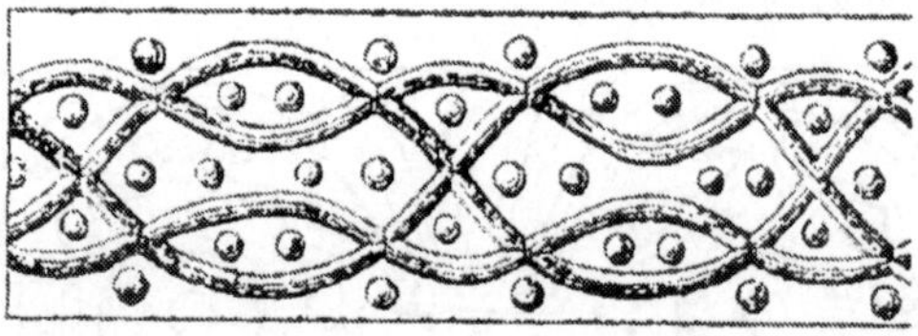

Fig. 13.

fig. 74). Some of his inscriptions are decidedly quaint, as for instance the two at **Shustoke**:—

OF FORE HE CAST VS INTO FIVE
REPAIRD OVR CHVRCH AND BELLFREE HERE

It is much to be regretted that we have lost the lines on the first (re-cast in 1736), which would have given the donor's name, and those on the 4th and tenor (re-cast in 1768); the tenor probably had a couplet. The Bagleys were alway remarkably weak in spelling.

Walsgrave 4th and 5th are somewhat unintelligible, but there can be no doubt that the one signifies a thirst on the part of the ringers rather than of the bells! In the other Bagley's Latin is hardly a success:—

4th (2nd line):— HARKEN DO YE HEARE OVR CLAPERES WANT BEERE
5th:— QVANTVM SVFFIIFIT BIBIERE MOLO CLANCVLA VOS MVSICA TONE

It only remains to note one departed bell of his of which a record remains; it hung in the Gosford Gate at Coventry, and was dated 1691.[1]

It should be noted that at Snitterfield the old 2nd bore in addition to William Bagley's name, the initials H B of Henry Bagley. It is open to question whether this is the second or Ecton Henry, who died in that year. He, at all events, cast the treble at **Grendon** in 1699 and the 3rd at **Corley** in 1702; these bells may have come either from Ectonor Chacomb. Other bells cast by William and Henry Bagley together have already been noted (p. 65)

HENRY BAGLEY III. (1706—1746).

Between 1703 and 1740 there is a great drop in the Bagley bells, and only two Warwickshire towers illustrate this period. William Bagley died in 1712, and the surviving Henry III. was much on the move. But Henry Bagley "of Buckingham" cast six bells for **Priors Marston** in 1721, of which the tenor has since been re-cast. From Witney or Chacomb came four bells, the 3rd, 5th, and 6th, to **Long Compton** in 1731; probably, I think, from the former place, as Henry Bagley of Witney, in his fly-sheet of that year (see above), gives such full details of the donors, who were the Earl and Countess of Northampton, Mr. E. S. England, and the Rev. John Brown. The same Henry also cast at Chacomb five bells in 1740-42:

1740.	Barton-on-Heath	bell.
1742.	Cherington	3rd and 4th.
	Stratford-on-Avon	3rd.
	Wootton Wawen	1st.

He introduced a new style of alphabet, of larger and heavier type, and altogether more of 18th century character, but not at all ineffective. In the use of ornaments he is somewhat sparing. The last year for his bells is 1746, and he seems to have spent at least six years at Chacomb.

[1] Harleian MSS. 7017, 290; *Vict. County History of Warwick*, ii., p. 207

MATTHEW BAGLEY III (1726—1782)

The last of the Bagleys is Matthew III (or IV), the son of William, born in 1700, whose long founding life covers a period of no less than 56 years. His last bell is dated 1782, and he died in 1785. All his bells were cast at Chacomb except for the migration to Wolverhampton in 1747-48, already noted, and on the whole he did a very fair business. His lettering is an enlarged version of that used by the Witney Bagley, with a stop of three roundlets between the words and occasional arabesque ornaments. There are thirteen of his bells in Warwickshire

1752	Wolford	5th.	
1763	Ratley	3rd	
1766	Whatcote	old 3rd	
1773	Warwick St Nicholas	8th	
1774.	Lighthorne	old 1st	
	Shotteswell	3rd and old 4th	
1775.	Barcheston	1st	
1778	Haseley	3rd.	(in the smaller type used by Henry III)
1779	Ufton	1st-3rd	
1782	Tysoe	5th	

None of these bells call for special comment, the inscriptions being mostly of the orthodox "Vicar and Churchwarden" type.

JAMES BAGLEY OF LONDON (1710—1719)

We have already had occasion to mention this James Bagley, the son of Matthew Bagley of London, who was at work either in partnership with his father or independently down to the time of the latter's death in 1716,[1] and for three years longer. The Bagley foundry in London was in the parish of St Giles', Cripplegate, on Windmill Hill. James' bells are not common, and are confined to the home counties (Essex, Middlesex, Kent, and Surrey). He however cast bells for Rochester Cathedral which implies a certain reputation. He claims our attention somewhat unexpectedly here, as one of his bells has found its way into Warwickshire, and now hangs in the tower of St Margaret's Church, **Ward End** (or Little Bromwich), on the outskirts of Birmingham. That the bell is second-hand is implied by its inscription —

THE ✲ ROYAL ✲ HOSPITAL ✲ AT ✲ GREENWICH ✲ 1716

which thus leaves no doubt as to its original home. Tradition says that one or more of the bells of this church were given by William Hutton the historian, about 1815, and he must be held responsible for the transaction—which it is hoped was a perfectly straightforward one—whereby the bell migrated from Greenwich to Birmingham. Though it does not bear James Bagley's name, his lettering is easily recognisable. His or his son's subsequent appearances in the Midlands have already been noted (p. 65.)

JOSEPH SMITH OF EDGBASTON (1701—1732)

With the beginning of the eigthteenth century we hail the advent of the first known founder resident in the county. Joseph Smith set up his foundry, according to tradition, in the district known as Chad Valley, Edgbaston, which since his time has probably been greatly transformed.[2]

---

[1] See Stahlschmidt's *Kent*, p. 101, for the story of his end.

[2] A writer in the *Birmingham Daily Gazette*, 21 April, 1856, under the initials J. A., says —"In answer to the enquiries made by 'W. A. J.' in *N. and Q.* 98 I may state that I was informed thirty years since by an old man that lived at Harborne Heath, that his father remembered a bell foundry standing opposite to the Swan, at Good Knaves End, at the bottom of Chad Hill, as it is called now. I have seen three peals of bells that were cast there." He goes on to give the inscriptions on Alvechurch, Halesowen and Northfield bells. I am indebted to Mr. W. F. Falkner for this extract.

His earliest bells that I can trace are dated 1701, his latest, 1732 The majority of these are in Warwickshire, where after the decline of the Bagleys he had a clear field, but even so they are chiefly confined to the northern part There are also many in South Staffordshire, a baker s dozen in Shropshire, about twenty in Worcestershire, and two in Leicestershire, ignored by North Among the whole rings cast by him are rings of six at Coleshill and Hampton, Madeley (Salop), Alvechurch, Halesowen, and Northfield (Worcs), and Alrewas, Handsworth, Pattingham, and Sedgley (Staffs), of these Coleshill, Hampton, Madeley and Northfield remain intact There are also rings of five at Castle Bromwich (one re-cast) Brinklow, Dunchurch, Rugby, and Willoughby, Sheriff Hales (Salop), King s Bromley, Forton, and Rushall (Staffs) In 1711 he appears to have cast bells for the new church of St Philip, Birmingham, which were soon replaced

In his inscriptions he mainly follows the lines of seventeenth-century founders, and we find GLORIA IN EXCELSIS DEO, GOD SAVE HIS CHURCH, etc, with considerable frequency, but his single bells seldom have more than churchwardens' names At Rugby we have adaptations of the Vulgate text of *Eph* iv, 4, *Matt* xviii, 19, and xvi, 18, and *1 John*, v 7 In his larger rings he usually places on the 3rd bell the statement IOSEPH SMITH IN EDGBASTON MADE ME but in some cases, as at *Alvechurch* and *Madeley*, he bursts into rhyme, if not poetry —

IF YOU WOULD KNOW WHEN WE WARE RVNN IT WAS MARCH THE 22 1711

and

IN MADELEY ALL THESE BELLS WAS RVNN BY IOSEPH SMITH OF EDGBASTON 1726

even higher flights are attempted on the well-known ring at *Northfield*, which I give here as they have never yet been accurately printed —

1 HENRY KNOWLES PARISH CLERK 1730 WE NOW ARE SIX THO ONCE BUT FIVE

2 AND AGAINST OUR CASTING SOME DID STRIVE 1730

3 BUT WHEN A DAY FOR MEETING THERE WAS FIXT 1730 JOSEPH SMITH MADE ME

4 APEARD BUT NINE AGAINST TWENTY-SIX 1730 SQUIRE SMITH

5 SAMUEL PALMER AND THOMAS SILK CHURCHWARDENS 1730

6 THOMAS JERVOISE ESR PATRON WILLIAM WORTH D D RECTOR
IT WAS WILLIAM KETTLE THAT DID CONTRIVE TO MAKE US 6 THAT WERE BUT FIVE 1730

[The coins and ornaments between the words are omitted]

Another gem of poetry is the treble at **Barford**

BY MISINFORMATION MADE WAS I
ITS THE FOUNDERS LOS PRAY THINK ON HE

Joseph Smith s bells are usually well ornamented with arabesques like those used by the Bagleys (Fig 11), and an effective scroll-border between the words (Pl XXIII Fig 2), by way of stop he generally uses impressions of various coins, mostly pence and half-pence His lettering is rather thin and narrow, but neat in appearance Occasionally as at Budbrooke and Sheldon, he uses an inverted shield with three bells and the letters I S among foliage (Pl XXIII, Fig 1)

The following is a list of his Warwickshire bells —

1708	Allesley	1st and 4th	1705	Brinklow	1-5	
1707	Anstey	3rd	1724	Budbrooke	2nd	
1722	Astley	5th	1717	Castle Bromwich	1st	2nd, 4th, 5th also old 3rd.
1706	Baddesley Ensor	small	1720	Coleshill	1-6	
1709	Barford	1st	1724	Dunchurch	1-5	

1728	Barston	4th	1727	Henley	1st, 6th
1711	Beaudesert	3rd	1711	Monk's Kirby	2nd
1703	Bickenhill	1st	1711	Rugby	1-5
1707	Do	5th	1723	Sheldon	1st
1728.	Binley	1st	1705.	Stretton on-Dunsmore	1st, 2nd
1706.	Exhall	old	1733	Tanworth	6th.
1706	Grandborough	2nd, 4th	1709	Water Orton	1st, 2nd
1725.	Hampton	1-6	1713	Willoughby	1-5

Those in other counties —

Leicestershire—

1711.	Ibstock	2nd	1718	Snarestone	1st

Shropshire—

1726	Madeley	1-6 (tenor 1727)	1726.	Willey	5th.
1722	Sheriff Hales	2-6	1723	Woodcote	bell

Staffordshire—

1711	Alrewas	1-6 (two re-cast)	1724	Pattingham	3-8.
1727.	Armitage	1-3	1723	Rushall	1-5
1709	Drayton Bassett	2nd	1720	Sedgeley	3-8
1729	Forton	1-5 (two re-cast)	1732	Smethwick	old bell.
1724	Lower Gornall	1st.	1710	Weeford	1st & 2nd
1701	Handsworth	1-6	1711	West Bromwich	2nd, 4th, 6th
1702	Hints	1-3	1706	Wolverhampton St John	1st
1705	King's Bromley	2-6			

Worcestershire—

1711.	Alvechurch	3-8 (tenor re-cast)	1725	Martin Hussingtree	1.
1718	Clent	1st	1730	Northfield	1-6
1707	Halesowen	3-5, 7, 8	1724	St Kenelm s (Romsley)	bell

His earliest bells are the ring at Handsworth (1701), his latest, the old bell of Smethwick Church, 1732, the total of thirty four years' labour is about 150 He does not appear to have left any successor, and Birmingham was not again represented in the church bell-foundry line until about 1868

THE BROMSGROVE FOUNDRY

A dangerous rival to Joseph Smith throughout the whole of his career was **Richard Sanders,** an inhabitant of the not-far distant town of Bromsgrove. His bells cover the period 1703—1738, occurring in both these years at Upton Snodsbury, near Worcester He is not, it is true, strongly represented in Warwickshire, but he maintained his reputation against his rival in his own county, where some fifty of his bells remain Nothing is known of his history except in connection with his bell-founding work,[1] but he has left several good rings of bells, notably the famous one at St Helen's, Worcester, with its couplets celebrating the victories of Marlborough, others at St. Nicholas and (formerly) St John, Worcester, Eckington, Norton by-Evesham, and other places In Warwickshire he cast rings for Salford Priors, Tanworth, and Tysoe, and some half-dozen single bells besides he is also found in Cheshire, Gloucestershire, Lancashire and Oxfordshire, and there are the remains of a ring by him at Kettering, Northants The Warwickshire list is —

1729	Alveston	3rd	1733	Stratford-on-Avon	old 3rd
1720	Barcheston	2nd	1717.	Do	8th
1722	Bilton	1st	1719	Tachbrook	2nd

[1] See *Assoc Archit Socs Reports*, xxv, p 587.

1715	Kinwarton	1st	1707	Tanworth	1 5
	Preston Bagot former bell		1719	Tysoe	1-6 (4th and 5th re-cast).
1735.	Salford Priors 3-8 (tenor re-cast)		1729	Wootton Wawen 6th	

His lettering is neat and effective, about an inch high, and he uses a plain cross, and arabesque borders between the words and lines One of his peculiarities is his fondness for "lower-case" lettering or Roman minuscules, such as we find at **Kinwarton**

Ieffery Hopkins Ch w 1715

This peculiarity, so far as I know, is only shared by one founder, Luke Ashton of Wigan, who was a contemporary of Sanders The latter has two trade-marks, one a plain circle with a bell and the letters R S, the other, a bell surrounded by a band with the words RICHARD SANDERS MADE THIS BELL (Pl. XXIII, Figs 3, 9) His inscriptions, so far as Warwickshire is concerned, do not call for much comment, but the second at **Tysoe** is unique in having a double row of small letters forming the alphabet, with a few odd letters and numerals thrown in at the end to fill up space, thus

56789 ABCDEFGHIKLMNOPQRSTUVWXYZ 1234
ABCDEFGHIKLMNOPQRSTUVWXYZ 1234

Alphabet inscriptions are, of course, common on bells of earlier date, but the use of numerals (unless the Newcombe bell at Haseley can be cited as a parallel) is unique before the days of patent steel bells

Sanders at his death in or about 1735 was succeeded by **William Brooke**, whose career extends to about 1750 His bells are few in number, and I only know of three in Worcestershire (Elmbridge, Moseley St Anne, Upton Warren), one in Leicestershire (Snibstone), and five in Warwickshire The latter include the three smaller ones at Meriden (1740), the old treble at Shustoke (1736), and the 3rd at Tachbrook (1740) In each case we have indications that, like Joseph Smith, he was a bit of a poet. The best specimen is the **Shustoke** treble (unfortunately damaged in the fire of 1886 and since recast) —

+ MR ROBERT MALLERON VICAR AS I DO TELL AND JOSIAS ALLEN CHVRCH WARDEN WHEN I WAS MADE A BELL W B: BROMSGROVE 1736

At **Meriden**, however, he indulges in an out-and-out pun on the 2nd.—

WHEN MY FIRST AND THIRD BEGIN TO RING
THEN I WAS BROKE BEFORE WE ALL DID SING WM BROOKE CAST ME 1740

His lettering differs from Sanders, being thicker and narrower, he uses a bell as trade-mark and sundry small ornaments.

THE EVESHAM FOUNDRY

I have already noted that one of the Matthew Bagleys died, and probably also worked, at Evesham, but as this is more or less conjectural, I have included this period under the general heading of the Bagleys But we have more definite evidence of a foundry here at the beginning of the next century, carried on by two founders named **William Clark** and **Michael Bushell** Their bells, indeed, centre more round Stratford than round Evesham, but the following facts are in favour of the Worcestershire town

In 1706 the great bell of Badsey Church (Worcs), which bears the name of William Clark, was conveyed thither from Evesham, according to the parish accounts In 1709 the registers of All Saints, Evesham contain the entry

Oct 18 Michael Bushell married Grace Phipps, per licence

I owe the latter fact to the kindness of the Rev J H Bloom, who also tells me that there is in the churchyard of St Lawrence a tombstone to Hannah, wife of Michael Bushell, who died 27 April, 1732, aged 43 If it was the same Michael, she must have been a second wife There is on the other hand an entry in the Churchwardens Accounts of Beoley (Worcs), under date 1711

Pd Mr Clarke the Bellfounder £1 1s 6d

this being apparently for a bell cast at Bromsgrove As, however, there are bells in that tower cast in 1711 by Richard Sanders of Bromsgrove (see above), it must be assumed that this Clarke was Sanders' foreman

The Warwickshire specimens of these founders' work are the 2nd to 5th at **Henley-in-Arden** and the ring of four at **Newbold Pacey** (all dated 1707), on none of which do their names appear Their characteristic mark is IHS in a square with a cross over the H, and they also use a plain cross Of the chronograms to which they were much addicted examples occur at Hinton, Gloucs, and Badsey, Worcestershire, but none in this county [1]

The 2nd bell at **Whatcote** bears the inscription

IOHN + CLARK + MED ME 1711

As this bell is later than any known by William Clark, I think it must be by his son or successor, to whom we may probably also assign a bell at *Wormington*, Gloucs, inscribed merely IOHN CLARK

THE WOOTTON FOUNDRY (BEDFORDSHIRE)

THOMAS RUSSELL (1715—1744)

In the eighteenth century there was a foundry carried on at Wootton, a village five miles south-west of Bedford, the originator of which was Thomas Russell a clock-maker He has supplied two rings of bells to Warwickshire, the five at **Hillmorton,** dated 1731, which still remain intact, and another five at **Napton,** cast in the same year, of which the tenor has been re cast by Warner He uses two types of lettering, one of medium size, something like the Rudhalls' (p 78), the other exceedingly small, only ⅜ of an inch high, the latter is employed in part on the Napton treble, and throughout on the 4th and tenor at Hillmorton the inscriptions being arranged in double lines throughout In the latter case they are only a list of the contributors to the bells with the amounts they gave, and on the other three bells we have the founder s or churchwardens names, with a star at intervals. The Napton treble has —

+ THOMAS RUSSELL MADE ME (*scroll*) WILLIAM REYNOLDS AND IOHN MARKHAM ✻ CHURCHWARDENS

with a plain cross, a scroll ornament, and a double triangle or six-point star [2] The other three have —

THOMAS RUSSELL OF WOOTTON MADE ME 1731

with scrolls between the words The extreme limits for Russell's bells appear to be 1715 and 1739, and he d ed in 1744

THE ALDBOURNE (WILTS) FOUNDRY

(1) THE CORS

It is a matter for some surprise that we should find in Warwickshire a ring of bells from so remote a foundry as that of Aldbourne in the North Wiltshire Downs, from which part

[1] See *Assoc Archit Socs Reports*, xxv, p 586
[2] Oddly described in *Bucks*, p 258, as a pentacle '

communication northwards must have been difficult in former times, it is hardly less so now[1] The parish in question, however, **Sutton-under-Bralles**, is near the southern extremity of Warwickshire.

The Aldbourne foundry was opened about the end of the 17th century by *Oliver Cor*, whose earliest recorded date is 1696 at Devizes St Mary, his latest, 1727, at Shalbourne, Wilts Between the years 1698 and 1719 we find the names of **William** and **Robert Cor** most frequently, and in 1724 Robert appears alone at St Mary, Marlborough, implying the decease of William before that date A *John Cor* occurs between 1728 (Amesbury) and 1750 (Marlborough), and with him the dynasty ends, the foundry passing into other hands

The ring of five at Sutton is dated 1701, and is remarkable for the extremely elaborate character of the ornaments with which the bells are all enriched The 1st in fact has no inscription, only ornament, the second has merely W C 1701, the third R C in curious large fancy letters (Pl XXIV, Figs 4, 5), and the fourth WILL COR 1701, all with ornaments The tenor has churchwardens' names, the initials in fancy capitals, and ROB COR The whole ring is thus the work of William and Robert together In all there are fourteen different patterns employed on these bells, all of the same style of 17th-century ornament, which it is impossible to reproduce in type, and I must therefore refer the reader to Part II for further details, and to Plates XXIV-XXVI for reproductions of some of them

One of the most interesting is the medallion (1)[2] with the Adoration of the Magi (Pl XXV 6), (3), (6), (7), (13) are cherubs or other figure subjects (Pl XXIV 2-3, XXV 3, 5), (4), (5), (8) and (12) are floral or quasi-floral ornaments (Pl XXV, 1, 2, 4, XXVI, 2), (10) and (14) are floral or arabesque borders (Pl XXIV 1, XXVI 1), and the list is completed by the Royal Arms (2=Pl XXVI 4), a coin of William III (11), and a monogram (C C ?) within a foliated border (9=Pl XXVI 3) Mr J R Jerram of Salisbury, to whom I am indebted for careful drawings, has discovered several of these on bells in Wiltshire, at Aldbourne, Malmesbury, and Tisbury, and I have found them at Lydiard Tregooze in the same county, But nowhere, I think, do they occur in such richness and variety as here, and some are peculiar to this ring. Mr Jerram thinks that Cor had come into possession of a lot of scraps of brass ornamentation in some way, and thought them suitable for adorning his bells

(2) ROBERT WELLS (1764—1794)

The foundry at Aldbourne was continued by *Edward Read* (1751—1757) from whom it passed to **Robert Wells** (1764—1794) Under him and his son *James* (1781—1825) the business for a long time flourished exceedingly, but at last fell on bad times and was finally bought by Mears of Whitechapel From Robert Wells we have in this county a ring of eight cast for the rebuilt church of **St. John, Deritend, Birmingham**, in 1776, and the Fire Bell at the **Guild Chapel, Stratford-on-Avon** They are inscribed like so many of the Aldbourne bells, on the sound-bow At Stratford he spells the name of his home ALBOURNE

It is to be hoped that it may be possible to give a more detailed account of this foundry when the investigation of Wiltshire bells and founders is completed

THOMAS PYKE OF BRIDGEWATER (1776—1783)

There was a foundry at Bridgewater, Somerset, in the 18th century, which lasted altogether from 1743 to 1831, being held by a succession of different founders Bayley and Street (1743—1773), Thomas Pyke (1776—1783), George Davis (1782—1799), and the Kingstons (1801—1831) Their bells are fairly common in Somerset, and also occur in Devon and Dorset, but it is a surprise to find one so far away as **Edgbaston**, to which church Thomas Pyke supplied a treble in 1781, recently re-cast

---

[1] Aldbourne is five miles from a railway station, Sutton the same, and even then the railway journey is not very direct

[2] The numbers in brackets refer to the description in Part II, *s v* Sutton

THE LATER GLOUCESTER FOUNDRY.

THE RUDHALLS (1684—1725)

The Gloucester foundry, continued for some years after Henry Farmer (p 47) by John Palmer, down to about 1665, apparently then came to an end for about twenty years But it was destined to arise with renewed vigour and establish itself firmly for 150 years, enjoying a reputation never surpassed or even equalled by any English firm, under the guidance of the famous family of Rudhall

Possibly an off-shoot of a well-known family, the Rudhalls of Rudhall, near Ross, **Abraham Rudhall I.** re-opened the foundry in 1684 His progress was slow at first, and comparatively few bells are found outside the county of Gloucester before 1700 It is curious to note how his reputation spread most quickly up the valleys of the Wye and Severn into Hereford, Salop, and Cheshire owing to the facilities of water-carriage The Avon being presumably less navigable, this is not the case with Warwickshire, where his bells and those of his successors are far fewer than in the West In Gloucestershire alone there are 675 Rudhall bells remaining—more than one third of the total number, in Hereford, Salop, Cheshire, and even Lancashire, as well as in Wales, nearly all the large rings are their work, as well as many smaller ones, and altogether they are said to have cast no fewer than 4,521 church bells. These figures speak for themselves, and there is no need to dwell more on the excellence of of their work

Their inscriptions are much less remarkable Limited to some ten or twelve sentiments of the kind that we should expect in the age of the Georges, such as GOD SAVE THE KING (or CHURCH), PEACE AND GOOD NEIGHBOURHOOD, PROSPERITY TO OUR BENEFACTORS (or TO THIS PARISH) they do not offer much variety or interest to the campanologist The last of the line, John Rudhall, drops these pious aspirations almost entirely, and contents himself for the most part with his name alone.

The succession of Rudhalls may be briefly noted as follows —

1 *Abraham Rudhall I.* (1684—1718)

From him we have the ring of three at Chesterton (1705), the ring of six at Kineton (1703, with treble of 1716 and tenor of 1717), the original six at Nuneaton (1703), the original ten at Warwick, St Mary (1702, put up after the fire of 1694), and two of 1703 at Leek Wootton

2 *Abraham Rudhall II* (1718—1736)

His only bells are Honington 4th and the ring of six at Alcester, cast in 1735, just before his death

3 *Abel Rudhall* (1736—1760)

Single bells at Polesworth (1740) and Tysce (1750)

4 *Thomas Rudhall* (1760—1783)

Single bells at Austrey (1779), Wootton Wawen (1760 and 1784), Wolverton (1771)

5 *Charles and John Rudhall* (1783—1785) No bells in Warwickshire

6 *John Rudhall* (1787—1830)

A ring of six at Bidford (1791), Dr Parr s ring of six at Hatton (1809), to which two trebles were added in 1817, single bells at Honington, Lea Marston, Wootton Wawen, Great Wolford The Hatton bells have been re cast, only the clock-bell of 1809 now remaining

Figs 14—18 illustrate Abraham Rudhall's trade-mark of a bell and the four ornamental patterns which the earlier members of the family placed on their bells, of the latter Fig 15 is the only one used by Thomas Rudhall

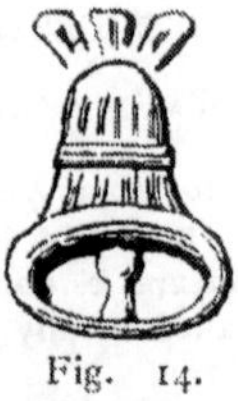

Fig. 14.

Fig. 15.

Fig. 16.

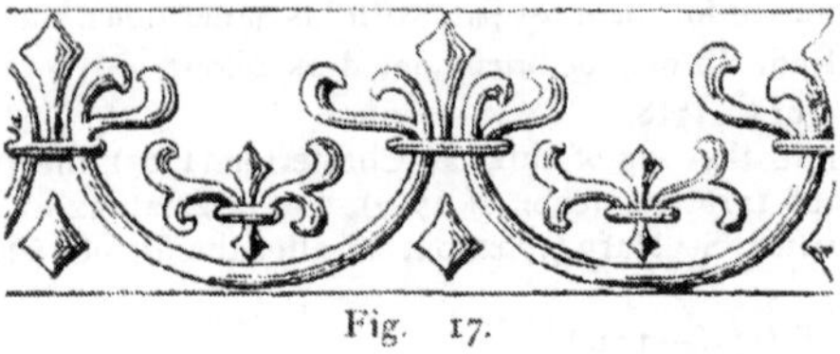

Fig. 17.

Fig. 18.

JOHN BRIANT OF HERTFORD (1782—1825).

This founder was at work at Hertford for over forty years, though the bells which he supplied to Warwickshire only cover a period of twenty. Stahlschmidt has described him as "the Herts. founder *par excellence*," though he was not the first founder in the county or even at Hertford. But he was undoubtedly an admirable craftsman, as is proved by the wide distribution of his bells, and the number of large rings which he cast Stahlschmidt collected much interesting biographical detail about him illustrative of his mental capacity, technical skill, and conscientiousness[1] It is sad to think that this worthy man ended his days in indigence, dying in an almshouse at St Albans in 1829, at the age of 81 His business was sold to Mears in 1825

In Warwickshire there are 21 of his bells remaining, including a ring of six and another of four, and in other counties over twenty large rings, including Barnstaple, Devon, Saffron Walden and Waltham Abbey, Essex, and St Alkmund, Shrewsbury[2] He uses a small neat type of lettering, something like Edward Arnold's, of which there are two sizes, and affected a set of curious little ornaments, consisting of a Calvary cross, a cross *patonce*, a diminutive bell, and a double triangle (Pl XXIII., Figs 4, 6, 7) At Waltham Abbey he introduces an old friend, the head of Edward III (p 8), a stamp which had already been in existence 400 years!

The Warwickshire list is —

1793	Ashow	1-4	1792	Newbold-on-Avon	1-6
1803	Churchover	3rd.	1809.	Nuneaton	4th
1805.	Coventry St Michael	10th	1808	Great Packington	bell
1792	Dunchurch	6th	1808	Shotteswell	1st.
1803	Ettington	4th.	1792	Stoneleigh	4th
1793	Leek Wootton	1-2	1811	Wormington	1st

The inscriptions do not call for much comment, with the exception of that at **Great Packington**, which is interesting for its historical allusions —

TRES OLIM CAMPANÆ E QVIBVS RVPTÂ QUADÂM VICTORIAM AD TRAFALGAR RESONANDO

A.D MDCCV IN UNAM FUSÆ A.D MDCCCVIII ✲ O

JOHN BRIANT HERTFORD FECIT 1808 ✲ GLORIA DEO IN EXCELSIS ✲

There is also a curious bit of theology on the tenor at Newbold On the Churchover and Nuneaton bells we may note the name of J. Over, whom Briant employed as his local agent and bell-hanger, he lived at Rugby For the Ettington bell he similarly employed one Waters of King's Sutton near Banbury.

THE EAYRES OF KETTERING

The name of Eayre, says North (*Northants*, p 47), is well known in the Kettering Registers of the seventeenth and eighteenth centuries One of the family, Thomas Eayre, was a clock-maker, as appears from the 4th bell in the Kettering ring, which was cast by Richard Sanders of Bromsgrove (p. 74) in 1714 From the fact that an outside founder was employed it would be inferred that there was then no foundry in the town, but the initials T E appear on the 2nd at East Farndon, Northants, with the date 1710, which seems to suggest that this Thomas Eayre had tried his hand at bell-founding He died in 1716, leaving two sons, Thomas, born 1691, and Joseph, of whom the latter subsequently opened a foundry at St Neot's

THOMAS EAYRE (1717—1757)

Not long after his father's death Thomas Eayre started a bell-foundry in Kettering, at first in partnership with his uncle John (who died about 1718) His bells, says North, soon became very plentiful in this and neighbouring counties, and there are several examples in Warwickshire The list is —

1730	Willey	2nd	1752	Stoneleigh	1st
1731	Honily	1-5	1756	Curdworth	2nd.
1741.	Monks Kirby	5th			

[1] *Herts* p 56

[2] The frequency of Briant's bells in the neighbourhood of Banbury is perhaps worth noting

All are inscribed in small very neat lettering, but the inscriptions present no special feature He sometime uses Calvary crosses, crowns, and other small ornaments like Briant's, and at Monk's Kirby an effective scroll-pattern North (*op cit* p 48) contributes other interesting information about Thomas Eayre, who died in December 1757, leaving a son Thomas, who carried on the foundry for a few years longer

EDWARD ARNOLD OF LEICESTER (1784—1800)

The other Eayre, Joseph, who set up a foundry at St Neot's about 1735, died in 1771-72, leaving his business to his nephew Edward Arnold, and thereby establishing a dynasty of founders which, with some changes of name and habitation, has lasted to the present day, with an ever-growing reputation, not only in the Midlands, but it may be said, throughout the world

Edward Arnold kept on the St Neot's foundry for twelve years, and in 1784 migrated to Leicester, where, except for one or two spasmodic efforts, no founding had been done for 140 years, *i e*, since Hugh Watts death in 1643 His bells are not very numerous, and there are only a few stray ones in Warwickshire —

1790	Arley	3rd	1795	Shilton	1st and 2nd
1791	Fillongley	6th	1798	Warwick St. Nicholas 7th	

He uses the same kind of lettering as the Eayres, and occasional scroll-patterns by way of ornaments (as at Arley)

His business at St Neot's he left in the hands of Robert Taylor, the first of a long series of eminent exponents of the founder's craft Arnold himself died about 1800, but Robert Taylor kept on the foundry at St Neot's until 1821 Mr Owen has collected much information about him and his family,[1] and informs us that a fire compelled Taylor's removal from St Neot's in that year He thereupon set up a foundry at Oxford, in which on his death he was succeeded by his sons William and John (born 1795 and 1797) respectively

WILLIAM AND JOHN TAYLOR OF OXFORD (1821—1854)

The Taylors' bell-founding business seems to have been carried on somewhat intermittently for some years William was more of a clock-maker than a bell-founder, and John in 1825 migrated to Devonshire and set up business at Buckland Brewer, where his son the late John William was born in 1827 He, however, paid occasional visits to Oxford, and returned there finally in 1835, from which time the foundry was continued down to 1850 The branch at Loughborough appears to have been opened by John about 1840, but few bells were cast there before 1850, and the Oxford foundry was finally closed in 1854 on the death of William Taylor

The fourth bell at Long Compton is one of the earliest products of the Oxford foundry being dated 1823 and the 3rd at Bourton-on-Dunsmore was cast there in 1827 Both are inscribed in the small neat capitals of Eayre and Arnold Several bells belong to the second period of the Oxford *régime* Cherington 1st, 2nd, and 5th (1842), Compton Wynyates (1847), Christ Church, Coventry (1851), Farnborough 2nd-4th (1844), Walsgrave 1st and 2nd (1843) Whichford 5th (1848) All are in the small Roman alphabet except those at Farnborough, where "Mixed Gothic," of a type much affected by the Taylors at this time, occurs, it is doubtless partly due to the ecclesiastical revival of taste

THE TAYLORS OF LOUGHBOROLGH

As we have seen, it was in 1840 that John Taylor first settled down at Loughborough, and established the business which under his son John William senior, and his grandson John William junior, has gradually built up such a mighty reputation John Taylor died in 1858, and

---

[1] *Hunts*, p 45

his son has lately passed to his rest, dying in November 1906 at the age of seventy-nine. The business is now in the hands of Messrs. J. W. Taylor junr. and E. D. Taylor. Of their work it is hardly necessary to speak in much detail. For the first thirty years or so they were but making their way, but since their production of the great ring of twelve for St. Paul's Cathedral in 1877, and of Great Paul in 1881, their reputation has been enormously enhanced, and they are now almost without rivals. In the latest improvements and appliances of the bell-founders' craft they always take the lead. For the most part their bells have been marked by a certain severity of style—since the Gothic outburst in the forties and fifties—but recently they have introduced more—and in some cases very effective—ornamentation, as well as more artistic lettering. Their present trade-mark is illustrated in Fig. 19. As an early specimen of their work the elaborately ornamented tenor at Prior's Marston is worthy of attention.

Fig. 19.

Of their many works in Warwickshire we can only mention a few of the more important. The earliest is the tenor at Prior's Marston (1845), followed by the ring of five at Kingsbury (1849); other complete rings, mostly of recent date, are Chilvers Coton (8 of 1907), Erdington (8 of 1904), Bishop's Itchington (5 of 1874), Ladbroke (5 of 1873), Warwick, All Saints, Emscote (8 of 1876-85). They have also augmented or partly re-cast the rings at Allesley (1901), Bedworth (1891), Berkswell (1898), Fillongley (1896), Kenilworth (1875), Church Lawford (1872), Oxhill (1878), Stoke (1902-05), Warwick St. Mary (1901), Whichford (1904), Whitnash (1892-96), Stratford (1887), and Sutton Coldfield (1884).

THE WHITECHAPEL FOUNDRY (1570 to Present Day).

This famous foundry, now perhaps the oldest-established business in England, has enjoyed a consecutive career without a break for over 300 years. Its history I do not propose to dwell on at length, partly because I have told it in greater detail elsewhere,[1] partly because it is not represented in Warwickshire before the middle of the eighteenth century. Up to that time its owners were as follows :—

1565—1575.	Robert Doddes (?)	1640—1675.	Anthony Bartlet.
1575—1607.	Robert Mot.	1675—1700.	James Bartlet.
1607—1616.	Joseph and William Carter.	1700—1738.	Richard Phelps.
1616—1632.	Thomas Bartlet.	1738—1752.	Thomas Lester.
1632—1640.	John Clifton.		

Thomas Lester it was who removed the foundry from its old site in the Whitechapel High Street to that which it now occupies in Whitechapel Road (No. 267, now 34). He does not seem to have been so successful with the business as was his predecessor Phelps, and in 1752 he took into partnership *Thomas Pack*, who had probably been his foreman. Previously, however, he had been privileged to cast a ring of ten (in 1751) for St. Philip's, Birmingham, of which six still remain. From this time the business seems to have rapidly improved, and bells with the two names become frequent. In 1757 they cast a ring of six for Claverdon, of which four remain, and the following year they provided the parish church of Birmingham with a ring of ten bells, of which five still exist. They also supplied two to Shustoke in 1768, the year before Lester died. Up to 1762 they employed the simple yet effective lettering which

Phelps had introduced, but apparently began to think it old-fashioned, and introduced a new and more up-to-date though commonplace alphabet of two sizes, the larger used for initials This type was adhered to by their successors for many years, down to 1837. They occasionally employ, as on the tenor at St Martin's, sundry small ornaments, such as a rose or scallop-shell but their inscriptions, if not limited to the simple (if ungrammatical) LESTER & PACK FECIT, are not to be commended either for their good taste or their poetic feeling

Shortly before his death Lester also took his nephew *William Chapman* into partnership, and from 1769 he and Pack managed the foundry for twelve years, until the latter s death in 1781 Under them the business continued to flourish, and they cast many important rings, such as Aylesbury, St Mary's, Shrewsbury, and notably the great ring of ten at St Michael's, Coventry, still intact all but the tenor They also cast an eight for Holy Trinity, of which the tenor, the sole survivor since 1856, has but recently disappeared Their Warwickshire list in full is —

1775	Aston	3—5, 7—9	(Original ring of eight)
1772-71	Birmingham St Martin	1—2	
1772	Do St. Philip	5 10	
1776	Coventry Holy Trinity		Former eight
1778	Do St John	2nd	
1774	Do St Michael	1—9	Also former tenor
1776	Polesworth	3rd	
1780	Wolfhamcote	1st	

To which should probably be added the priest's bell at Birdingbury, merely dated 1774, and the single bell at Stivichall, also merely dated, 1778

As examples of the style of inscriptions in which Pack and Chapman delighted, we may quote those at **St. Michael's, Coventry**, which occur again and again, usually in the same order —

(1) **AL THOUGH I AM BOTH LIGHT AND SMALL I WILL BE HEARD ABOVE YOU ALL**

(2) **IF YOU HAVE A JUDICIOUS EAR YOU LL OWN MY VOICE IS SWEET & CLEAR**

(3) **SUCH WONDROUS POW'R TO MUSIC'S GIVEN IT ELEVATES THE SOUL TO HEAVEN**

(4) **WHILST THUS WE JOIN IN CHEARFULL SOUND MAY LOVE AND LOYALTY ABOUND**

(5) **TO HONOUR BOTH OF GOD AND KING OUR VOICES SHALL IN CONSERT RING**

(7) **YE RINGERS ALL THAT PRIZE YOUR HEALTH AND HAPPINESS**
BE SOBER MERRY WISE AND YOU LL THE SAME POSSESS

(8) **YE PEOPLE ALL WHO HEAR ME RING BE FAITHFUL TO YOUR GOD & KING**

(9) **IN WEDLOCK BANDS ALL YE WHO JOIN WITH HANDS YOUR HEARTS UNITE**
SO SHALL OUR TUNEFULL TONGUES COMBINE TO LAUD THE NUPTIAL RITE

Pack died in 1781, and for a year William Chapman was founding alone His name occurs on the tenor at Willoughby, of that year, but there are only a very few other examples Durham Cathedral 3rd, St Osyth, Essex, 1st, Otley, Yorkshire 8th, two bells in Kent, and one in Scotland

The story has often been told of Pack's visit to Canterbury in 1762, when he took up a a young man named *William Mears*, and taught him the business, and we find this Mears, after four years' work on his own account taken into partnership by Chapman in 1782 The name has continued in the firm ever since, though there has been no Mears in it since 1865 Bells by Chapman and Mears are not common as the former died in 1784, and there are none in this county Between 1784 and 1787 William Mears was alone and to this period belong the treble and tenor at Lapworth (1789) In 1717 he took into partnership his son Thomas, and the two cast the 4th at Wolston in 1789, and the 9th at St Martin s, Birmingham, in 1790

William Mears died in 1791, and his son *Thomas* took sole charge of the foundry for 15 years In 1806 he took into partnership his son Thomas, and for four years the formula THOMAS MEARS & SON appears on the bells His almost invariable form of inscription is THO[s] MEARS OF LONDON FECIT, the date being placed before or after We seldom find any other inscriptions, except on tenors, which have names of incumbents and churchwardens, and occasionally longer inscriptions in prose or verse He is fond of what is known as "the Whitechapel pattern,' introduced by Lester, which consists of alternative loops and lozenges, of varying length, with a horizontal V at each end His bells are not numerous, comprising only the original ring of six at Sutton Coldfield (1795), of which two remain, and one at St Philip's, Birmingham (1796) His son, Thomas II, who succeeded him in 1810, had a much longer and more prosperous career

Thomas Mears II enjoyed almost a monopoly in bell-founding during the thirty-three years of his active life, and the prosperity of his business was increased by the requirements of the many new churches springing up in London and elsewhere His bells differ little in their characteristics from his father's, up to 1837 he usually describes himself as T MEARS, but from that year onwards he gives his full name, and discards the larger initial letters Good as his work is it has hardly any interest except for the ringer

His Warwickshire list is a fairly long one, including four of 1814 at Aston, five of 1811 at Harbury, three of 1826 at Middleton, the original six at Leamington (1830), and several single bells[1] or couples a total of 23 exclusive of those in modern Birmingham churches The two trebles at Salford Priors (1836) appear to have been cast by him at Gloucester, whither he went in 1835 to wind up Rudhall s business (p 78) He appears to have opened a branch there for about six years, whence he supplied a few bells to the Western Midlands, the type of lettering on which is not his own but John Rudhall's

On the death of Thomas Mears in 1844 his sons *Charles* and *George* took up his business They made several changes in the style of inscriptions, dropping the FECIT, dispensing with stops, and sometimes even with the date, as at Warwick St Nicholas Most of their bells are simply inscribed

C & G MEARS FOUNDERS LONDON

with the date, in a set of lettering corresponding to their father's smaller set, which their successors have adhered to down to the present day Sometimes, however, as at Baddesley Ensor, they indulge in Gothic type, or in black-letter inscriptions Most of their bells in Warwickshire are to be found in modern churches such as Keresley or Shirley Street, but their names appear on the first seven bells at Holy Trinity, Coventry, a re-casting of their predecessor's work in 1856 Charles Mears died in 1855, but George kept up the style of inscription for two years longer, and in 1858 his initial alone appears, with the addition of a "Co in 1862 He cast five bells for Sherborne and three for Southam in 1863, in which year he took into partnership Mr Robert Stainbank Under the latter the business, which had been declining, again rose to prosperity

With the exception of a few bells of 1868, of which the little ring of five at Radway is an example, with the name of R Stainbank in Gothic letters, all bells cast by this firm since 1864 have borne the now familiar name MEARS AND STAINBANK George Mears, however, died in 1873 and Robert Stainbank in 1883, and since the latter year the business has been in the hands, first of Mr A S Lawson, who died in 1904, and then of Mr A Hughes.

The work of this firm in the county includes the new ring of eight at Rugby (1896), a

[1] The most noteworthy of these is the tenor at St Mary, Warwick (1814)

small ring of three at Combrooke (1867) and miscellaneous additions, such as the two trebles at Leamington (1900) and first three at Warwick St. Nicholas (1887). They are doubtless handicapped in the Midland district by the fame of the great Loughborough and Birmingham firms.

THE WARNERS OF CRIPPLEGATE, LONDON.

This firm, originally started by "Old John Warner," in the eighteenth century, cast very few church bells down to the year 1853, since which time they have gradually built up a considerable reputation. Their offices are still on the original site in Jewin Crescent, Cripplegate, though the works have lately been removed to Spelman Street, Spitalfields. Like the Whitechapel firm they have never been able to gain much of a footing in the Midlands, as compared with the local foundries, and their connection is chiefly with their native county of Essex and the South of England. There is no complete ring by them in Warwickshire, except the small ring of eight at Ullenhall new church (1874)[1]; otherwise the largest number is five out of the eight at Nuneaton in 1873. Bells by them at Milverton (1863) and Weethley (1857) are inscribed in the plain block capitals which they affected down to 1867, and which are much more effective than the somewhat feeble variety of Gothic which they have employed for the last forty years. By way of compensation, however, they have dropped the objectionable "PATENT" which, accompanied by the Royal Arms, disfigured their earlier bells.

THE BIRMINGHAM FOUNDRIES.

WILLIAM BLEWS AND SONS.

This firm was established in the 'sixties, and for about twenty years carried on business with much success, turning out some excellent bells. Their masterpiece is certainly the re-casting of the great tenor at Brailes, with its admirable reproduction of the old inscription (see p. 23). There are also a ring of five by them at Avon Dassett (1869), and eight of the same date at Bishop Ryder's church, Birmingham.[2] Their inscriptions are always in "Modern Gothic" of a very fair type. In 1887 the foundry came to an end with the death of William Blews on January 30th, and the business was sold to Mr. Charles Carr.

CARR OF SMETHWICK.

Mr. Charles Carr, of the Woodlands Foundry, Smethwick, has done much good work since 1887, chiefly in the way of additions to rings, as at Castle Bromwich, Edgbaston and Rowington.

BARWELL OF BIRMINGHAM.

Fig. 20.

The firm of Barwell, of Great Hampton Street, Birmingham, was established in 1784, but does not appear to have taken up bell-founding before 1870, in which year they cast a ring of six for Lydbury North in Shropshire. During the last few years their reputation has been steadily on the increase, and the amount of work they have done in the county is now considerable. It includes rings of eight at St. Michael, Boldmere (1906), six at Hatton (1885) and Knowle (1897), three at Exhall by Coventry (1900), and parts of the rings at Solihull and Withybrook, as well as single bells in Birmingham and elsewhere. Their trade-mark is given in Fig. 20.

[1] Described as "the lightest ring of eight in England" (*Bell News*, 21 July, 1883).
[2] "The first eight ever cast in Birmingham" (*Bell News*, 19 Feb., 1887).

LLEWELLYN AND JAMES OF BRISTOL

From this firm, whose reputation is naturally more confined to the neighbourhood of Bristol, we have two bells at Lighthorne, cast in 1890

BOND OF BURFORD, OXON

This foundry supplied a bell to Whatcote in 1897 and another to Shotteswell in 1906 Though not common, even in their own neighbourhood, their work seems to be pretty good

NAYLOR, VICKERS & CO, SHEFFIELD

In the 'sixties steel bells were cast by this firm, examples of which may be seen in several of the Midland Counties, there being three at Caldecote, cast in 1868 They all bear a running number and the words " E RIEPE S PATENT," and can hardly be described as beautiful objects, owing to the fearful rust which accumulates on them; as to their tone I cannot speak The firm is now the well-known one of Vickers, Maxim & Co, which devotes all its energies in another direction It is, however, worth noting that the combination of gun founding and bell-founding has historic precedent, there having been a well-known foundry at Bury St Edmund s in the fifteenth century, which combined both functions

We have now accounted, more or less satisfactorily, for every bell in Warwickshire, with but two exceptions, for which I am still at a loss to find a founder These are (1) **Atherstone-on-Stour** 3rd, inscribed —

IESUS BE OVR SPEDE 1627 RM HP

The lettering is thick and plain, I have not met with it elsewhere, and cannot assign it to any known founder of the period, in the neighbourhood or elsewhere (2) **Barton-on-Heath** sanctus, inscribed —

IOHN KERRY 1672

in thin plain lettering, somewhat rough, It might possibly be the work of John Martin, but this is exceedingly doubtful, as he seldom succeeded in penetrating into the territory of the Bagleys and Keenes Failing him, the most likely founder is Richard Keene (see p 59), but the lettering is not like that which he uses elsewhere

II RINGING CUSTOMS AND PECULIAR USES

Of these there are on the whole a very fair number of survivals in Warwickshire, more perhaps than in some more rural counties, such as Shropshire Considering the rapidity with which old ringing customs are dying out in all parts of the country from various causes, it is a matter for satisfaction that so many remain as at Allesley, Coleshill, and Kineton and that there is sufficient material for a separate chapter on the subject.

Into the history and meaning of the older customs I do not propose to enter, and they have been ably discussed by several of my predecessors, such as Messrs North, Stahlschmidt, and Cocks [1] But although full details are given under the heading of each parish of the uses retained in each individual case, the student of bell-lore will perhaps be grateful for a summary which will enable him to dispense with the necessity of a prolonged search for the information he may require

Apart from change ringing and the recognition of secular festivals or anniversaries, all of which are of comparatively modern introduction, it may be laid down that all "uses" of our church bells were originally associated with some religious idea or custom, even though that is not now apparent The Curfew Bell, which is popularly associated with the well-known enactment of William the Conqueror, and its correlative the early morning bell, are really survivors of the morning and evening "Ave Peals" Similarly the Pancake Bell was originally associated with the preparations for the Lenten Fast But it is doubtful whether ringing on the 5th of November can fairly be regarded as coming under the same category! In the case of Sunday uses the connection is more apparent, though the original meaning of many customs has become obscured by time and vicissitudes of religious beliefs and practices Even the Passing Bell, originally an admonition to prayer for the departing soul, is now deferred till some hours later, usually to suit the Sexton's convenience, or is even combined with the funeral ceremonies

In the succeeding account the reader is warned that it has unfortunately been impossible to obtain complete returns from all the parishes, and that in some cases the information received has been too vaguely expressed for statistical use, or is now out of date But the present Editor has been fortunate enough to obtain replies from over half of the total number of beneficed clergy in the county, and trusts that enough evidence has been thus obtained to make his statistics fairly representative

I SUNDAY USES

The normal pre-Reformation arrangement of services was Mattins at 8 a m. and Mass at 9, though this was not invariable Traces of either or both of these bells exist in several cases, but the usage has been somewhat obscured by the fairly general introduction of early celebrations at 8 a m In many of the returns where the ringing of a bell at that hour is reported, it is not clear whether this refers to the use of a bell for services only or whether one is rung independently Sometimes several bells are chimed in place of the one The following summary will indicate the various uses of early ringing of which information has been received [2]

Ringing at 7 a m Marton Southam in Summer only

Ringing at 7-45 a m Dunchurch and Nether Whitacre (? for celebrations) [3]

Ringing at 8 a m when there is no service Coleshill and Kineton

---

[1] Tyack's *Book on Bells* may also be profitably consulted

[2] In all cases one bell only is used except where definitely stated otherwise

[3] Cases where the bell is definitely stated to be rung for Celebrations are not included, as it is assumed that it is not rung otherwise

Ringing at 8 a m (whether for service is not specified) Ashow, Austrey, Barcheston, Barston, Bickenhill, Bidford, Butler's Marston, Long Compton, Cubbington (2nd bell), Combrooke, Fillongley, Frankton, Henley-in-Arden, Knowle, Offchurch, Rowington, Shotteswell, Snitterfield, Wishaw, Wootton Wawen

Chiming (two or more bells) at 8 a m Allesley (1st and 2nd), Berkswell, Chilvers Coton, Exhall by Coventry (in Winter 8-30) Farnborough, Wolvey (1st and 2nd), St Mary, Warwick (for service)

Ringing at 8 and at 9 (survival of Mattins and Mass Bells) Cherington (two bells at 9), Fenny Compton, Hampton-in-Arden (two at 9), Middleton (two at 9), Ratley formerly, Tachbrook, Whitnash

Ringing at 9 a m only Ansley, Grandborough, Honington, Southam Stretton-on-Dunsmore, also Rugby formerly (4th and 5th) At Grendon the first or first two bells are rung as *Sermon Bell* (see below)

The following may also be noted as peculiar uses

Ilmington Ringing at 8, 9, and 10, at 9 the bells are chimed on 1st Sunday in month

Newbold-on-Avon Ringing at 7 and 8 a m

Solihull Ringing at 6, 7, and 8 formerly

Southam Ringing at 7 8, and 9, at 7 in Summer only, at 8 now rung for celebrations

Tanworth Chiming or tolling at 8 and 10 (Mr. Tilley noted in 1881 ' Bells 1 and 2 rung at 8 a m and 2 p m ")

Warwick St Nicholas Formerly each bell tolled eight times at 8 a m, followed by 3×3 strokes on the 7th

For Mattins and Evensong the ordinary usage is ringing or chiming for a period varying from three-quarters of an hour to ten minutes, followed in most cases by " tolling in " on a single bell Ringing on all occasions is reported in nine cases (Berkswell, Dunchurch, Edgbaston, Fillongley. Nuneaton, Rugby, Solihull, Stratford, Warwick St Mary), chiming in 58, in thirteen the practice is variable or alternating, and at Bedworth, Wellesbourne, and Sherborne ringing is confined to Festivals (see below) In a few cases ringing or chiming is combined with tolling, as at Ettington, Middleton, Salford Priors (each for 30 minutes) and Nether Whitacre At Warwick St Nicholas nine strokes are given on the 7th bell before chiming begins.

The use of what is known as the Sermon Bell is fairly common though it takes various forms Its original purport was to announce that a sermon was to be preached, but in many cases it has lost that significance, and has become a mere form of " tolling-in " after chiming At Allesley, Ilmington, Lapworth, and Tanworth the Sermon Bell is rung as early as 10 a m, as a " Warning Bell," and at Grendon at 9 (see above) The name of Sermon Bell is expressly given to the tenor when rung just before the beginning of the service in the following instances Ansley, Avon Dassett, Brinklow (formerly), Coleshill, Coventry Holy Trinity and St. Michael (8th bell used in morning), Cubbington Fenny Compton, Kenilworth, Newbold-on-Avon, Rowington, Rugby (formerly), Sherborne, Shilton, Wappenbury, Warwick St Nicholas, Weston-under-Weatherley, and Wishaw, at Warmington the 2nd is used followed by the treble The tenor and treble are used successively for tolling in at Butler's Marston, Kenilworth, Kineton, Newbold-on-Avon, and Solihull, the 4th and treble at Farnborough The Sermon Bell *before chiming* occurs at Austrey, Barston, and Tachbrook, at Cherington it is rung from 10-35 to 10-45 after five minutes chiming, except on " Sacrament Sunday The treble only is used for tolling in, sometimes called the " ting-tang " or " Priest's bell," at Allesley, Beaudesert Bidford, Chadshunt, Cherington, Harborough, Haseley, Ipsley, Long Itchington, Offchurch, the little bell or sanctus at Brailes, Long Compton, Shotteswell and Oxhill formerly But this bell is rarely found in Warwickshire churches At Rugby the 2nd bell was formerly used for tolling in when there was no sermon At Ettington the tolling-in bell is called the " Surplice Bell " The tenor is used alone but not called the Sermon Bell at Austrey, Coventry St John, and

Stoke, at Bickenhill, Chilvers Coton, Coughton, Curdworth, and Southam the use is not definitely specified

The only reported use of a bell during service is at Aston Cantlow, where the old custom of ringing at the consecration in the Holy Communion service has been revived But a bell at the conclusion of morning service is more general At Barcheston it is rung after a mid day celebration only The object of such a bell is to indicate service in the afternoon, and is a relic of the slack times of pluralism and non-residence, when services were not only few but uncertain (see also explanation given under Beaudesert, Offchurch, and Tysoe in Part II) It is sometimes (as at Barston and Kineton) known as the Pudding Bell, as it was supposed to be for warning housewives to prepare the Sunday dinner This bell is now rung at Ashow ("Rector's Bell"), Austrey, Barston, Beaudesert (2nd bell), Butler's Marston (1st), Cherington, Cubbington, Fenny Compton, Frankton, Grendon (two bells), Haseley, Honington, Ilmington, Long Itchington, Kineton, Offchurch (tenor), Oxhill, Ratley, Tysoe, Ufton, and at Rugby and Wolston formerly At Haseley it is also rung after Evensong, and at Coventry St. Michael it was formerly rung from 1 to 2 p m At Tanworth and Rugby bells were formerly rung at 2 p m (in the latter case the 4th and 5th) At Tanworth a bell is also rung at 5 and 6 p m on Sundays

The only parish with any week-day uses worth noting is Curdworth, where for daily services the bell is tolled 33 times (representing the years of our Lord's life), ordinarily the treble is tolled, the 2nd on Festivals, and the 3rd for celebrations At Rugby the old bells are chimned for week-day services, at Tysoe the priest's bell is used At the latter place a bell used to be rung on week-days at 8 a m, when there was a service during the day

II CHURCH FESTIVALS, GOOD FRIDAY, AND NEW YEAR'S EVE

Special ringing on the great Festivals is reported in 73 instances, of which 34 specify ringing on Christmas Eve (at midnight or earlier), 10 on Christmas morning (Kineton at 6 a m, Rugby after morning service), and 24 report ringing at Christmas without further detail Ringing at Easter is definitely specified in 32 instances, sometimes, as at Coventry St John and Tachbrook, late on Easter Eve, but more usually early on Easter Day (Fillongley 7 a m) Ringing at Whitsuntide is reported in 15 instances, on Trinity Sunday at Allesley, Barston, Bilton, and Hampton, on Ascension Day at Anstey, Hampton, Oxhill, Shilton, Stratford, and Warwick St Nicholas, on Epiphany at Anstey and Shilton At Coventry St John there is ringing at 7 30 a m and before Mattins and Evensong on all Festivals The Patronal Festival is observed by ringing at Anstey (St James, 25 July), Exhall by Coventry (St Giles, 1 Sept), Sherborne (St Michael, 29 Sept), Shilton (St Andrew, 30 Nov), Warwick St Nicholas (6 Dec), and Wellesbourne (St Peter, 29 June), at Oxhill on the Sunday after St Lawrence's Day (10 August) Ringing on St Thomas' Day is reported in no less than nine instances, usually at 6 a m Bidford, Ettington, Fenny Compton, Frankton, Harbury Kineton, Southam, Tachbrook, and Wellesbourne formerly This is, or was, in connection with the distribution of local charities which took place on that day At Solihull ringing formerly took place on All Souls' Day (2 Nov) when a dole was distributed At Bidford and Sutton Coldfield there is ringing on Trinity Monday, at Warwick St Nicholas on Easter Tuesday, known as "Churchwardens' Day," at Middleton on St George's Day, but apparently with a secular reference The bells are rung for Harvest Festivals at Bedworth, Coleshill, Rowington, Stratford, and Tachbrook, and at Bedworth also on the first Sunday in August, "Wake Sunday," "Sunday School Sunday," and on the occasion of the Bishop's visit Ringing once or twice a week is usually indulged in during November and December by way of practice for Christmas, or else during Advent only, of this 21 instances are reported, that at Tachbrook taking place on the Sundays in Advent after Evensong

Special Good Friday uses are not common, at Offchurch the treble is rung at 8 a m, and at Shotteswell the treble is rung to announce the distribution of a dole At Stratford the tenor is the only bell used on this day On New Year's Eve ringing in some form takes place in 78 instances The usual practice is to ring from 11-30 to 12-30, or thereabouts, sometimes with a break at midnight to allow the clock to strike; this is done at Alveston, Bedworth, Cubbington, Ettington, Solihull and Nether Whitacre At Allesley, Chadshunt, Butler's Marston, and Coventry St John ringing does not begin till midnight A much more effective method is to ring a muffled or half-muffled peal before midnight and then an "open" one; this is done at Aston Cantlow, Bidford, Dunchurch, Farnborough, Fillongley, Lapworth, Oxhill, and Rugby But in the majority of cases the method is not specified At Kineton and Whitnash the bells are also rung on New Year's Day (Kineton 9 a m)

III SECULAR AND SOCIAL FESTIVALS

Under this heading we may include Weddings, though religious functions, the ringing on such occasions being a purely personal matter, according to the desire of the parties concerned, and paid for by them In 72 parishes ringing is more or less customary, but the only peculiar use specified is at Grandborough, where the peal is repeated at 5 a m next day; nor is there any instance of ringing when Banns are published

Ringing on the 5th of November (Gunpowder Plot Day) is exceptionally common in Warwickshire; it is still kept up at Allesley, Ansley, Ashow, Avon Dassett, Barston, Bidford, Bilton, Brinklow, Butler's Marston, Combrooke, Farnborough, Fenny Compton, Frankton, Grendon, Hampton, Ilmington, Lapworth, Middleton, Newbold on-Avon, Oxhill, Shotteswell, Tachbrook, and Wormleighton—in all, 23 instances On May 29th (Restoration Day) it is much rarer, only occurring at Ansley, Hampton, and Middleton At Curdworth both days were formerly observed; at Ipsley the former

Royal Anniversaries are celebrated by peals as follows —Birthdays at Ashow, Coventry St Michael, and Ilmington formerly; Sovereign's Birthday only at Ansley, Bedworth, Butler's Marston, Coleshill, Coventry Holy Trinity, Farnborough, Hampton, Kenilworth, Oxhill, Rugby, Southam, Warwick St Mary and St. Nicholas, and Wootton Wawen; also at Curdworth and Solihull formerly Ringing on Coronation Day (9 Aug) at Brinklow, Coleshill, and Hampton; at Coleshill and Rugby also on Accession Day (22 Jan) Empire Day (24 May) is celebrated at Coleshill and Kenilworth; St George's Day at Middleton, and at Stratford there is ringing on the same day (23 April) to celebrate Shakespeare's birthday November 9th is celebrated as Mayor's Day at Coventry St Michael, Stratford, Sutton Coldfield, and Warwick St Mary and St Nicholas At Coventry Holy Trinity there is also ringing on the occasion of a proclamation of peace (as in June, 1902) at the Bishop's visit, and the annual Bluecoat Sermon; at Warwick St Mary and St Nicholas for the Assizes and for the Meeting of the Chamberlains of St Nicholas Meadow; at Coughton on the Squire's birthday At Rugby the 20th of October is celebrated as Lawrence Sheriff's Day by ringing at 6 a m, 1 p m and 7 p m At Warwick St Mary there is ringing on the occasion of the Midsummer Sunday School Feast At Nuneaton, Stoke, and Tysoe the Anniversary uses have not been specified

IV FUNERAL USES

Of all special ringing customs, ancient and modern, these seem to have been the most universal, and are the most generally kept up, though not always as carefully as they might be The uses include the Passing Bell or Death Knell, rung immediately or at a specified interval not exceeding twenty-four hours after death, which usually comprises tolling at intervals of a minute for a few minutes to an hour, with "tellers" at the beginning and end, or other methods of denoting age and sex On the day of the funeral itself the uses are practically limited to tolling before (and sometimes after) the ceremony, with occasional quick ringing or chiming on the approach of the procession Muffled peals are sometimes rung on special occasions

There is an interesting record of the mediaeval custom given in Smyth's *Lives of the Berkeleys*,[1]

[1] Edited by Sir John Maclean for the Bristol and Glouc Arch Soc 1883, ii, p 175 See also Ellacombe, *Bells of the Church*, p 227

with reference to funeral peals rung in Coventry on the occasion of the death of the Lady Isabel Berkeley in 1516. This may be a convenient place to introduce it. "There was ryngyng daily with all the bells contynually, that is to say, at St Michael's xxxiii peles, at Trinitie xxxiii peles, at St Johns xxxiii, at Babyllake, because hit was so nigh, lvij peles, and in the mother church xxx peles, and every pele xij^{d}."

The varieties in the use of the Passing Bell are very great, but I will endeavour to summarise them as briefly as possible. The method of ringing has not always been clearly specified in the returns which have reached me, but the following statistics may be taken as accurate so far as they go.

In eighteen instances the knell is tolled immediately or as soon as possible, and in twenty others the time given is "on receipt of notification of death," which amounts to much the same thing. Other uses vary between one hour after (Ashow, Butler's Marston, Farnborough, Ilmington, Oxhill, and Sherborne), 8 a.m. next day (Chadshunt, Corley, Cubbington, Haseley, Wappenbury, Weston), 9 a.m. next day (Brinklow sometimes, Frankton, Henley, and Wolvey), noon next day (Newbold-on-Avon), on the same day before sunset (Atherstone-on-Stour), within twelve hours (Barston), same or following day (Bulkington, Grandborough (before noon), Shotteswell, Nether Whitacre), twelve hours after (Bedworth, Coventry St John), within 24 hours (Bidford), between 8 a.m. and 8 p.m. (Beaudesert). Sometimes, as at Warwick St Nicholas, it is deferred till the day of the Funeral. In nineteen instances the time of ringing is not specified.

The total number of parishes in which the use of the Passing Bell is reported is 86, and in 26 of these the bell (usually the tenor) is simply tolled, without any tellers. The time as already noted varies from a few minutes (at Beaudesert and Solihull) to one hour; the tellers, when in use, are generally given at the beginning, and sometimes repeated at the end, as definitely noted in eleven instances. At Coventry Holy Trinity and St John the bells are first tolled singly in succession and then in pairs ("single and double tolling"); at St Michael's three strokes are given on the tenor, then 60 on the 1st and 2nd alternately, ending with twelve on the tenor, and tellers. Sometimes distinctions of sex or age are noted by the bell used[1]. At Bilton the 4th is used for an adult, the 1st for a child; at Rugby, tenor for adult, treble for child; at Nuneaton the 6th or 7th for a child; at Chilvers Coton a large and a small bell; at Warwick St Nicholas the 6th, 7th, or 8th for a child, woman, and man respectively. At Rowington only a few strokes are tolled in the case of a child. At Tanworth this is done when tolling for funerals. The age is indicated by tolling the requisite number of strokes at Aston Cantlow, Barcheston, Barston, Bulkington, Lapworth, Newbold Pacey, Sherborne, Solihull, Warwick St Nicholas, Nether Whitacre, and Whitnash, and at Exhall-by-Coventry after the funeral.

But the more usual method of distinguishing sex, if not age, is by tellers. The normal custom is 3×3 strokes for a man and 3×2 for a woman, including children, usually before and after tolling. This we find practised in 41 instances. Sometimes 3×1 are given in addition for a child, and this we find done in thirteen instances (at Nether Whitacre only for infants under three). At Barston, Beaudesert, Bidford, Lapworth, Lillington, and Nuneaton the tellers are repeated *on each bell*; at Exhall-by-Coventry 3×3 is sometimes rung for all alike, and at Sherborne and Walton d'Eivile two strokes and 2×2 respectively are rung for a child. At Burton Dassett the tellers are three, two, and one *single* strokes respectively. Other abnormal uses are as follows:—

Allesley: 3×6 on each bell, followed by 15 strokes for male; 2×6 on each, followed by eleven strokes for female.

Bedworth: 12×3 male; 12×2 female or child.

Bickenhill: 6×6 male; 6×5 female; 6×4 child.

Hampton: 3×6 male; 2×6 female; 1×6 child.

Leamington Hastings: 1×3 male; 2×3 female; 3×3 child[2].

---

[1] This is a very common practice in Essex.

[2] Maintained by some to be the correct version.

Tolling at funerals is reported, in one form or another, in 57 instances At Allesley and Caldecote the bells are occasionally chimed before the ceremony, at Ilmington and Solihull this is done in the case of ringers and their families, at Kineton regularly, at Coleshill, Curdworth and Middleton formerly At Over Whitacre chiming takes place afterwards Tolling at Curdworth takes place at 7 a m (with tellers) as well as before the service, at Coughton, Oxhill, Tysoe, and Warwick St Mary and St Nicholas at 8 a m , at Newbold Pacey at 9 a m , and at Atherstone-on-Stour every two hours from 8 a m to 2 p m At Tysoe and Cherington tolling take place two hours before the service, known respectively as the "Bearers Bell" and the "Inviting Bell" The time for tolling before the service varies from 15 minutes to an hour, usually at minute intervals (at Henley every five minutes), and often as at Beaudesert and elsewhere, concluding with a few quick strokes At Kineton tolling continues for two hours followed by chiming, and tolling for thirty seconds At Brinklow this is known as the "Bidding Bell" At Bilton, Coventry St John Fenny Compton, Grendon, and Warwick St Mary and St Nicholas tellers are given after the service, at Exhall-by-Coventry the age of the deceased, at Alveston and Chadhunt the bell is rung quickly at this time Tolling afterwards is definitely reported in twenty-three instances At Burton Dassett the tenor is merely rung up and down before and after At Kineton the use is Tenor tolled for two hours and chime for 15 minutes before, toll for 30 seconds after At Tanworth the custom varies with the age of the deceased Muffled peals for various personages are rung at Bedworth, Birmingham St Martin (Sovereign), Butler's Marston and Nuneaton (Royalty), Coventry Holy Trinity (24 Jan for Thomas Smith) and St. Michael (13 Jan by bequest), Grendon, Ilmington (Ringers), Kenilworth, Stoke, Stratford, Sutton Coldfield, Warwick St Nicholas (Royalty, Warwick family, and Ringers) and Wellesbourne

V MISCELLANEOUS USES

The Morning Bell and the Curfew I have already noted as survivals of the old "Ave peals" They are now rapidly dying out all over the country, but there are a fair number of survivals in Warwickshire, especially in the case of the Curfew, which is still rung in eighteen instances Allesley, Austrey, Brailes, Coleshill, Coventry Holy Trinity, Curdworth, Kenilworth, Kineton, Kingsbury Knowle, Nuneaton, Offchurch, Solihull, Southam Stratford (Guild Chapel), Tanworth, and Warwick St Mary and St Nicholas It was also formerly rung at Bickenhill, Harborough Magna, and Rugby The usual hour for ringing is 8 p m , on Saturday at 7, and in most places it is only rung in the winter, beginning at Michaelmas or in October, and continued to Lady-Day The tenor bell is generally used, but at Holy Trinity, Coventry the 3rd, at Kenilworth the 5th, at Kineton the 4th, at Nuneaton and Warwick St Nicholas the 7th, at Solihull the 6th, at Warwick St Mary the 8th, and at Southam the 4th or 5th are used The day of the month is tolled in strokes afterwards at Coleshill, Curdworth (on 1st) and Solihull

The early morning bell is kept up in five instances at Allesley and Nuneaton the 4th at 5 in summer, 6 in winter, at Coleshill the 1st or 2nd at 7, at Kineton and Stratford (Guild Chapel) at 6 a m At Exhall by Coventry two bells are rung daily at 9 30 a m , at Brailes a bell is rung at noon, at Coleshill and Southam the 1st or 2nd at 1 p m , and at Warwick St Mary the 3rd At St Michael, Coventry, a bell was formerly rung at 6 a m and 6 p m (see under St John s in Part II) and also at 9 p m , and at Warwick St Nicholas the morning bell at 5 a m At Tanworth there were formerly bells daily at 9 a m 1 p m and 8 p m ,[1] but the two former were discontinued in 1879 There was formerly also a daily bell at Tysoe

There are thirteen instances of ringing the Pancake Bell on Shrove Tuesday at Allesley (3rd at 11), Bedworth (tenor at 11), Bidford (3rd and 4th at noon) Coleshill (4th and 5th at 11),

[1] Hannett, *Forest of Arden*, p 110

Coventry Holy Trinity (4th at 11-30), Grandborough (5th from 11 to 12), Grendon (2nd and 5th at 11-15), Hampton (5th at 11), Solihull (8th at 11), Tachbrook (noon), Tysoe and Warwick St Mary (6th from 11 30 to 12-30) and St Nicholas (4th at 11) It was also rung within memory at Ashow, Austrey, Brinklow, Coventry St Michael, Frankton, Rugby, Sutton Coldfield, and Tanworth

A bell is rung for Easter Vestry Meetings in 25 parishes

The Gleaning Bell, formerly common in many parts of England, has now died out entirely, as the result of the changes in agricultural conditions It is still kept up in corn-growing districts, as in North Essex, where seventeen instances are recorded In Warwickshire it was formerly rung at Cubbington, Ettington, Farnborough, Frankton, Harborough, Ilmington, Leamington Hastings, Offchurch, Tysoe, and Wolston, and has only recently been dropped at Tachbrook, and at Ratley, where it was rung at 8 a m and 1 p m

In cases of Fire the treble and tenor are rung at Coleshill and Kenilworth, and at Ilmington the 4th, at Tysoe the 1st and 5th (formerly the sanctus bell), at Stratford-on-Avon the two bells of the Guild Chapel The little Fire-Bell at Warwick St Mary, dated 1670, is now disused and unhung

The only "peculiar uses" of Warwickshire bells with which I have met beyond those already noted, are at Bilton and Tysoe (sanctus) for Choir Practices, and at Newbold Pacey for the annual Choir Supper

PRINCIPAL RINGS IN WARWICKSHIRE

	Weight of tenor Cwts	Diam of tenor ins	Diam next bell ins	Diam of treble in	Date and Founder of tenor
(1) RINGS OF TWELVE					
Birmingham St Martin . .	35	58	53	27½	Lester and Pack, 1758
(2) RINGS OF TEN					
Aston	20¼	48	43	28½	T Mears, 1814
Birmingham St Philip .	29	55½	50	31	Lester and Pack, 1757
Coventry St Michael	31¼	56½	50½	33	Briant, 1805
Solihull . .	19¼	48½	42⅜	27	H. Bagley, 1685
Warwick St Mary	21¼	54¼	48	26¾	T Mears, 1814
(3) RINGS OF EIGHT					
Bedworth	14¼	42½	38½	24½	Taylor 1891
Bir'ngham St John, Deritend	—	—	—	—	R Wells, 1776
Do. Bishop Ryder	—	—	—	—	Blews, 1868
Chilvers Coton .	13¼	42½	37½	24½	Taylor, 1907
Coventry Holy Trinity . . .	23¼	51	44	31	Taylor, 1898
Erdington	15¼	44½	39½	26¼	Taylor, 1904
Leamington	12¾	40½	38½	26	Mears and Stainbank, 1902
Nuneaton . .	14¼	44½	40	28½	Warner, 1873
Rugby	24¾	52	45	33	Mears and Stainbank, 1896
Salford Priors . .	15¼	43	38½	27	Mears and Stainbank, 1867
Stoke-by-Coventry .	13¼	42¼	38½	25½	Taylor, 1905
Stratford-on Avon	18	44	39¼	27½	R Sanders, 1717
Sutton Coldfield .	23¼	50½	44½	29	Taylor, 1884
Sutton Coldfield, St Michael (Boldmere)	13¾	43¾	39½	27⅜	Barwell, 1906
Warwick, All Saints (E'scote)	16¼	44½	39¼	26	Taylor, 1876
Do St Nicholas	15¾	43½	40	28	M Bagley, 1773
(4) RINGS OF SIX.					
Brailes .	32	58	51	37½	Blews 1877
Monk's Kirby	23	53	47	35	Watts, 1618

[These two are included as being of exceptional weight]

PART II.

THE INSCRIPTIONS ON
THE CHURCH BELLS OF WARWICKSHIRE,

THEIR HISTORY AND USES,

ARRANGED ALPHABETICALLY BY PARISHES

PART II

THE INSCRIPTIONS ON THE CHURCH BELLS OF WARWICKSHIRE

ALCESTER. ST NICHOLAS Six bells

1. GOD SAVE THE CHURCH & KING A [bell] R 1735 (29 in
2. PROSPERITY TO THIS PARISH A [bell] R 1735 ($30\frac{1}{8}$ in
3. PROSPERITY TO ALL OUR BENEFACTORS A [bell] R 1735 †††††††† ($31\frac{1}{2}$ in
4. PROSPERITY TO THE CHURCH OF ENGLAND A [bell] R 1735 ($34\frac{1}{4}$ in
5. WE WERE ALL CAST AT GLOCESTER BY AB. RUDHALL 1735 *(border as 3rd)* (36 in
6. IOHN QUINTON & THOMAS TONG CH WARDENS 1735 *(border as 2nd)* ($39\frac{1}{4}$ in.

The ring is by Abraham Rudhall, who died in February 1735-6 Borders on 3rd and 5th, Fig. 18, on the others, Fig. 17.

Mr Falkner notes "Belfry dark, bells very greasy"

Browne Willis' list of bells in Worcester Diocese about 1750 (Cole MSS, Brit Mus Add. 5828 fol 268) gives "Alchester 6 Bells"

Inscriptions given in *Notices of Warwickshire Churches* (1849), ii p 110

The church (but not the tower) was re-built 1727—1734

Best thanks to Mr W E Falkner

H. T. T, 27 July, 1881

ALLESLEY ALL SAINTS Six bells

1. IOHN ● STONE ● AND ● NICHOLAS ● RIDER ● CHVRCH ● WARDENS ● 1708
   Below, double row of arabesques ($25\frac{1}{2}$ in
2. S A N N A ($26\frac{1}{2}$ in
3. ✠ S ADELE BREE RECAST ME ✠ 1901
   Below, vine-pattern all round and Taylor's trade-mark (Fig. 19) (30 in
4. *As No. 1 with a coin after date* (32 in
5. ✠ BE YT KNOWNE TO ALL THAT DOTH ME SEE THAT NEWCOMBE OF LEICESTER MADE MEE 1610 ($35\frac{3}{4}$ in
6. ✠ I HOPE IN GOD ✠ *(Scroll ornament)*

Below, vine-pattern all round, and

(a) Taylor's trade-mark *(b)* **EUPHEMIA L. LANCASTER GAVE ME**
W. BREE D D RECTOR
A. KIRBY } CH WARDENS 1901
T. WRIGHT } (40¼ in

Hung in Taylor's new H-frames, but the arrangement is awkwardly planned, the trap door being immediately under the tenor, which it is hardly possible to squeeze past!

Up to 1901 there were only five bells, in that year the then 2nd was re-cast, and a new tenor added, making six. The old bell was inscribed —

SANCTA KATERINA ORA PRO NOBIS

and was similar in type to the 3rd at Lapworth (see p 10)

The 1st and 4th are by Joseph Smith of Edgbaston,[1] arabesques like Bagley's (Pl XXII, Fig 11), the 2nd is probably by Thomas Newcombe of Leicester (see p 30)

Border on 5th Pl XXII, Fig 3, afterwards used by Oldfield of Nottingham (see p 38).

		cwt	qrs	lbs		cwt	qrs	lbs
Weights —	1)	3	0	15	4th)	5	3	27
	2)	3	3	8	5th)	8	0	21
	3)	5	0	27	6th)	12	0	0

1552 iiij^or belles in the steple."

1750 (Browne Willis) "Allelsley 5 Bells"

CUSTOMS

On Sundays, 1st and 2nd bells rung at 8 a.m Tenor as Sermon Bell at 10 a m.

Bells chimed for services 10-40—10-55, followed by treble for five minutes

Death Knell as soon as convenient, tellers, for males, three strokes on each bell, followed by 15, for females, two stroke on each, followed by eleven Chiming occasionally at Funerals

Ringing during Advent preparatory for Christmas; on Christmas Eve from 11-30 p m to 12-30 a m, on Christmas Day, Easter Sunday, Whit Sunday, and Trinity Sunday at 10 a m, on New Year's Eve from 11-55 p m. to 12-30 a m Also on November 5th

The 4th bell is rung daily at 5 a m from March 25th to September 29th, and at 6 a m for the rest of the year

Curfew daily throughout the year at 8 p m

Pancake Bell on Shrove Tuesday at 11 a m (3rd bell)

Bell formerly rung for Vestry Meetings.

As will be seen, the customs here are of considerable interest, and all praise is due to those who have ensured their continuance

Many thanks to Rev W Bree, Rector

H T T, 19 May, 1883, H. B W, Sept, 1907

ALNE, GREAT. ST MARY MAGDALENE One bell.

1 ALL PRAYSE AND GLORY BE TO GOD FOR EVER 1670 I M

By John Martin of Worcester, small type and border also occurring at Temple Grafton. For border and trade-mark see Plate XXI, Figs 2, 8

[1] Mr Tilley read the date on the 4th as 1703, he *may* be right, but it is more likely to be the same as the treble

In a small octagonal tower at W end of church
1552 "Itm there . . ij belles"
H. T T, 27 July, 1881

ALVESTON

ST JAMES — Three bells

1. *Above, scroll-pattern all round*

CANTATE DOMINO ✤✤ CANTICVM ✤✤ NOVVM H ✤ B
1668

2 THOMAS ✤ WELLS THOMAS ✤ HIGGINS 1616 ✤ GOD ✤ SAVE ✤ NOBEL ✤ KINGE ✤ IAMES ✤ ANO
THOMAS ✤ TOVNSEND

3 ✠ GEORGE HINE ROBART BEESON 1729 R S • ✠

Treble by Henry Bagley, narrow scroll borders (*Bucks*, fig 71)
2nd by Henry Farmer of Gloucester (see p 47), fleur-de-lys, Pl XIX, 7
3rd by Richard Sanders of Bromsgrove
Several members of the Townsend family are buried in the church

1552 'ALUUSTON. Itm there . ij belles'
1750 Browne Willis gives '1 bell' *(sic)*

CUSTOMS

Bells chimed on Sundays for 11-0 and 6-30 services, one bell for services at 8 a m and 3-30 p m
Ringing during Advent and on New Year's Eve at 11-30 p m, and for a few minutes after midnight, also for Weddings by request.
"Minute bell" tolled before funerals and a bell rung fast for two or three minutes afterwards
Best thanks to Rev P Llewellyn, Vicar, and to Mr W E Falkner
H T T, 3 Aug, 1881

ANSLEY

ST LAWRENCE — Three bells

1 ✠ M A R G A R E T A

2 FEARE GOD HONOR THE KING
1668

3 ✠ BE YT · KNOWNE · TO ALL THAT DOTH · ME · SEE THAT NEWCOMBE OF LEICESTER MADE MEE · 1609

1st By Thomas Newcombe of Leicester (see p 30) Cross and shield, Plate XVI Figs 2, 3
2nd By George Oldfield of Nottingham (p 63), border as Allesley 5th, trade-mark, Plate XXII, Fig 1 (with G for H)

1552 'ANSTLEY Itm there iij belles in the steple'
'M[d] that the p'ishe have solde sithence the last S'vey to the relief of the poore inh'itaunts there this p'cell folowing . a bell ou and besyd the iij aforesaide'
1750 (Browne Willis) 'Awsley 3 Bells'

CUSTOMS

A bell rung on Sundays at 9 a m for five minutes (the old mass bell) Bells chimed for services, for ten minutes, ten minutes, and last five
Death-knell with tellers 3×3 and 3×2, as soon as possible after notice given
Ringing on Christmas Eve, New Year's Eve, May 29th, and November 5th, Sovereign s Birthday and for Weddings

Bartlett in *Manduessedum Romanorum* (Nichols, *Bibl Topogr Brit* ix, No 1, p 146), states that "the sum of 6*s* 8*d* yearly was charged upon a small cottage and croft late in the occupation of George Izon, to find bell-ropes for the church bells, but by whom is not now known, which cottage and croft about 1765 was purchased of the parish by the late John Ludford, Esq, for £30, which [together with other bequests] was expended in rebuilding the Poor's houses, and the income is now paid by the Overseers of the Poor" Thus the endowment for the bell-ropes has lapsed, having been diverted to other purposes

Best thanks to Rev C Heaton, Vicar

H T T, 22 July, 1876

ANSTEY. ST JAMES Four bells.

1 **J. WARNER & SONS LONDON 1876** (22½ in

2. **CAST BY JOHN WARNER & SONS LONDON 1876**
On Waist —Royal Arms and PATENT (24¾ in

3 DANIEL● PETTIFER● AND IOHN● FARNDON● CHVRCH● WARDINGS 1707●✝✠✠✝✠✠✝✠✠✝ (26½ in.

4 **CAST BY JOHN WARNER & SONS LONDON 1876** (28½ in

Four very small bells, for which there is hardly room in the little octagonal tower, they are hung in two tiers, the first and third above. Warner's bells have angular cannons. The 3rd is by Joseph Smith (arabesques as Pl XXII, 11), previous to 1876 it was the only bell in the tower The new bells were given by Lady Adams of Anstey Lodge

No Edwardian Inventories

CUSTOMS

Bells chimed for Sunday services *Sermon Bell* for last five minutes, when there is a sermon
Death Knell at intervals of a minute for an hour, with tellers at beginning and end (3×3 for male, and 3×2 for female) Tolling at Funerals
Ringing on Christmas Day, Epiphany, Easter Sunday, Ascension Day, Whit Sunday, and Patronal Festival (25 July), also for Weddings by request

Best thanks to Rev T C Pyemont, Vicar

H T T, 26 Aug, 1876, H B W, Sept, 1907

ARLEY ST WILFRED Three bells

1 ✠ ROBART ✠ NEWCOME (28 in

2  IHS : NAZARENVS *(border)* REX IVDEORVM *(border)* FILI DEI *(border)* MISERERE MEI *(border)* 1625 (30½ in

3 THO CLARK CHURCHWARDEN *(scroll)* EDWD ARNOLD LEICESTER FECIT 1790 *(scrolls)*
On the waist, arabesques (34 in

1st by Robert Newcombe, dating about 1590, a similar bell at Pytchley, Northants cross Plate XVI, Fig 2, see p 31

2nd by Watts, "Acorn" border (Pl XVII, Fig 7) The S in IHS is reversed here, as invariably elsewhere

3rd After WARDEN and the date are ornamental scrolls, and on the waist arabesques like Bagley's (Pl XXII, 11) The 9 of the date is reversed The cannons are elaborately ornamented

1552 'iij belles and a small bell'

'Md that the p'ishe have sold sithens the last s'vey our and above the forsaid p'cells their things folowing two hand bells.

H T T, 1876, H B W, Sept, 1907

ARROW HOLY TRINITY One bell

1 HENRY *(border)* BAGLE *(border)* MADE *(border)* MEE *(border)* 1657 *(border)* ✤✤ *(border)*

1552 'Itm there ij bells

1750 (Browne Willis) '1 Bell'

H T T, 19 Oct, 1881

ASHOW ST MARY Four bells

1 J BRIANT HARTFORD FECIT 1793

2 *The same*

3 J BRIANT HARTFORD FECIT 1793 WM BADAMS C WARDEN

4 JOHN BRIANT HARTFORD 1793 H IORONS C WARDEN

Tenor 7 cwt This ring is mentioned in a list of "entire peals" cast by John Briant (North and Stahlschmidt, *Church Bells of Herts*, p 65) John Briant was fond of spelling the name of his native town as above

1552 'ASHOO iij belles and a sacring bell

1750 '4 Bells

CUSTOMS

On Sundays a bell rung at 8 a m, chiming for morning and evening services "Rector's bell" rung after morning service

Ringing on Christmas Day and New Year's Eve, on November 5th and Royal birthdays, and for Weddings

Death Knell one hour after death, tolling at Funerals when requested

H T T., 8 Oct 1878

ASTLEY. ST MARY Five bells

1 ✠ BE YT KNOWNE TO · ALL THAT DOTH ME SEE THAT NEWCOMBE OF LEICESTER MADE MEE 1607
(border after date and above inscription)

The same with border below

As No 1, no border above

As No 2

IOSHVA ● MERRY ● CHVRCH ● WARDEN 1722 ● ● ●

On sound-bow, border of scrolls all round

2nd, 3rd and 5th much chipped at lip, the 4th a maiden bell
5th By Joseph Smith of Edgbaston, scrolls, Pl. XXIII, 2
H T T 17 July, 1876

ASTON. SS PETER AND PAUL Ten bells

THIS TREBLE BELL WAS PRESENTED TO THE PARISH OF ASTON BY THE
Below --) INTEREST OF JOB PERRENS JOSHUA SHORT & W^M HASSAL 1814
T MEARS OF LONDON FECIT (28½ in

PEACE & UNANIMITY WITH ALL THE WORLD T MEARS OF LONDON FECIT 1814 (30 in

PACK & CHAPMAN OF LONDON FECIT 1775 (31 in

OUR VOICES SHALL IN CONSORT RING TO HONOUR BOTH OF GOD & KING
Below —*As on 3rd with date* 1776 (32½ in

YE PEOPLE ALL WHO HEAR US RING BE FAITHFULL TO YOUR GOD AND KING
Below, as last (34½ in

PEACE AND GOOD NEIGHBOURHOOD T MEARS OF LONDON FECIT 1814 (36½ in

MUSIC IS MEDICINE TO THE MIND PACK & CHAPMAN OF LONDON FECIT 1776 (39 in

JAMES COOKE ESQ^R SECRETARY PACK *etc* (40 in

YE RINGERS ALL THAT PRIZE YOUR HEALTH & HAPPINESS BE SOBER MERRY WISE & YOU'L THE SAME POSSESS ● ● ● ●
Below, as on 4th (43 in

THE REV^D B SPENCER L L D. VICAR JOS^H ARMISHAW THO^S PERRENS JN^O DEYKIN CHURCH WARDENS 1814
Below —THOMAS MEARS OF LONDON FECIT (48 in

	cwt	qrs	lbs		cwt	qrs	lbs
Weights —1)	4	3	0	6)	8	2	16
2)	5	1	0	7)	10	1	9
3)	5	3	20	8)	11	0	24
4)	6	2	11	9)	14	3	14
5)	7	2	21	10)	20	3	3

1552 'Astone v belles oon of them broken"
1760 'Aston-juxta-Birmingham 5 Bells'
For records of ringing here see *Church Bells*, 9 May, 1874, and 25 January, 1889
H T T, 24 Oct, 1881

ASTON St James. One bell

Church built 1791

ASTON St Mary One bell

Church built 1863

ASTON CANTLOW St John Baptist Five bells

1 IOHN GIBBES WILL BARDSHA C W
1 6 2 9

2 *Above, border of arabesques*

✠ IOSIAH FVLLWOOD GENTLEMAN THOMAS ADKINS CHURCHWARDENS

Below, shield, and border of arabesques, below shield, the date 1626

3 ✠ ✱ SANA MANET CHRISTI PLEBISQVE RELIGIO VANA 1626

4 ✠ AD LAVDEM CLARE MICHAELIS DO RESONARE

5 HENERY INGRVM IOHN BARTLAM C=W RICH KEENE MEDE MEE 1681

1st, 2nd, and 3rd by Thomas Hancox of Walsall, see p 51. The lettering on the 3rd is thinner and larger than that on the others, with a G in Gothic form The 1st has a fleur-de-lys (Pl. XIX, 7) as stop and the border Pl XX 1—3 and a plainer running border (Pl. XX 5) before and after the date, the 2nd arabesques (Pl XX 7) above and below the inscription, initial cross (Pl XIX, 8), and on the waist a shield with T H and anchor (Pl XIX 4), below which is the date On the 2nd the S is reversed On the 3rd plain initial cross followed by a star (Pl XX, 9), a bell (Pl XIX, 5) before and after date, and running border (Pl. XXII, 3), below, trade-mark as on 2nd but heart-shaped (Pl XIX 2) The 3rd is much flattened by chipping The date on the 1st *may* be intended for 1626 (as 2nd and 3rd), the 6 being inverted.

4th. By a Worcester founder, c 1400—1420, with cross Pl V 12, and heads of King and Queen as stops (Pl. V, 13, 14, see p 9). Lettering, Pl V. 15—24 The diameter of this bell is 40½ in

5th · Letters as on 1st and 2nd, Keene was a Woodstock man (see p 60)

1552 · 'ASTON CANNTLOWE, iij belles one litle bell'

Mᵈ that the p'ishe have solde sithe the Last S'vey to the mayntenᵃnce of theire churche and the Relief of the poore oon bell

1750 '5 Bells'

Customs

Passing Bell immediately after death, with tellers, 3 × 3 for male and 3 × 2 for female, the age being tolled on the tenor At funerals the tenor is raised and lowered after the service

Ringing on New Year's Eve muffled peal at 11-45, followed by an open one at twelve o'clock

Pancake Bell rung on Shrove Tuesday until about thirty years ago

"Priest's Bell" (? treble) rung at the Consecration in the Communion Service

Best thanks to Rev F A Applewhaite, Vicar, and to Mr Falkner

Josiah Fulwood, whose name appears on the 2nd bell, must have been one of the well-known local family of that name, some of whom resided here But his name does not occur in the Warwickshire visitation of 1619 (see pedigree on p 237 of the *Harleian Soc* volume)

H. T T, 27 July, 1881

ATHERSTONE. ST MARY One bell

1 ⁂ IH NAZARENUS REX IUDEORVM

By Johannes de Stafford (of Leicester), see p 14 and Plate VII, Figs 16—19 The first N and the S are reversed as is also the Z, which is also on one side

There does not appear ever to have been more than one bell here

H. T. T, 5 July, 1876

ATHERSTONE-ON-STOUR ST. MARY Three bells.

1 ✠ MARIA MATER DEI MESERERE MEI

2 ✠ IHESU S CAMPANAM S TIBI S SEMPER S PROTEGE S SANAM

3 IESVS BE OVR SPEDE 1627 R M H P

1st and 2nd probably both of the 14th century and from the Gloucester foundry See p 5 and Pls III—IV The cross on the 1st is a small version of that on the 2nd (see Pl II, Figs 13, 19 The T on the 1st is reversed the letters on the 2nd are ornamented

3rd By an unknown founder, plain thick lettering, about 1 in high unknown elsewhere (see p 86) The initials are probably those of churchwardens (a Henry Palmer was Churchwarden in 1611 and 1632)

The old church had no tower and the bells hung in a small wooden turret New church built 1876 The treble is hung above the others, and is noted by Mr Tilley as a cylindrical bell

1552 'ADERSTON SUP' STOWER iij belles one hande bell'

1750 'Altherston 1 bell' *(sic)*

CUSTOMS

On Sundays one bell at 8 a m (for Holy Communion), three for later services

Ringing on Christmas Eve and New Year's Eve, also for Weddings by request

Death-knell on the day of death, and at funerals tolling every two hours from 8 a m to 2 p m

Best thanks to Rev T A Lewis, Rector

H T T, 22 March, 1875, and 3 March, 1893

ATTLEBOROUGH HOLY TRINITY Three bells

There was an ancient chapel here in the parish of Nuneaton, which was in existence in in Edward VI's reign, as the Inventory of 1552 implies "Itm there a oon bell in the steple" This fell into ruins, and the present church was erected in 1842

AUSTREY. St Nicholas Five bells

1  **GOD** (*border*) **SAVE** (*border*) **THE** (*border*) **KING** (*border*) **1632** (*border*) (31 in.

2.  **WILLIAM** (*border*) **CROSS** (*border*) **THOMAS** (*border*) **TAYLOR** (*border*) **C** (*border*) **ANNO** (*border*) **DM** (*border*) **1632** (*border*) (32 in.

3 RECAST AT GLOCESTER BY THO^S RUDHALL 1770 (34 in.

4  **IHS NAZARENVS** (*border*) **REX · IVDEORVM** (*border*) **FILI DEI** (*border*) **MISERERE . MEI 1632** (*border*) (37½ in

5  **CVM SONO · SI NON VIS** (*border*) **VENIRE** (*border*) **NVNQVAM AD PRECES** (*border*) **CVPIES · IRE** (*border*) **1632** (*border*)

Below, arabesques all round (41 in.

All by Hugh Watts, except the 3rd, which probably originally bore his other stock inscription "Celorum Christe, etc." On the 1st the HE are conjoined, "Acorn ' borders (Pl XVII 7) throughout, arabesques (Pl XVII 8 on tenor) Treble hung above the rest, said to be cracked in 1876 (H T T), but I could detect nothing wrong

1552 'ALSTREY iiij^or belles in the steple'

Customs

On Sundays, treble at 8 a m and after Morning Service Before Morning Service treble rung as Sermon Bell 10-30—10-45, bells chimed for ten minutes, then tenor for five, similarly in the evening

Ringing on Christmas Day, Easter Day, Whit-Sunday, and New Year's Eve, and for Weddings by request

Death Knell on tenor for twenty minutes, with usual tellers at beginning and end Tenor tolled for an hour at funerals

Curfew at 8 p m on tenor Pancake Bell formerly at 11 a m on Shrove Tuesday (2nd and 4th bells).

Treble rung for Vestry meetings

Best thanks to Rev I. J. Rosser, Vicar.

H T. T, 3 Oct, 1876 H B. W, May, 1908

AVON DASSETT. St John Baptist Five bells

1—5 WILLIAM BLEWS AND SONS BIRMINGHAM 1869

1 *On waist* —ASCRIBE UNTO THE LORD WORSHIP AND POWER

2 *On waist* —ASCRIBE UNTO THE LORD THE HONOUR DUE UNTO HIS NAME

3 *On waist* —BRING PRESENTS AND COME INTO HIS COURTS

4 *On waist* —O WORSHIP THE LORD IN THE BEAUTY OF HOLINESS

5 *On waist* —LET THE WHOLE EARTH STAND IN AWE OF HIM PSALM 96 7 8,9
0

Nothing is known of the predecessors of this ring

1552 'iij belles a saunce belle.'
1750 'Dasset p'va 3 Bells'

CUSTOMS:

Bells chimed for services on Sundays, tenor rung as "Sermon Bell."
Death Knell for one hour, tenor tolled for funerals.
Ringing on New Year's Eve, 5th of November, and for Weddings
Thanks to the Captain of Ringers.

H. T. T, 14 June, 1887.

BADDESLEY CLINTON St. Michael. Three bells

1 Sancte Nicolae Ora Pro W Nobis H

2 HENRY BAGLEY MADE MEE 1678 *(border at end)*

3. S T O M A

Treble By William Hasylwood of Reading, whose initials appear before and after *Nobis*, date about 1500 The black-letter minuscules are very thick and clumsy, but the capitals are well formed, except the Roman W See p 26 and Plate XIV, Figs 1-6 The tower dating from the time of Henry VII, the bell was probably put up at the same time

Tenor By Thomas Newcombe, with his shield Pl XVI, Fig 3, as at Ansley

1552 'iij belles a handbelle and a sacring bell'
1750 'Badesley Clinton cap 1 bell' (*sic*)

Bells chimed for half-an-hour before services on Sundays
Death Knell rung when notice is given, at funerals a bell tolled before and after the service
Thanks to the Rev H T Robson, Rector.

H T. T, 5 Oct, 1874

At the Hall is said to be a chapel-bell of foreign workmanship with the inscription IESVS IS NAME 1546

BADDESLEY ENSOR St Matthew 1+1 bells

1 G AND G MEARS FOUNDERS LONDON 1846

S RICE ● GOODE ● CHVRCH ● WARDING ● 1706

Smaller bell by Joseph Smith of Edgbaston, brought from the old church in 1846 It weighs between one and two cwt, the larger is 14 cwt 2 qrs 11 lbs

H T T, 25 July, 1876

BAGINTON St John Baptist Two bells

1 *No inscription*

2 PRES ✠ THE ✠ LORD

"Both very small, but quite fill the little tower" (H T T) The tower is hardly more than a turret, placed on the roof at junction of nave and chancel

2nd, by one of the Newcombes, see p 37, the stop is *Leics* fig 43

1552 'BAGINTON, ij small belles and a handbelle'

H T T, 19 Sept, 1874

BARCHESTON — St Martin. — Three bells

1 **WILLIAM . BALDWIN GORGE SNOW CHURCH : WARDENS MATHEW BAGLEY : MADE MEE 1775**

2 ✤ **DANIEL PERRY THOMAS GRIMET CW^s 1720** *(border)*

3 BARTHOLOMEW ATTYN MADE MEE 1596

2nd By Richard Sanders of Bromsgrove, with two trade-marks, the first a plain circle with R S and a bell, the second a bell surrounded by the words RICHARD SANDERS MADE ME; after the date, arabesques See Pl XXIII, Figs 3, 9

3rd. By Bartholomew Atton of Buckingham, see p 46, and for the lettering, Pl XIV, Figs 7-12

Pits for four bells, but there do not seem ever to have been more than three

1552 · 'iij belles a sanctus bell'

1750. '3 Bells'

CUSTOMS

A bell rung after Mid-day Celebration on Sundays, also at 8 a m

Ringing on Festivals when possible, as also for Weddings

Death Knell on notification of death, age denoted in tolling

Many thanks to Rev. C F Turner, Rector

H T T, 20 Apr, 1887

BARFORD — St Peter. — Three bells

1 ✠ BY ● MIS ● INFORMATION ● MADE ● WAS ● I ITS THE FOVNDERS LOS PRAY ● THINK ● ON ● HE ● 1709

(Immediately below, on same band, a continuous scroll) (27 in

2 *Above, a cable-moulding* (29¾ in.

PRAISE THE LORD YE PEOPLE 1639 H B ✤

3 *Above, bits of interlacing fleur-de-lys border all round* (Fig 9)

WILLIAM WALGRAVE CHVRCH WARDEN 1661 (31⅜ in

1st By Joseph Smith of Edgbaston One would be glad to know more of the history of this bell, and the founder's misadventures

2nd and 3rd By Henry Bagley, for the 2nd cf Halford 3rd and see p 67 The ornaments on the 2nd are *Bucks*, Pl. XXXII Figs. 2, 4, on the 3rd Fig 9 and *Bucks*, Pl XXXII 2

1552 'iiij belles a little bell

1753 '4 Bells'

There is a tradition that one of the bells was stolen by Sherborne parish

Inscriptions given by Sweeting in Brit Mus Add MSS 37180

Best thanks to Mr W E Falkner

H T T, 3 Aug, 1881

BARSTON ST SWITHIN (Five bells

1. ABRAHAM FISHER CAVE MEE WILLIAM BAGLEY MADE MEE 1691 (22 in

2. MATTHEW BAGLY AND WILLIAM BAGLY MADE MEE 1689 (23½ in

3 *No inscription* (24 in

4 ● M[R] ● ROBERT ● BOYSE ● MINESTER ● 1728 ● (27 in

5 WILLIAM SHAGTHWALL AND IOHN EATON C W MATTHEW BAGLEY MADE MEE

Below —1683 *On the sound-bow, impression of coin* (30½ in

Border on 1st, Fig 13, on 2nd, bits of the same, and on 5th, bits of another ornament between the words The A has a hooked top throughout

The 3rd is a fourteenth-century bell; round the top is a plain band

4th by Joseph Smith, border Pl XXIII. Fig 2

Pits for six bells, rather dirty, stays broken off A very light ring, the tenor only about 5 cwt

1552 'Itm there . iij belles'

CUSTOMS —

On Sundays bells chimed for services preceded by a Sermon Bell and followed by another for the last five minutes, also a bell rung at 8 a m. Until 1894 a bell was rung after Morning Service, known as the Pudding Bell

Ringing on Principal Festivals and New Year's Eve, also for Weddings on payment of fee, on November 5th in the evening (formerly at 5 a.m, the ringers receiving 5s from the Churchwardens)

Death Knell within 12 hours after death, *each* bell tolled three times for male, twice for female, age on tenor

Many thanks to Rev E K Graham, Vicar

H T T, 1876 H B W, Sept, 1907

BARTON-ON-HEATH ST LAWRENCE 1+1 bells

1 **IOHN BRAINE · EDWARD WILLIAMES · CHVRCH · WARDENS HENRY BAGLEY MADE MEE 1740** (36½ in

S IOHN KERRY 1672 (15½ in

Large bell hung in iron frame with cannons off, small bell hung above it, rung by lever; edges much chipped Tower very small

Founder of smaller bell doubtful, perhaps Richard Keene, see p 86 The N is reversed

1750 '1 Bell"

H T T, 30 May, 1888, H B W, Apr, 1907

BAXTERLEY One bell

1 W BLEWS AND SONS BIRMINGHAM 1875

The present bell replaces two old ones, inscribed respectively

+ ABO HOƎƎQ VTSЯ ✤ XX 1986

+ AVE MARIA

Of these the smaller was by Robert Newcombe (see p 31), the cross and fleur-de lys are Pl XVI, Figs 4, 5 The lettering on the larger (Pl II, Figs 18, 19) is found on the bell at Wyken, but the cross there is different, here it is quite plain See p 5 The "rings" with the inscriptions from these two bells were preserved by Canon Ellacombe, and rubbings which he took from them are in his collection at the British Museum, labelled "Kingsbury" (Add MSS 33203) See also *Trans Birm and Mid Inst* 1878, p 18

1552 'BAKSTERLEY, iij belles in the steple'
H T T, 9 Sept, 1876

BEARLEY — St Mary the Virgin — One bell

1 MARIA ⚜ [Q] ✠ [K] ⚜ MARIA ⚜ [Q] ✠ [K]

The two old bells one mediaeval from the Worcester foundry (probably by Nicholas Grene, *c* 1530, see p 11), were re-cast into one by Blews in 1875, with the old inscription imitated from the larger one "The two old bells weighed together 2 cwt 1 qr 4 lbs, the new bell weighs 2 cwt 1 qr 5 lbs, clapper 13 lbs, our work about the bell 25½ lbs, the two old bells were re-cast into one with devices as near as possible like those of the larger bell" (Information given to H T T by the founders, 28 July, 1881)

The inscription on the old mediaeval bell was as follows —

✠ airam ✠ [K] ⚜ airam ● [K] ✠ airam ⚜ [K]

the word maria being reversed in each case (K=head of King, Plate V, Fig 13) It resembled the larger bell at Morton Bagot (Plate VI, Figs 1, 2, and VII, Fig 4) The letters on the present bell are said by Mr Tilley to resemble those on Plate II of Ellacombe's *Church Bells of Somerset*, *i e*, Robert Norton s (of Exeter) It will be seen that they do not reproduce the old inscription at all accurately The inscription band of the old bell was preserved by Canon Ellacombe, and a rubbing from it is in the British Museum (Add MSS 33,203), but its present whereabouts are unknown

1552 'Itm there ij belles'
1760 'Brearley 2 Bells'
H T T, 27 July, 1881

BEAUDESERT — St Nicholas — Three bells

1 ✠ AVE MARIA GRACIA PELNA (23 in

2 ✠ IHESUS NAZSARINUS REX · IUDEORUM (26 in

3 ● THE ● THENTH YEAR ● OF THE ● REIGN ● OF QVEEN ● ANNE ● 1711 ●
Below, border of scrolls all round (29 in

1st and 2nd probably by a local founder, dating about 1350 The bell at Whitchurch is of similar type, and has the same initial cross See p 4 and Plate II Figs 1-8 'Two small cylindrical bells' (H T T)

3rd By Joseph Smith of Edgbaston, the coins between the words are half-pence, scrolls, Pl XXIII, Fig 2

1553 'BEWDESERTE Itm there iij bells'
1750 '3 Bells

See *Notices of Warwickshire Churches* i p 155

CUSTOMS

Bells chimed for services on Sundays, with tolling in for last five minutes on treble, the 2nd bell rung after Mattins to announce that there will be Evensong (a relic, says the Rector, of the days when the church was served from Henley-in-Arden, the Rector being non-resident)

Death knell as soon as possible, between 8 a m and 8 p m, tellers 3 for man, 2 for woman, one for child, on each bell, followed by tenor for two or three minutes

At Funerals the tenor tolled as "minute bell" for fifteen minutes, followed by a dozen or so quick strokes

The 2nd is rung for about five minutes before Vestry Meetings

Best thanks to Rev J S Turner, Rector

H T T, 16 March, 1881, 20 July, 1891

BEDWORTH — ALL SAINTS — 8+1 bells

1. **J TAYLOR & C° FOUNDERS LOUGHBOROUGH 1891** (24½ in

2 *The same* (25 in.

3 *The same* (27 in

4. *The same* (29½ in

5. *The same*

On waist.—**I.H.S. NAZARENUS REX IUDEORUM FILI DEI MISERERE MEI 1627**

RECAST 1891 (32½ in

6.  **IHS NAZARENVS IVDEORUM FILI DEI MISERERE MEI 1629** (33¾ in

7 *As 1—4, with band of ornament below inscription*

On waist —**CUM CUM AND PRAIE 1639**

RECAST 1891 (38½ in

8 *As 1—4*

On waist —**GLORY TO GOD IN THE HIGHEST 1891** (42½ in

S *No inscription.*

	cwt	qrs	lbs		cwt	qrs	lbs
Weights —1)	3	1	5	5)	6	3	23
2)	3	2	14	6)	6	2	14
3)	4	1	14	7)	10	3	23
4)	5	0	18	8)	14	0	18

Formerly three bells, of which the 2nd forms the present 6th All three were by Watts of Leicester, the old treble being inscribed like the present 6th, except the date (1627), the old tenor as indicated on the present 7th The small sanctus bell hangs in a turret at the east end of the nave

Mr Tilley, in 1876, noted that the 2nd and 3rd had been quarter-turned, the one much deepened and the other much sharpened

1552 'iij bells, a saunce bell and a handbell'
1750 · '4 Bells'

CUSTOMS

On Sundays bells chimed for services (except as below), with a single bell for the last two minutes, single bell at 8 a m (for H C), and treble for daily services

Ringing on Christmas Day, Fourth Sunday in Lent (Mothering Sunday), Easter Sunday, Whit-Sunday, Sunday before August Bank Holiday, Wake Sunday, Sunday School Sunday, Harvest Festival, or special occasions such as the Bishop's visit, all at mid day, on Christmas Eve and New Year's Eve 11-30 p m to 12-30 a m , also on King's Birthday and for weddings

Death Knell on tenor, twelve hours after death, tellers 12×3 for man, 12×2 for woman or child At funerals the tenor is tolled every few seconds for half-an-hour previously, muffled peals are occasionally rung

The Pancake Bell is rung on Shrove Tuesday at 11 a.m (tenor used)

The small bell in the turret at the E end of the nave is not used

A full peal of 5020 Grandsire Triples was rung on the completion of the ring of eight in 1892, and a full peal of Steadman Triples in 1907.

There is a local distich to this effect ·—" Coventry Janglers
Bedworth Egg-shells
Coton cracked Pancheons,
Nuneaton merry Bells"

It may be assumed that its inventor hailed from the last named place!

Many thanks to Rev Canon F R Evans, Vicar

H T. T, 15 Aug, 1876

BENTLEY. See SHUSTOKE

BERKSWELL ST JOHN BAPTIST 6+1 bells

1 CHRISTINA ELIZABETH FEENEY ✻ WIFE OF JOHN FEENEY ✻ 1898 ✻
Below band of vine-pattern all round (as at Allesley), and Taylor's trade-mark (30¼ in

2 JOHN FEENEY ✻ THE MOAT ✻ BERKSWELL ✻ 1898 ✻
Below, as the last. (30¼ in

3. **GALFRIDVS ◆ GILES ◆ ME ◆ FESIT ANNO ◆ DM ◆ 1584** (34 in

4 ✣ AVE · MARIA GRA PLENA (36 in

5   Nomen Magdelene Geret Melodie  (38½ in

6 TO THE MEMORY OF JOHN FREDERICK FEENEY ✻ DIED IN EDGBASTON 1869 *Below, as No 1* (45 in

S *No inscription*

Formerly three bells only, the first two and tenor being added by Taylor of Loughborough in 1898, each has his trade-mark (Fig. 19) on the waist

3rd Coarse rough letters, the only other known bells by this founder are the two broken ones at Weston-under-Weatherley see p 47

4th By Johannes de Stafford (see p 14, and Pl VII, Figs 16-19)

5th Probably cast by Newcombe and Watts in partnership, about 1600, see p 35 Of the four stamps the first cross appears to be *Northants*, fig 17, also found at Heyford in that county the second is Newcombe s, Pl XVII, 2, the two stamps before *Nomen* are the Brasyer lion s head (Fig 7) which was used by Newcombe, and Watts' Brasyer shield (Pl XVIII 11) The word *Campana* is omitted in the inscription

	cwt	qrs	lbs		cwt	qrs	lbs
Weights —1)	5	3	15	4)	7	2	6
2)	5	1	27 ?	5)	9	3	9
3)	7	1	7	6)	16	2	7

1552 'BARKSWELL, Itm there iij belles'
1750 ' 5 Bells'

CUSTOMS '

On Sundays bells chimed at 8 a m, a peal for morning and evening service
Ringing on New Year's Eve, also on Sunday after election of new churchwardens
Death Knell as soon as notice given, before sunset, tellers 3×3 for male 3×2 for female
A bell rung for Vestry Meetings
The small Priest s bell is not now used

Best thanks to Rev H C A Back, Vicar.

H T T, 1876, H B W, Sept, 1907.

BICKENHILL ST PETER Five bells

1 M[R] CARVER MINISTER 1703

Two coins on sound-bow (27½ in

2 M[R] SAMVEL COX AND M[R] IOHN SHAW CHVR WAR 1703 (28¾ in

3 *Above, arabesques inverted*

IESVS BE OVR SPED 1636

Below —  (30 in

4 SOLI DEO GLORIA PAX HOMINIBVS 1650 C W T D

Below,  (32 in

5 M[R] HENRY KARVER VICAR IOHN HINSHAW AND IOHN BARBONE CHVRCHWARDENS 1707 (37½ in

Bells recently rehung by Barwell

1st, 2nd, and 5th by Joseph Smith, with arabesque ornaments between words

3rd by Thomas Hancox (see p 53), letters as Aston Cantlow 3rd, cross Pl XXI 7, the same as John Martin's on the 4th, fleur de-lys before the date heart-shaped trade-mark

(Pl XIX 2) on waist Border above inscription (arabesques), after date narrow running border (Pl XXII 3), followed by border with medallions (Pl XX 1-3) as on Aston Cantlow 1st

4th By John Martin of Worcester, thick letters, cross and trade-mark Pl XXI, Figs 3, 7, between the words narrow running border, Pl XXI, Fig 8 The N is reversed

1552 'BYKNELL, iij belles in the steple'

1750 'Bignell 5 bells'

CUSTOMS

Curfew rung formerly

Death Knell with tellers, said to be 6×6 for man, 6×5 for woman, and 6×4 for child

Bell rung every Sunday morning at 8 a m, "ringing in" for last five minutes before services

Ringing for Weddings when paid for

Bell rung for Vestry Meeting (by the Vicar)

Thanks to Rev J C B Walter, Vicar

H T T, 4 March, 1876, H B W, Sept, 1907.

BIDFORD ST LAWRENCE Six bells

1 **COME AWAY MAKE NO DELAY 1791**

2 **FEAR GOD HONOR THE KING 1791**

3 **PEACE AND GOOD NEIGHBOURHOOD 1791**

4 **1791**

5 **IOHN HURST HENRY BIDDLE & MARK OSBORNE CHURCH WARDENS 1791**

6 **INO HURST HENRY BIDDLE MARK OSBORNE & THOS SALE CHURCH WARDENS 1791** (42½ in

The ring is by John Rudhall of Gloucester

Weights —1)	5½ cwt	Note—D sharp	4)	8 cwt	Note—A sharp
2)	6 "	C sharp	5)	9¾ "	G sharp
3)	7 "	B	6)	13 "	F sharp

Bells hung awkwardly in two tiers, the upper three very difficult to reach

1552 'BYDFFORDE, iij belles one sance bell'

1750 '5 Bells'

The late Rev T P Wadley, of Naunton Beauchamp, Worcs, recorded the inscriptions on the old bells as —

(1) "God and King"

(2) "Peace Good-will"

(3) 'Religion Death and Pleasure make we ring"

These are obviously inaccurate, but they seem to be Rudhall's bells

CUSTOMS

A bell rung at 8 a m every Sunday Treble rung as "Priest s Bell' every Sunday for five minutes before Matins and Evensong

Ringing at Christmas, Easter, and Whitsuntide, at 6 a m on St Thomas' Day, on New Year's Eve a muffled peal followed by an open one

Ringing on Trinity Monday, November 5th, and for Weddings

Death Knell within 24 hours, with usual tellers (on each bell)

Pancake Bell on Shrove Tuesday at noon (3rd and 4th bells)

The bells were brought to Bidford by water in 1791, and a villa on the banks of the Avon is named "Bell Court" with reference to this

Best thanks to Rev W E Hobbs, Vicar, and Mr W E Falkner

H T. T 29 Jan, 1878

BILLESLEY. ALL SAINTS One bell

1 **RICHARD SANDERS MADE MEE**
1721 (12 in

A very small bell, by R Sanders of Bromsgrove, hanging in a small turret at W end, date very indistinct

The church was erected in 1692, but there was an ancient chapel here before that time

1750 'Billsley 1 bell'

H T T, 15 Nov, 1881

BILTON. ST MARK Five bells

1 ✠ **THE GUIFT OF THE HONOURABLE COUNTES OF WARWICK**
On waist **1722** O (27 in

2 ✠ Sancta Katerina Ora Pro Nobis ✠ (29 in

3 ✠ Vox Augustini Sonet In Aure Dei (30½ in

4 Beata Katerina Ora Pro Nobis (33 in

5 HENRY ✤ BAGLEY ✤ MADE ✤ ME ✤ 1662 ✤ ✤ ✤ (35½ in

1st By Richard Sanders of Bromsgrove trade-mark Pl XXIII, Fig 9 The Countess of Warwick who gave the bell was the daughter of Sir Thomas Myddleton of Chirk Castle, and wife of the 6th Earl of Warwick and Holland who died in 1701 She married Joseph Addison (of the *Spectator*) in 1716, and died in 1731

2nd Probably by John Sturdy or John Kebyll of London (see p 23), cross Pl XI, Fig 3, crowned capitals, Pl XI, Figs 6-14

3rd and 4th By John Danyell of London, c 1460 (see p 24), crosses on 3rd, Pl XIII, Figs 1, 12, foundry shield = Royal Arms (Pl XIII, 11) Crosses on 4th, Pl XI, 16, Pl XIII, 12, Royal Arms as on last, but crowned Capitals on both, Pl XIII, Figs 2-6

Weight of tenor about 9 cwt, borders of interlacing fleurs-de-lys, Fig 9

1552 'BYLTON, iij belles and oon lytle bell ij handbelles'

[The three existing mediaeval bells thus formed the original ring]

1750 '5 Bells'

See Watt, *Rugby Past and Present*, p 285

CUSTOMS

On Sundays bells chimed for Morning Service, rung in evening.

Ringing at Christmas, on Whit-Sunday Trinity Sunday, and New Year's Eve, also on November 5th, and for Weddings occasionally

Death Knell as soon as convenient, usual tellers, followed by fifteen minutes' tolling, 4th bell for an adult, treble for a child At Funerals, 4th bell tolled slowly for ten minutes beforehand, with tellers at conclusion of service

A bell rung for Choir Practice
See *Bell News*, 18 Oct, 1884
Thanks to Rev. W O Assheton, Rector
H T T, 1875, H B W, June, 1908

BILTON, NEW. St Oswald One bell

Church built 1867, parish formed out of Bilton

BINLEY St Bartholomew One bell

1 THOMAS ● SHEARES ● CHVRCH ● WARDEN ● 1728

Below, border of scrolls all round

By Joseph Smith
Present church consecrated 1778
1552 'two belles'
H T T 1 Sept, 1876

BINTON. St Peter One bell

1 HENRY BAGLEY MADE ME 1669

There are three varieties of borders between the words, *Bucks*, Pl XXXII 2, and Fig 71, and Fig 9 of this work (p 68)
1552 'Itm there ij belles.'
1750 '2 Bells'
H T T, 15 Nov, 1881

BIRDINGBURY St Leonard 1 + 1 bells

1 ✠ A B C C E F G H I K 1615 (32¼ in

S. 1774

Larger bell probably by Edward Newcombe cross Pl XVI, Fig 2, cf Morton Morrell and Warmington, and see p 37
Smaller by Pack and Chapman of London, about 18 in diam, hung with lever
1552 'iij belles and a saunce belle'
H T T, 10 Oct, 1878, H. B W, June, 1908.

BIRMINGHAM St Martin Twelve bells

1 PACK & CHAPMAN OF LONDON FECIT 1772 (27½ in

2. ROB^T THOMPSON & JAM^S BUTTLER C^H WARDENS PACK & CHAPMAN OF LONDON FECIT 1771 (29½ in

3 THO^S LESTER & THO^S PACK OF LONDON FECIT 1758 (30⅝ in

4 WILLIAM BLEWS AND SONS FOUNDERS BIRMINGHAM

On waist —(*a*) RECAST 1870 (*b*) REV W WILKINSON, DD RECTOR
W W RIDDELL }
JOHN GOUGH } CHURCHWARDENS
LAUS DEO (31¾ in

5 *The same* (33⅞ in

6 RICH^D DOVEY RECTOR THO FAULCONBRIDGE & RICH^D ANDERTON CH WARDENS

Below —LESTER PACK & CHAPMAN OF LONDON FECIT 1769 (35⅜ in
8-2-12

7 LESTER AND PACK FECIT 1758 YE RINGERS ALL THAT PRIZE YOUR HEALTH AND HAPPINESS BE SOBER MERRY WISE AND YOULL THE SAME POSSESS
9—3—12 (37½ in

8 TO HONOUR BOTH OF GOD AND KING OUR VOICES SHALL IN CONSORT RING LESTER & PACK FECT 1758
11—3—6 (40½ in.

9 RECAST IN THE YEAR 1790 IOHN DADLEY & HENRY PARKER CH WARDENS
15-1-17 (44¼ in

10 OUR VOICES WITH JOYFUL SOUND MAKE HILLS AND VALLEYS ECHO ROUND LESTER AND PACK OF LONDON FECIT 1758
17—3—2 (46½ in

11 RICH^D DOVEY RECTOR THO^S FAULCONBRIDGE & RICH^D ANDERTON CH WARDENS 1769 LESTER PACK & CHAPMAN OF LONDON FECIT
27-3 6 (53 in

12. THE REV^D RICH^D DOVEY RECTOR CARTER BARTON & CHRIST^R SIDMAN CH . . WARDENS 1758 OoOOOOOOOOOoo ❀ O ❀ LET YOUR CEASELESS CHANGES VARY TO OUR GREAT MAKER STILL NEW PRAISE □ LESTER & PACK OF LONDON FECIT
35-0-8 (58 in

Cannons wanting on 3rd, 7th, 11th, and 12th Weights incised on the 6th—12th
The present weights are given as —

	cwts	qrs	lbs		cwts	qrs	lbs	
1)	6	1	0	7)	9	3	12	
2)	6	2	0	8)	11	3	6	
3)	6	2	16	9)	15	1	17	
4)	7	0	0	10)	17	3	2	
5)	7	2	14	11)	27	3	16	
6)	8	2	12	12)	35	0	8	Note, D flat

The old 4th and 5th were by Lester and Pack, 1758, probably inscribed like the 3rd; weights 6 cwt 3 qrs 25 lbs, and 8 cwts 20 lbs The date on the 2nd *may* be 1777

Among the coins on the tenor is a "Spanish Dollar," probably a coin of John V of Portugal (see Deedes and Walters, *Church Bells of Essex*, p 135), the ornaments below are a large rosette and a helmet supported by two eagles (*op cit*, Pl XXXIII, Fig 6)

1552 'BYRMYCHAM, Itm there . iij^or belles w^t a clock and a chyme'
1760 '8 bells' (*sic*)

There were six bells previous to 1758, put up in 1682, the founder's name is not given, but it was probably Henry Bagley An entry in the Parish Books (which are extant from 1676 onwards) says "The Six Bells now in the Steple were new cast Samuel Banner & John Rogers being then Churchwardens being in the yeare 1682 and wayd as followeth" —

	c	q	l
1 Bell wayd	6	3	5
2 Bell	7	1	2
3 Bell	8	3	23
4 Bell	10	0	8
5 Bell	12	1	24
6 Bell	17	3	9
In all	63	1	15

The following entries are also of interest —

April 7th, 1702 "Its this day ordered att a Publick meeteing of the Parishon^rs of Birmingham That the Twenty pence that hath used to be paid to the Church-wardens for the Ringing the Bell to any funerall shall not be paid for the future by any person"

15th March 1737 Memorandum that at a publick meeting held in Vestry this day by the inhabitants of the Town of Birmingham it is agreed that as great Illconveniences have attended the Ringing of State Days and Holidays at Both Churches in the said Town it is now ordered & agreed that there shall be ringing only at one Church in a Day and that such ringing shall be at each Church by Turns the First Day to begin at St Martin's Church and the next at St Phillips

4 July 1752 To cash received of the Chapel Warden of Bloxidge (Bloxwich) for a Bell and Clapper 52 8 0

1st November 1757 at a second Vestry Meeting after proper notice given in St Martins Ch in Birming^m it is further agreed to give orders to Messrs Lester and Pack to cast for the use of the said Parish Eight Bells and to be of the weight of St Georges in the East, Middlesex, which weight is 61 7CT 0 0

[A meeting in reference to the bells had been held on July 19th in the same year]

The above information is derived from J T Bunce's *Old St Martin s, Birmingham*, p 35 ff A further account of the bells (subsequent to the alterations of 1870) is given in *Church Bells*, 7 January, 1871

CUSTOMS —

Bells rung for Sunday Morning Services, chimed at other times with Ellacombe's apparatus Ringing on Church Festivals, for Weddings by request
Muffled peals rung on death of Sovereign

A Croft of land was originally bequeathed for the purpose of providing bell-ropes, its locality is not given, but it is probably valuable property now-a-days!

On the walls of the Ringing Chamber are numerous peal-boards, the St Martin's Ringing Guild being an old-established well-known company They are too numerous to give in detail, but those previous to 1880 are given in *Church Bells*, 23 and 30 May 1874, 24 April 1880. An account of ringing done here between 1755 and 1888 is given in the same periodical, 25 Jan 1889 For a ringer's opinion of these bells, see *Bell News*, 29 Sept. 1883, also 9 July, 1887 See also for the chimes Bunce, p 36

Best thanks to Rev Canon Denton Thompson, Rector

The Rev W Wilkinson, D D (see 4th bell), of Trin Coll, Dublin was the well-known Rector of Birmingham from 1866 to 1897 He was Rural Dean 1874-92 and Hon Canon of Worcester 1871-97.

H T T 25 July, 1892

BIRMINGHAM. ST PHILIP (PRO-CATHEDRAL) Ten bells

1 THOMAS LESTER OF LONDINI FECIT 1750 (31 in

2 THOMAS LESTER OF LONDON FECIT 1751 (32 in

3 AT PROPER TIMES MY VOICE ILL RAISE AND SOUND TO MY SUBSCRIBERS PRAISE

Below —T LESTER FECIT 1750 (34 in

4 *As No 2, but no ornament* (35 in

5 PACK & CHAPMAN OF LONDON FECIT 1772 (*loop-pattern as on 2nd*) (37 in

6 MESSRS CLAUD JOHNSON & GEORGE STUBBS CHURCH WARDENS 1796 THOMAS MEARS OF LONDON FECIT (40 in

7 *As No 1* (41 in

8 T. MEARS OF LONDON FECIT 1823 (*loop-pattern as on 5th*) (44 in

9 THOMAS LESTER FECIT 1750 (50 in

10 IN WEDLOCK BANDS ALL YE WHO JOIN WITH HANDS YOUR HEARTS UNITE SO SHALL OUR TUNEFULL TONGUES COMBINE TO LAUD THE NUPTIAL RITE

Below —PACK & CHAPMAN OF LONDON FECIT 1772 (*loop-pattern as on 5th*) (55½ in

Bells very grimy and encrusted with accumulated deposits which largely obscure the lettering The tower is said to be in an unsafe condition and the bells are no longer used for ringing, in fact the treble only is used for services, and the tenor tolled for funerals, the rest being silent except for the clock chimes

	cwts	qrs	lbs		cwt	qrs	lbs
Weights —1)	5	3	22	6)	11	0	11
2)	6	1	14	7)	13	2	8
3)	7	0	10	8)	16	2	9
4)	7	2	13	9)	21	0	13
5)	9	0	13	10)	29	0	18

The church was first built in the year 1711, and it is said that the original ring of bells was by Joseph Smith, but at all events the following extracts from the Vestry Minutes throw some light on their history

"3rd Aprill 1727 By an order of a generall meeting this day it was agreed that Joseph Smith shall receive the mettle from Mr Bradburn in order to cast a Bell for the parish church of St Phillips in Birmingham to be done with all expedition "

"At a meeting 13th day of June 1727, ordered that a fframe of good Timber be erected & fixed in the Steeple of the New Church for Hanging of Eight Bells, & that the Two Bells already made be hung there with all convenient speed "

[For another extract, dated 15 March 1737, see under St MARTIN S]

The above are quoted from Bunce's *History of St Martin's*, p 44 It seems probable that Joseph Smith supplied one or two bells originally, and a full ring of eight in 1727. About 1750-51 the latter were increased to ten, to which reference is made in Vestry Minutes of 12 February 1750-1 and 4 June 1751. Of this ring by Thomas Lester, six still remain

Browne Willis in or about 1760 mentions the ring of ten bells

In the ringing-chamber are several peal-boards, one of 1844, recording peals of 5184 and 5160 changes, others more recent (28 February, 1893, 3 September, 8 December, 1894, 14 December, 1895, 22 February, 7 March, 16 May, 1896) See also *Church Bells*, 30 May, 1874

An old chime-barrel is still preserved in the tower

It is stated that when the new bells were put in in 1751 a ' Bell Wake" was held in Navigation Street, and this was kept up for many years

H B W, 18 March, 1908

BIRMINGHAM St John, Deritend Eight bells

1 WE ARE PLACED HERE BY SUBSCRIPTION IN THE YEAR MDCCLXXVI THO COX MINISTER

2 HEALTH & HAPPINESS TO ALL OUR WORTHY SUBSCRIBERS R WELLS FECIT MDCCLXXVI

3 R WELLS ALDBOURNE FECIT

4 MAY THE TOWN OF BIRM^{M} BE EVER HELD IN ESTEEM FOR ITS MANUFACT R WELLS FECIT

5 *As No 3, with date* MDCCLXXVI

6 WISDOM TO THE COUNCIL OF THE STATE & SUCCESS TO THE BRITISH FLEET R WELLS FECIT MDCCLXXVI

7 MAY GREAT BRITAIN EVER STAND UNRIVALLED IN HER COMMERCE R WELLS F MDCCLXXVI

8 *As No 5, with addition of* OF *after* WELLS

A ring of eight by Robert Wells of Aldbourne (see p 77), put up in the rebuilt church in 1776 All the inscriptions are on the sound-bow as is usual with this founder Mr W E Falkner, who kindly examined the bells, reports them as very difficult to read, owing to corrosion in particular he is doubtful about the 5th The bells were rehung by Blews in 1872

In the Additions to Dugdale (Brit Mus Add MSS 29264, fol 160) 'The Tower in 1777 received Eight very musical Bells" See also *Gentleman's Mag Topogr* xiii p 56=*Gent Mag* 1818, i p 498

For peal-boards see *Church Bells*, 23 May, 1874

BIRMINGHAM All Saints One bell

Church rebuilt 1833

All Saints Small Heath One bell

Church built 1875, one bell of that date by Barwell, diam 24 in, weight 3 cwt

Bishop Latimer Memorial One bell

Church built 1904, a ring of ten bells in prospect, of which the 4th, inscribed —

HOOPER | BISHOP AND MARTYR | BORN 1495 | MARTYRED 1555

was supplied by Taylor of Loughborough in 1905

BISHOP RYDER MEMORIAL — Eight bells

Church built 1838 A ring of eight bells by W Blews put up in 1869 (see *Builder's Weekly Reporter*, February, 1869) "The first eight ever cast in Birmingham" (*Bell News*, 19 Feb, 1887)

CHRIST CHURCH

Church built 1805, destroyed 1898, when the bell was transferred to the new church of St Agatha, Sparkbrook

CHRIST CHURCH SPARKBROOK — One bell (?)

Church built 1867

CHRIST CHURCH, SUMMERFIELD — One bell (?)

Church built 1883

EMMANUEL — One bell (?)

Church built 1865

HOLY TRINITY, BORDESLEY — One bell (?).

Church built 1823

ST AGATHA, SPARKBROOK — One bell

Church built 1901 The bell came from Christ Church

ST AIDAN — One bell

Church built 1896, one bell by Carr of Smethwick, diam 30 in, weight 5cwt 1qr 24½lbs

ST. ALBAN — One bell (?)

Church built 1871.

ST ANDREW, BORDESLEY — One bell

Church built 1846, bell supplied by Messrs Barwell 1908, diam 28½ in, weight 4¼ cwt Also a set of tubular bells

ST ANNE, DUDDESTON — One bell

Church built 1868, one bell by Taylor of Loughborough, weighing 4 cwt

ST ASAPH

Church built 1868, the bells supplied in that year by W Blews (number not stated)

ST BARNABAS — One bell (?).

Church built 1857

ST BARTHOLOMEW — One bell (?)

Church built 1749

ST BASIL, DERITEND — One bell (?)

Church built 1885

ST CATHARINE, NECHELLS — One bell (?)

Church built 1878

ST CHRYSOSTOM One bell

Church built 1887

ST CLEMENT, NECHELLS One bell

Church built 1858

ST CUTHBERT One bell

Church built 1872, one bell by Carr of Smethwick, diam 25in, weight 3cwt 2qrs 10lbs.

ST DAVID. One bell (?).

Church built 1865

ST EDWARD One bell

Church built 1899

ST GABRIEL One bell

Church built 1869 one bell of 1882 by Barwell, diam 25in, weight 3cwt 1qr 25lbs

ST GEORGE

Church built 1820. Number of bells not reported, but the treble is by Thomas Mears, 1839

ST JOHN EVANGELIST, LADYWOOD One bell

Church built 1852

ST JUDE One bell

Church built 1851, one bell of 1878 by Barwell, diam 22in, weight 2cwt 2qrs 4lbs

ST LAWRENCE One bell

Church built 1842, one bell of 1903 by Barwell, diam 24in, weight 3cwt 14lbs

ST LUKE One bell.

Church built 1842; one bell by Thomas Mears, weight ¾cwt

ST MARGARET, WARD END

See WARD END

ST MARK One bell

Church built 1841.

ST MARK, SALTLEY One bell (?)

Church built 1899

ST MARY One bell

Church built 1774.

ST MATTHEW, DUDDESTON One bell

Church built 1875

ST MATTHIAS One bell (?)

Church built 1855

ST NICHOLAS One bell (?)

Church built 1867

ST OSWALD One bell (?)

Church built 1892

ST PATRICK — One bell

Church built 1896, one bell of that date by Mears and Stainbank, weighing 1 cwt

ST PAUL — Two bells

Church built 1777, two bells of 1874 by Barwell Diam 27 in and 32¾ in Weights 4 cwt 2 qrs. 10 lbs and 7 cwt 20 lbs

ST PAUL, LOZELLS — One bell (?)

Church built 1880

ST PETER — Two bells

Church built 1901, two bells, one by Thomas Mears, 1837, said to be from the old church of St Peter, Dale End (1827—1900), the other by Barwell, 1902 They appear to be the 6th and tenor of a ring of eight, diam 40½ in and 50½ in., weight 12 cwt 3 qrs 3 lbs and 21 cwt 24 lbs

ST SAVIOUR — One bell

Church built 1874, one bell of that date by Barwell diam 30 in, weight 6 cwt 2 qrs 18 lbs

ST SAVIOUR, SALTLEY

Church built 1859 has eight tubular "bells"

ST SILAS, LOZELLS — One bell (?)

Church built 1845

ST STEPHEN — One bell

Church built 1844

ST THOMAS — One bell (?)

Church built 1826

BISHOPTON — ST PETER. — One bell

The bell hangs high up in an open turret at the west end, and is uninscribed It is probably the one which hung in the old church It was inspected through a telescope by Mr. Falkner, July, 1908 Mr Savage kindly contributes an extract from Wheler's MS *Collectanea*, p 46 "The Bell belonging to Bishopton Chapel is in the Granary of the Manor Farmhouse, belonging to Joshua Smith Simmons Smith, Esq, and occupied by Mr Thomas Jacksons, where I examined it the 15 July 1833 It is a small bell without any date or inscription It formerly hung in a kind of open tower springing from the roof over the junction of the Nave and Chancel"

See also *Gentleman's Mag*, 1810, i. p 315 (*Gent Mag Topog* viii p 38)

BOLDMERE See SUTTON COLDFIELD,

BORDESLEY See BIRMINGHAM.

BOURTON-ON DUNSMORE — ST PETER — Three bells

1 ✠ S A N N A L 

2 ✠ A B C D E F G H I K L M N O P Q R S T ✠

3 R. TAYLOR & SONS OXFORD MDCCCXXVII

1st and 2nd by Thomas Newcombe (shield, Pl XVI 3, on 1st), cross, Pl. XVI 2

1552 'BURTON & DRAICOTT, iij belles a saunce bell and ij handbelles'
'Note that oon of the said handbells is stollen'

1750 'Burton on-Dunsmore, 4 Bells'

H T T, 10 Oct, 1878

BRAILES St GEORGE. 6+1 bells

1. *Above, border of interlacing fleurs-de-lys* (Fig. 9)

✠ I ◆ AM ◆ HEE ◆ FOR ◆ RICHARD ◆ PVRDI ◆ MADE ◆ MEE ✠ ✠ ANNO DOMINI

Below —(*a*) 1624 (*b*) *Arms of James I* (*c*) *Arms of Charles I as Prince of Wales.*
R🔔P (37½ in.

2 In Multis Annis Resonet Campana Iohannis 

  (39½ in

3 WILLIAM BLEWS AND SONS FOUNDERS BIRMINGHAM 1877

Below —(*Figure of St George and the Dragon*)

GLORY TO GOD IN THE HIGHEST
RECAST AT THE EXPENSE OF
REV CANON THOYTS MA
VICAR OF HONINGTON
T SMITH BA VICAR
H T SHELDON ESQR } CHURCHWARDENS (43½ in
J SPENCER

4 IME NOT THE BELL I WAS, BUT QUITE ANOTHER, IME NOW AS RITE AS MERRY GEORGE MY BROTHER

Below —1668 RICH· KEENE ME FECIT NATHANIELL HIL WILLIAM POELL C.W

RECAST 1900
F E GARRARD, VICAR
G FINDLAY } CHURCHWARDENS
W H BUCKINGHAM

MEARS & STAINBANK FOUNDERS LONDON

On the sound-bow, four impressions of coins from old bell (46 in.

5. ILE CRACK NO MORE NOW RING YOVR FILL MERRY GEORGE I WAS AND WILL BE STILL ◊ IOHN OKELY RIC CAPELL C W

Below — R 1671 K (51 in

6 ✠ Gaude Quod Post Ipm Scandis Et Est Honor Tibi Grandis In Celi Palacio

On waist —(*a*) HAEC ET ALTERA EX IMPĒSIS
ERNESTI THOYTS VICARII DE HONĪGTŌ
RENOVATAE SUNT
T SMITH VICARIO
H J SHELDON ET
J SPENCER ECCL GARDIANIS

(*b*) GULIAL BLEWS FILIIQ CAMPANARII
BIRMHAM MDCCCLXXVII (58 in

Sanctus, *No inscription, mediaeval*

The old 3rd was inscribed

THOMAS TARVER AND THOMAS WILLS CHURCH WARDENS ZACHARIUS RICHARDSON IOHN CLARK MATTHEW BAGLEY MADE ME 1752

The inscription on the old 4th and 6th have been reproduced with admirable accuracy, that on the 6th in exact facsimile of the old tenor

Treble It will be noted that the name here is Richard Purdue, but the only records we have at this period are of a Roger (cf Ellacombe, *Church Bells of Devon*, p 56) Either we must assume that Roger Purdue forgot or bungled his own name, or else the Brailes bell and others in the neighbourhood (see p 48) are by an otherwise unknown Richard The name does not appear in full elsewhere By a somewhat unpardonable oversight, this discrepancy has been overlooked in the Introduction

The 2nd is by Henry Jordan, of London (p 25), with capitals as on the old tenor, but not crowned, stamps, Pl XI, 15-17 This bell is hung above the rest

5th and old 4th by Richard Keene as indicated

The inscription on the tenor is referred to by Dr Thomas in his 1730 edition of Dugdale (ii p 555) "On the great bell here are the Arms of Underhill, a chevron between three trefoils, and round it this inscription in Saxon characters, *Gaude*, etc" See also Introduction, p 23, and Plate XII The founder is John Bird, of London, c 1410

The weight of the tenor is popularly said to be 35 cwt, but is given by Messrs Blews as 31 cwt 22 lbs, Note C, the 3rd bell as 14 cwt 2 qrs 19 lbs Note F (letter to Mr Falkner, 4 July, 1889) The present 4th weighs 17¼ cwt

1552 BRAYLLIS, vj belles a saunce belle' 1750 'Brayles 6 Bells'

The Sanctus-bell still hangs in its original position, though the present cot only dates from 1877, it is still used for "ringing in" before services

Mr Falkner states that the treble used to be rung on Sunday mornings for Sunday School.

It is stated that the Curfew is rung at 8 p m, and a bell daily at noon

There was also formerly a bell rung daily at 6 a m

There are or were chimes here playing five tunes, at 12, 4, 6, and 9

The bells are not now regularly rung.[1] The tenor is said to take three men to raise, and it is also stated that 15 men were required to ring the bells from the ground floor, but they are now rung from the upper stage.

The Rev. E. Thoyts (see 3rd bell) of Oriel Coll., Oxf., M.A., 1877, was Vicar of Honington 1877-79. The Rev. T. Smith, of Corpus Coll., Camb., was Vicar of Brailes 1856-86.

Mr. H. A. Evans, in his *Highways and Byeways in Oxford and the Cotswolds*, p. 136, records a tradition about the great bell, that it was "dug up" in the neighbourhood of Gallows Hill, on the Banbury road; he explains this by the fact that when the bell was taken to be recast, the conveyance broke down, and it lay some time by the roadside. But would it have gone to Birmingham via Banbury?

An account of the bells is given in the *Evesham Journal*, 27 February, 1892; see also *Bell News*, 27 April, 1907, where some curious statements are made.

H. T. T., 17 January, 1876, and April, 1887; H. B. W., 2 Oct., 1908.

At WINDERTON, a Chapel-of-ease to Brailes, are a hour bell and two quarter-bells, put up in 1877, by Messrs. Mears and Stainbank. The hour bell weighs 10 cwt. 1 qr. 8 lbs. (diam. 39 ins.), the quarters, 5½ and 6¾ cwt. (diam. 30½ ins. and 30 ins.)

BRINKLOW — ST. JOHN BAPTIST — Five bells

1 THOMAS MVSTON RECTER 1705
Below, border all round coins on sound-bow

2 MR ● IOHN FAIRFAX AND HUMFRY LESTER CHVRCH WARDINGS 1705

3 JOSEPH SMITH IN EDGBASTON MADE ME 1705

4 IHS NAZARENVS REX IVDEORVM FILI DEI MISERERE MEI 1705

5 MY MOVRNFVLL SOVND DOTH WARNING GIVE THAT HEARE MEN CANNOT ALLWAYES LIVE 1705 ● ●

All five by Joseph Smith; arabesques like Bagley's (Fig. 11); said to be out of repair.

1552 'BRYNKLOWE, iiij^or bells and a saunce bell.'
1750 '6 Bells.'

CUSTOMS:—

Bells chimed for Services on Sundays; tenor formerly rung for half-an-hour as 'Sermon Bell.'

Ringing at Christmas and other Festivals (not on Ascension Day), on New Year's Eve, also on November 5th, and for Weddings by request. Peals were rung on the recent occasions of Jubilee and Coronation.

Death Knell on receipt of notice or next morning at 9 a.m.; usual tellers formerly (on tenor). At Funerals "Bidding Bell" chimed an hour previously.

Pancake Bell formerly at 11 a.m. on Shrove Tuesday (3rd bell); now discontinued for over twenty years.

Best thanks to Rev. R. P. Watson, Rector.

H. T. T., 1 Sept., 1876.

BROMWICH, CASTLE See CASTLE BROMWICH.

BROMWICH, LITTLE See WARD END.

[1] See, however, for an account of recent attempts, *Stratford Herald*, 25 June, 1909; *Evesham Journal*, 26 June, 1909.

BROWNSOVER ST MICHAEL AND ALL ANGELS One bell

1  **IHS NAZARENVS ⁂⁂ REX IVDEORVM ⁂ FILI DEI MISERE MEI 1636**

By Hugh Watts, arabesques (Pl XVII, Fig 9) between the words

Formerly two bells (see below) H T T noted, 25 April, 1876, that the bell was then on the ground, the Chapel being under restoration

1552 'BROUNSOVER, ij small belles'

In the Rev W O Wait's *Rugby Past and Present*, p 206, it is stated "that for many years one of the two bells, which was cracked, stood on the north side of the Communion Table, it was generally thought to have been brought from Clifton. Upon it was the following inscription

CUM SONO SI NON VIS VENIRE NVNQUAM AD PRECES CUPIES IRE 1631

This bell was recast, and is now in a turret, built for the purpose, in the stable yard of Brownsover Hall The other bell, which hangs in a bracket on the west face of the chapel bears this inscription" [as above] The old bell was obviously by Hugh Watts (see p 43), and bore the Brasyer shield, according to a note supplied by Mr H J Elsee to the late Dr Raven

Best thanks to Rev T D Lane of Clifton

H T T, 25 April, 1876

BUBBENHALL ST GILES Three bells

1. ✠ A ✠ A B D C B D B D C E F G

On the sound-bow impressions of coins

2 RICHARD LOVCK ✠ AND ✠ WILLIAM ✠ CLARKE ✠ CHVRCHWARDENS ✠ 1670 ✠ H ✠ B

3 T MEARS OF LONDON FECIT 1813 (30 in.

1st by one of the Newcombes, cross, Pl XVI, 2

2nd by Henry Bagley, floral scroll, Pl XXII, 10 = *Bucks*, Pl XXXII, 2, and bits of ornament between words, the same as on Barston tenor

1552 'BUBNELL iiij^or bells and a saunce bell'

'Note that oon of the iiij^or bells afore saide is not as yet paid for, as they saie'

H. T. T, 15 May 1889, H B W, June, 1908

BUDBROOKE ST. MICHALL. Three bells

1  **GOD** (*border*) **SAVE** (*border*) **THE** (*border*) **KING** (*border*) **1637** (*border*) ($24\frac{7}{8}$ in

2 MR THOMAS NORTON VICAR IHON WEBB ● IOSEPH ● AVERY CHVRCH WA 1724

Below —  *and border of scrolls* (Pl XXIII 2) (27 in.

3 A C S I O H I [K]  (31¼ in

1st By Hugh Watts, 'Acorn' borders (Pl XVII, 7), HE of THE conjoined

2nd By Joseph Smith, with trade-mark Pl XXIII, Fig 1, coins (half-pence) of Queen Anne

3rd By Edward Newcombe and Watts in partnership, lettering (Pl VIII) as at Mancetter and St John Coventry (very much worn, as on Little Packington 1st), head of Edward III, as at Stoneleigh, and the Watts-Brasyer shield Date about 1600 The letters appear to be quite without meaning, and are not easy to read, the last in particular being very doubtful (See p 34)

Frames, ladders, and flooring in bad condition

1552 'Itm there ij belles'

1750 '3 Bells.'

See also *Notices of Warwickshire Churches*, i, p 110

No customs.

Thanks to Rev. O Hunt, Vicar

H T T, 16 June, 1882 H B W June, 1908

BULKINGTON St James Four bells

1 **IESVS ✿✿✿✿ BE ✿✿✿✿ OVR ✿✿✿✿ SPEEDE ✿✿✿**

[IG] **1614** (30 in

2 **✠ BE YT KNOWNE TO ALL THAT DOTH ME SEE THAT NEWCOMBE OF LEICESTER MADE MEE 1605** (32½ in

3 ✱ IOHN ✤ GAMMAGE ✤ AND ✤ IOHN ✤ LOLE ✤ CHVRCH : WARDENS ✤ HENRICVS : BAGLEY ✤ ME ✤ FECET ✤ 1676 (36¼ in

4 | Vox | dni | ihu xpi | vox | exultacionis | & | salutis | (41 in

1st By John Greene of Worcester (see p 55), border between words (Pl XX, 8) as used by Hancox at Mancetter, trade-mark Pl XXI, Fig 4

3rd Cross as at Lillington and Pillerton (Pl XXII, Fig 7); bits of pattern and fleur-de-lys between words

4th Probably by one of the Newcombes, cf Butler's Marston, and for the lettering see Plate XVII, figs 4, 5 See above, p 35

Bells in good order.

1552 'iiij^or belles and a saunce belle'

1750 '4 Bells'

Customs —

Bells chimed or rung for half-an-hour before Sunday services

Ringing on Christmas Eve and several evenings previously, also on New Year's Eve at midnight

Death Knell on morning of death or following morning according to time of notice given; tellers 3×3 and 3×2, age of deceased denoted by tolling

Thanks to Rev G S Brewer, Vicar.

H T T., 15 July, 1891, H B. W., May, 1908

BURMINGTON — SS Barnabas and Nicholas — One bell

1 ✠ PRAISE ⚜ THE ⚜ LORDE 1592

By Robert Newcombe of Leicester, see p 31 Cross and fleur-de-lys Pl XVI, Figs 4, 5 Turret dark and dirty, and difficult of access Diameter of bell about 30 in

1552 'iij belles one little bell'

There is a tradition here of bells being sold in 1692, but it is more likely to have been in 1592 when the present one was obtained

H T T, 20 April, 1887, H B W, October, 1908

BURTON DASSETT — All Saints — Six bells

1 CANTATE *(border)* DOMINO *(border)* CANTICVM *(border)* NOVVM *(border)* 1686 *(border)* ($29\frac{3}{4}$ in

2 HENRY *(border)* BAGLY MADE *(border)* MEE *(border)* 1686 *(border)* (31 in.

3 FEARE *(border)* GOD *(border)* AND *(border)* HONOR *(border)* THE *(border)* KING *(border)* 1686 *(border)* ($32\frac{7}{8}$ in

4 MATHEW *(border)* BAGLY *(border)* MADE *(border)* MEE *(border)* 1686 *(border)* ($35\frac{1}{8}$ in

5 BE IT KNOWNE TO ALL THAT DO MEE SEE THAT BAGLY OF CHACOM MADE ME 1686 ($37\frac{5}{8}$ in.

6 *Above, a double row of scroll-ornament as before*

THOMAS MAKEPEACE *(border)* AND *(border)* ROBERT *(border)* LADBROOKE CHVRCHWARDENS 1686

On waist and sound bow, five and six coins respectively ($41\frac{3}{4}$ in

One of the latest rings by Henry and Matthew Bagley in partnership (see p 69), all N's reversed, borders thoughout, the scroll, fig 10 (see p 68). H. T T noted in 1875 "1st and 2nd hung above the rest," apparently this is not so now, the bells having recently been rehung.

1552 'Darset Magna iij^or^ belles a saunce belle'

1750 'Dasset Magna 6 bells'

There is a tradition that Cromwell watched the battle of Edge Hill from this tower, and escaped by slipping down a bell-rope!

Customs

Bells rung or chimed for Sunday services

Ringing on Christmas Eve and New Year's Eve, also one night weekly from November 5th to Christmas, for Weddings by request

Death knell as soon as possible after death, on tenor, the tellers are merely three strokes before and after for a man, two similarly for a woman, and one for a child At Funerals the tenor is rung up and then tolled, and also rung up and down after the ceremony.

A bell rung for five minutes before Easter Vestry Meetings

Many thanks to Mr W E Falkner, also to Rev W Westacott, Vicar

H T T, 18 September, 1875

BURTON HASTINGS. St. Botolph — Three bells

1 BRYANVS ELDRIDGE ME FECIT 1657

2 HENRY ✠✠✠✠ BAGLEY ✠✠✠✠ MADE ✠✠✠✠ MEE ✠✠✠✠ 1657

3 ✠ PRASE ✤ GOD ✤ ONLI ♛

1st By Bryan Eldridge of Chertsey, see p 58

2nd arabesques, Fig 11

3rd By one of the Newcombes, see p 37, and cf. Wroxhall 2nd. Marks Pl XVI 2 and XVII 3, *Northants* 86

1552 'iij belles in the steple.'

H T T, 19 August, 1876

BUTLER'S MARSTON. SS Peter and Paul — Five bells.

1 *Above, narrow border, Bucks,* fig 71

✤ WILLIAM ✤ ABRAHAM AND ✤ WILLIAM ✤ LOGGIN ✤ 1662 ✤ ✤✤ ✤✤ (30½ in

2 ✠ SANCTA KATHERINA · ORA : PRO NOBIS (32½ in

3 HENRY *(scroll)* BAGLEE *(scroll)* MADE *(scroll)* ME *(scroll)* 1652 ✤ ✤ (34½ in

4 HENRY ✤ BAGLEE *(border)* MADE *(bit of border)* MEE *(border)* 1652 *(border)* (39 in

5 Vox dni ihu xpi vox exultacionis et salutis  (44 in

1st, 3rd, and 4th by Henry Bagley Border on 3rd, *Bucks*, Pl XXXII 2, on 4th, narrow floral border as on 1st (*Bucks*, fig 71) William Loggin died March, 1714 (Brit Mus. Add MSS 29264, fol 220), the Loggins were a well-to-do family in the parish. The Abrahams lived at the Manor House by the church See Miller, *Rambles round Edge Hill*, p 157

2nd by Robert Hendley of Gloucester (p 7), cross and lettering, Pl V 1—9

5th By Edward Newcombe and Watts in partnership (see p 35), with the Brasyer-Watts shield, cf Bulkington 4th, and see Pl XVII 4, 5

Bells re-hung by Taylor in 1891 at the cost of the Rev J C Gardner, then Vicar Weights given as 7, 9, 11, 15, and 20 cwt, but more accurately they are 6, 7, 8, 11, and 15 cwt

1552 'iiij^or belles one litle bell' 1750, '2 bells' (*sic*)

Customs

- On Sundays bells rung or chimed for twenty minutes before services, followed by tenor and treble successively, each for five minutes, treble rung every Sunday at 8 a m, and also immediately after Morning Service
- Ringing on Christmas Eve for half-an-hour after midnight, also for half-an-hour at midnight on New Year's Eve, for Weddings occasionally, on King's Birthday and November 5th
- Death-knell about an hour after death, tenor rung as minute bell for 15 minutes Muffled peals on burial of any of Royal Family

Treble rung for Vestry Meetings.

Best thanks to Rev. A. P. Dodd, Vicar, and to Mr. Falkner.

H. T. T., 17 Feb., 1875.

CALDECOTE. SS. THEOBALD AND CHAD. Three bells.

1. **NAYLOR VICKERS & C° 1868 SHEFFIELD RIEPE'S PATENT N° 601**

2. *The same, with* **N° 600**

3. *The same, with* **N° 628**

1552; 'CALCOTT. ij belles and a handbell.'
1750: '1 Bell.'

CUSTOMS:

On Sundays bells chimed for all services, including Celebrations at 8 and 11-30.
Ringing for Weddings; ringing or chiming at Funerals; Death-knell tolled.

Thanks to Rev. J. K. Fenton, Rector.

H. T. T., 5 July, 1876.

CASTLE BROMWICH. SS. MARY AND MARGARET. Six bells.

1. IOHN ● THORNTON ● THOMAS ● SADLER ● TRVSTEES ● 1717 (scroll)
Below, scroll-border all round, and on sound-bow a border of simpler narrow scrolls. (26 in.

2. IOHN ● BANNER ● ROLAND ● BRAWBRIDGE ● TRVSTEES 1717 ● (scroll) ●
Below, borders as on last. ($26\frac{1}{2}$ in.

3. **WILLIAM SADLER ISAAC SADLER TRUSTEES. 1717.**
On waist:—**RECAST BY "CHARLES CARR"**
GOLD MEDALLISTS.
SMETHWICK.
1893. ($29\frac{1}{2}$ in.

4. IOHANNES ● BROOKE ● S ● T ● B IOHN CHETTOCK ● CHAPPEL ● WARDEN 1717 ●●
Below, borders as on 1st. (31 in.

5. S^R ● IOHN ● BRIDGEMAN ● (scroll) ● BARONET ● (scroll) ● 1717 (scroll)
Below, borders as before. ($34\frac{1}{2}$ in.

6. *On waist:*—(*a*) **DEO**
18 A D 93
LAUS
I CELEBRATE THE WEDDING DAY
OF GEORGE OF YORK AND PRINCESS MAY

(*b*) **FOUNDED BY "CHARLES CARR"**
GOLD MEDALLISTS.
SMETHWICK.

($39\frac{1}{2}$ in.

Formerly a ring of five by Joseph Smith; the third of these was re-cast and a tenor added in 1893. The old 3rd was inscribed

WILLIAM ● SADLER (*scroll*) ● ISAAC ● SADLER ● TRVSTEES ● 1717 ● (*scroll*) ● (*scroll*)

Weights of new bells 3rd, 6½ cwt., tenor, 11¾ cwt Borders, Pl XXIII 2

1760 '5 Bells'

H T T, 26 Oct, 1881, H B W, March, 1908.

CHADSHUNT ALL SAINTS Six bells.

1 PROCAROLO NEWSHAM HANC RESVNO MVSAM 1693 (26⅝ in

2 NVMEN INEST NVMERIS RICHARD HVNT VICAR 1669 (28⅝ in

3. THOMAS GOODWIN GENT ◆ WILLIAM BEARS C W 1669 (30 in.

4 IN MEDIO TVTISSIMVS IBIS 1669 (33¼ in.

5 AMICI MVSARVM MEI GENITORES 1669 (36 in

6 VITAM EXHILARO MORTEM CONDOLEO WILLIAM DAVIS THOMAS WARD C W 1693 (41⅛ in

A ring of six by Richard Keene of Woodstock (p 59) All cannons off Letters on *paterae*, clearly marked, for the two varieties of type, cf. Wolford.

1st The Newsham family is mentioned in connection with Chadshunt in the reign of Henry I [1] This Charles Newsham was born in 1633, married Elizabeth Hide, and died 10 May, 1705 RESVNO may be either for RESVMO (*i e*, "I resume the poetical effusions on my earlier bells") or RESONO The same inscription is found on the 2nd at Water Stratford, Bucks (see Cocks, *Bucks*, p 585) It probably came there from Chadshunt when Keene increased the ring in 1693, as it bears the date 1669, and was here replaced by a bell with the same inscription

2nd An allusion to 'Divine Poesy"

4th Probably the motto of one of the "friends of the Muses," mentioned on the 5th bell

6th EXHILARO, *i e*, "make cheerful'

Bells re-hung by Bond of Burford 1906

1552 'CHADSON iij belles ij saunce belles'

In the MS additions to Dugdale (Brit Mus Add. MSS 29264, fol 249) is the note '3 Musical Bells' (*sic*)

CUSTOMS

Bells rung for Sunday services when possible, small bell for last five minutes

Midnight peals at Christmas and on New Year's Eve Ringing for Weddings. Practice ringing from November 5th to Christmas

Death-knell at 8 a m on day following, tellers 3 for man, 2 for woman, 1 for child, then brisk tolling for 15 minutes At Funerals the tenor is tolled previously and rung briskly afterwards

A bell rung for Vestry Meetings

Many thanks to Mr W E Falkner and to Rev F Woodward, Vicar

H T T, 19 Sept, 1875

CHARLCOTE ST LEONARD. Two bells

1 WILLIAM BAGLEY MADE MEE 169[?]

[1] See for this family's pedigree, *Warw Ant Mag*, part 2, also Brit Mus Add MSS 29264, fol 242ff, and Add MSS 28564, fol 25

2 RICHARD LEGWIS IOHN DIKINS CHVRCH WARDENS 169Γ

Bells removed from the old church to the new, both by William Bagley, whose spelling like that of other members of the family, was somewhat weak LEGWIS presumably is for LEWIS, DIKINS for DICKINS The 7 of the date is reversed in each case

1750, '5 Bells' (*sic*)
Notes and Queries, 3rd Ser, X (1866) p 143
H T T, 3 Aug, 1881

CHERINGTON. St. Nicholas Five bells

1 **E TIMMS C WARDEN W & J TAYLOR FOUNDERS 1842**

2 **EDW^D TIMMS C WARDEN W & J TAYLOR FOUNDERS OXFORD 1842**

3 *On crown* —1742
WILLIAMS DICKINGS NICKLAS HOLTOM THOMAS ATTWOOD C W H B M^A ME

4 *On crown* —1742
W DICKINGS N HOLTOM T ATTWOOD CHURCH WARDENS H BAGLEY MADE ME

5 **THE REV^D POWER TURNER RECTOR EDW^D TIMMS C WARDEN 1842** ✠ ✠

3rd and 4th cast by Henry Bagley III at Chacomb (see p 71)

1552 'iiij bells and a litle bell.'
Mem the p'ishe hathe solde sythe the last survey one bell to the Amending of highe ways & the Repac ons of theyr churche

1750 Cherrington 5 bells'

Up to 1842 there were only three bells, according to the present Rector, but this is at variance with Browne Willis' statement

Customs

On Sundays one bell rung at 8 a m, two at 9 a m ("Mattins and Mass Bells') For services, bells chimed for five minutes then Sermon Bell for ten (except on Sacrament Sundays), chime for ten minutes, and toll in on treble for five

A bell is rung for five minutes after Morning Service

Ringing on Festivals, and two or three times weekly from November to Christmas, also for Weddings by request

Death-knell as soon as notice is given, usual tellers At Funerals the "Inviting Bell is rung two hours previously to give notice to bearers (as at Tysoe), tolling for half-an-hour before the ceremony, and again afterwards

A bell is rung for Vestry or Parish Meetings

Modern Belfry Rules

Best thanks to Rev H O Barratt Rector
H T T 20 June, 1879

CHESTERTON St Giles Three bells

1 GOD SAVE THE QVEEN A R 1705

2 GOD SAVE THE QVEEN & CHVRCH A R 1705

3 WILLIAM PEYTO ESQ[R] GAVE THE CASTING OF VS ALL 1705

All by Abraham Rudhall of Gloucester, narrow running border (Fig 16) on 1st and 2nd

1552 'Itm there ij belles'
1750 '5 bells'

The Peyto family became owners of Chesterton about 1354 Dugdale (i p 471) gives an account of them down to 1658 which is continued in Brit Mus Add MSS 29264, fol 188ff This William Peyto was M P for the county 1722-1727, died Jan 1734, and was buried at Chesterton, being the last of the family in the main line The property then went to Lord Willoughby de Broke There is a very interesting account of him, especially of the end of his life, in the MS above referred to

H T T, 19 Sept, 1875

CHILVERS COTON ALL SAINTS Eight bells

1 GLORY TO GOD IN THE HIGHEST

Below all round, vine border, on waist — O 1907 (24½ in

2. ON EARTH PEACE GOODWILL TOWARD MEN

Below as on last (25½ in

3 MAKE THEM TO BE NUMBERED WITH THY SAINTS

Below as No 1 (27½ in.

4  CELORVM CHRSTE PLATIAT TIBI REX SONVS ISTE 1616

On waist, Taylor's trade-mark as before, and RECAST 1907 (29¼ in.

5  IHS NAZARENVS REX · IVDEORVM FILI. DEI MISERERE. MEI 1639

Below, Watts' arabesque pattern all round, on waist as last (32 in.

6.  GOD *(border)* SAVE *(border)* THE *(border)* KINGE *(border)* 1616

On waist as No 4 (34 in

7 RING OUT THE FALSE RING IN THE TRUE

Below as No 1 (37½ in

8 RING OUT THE DARKNESS OF THE LAND RING IN THE CHRIST THAT IS TO BE

Below as No 1 (42½ in

This new ring by Taylor of Loughborough, whose trade-mark occurs on the waist of each, was dedicated on Sunday, February 2nd, 1908, by the Dean of Hereford the cost having been

£312 [1] The first peal on them was rung on Saturday the 8th Previously there were only three bells all by Hugh Watts of Leicester, of which the 2nd had long been cracked The inscriptions on these three have been exactly reproduced on the new bells That on the 6th (old tenor) is in the Brasyer lettering, with the 'acorn' border (Pl XVII 7) between the words, the letters on the old treble were smaller than on the 2nd

The Vicar describes the old 1st and 3rd as 'of very poor tone and false harmonies'

The old bell frame, dated 1601, with the inscription 'ANNO 1601 TC TC' has been worked up into a new altar for the church

Weights of new bells —1)	3	2	27	F sharp	5)	6	0	3	B
2)	3	3	14	E sharp	6)	7	0	23	A sharp
3)	4	1	7	D sharp	7)	9	1	12	G sharp
4)	4	3	10	C sharp	8)	13	1	24	F sharp

The three old bells weighed respectively 4, 5, and 6 cwt (diams 27, 29, and 31 in)

1552 'CHILVERSCOTTON Itm there . ij belles in the steple'
'M^d that the p'ishe have solde sithence the last s^rvey oon broken bell to the mending of highewaies and rep'ac'ons of their church'

1750 '4 Bells'

CUSTOMS —

On Sundays bells chimed for 30 or 40 minutes before services, with single bell for last five minutes, also chimed at 8 a m

Death Knell with usual tellers; larger bell for adults, smaller for child

[These refer to the old ring of three, doubtless ringing will now be regularly practised].

Many thanks to Rev R Chadwick, Vicar, Mr W E Falkner, and Messrs Taylor

H T T, 18 Sept, 1876

CHURCH LAWFORD. ST PETER Four bells

1  **MARKE** (*border*) **BREWSTER** (*border*) **GAVE** (*border*) **THE** (*border*) **GREAT** (*border*) **BELL** (*border*) **OF** (*border*) **THIS** (*border*) **RINGE** (*border*) **1621** (28½ in

2 **J: TAYLOR & C^O FOUNDERS LOUGHBOROUGH 1872**
On waist —**GLORIA DEO SOLI** (29½ in.

3 *As No 2*
On waist —**OMNIA FIAT** (*sic*) **AD GLORIAM DEI** (31½ in

4. **JOHN TAYLOR & C^O FOUNDERS LOUGHBOROUGH 1872**
On waist —**HANC PETRI CAMPANA SERVA SANCTISSIMI** (35½ in

Treble by Watts of Leicester, with Brasyer shield, and bits of 'acorn' border between words The inscription on the waist of the 3rd is characteristic of Tobie Norris of Stamford (p 60), but there is no evidence that it is reproduced from an old bell, and he would not have been guilty of the false concord! The tenor is even worse in this respect, being an inaccurate version of the old inscription which was also ungrammatical! (See below)

Weight of bells —1)	4	3	14	3)	5	2	27	
2)	5	1	4	4)	8	1	0	Total 24 cwt 17 lbs

[1] See *Nuneaton Chronicle*, 7 Feb, *Bell News*, 22 Feb

1552 'CHURCHE LAWEFORDE Two belles in the steple'
1760 '3 Bells'

Mark Brewster, who gave the 'great bell,' is probably identical with the donor of the tenor at Marston Trussel, Northants, dated 1623 (see North's *Northants*, p 333) He was a wool-merchant of London, and died at Moscow in 1612, leaving a bequest for the bell above-mentioned, there is a monument to him in Marston Trussel church

From the Rev W O Wait's *Rugby Past and Present* (p 237) we learn that previous to 1872 (when the church was rebuilt) there were only three bells, and that they were inscribed as follows

1 GLORIA DEO SOLI 1741

2 Hanc Petri campana serba sanctissime sanc

3 *Present treble*

This will account for the present treble being described as 'the great bell,' if it was formerly the tenor, but the other two must have been very small I will not venture any conjecture as to the founder of the first, the inscription has been reproduced on the present 2nd, as has that on the old 2nd with less success on the present tenor It is possible that the last-named was really inscribed in Gothic capitals, not black-letter, but the inscription is not sufficiently characteristic of any foundry to hazard a guess as to where the bell was cast

Mr Wait also states that a small hand-bell, two inches in diameter, was found in the rebuilding of the church

H T T, 8 March, 1887

CHURCHOVER. HOLY TRINITY Four bells

1  **GOD** *(border)* **SAVE** *(border)* **THE** *(border)* **KING** *(border)* **1622** *(border)*

2  **IHS: NAZARENVS** *(border)* **REX IVDEORVM FILI. DEI** *(border)* **MISERERE MEI** *(border)* **1622**

3 J VOILE C WARDEN J BRIANT & J OVER HERTFORD FECERUNT 1803

4 ✠ S I O K A N N E S 

1st and 2nd by Watts, HE of THE conjoined

3rd J Over was a bell-hanger at Rugby, and acted as Briant's agent (see p 80)

4th By one of the Newcombes (see p 34) stamps, Pl XVI 2, *Leics* 43, and Fig 7, usual Newcombe lettering The H in IOHANNES is replaced by a K

1552 'CHURCHWAUER iij belles and saunce belle'
1750 '5 Bells

H T T, 13 Oct, 1897

CLAVERDON ST MICHAEL Six bells

1 LESTER & PACK OF LONDON FECIT 1757

2. RECAST BY JOHN WARNER & SONS LTD LONDON 1892

3 1757

4 *As No 1*

5 IN WEDLOCKS BANDS ALL YE WHO JOIN WITH HAND YOUR HEARTS UNITE
(2nd line) —

SO SHALL OUR TUNEFUL TONGUS COMBINE TO LAUD THE NUPTIAL RITE
LESTER & PACK OF LONDON

(3rd line) —

FECIT 1757

6 THOMAS LESTER & THOS PACK OF LONDON 1757 RECAST BY JOHN WARNER & SONS LTD LONDON

On waist — LAUS DEO
1892

Tenor 13 cwt The whole ring originally by Lester and Pack, 1757, the inscription on the old 2nd has not been preserved, but was probably the same as the 1st (cf *Notices of Warwickshire Churches*, ii p 34) The date on the 3rd is incised

Clock strikes on tenor

The inscription on the old 6th was

THOMAS LESTER & THO[S] PACK OF LONDON 1757 ✧◇◇✧ *(border continuous)*,
the date being incised

1552 'CLAREDON It'm there iij belles' 1750 '6 Bells'

See *Notices of Warwickshire Churches*, ii p 34

H T T, 24 Jan, 1882, 26 Aug, 1904

CLIFTON. St Mary Five bells.

1 *On waist* —*(a)* TO THE GREATER GLORY OF GOD
AND IN MEMORY OF THE REIGN OF QUEEN
VICTORIA
1837—1901
THIS BELL IS ADDED TO THE PEAL NOW REHUNG
1903
(b) Barwell's trade-mark (30½ in

2  IHS NAZARENVS *(border)* REX IVDEORVM *(border)* FILI DEI *(border)* MISERERE MEI *(border)* 1624 *(border)* ✝ *(border)* (31 in

3  MILIK IIHIGI *(border)* FIEIDICIBIAI *(border)* IXIWIVITISI *(border)* IRIQIPIOINI *(border)* 1640 *(border)* (32½ in

4 HENRICVS BACLEY ME FECIT 1670

On waist —(*a*) **RECAST 1903** (*b*) *Barwell's mark*

CHARLES PEAT SHEPPARD M.A. VICAR'
SIR PHILIP ALBERT MUNTZ BART M P. }
THOMAS SUTTON TOWNSEND ESQ J P. } **CHVRCHWARDENS**
WILLIAM HARRATT PARISH CLERK (35 in

5. SOLI DEO GLORIA PAX HOMINIBVS 1655 I M (39 in

Formerly four bells, the old 3rd, which was cracked, recast with inscription reproduced (but not in facsimile, the borders between the words being also omitted), and new treble added 1903

2nd and 3rd by Hugh Watts, the 3rd in thin medium sized letters, there are similar bells at Newton Regis and Seckington (see p 44) The 2nd is of the usual type, with a small cross crosslet in the middle of the border after the date ' Acorn" borders on each bell, and on the 3rd arabesques below the inscription

5th by John Martin of Worcester, cross and ornament between words, Pl XXI, Figs 6, 7 ' Poor tone' (H T T)

Frames for eight bells, all of iron, by Barwell, whose name appears on the stock of each bell, the cannons have all been replaced by ugly circular caps screwed to the stocks

Weight of new treble, 5 cwt 2 qrs 3 lbs, of new 4th, 8 cwt 1 qr 17 lbs.

The cost of the two new bells was £227 5s $3\frac{1}{2}$d, including value of old metal

1552 ' iiij or belles and a saunce belle'

' Md that oon bell is sold to bild their bridge sithe the last s'vey'

See Wait, *Rugby Past and Present*, p 194

No Customs

Many thanks to Rev F D Lane, Vicar

H T T., 22 Jan, 1892 H B W, June, 1908

COLESHILL SS PETER AND PAUL Six bells

1 *Above, border as Plate XXIII, Fig 2*

THE ● GIFT ● OF ● HENRY ● SMITH ● OF ● COLESHILL ● GENT ● 1720

Below, border as before (Diam $28\frac{1}{4}$ in

2 ● GOD ● SAVE ● HIS ● CHURCH ● 1720 ●

Below and on rim, border as before

3 IOSEPH ● SMITH ● IN ● EDGBASTON ● MADE ● ME ● 1720 ●

Borders as on last

4 ● IOHN COLE AND THOMAS BRVCE ● ● CHVRCH ● WARDENS ● 1720 ●●

Borders as before

5 Mr DIGBE ● COATS ● RECTER ● ● 1720 ● ●●●

Borders as before

6 MY ● MOVRNFVLL ● SOVND ● DOTH ● WARNEING ● GIVE THAT HEAR MEN ● CAN NOT ● ALLWAYS LIVE 1720

Borders as before (Diam 40½ in.

On each bell, Joseph Smith's trade-mark (Pl XXIII 1) as at Sedgeley, Staffs, and Sheriff Hales Salop The coins between the words appear to be Charles II s

Weight of tenor, 16¾ cwt Bells rehung in 1907 in memory of J K D Wingfield Digby, M P, to whom a tablet is placed in the Ringing Chamber

1552 'COLSHULL Itm there iij belles
'Md that the p'ishe have sold sithence the last S'vey oon of the forsaid belles to repaere their steple'

Dugdale (ii p 1014) notes that the spire was injured by lightning about the year 1550

1750 'Colshill 6 Bells'

CUSTOMS —

Bells rung or chimed on Sundays for services, with 'Sermon Bell' for last five minutes Treble rung at 8 a m when no early service

Ringing on Festivals (Easter, Whitsuntide Christmas) and for Harvest Festival on New Year's Eve the new year is rung in with a peal Also on Accession Day (January 22), Empire Day (24 May) Coronation Day (9 August) and King's Birthday, for Weddings by request

Both ringing and chiming formerly customary at Funerals, but now discontinued

Treble or 2nd bell rung daily at 7 a m and 1 p m Curfew rung on 5th at 8 p m with day of month on tenor

Pancake Bell at 11 a m on Shrove Tuesday (4th and 5th bells)

A bell rung for Vestry meetings

Treble and tenor rung in cases of Fire

Best thanks to Rev F W Wingfield Digby, Vicar

Mr Tilley notes that the tower was built in 1412 and eight bells hung in it [this is surely wrong] they were rehung in 1620, and two sold, the rest were recast in 1720, which would have reduced the ring to five owing to loss of metal, but a new treble was given by Henry Smith, of Coleshill

The Rev D Coats (5th bell) was Prebendary of Lichfield and Principal of Magdalen Hall, Oxford, he died Jan 1745

H T T 14 June 1882

COMBROOKE St MARGARET Three bells

There are here three small bells cast by Mears and Stainbank in 1867 which replace a mediaeval bell, of which a record has been preserved in Mr Kimber's drawings of bell-inscriptions at the Whitechapel foundry It had no inscription, but three medallions round the shoulder. (1) occuring twice, with IHS, (2) with quatrefoil rosette, (3) with interlacing triangles See Fig 4, p 28 The date was probably about 1500-1530, cf a similar bell at Ford, Shropshire The present bells hang in a small open turret and are very awkward to reach, the attempt would hardly appear to be worth making They weigh respectively 1 cwt 1 qr 5 lbs, 1 cwt 3 qrs 8 lbs and 2 cwt 1 qr 16 lbs (diam 19, 20 and 22 in)

1552 'CUMBROKE ij belles one little bell'

On Sundays a bell rung at 8 a m , chiming for services
Death Knell immediately on receiving notice, tellers, 3 male, 2 female, 1 for child
Tolling at Funerals Ringing for Weddings and on November 5th
A bell rung for Vestry meetings
Thanks to Rev T Lloyd, Vicar

COMPTON, LITTLE.

Parish formerly in Gloucestershire, now transferred to Warwickshire though still in Gloucester diocese There are five bells by Rudnall dated 1720 (one re-cast 1810), an account of which is given by Ellacombe in his *Church Bells of Gloucestershire*, p 163

COMPTON, LONG SS PETER AND PAUL 6+1 bells

1 **IAMES WALKER ✤ ANTHONEY RAWLINS ✤ 1652 ✤ R K** *(border)*

2 **THOMAS SHEPPARD ✤ RICHARD BVLLER ✤ C W ✤ I K 1652 ✤**

3 **HENRY BAGLEY MADE MEE OCTOBER 1731 IAMES TAPIN BENEFACTOR**

4 **JOHN FOWLER & WILLIAM TAYLOR C W ✠ WIL^M & J TAYLOR FOUNDERS OXFORD 1823**

5 **ANTHONY NEWMAN IOHN WALKER CHURCH : WARDENS IAMES TAPIN BENEFACTOR 1731 ·**

6 **IAMES COMPTON EARL OF NORTHAMPTON · ELIZABETH COMPTON : COUNTIS NORTHAMPTON · ···· ·**
EDWARD SHELDON ESQVIRE IOHN BROWN VICKOR BENEFACTERS HENRY BAGLEY MADE MEE 1731 (40 in.

S *(Unintelligible six small minuscule letters and a fleur de-lys)* (13¾ in

Belfry dirty and neglected Sanctus bell rung by lever The third bell is cracked

The 1st and 2nd are apparently by Richard and James Keene, of Woodstock, in partnership, the latter died in 1654. See p 59 The fleur-de-lys is Pl XIX, Fig 7, also used by Hancox, the border at end of 1st is *Bucks*, p 164, fig 62

4th the type is like John Briant s

6th the stops are dots variously grouped See p 71 Bagley's list gives the name Sheldon incorrectly as S England

Sanctus · inscription unintelligible, probably of the 16th century, see p 27 and Pl XV, Fig 1 This formerly hung in its original cot, still existing on the E end of the nave

1552 · 'LONGE COMPTON iiij belles a saunce bell a little bell'
1750 'Compton Longa 6 bells

Passing bell rung at time of death tolling at Funerals
A bell every Sunday at 8 a m , chiming for services, sanctus bell rung for the last five minutes
Ringing on Festivals

James Compton, 5th Earl of Northampton (see tenor), was summoned to the House of Lords as Baron Compton in 1711 He married Elizabeth, Baroness Ferrers, and died 3 October, 1754

Edward Sheldon of Weston House was born in 1679, and married Elizabeth Shelley. He was descended from the Sheldons of Beoley and Steeple Barton See Dugdale i p 584, and Brit Mus Add MSS 29,264, fol 215

Best thanks to Rev W Crompton, formerly Vicar

H T T, 20 June, 1879, H B W, April, 1907

COMPTON VERNEY

One bell

1 W & P TAYLOR FOUNDES OXFORD 1852 *(head)* ✠

(27 in.

In a turret on the roof of the church and very difficult of access, requiring two long ladders The stamp after the date appears to be the head of a cherub The P as founder's initial appears to be a mistake for J

Many thanks to Mr W E Falkner

COMPTON WINYATES

One bell

1 ✠ O WILLIAM & JOHN TAYLOR OXFORD FOUNDERS O

On sound-bow —THIS BELL WAS RECAST IN THE YEAR OF OUR LORD 1847 FROM A BELL GIVEN TO THIS CHURCH BY WILLIAM COMPTON FIRST EARL OF NORTHAMPTON IN THE YEAR OF OUR LORD 1628

The original bell was probably by James Keene

1760 'Compton Vineyard 1 bell'

William Compton, son of Sir Henry Compton, Knt, was born about 1580, and was created Earl of Northampton in 1619, and Knight of the Garter He died in 1630, and was buried in this church See Colvile's *Worthies of Warwickshire*, p 133

H T T, 17 Jan, 1876

COPSTON MAGNA St John.

One bell

1 C & G MEARS FOUNDERS LONDON 185-

The bell hangs in an open gable-cot at a considerable height, and would be difficult to reach even if a ladder were available The last figure of the date, being on the south side of the bell, is unfortunately hidden by the wheel but the rest of the inscription could be clearly seen with glasses The date must be between 1850 and 1856

H B W, May, 1908

CORLEY

Five bells

1 GOD SAVE THE KING 1641 (22 in

2 ✠ GLORIA TIBI DOMINE (24 in

3 HENRICVS BAGLEY ME FECIT 1702 (24⅓ in

4 *No inscription* (28 in.

5 IESVS BEE OVR SPEED WILLIAM HALLEY FRANCIS MILLER WARDENS | 1631

On waist —(T H) (30¼ in

1st By Hugh Watts, lion's head (Fig 7) in place of shield, arabesques (Pl XVII 9) between words, HE of THE conjoined

2nd By Johannes de Colsale, *c* 1410 (see p 18), similar bell at Stoke See Plate IX, Figs 6 8

3rd Cast at Chacomb or Ecton (see p 71) arabesques (Fig 11) between words

4th Three rows of beading in place of an inscription-band, H T T notes 'probably an ancient bell' but it looks to me of more recent date

5th By Thomas Hancox (see p 52), borders, Plate XX, Fig 6=Fig 8 on p 54, after SPELD, HALLEY, and MILLER, after WARDENS unintelligible pattern, after date a broad cable-pattern (Pl XX 4), on waist, shield with anchor and I H (Plate XIX, Fig 2) Small letters, a reduced version of the ordinary type (see p 54)

The bells hang in a curious low wooden turret over the east end of the nave, practically invisible from outside, and are approached from the west end along the roof They are very cramped in the limited space A light ring, the total weight being computed at about one ton

1552 Itm two belles' [Query, the present 2nd and 4th ?]
M[d] that there was oon bell solde to relyve the poor before the last s[r]vey

The bells are rung two or three times a week during Advent

Death-knell for one hour at 8 a m on following morning tolling at Funerals

The Churchwardens Accounts appear to contain nothing of interest except payments for 'ile' for the bells

Best thanks to Rev V K Fortescue, Rector

H T T, 29 July, 1876, H B W May, 1908

COUGHTON ST PETER. Six bells

1 MATTHEW ●● BAGLEY ●●● MADE (Fig 11) MEE (Fig 11) 1686
Below, border of complete arabesques (Fig 11) *all round* (29 in.

2 CANTATE : DOMINO CANTICVM NOVVM 1686 (30⅜ in.

3 *As No 1, with border as 2nd throughout and after date* (32½ in

4 HENRY (*border as 1st*) BAGLEY (*border*) MADE (*border*) MEE (*border*) 1686 (*border*) ● (35 in.

5 FEARE GOD AND HONNOR THE KING 1686 (*border*) (37¼ in

6 CAMPANA (*arabesques*) GRAVIDA (*arabesques*) ● PEPRIT (*arabesques*) FILIAS (*arabesques*) 1686 (*arabesques*) (*Eight coins on sound-bow*) (42 in

Borders the same throughout (Fig 11, slightly varied), but on the 1st and 4th the upper part has been cut away in each case A joint ring by the two Bagleys, probably their last production before they separated (see p 69) The last word on the tenor *may be* FELIAS The jest on this bell, which is perpetrated on another of Bagley s bells at Dodford Northants, implies the recasting of its predecessor into two bells Probably there were five before 1686

Bells rehung in 1893

1552 'Item there ij bells' 1750 '6 bells'

See *Notices of Warwickshire Churches*, ii p 145

CUSTOMS —

Bells chimed for Sunday services with tolling in for last five minutes

Ringing on greater Festivals, Christmas Eve, and New Year's Eve, also on the birthday of Sir William Throgmorton, the Squire.

A bell tolled at 8 a m on the day of a funeral

Best thanks to Rev C F Eagles, Vicar, and to Mr Falkner

H T T, 19 Oct, 1881

COVENTRY — CHRIST CHURCH — One bell

1 W & J TAYLOR FOUNDERS 1851

Below, figure of ox to left (for Oxford?)

The steeple of the church was left standing when the Monastery of the Greyfriars was dissolved, but no new church was consecrated until 1832 There was probably no bell during the intervening period

H T T, 21 July, 1891

COVENTRY. — HOLY TRINITY — Eight bells

1 *On sound-bow* —C & G MEARS FOUNDERS LONDON (31 in

2 *The same* (32 in

3 *The same* (34 in

4. *The same* (36 in

5 *The same* (39 in

6 *The same* (41 in

7 THESE SEVEN BELLS WERE RECAST A D 1856
On sound-bow, as before (44 in

8 **J TAYLOR & C° FOUNDERS LOUGHBOROUGH.**
On waist —**VOX MEA AD GLORIAM SANCTÆ TRINITATIS CLAMAT**
ADESTE FIDELES
RECAST 1898.
REV CANON BEAUMONT, VICAR
JOHN POWERS
WALTER HEWITT } **CHURCHWARDENS**
ALBERT HORTON
W P. COLLINGBOURNE ACCOUNT CHURCHWARDEN (51 in

The old tenor was cracked in 1891, a piece broken out of the sound-bow, and the crack sawn off smooth (H T T) It was inscribed

THE REV^D JOSEPH RANN L L B VICAR WILLIAM GRANT EDWARD KING JOSEPH CATTELL & ROBERT JARVIS CHURCH WARDENS 1776

Below —PACK & CHAPMAN OF LONDON FECIT

Diam 50 in, weight 20 cwt 18 lbs. Weights of present ring

	cwt	qrs	lbs		cwt	qrs	lbs
1)	6	1	6	5)	10	0	8
2)	6	3	14	6)	11	2	21
3)	7	1	20	7)	13	-	17
4)	8	1	3	8)	23	1	15

According to Sharp, *Hist of Coventry* (*ed* Fretton, 1871), p 113ff there are no records of the bells before 1563 He quotes the following —

1563 Pd for mendynge Saunse Bell
1573 [A similar entry]
In the same year the Parish purchased of the Mayor and Corporation for £20 a large bell from the dissolved monastery of the White Friars —
Item payed for drawynge the bell from the fryers ij^s
Item payed for mendynge the churche wall where the bell was broughte in xij^d
Item payed for hangynge the bell . xxvj^s viij^d
Item payed for planks to laye over the hole of the steple under ye bells ij^s vj^d
[Sundry other charges for clapper, brasses, ropes, and baldrick]
1574 Receyved of Mr Maior and the reste of yo'r worshyppes for the of the vestrye towards the pavenge for the greate bell – xvj^{li} v^s iiij^d
Item payed to Mr Maior and his brethren for the grete bell at the p'ler dore xx^{li}
1577 A bell recast at Leicester this year for £7
1579 A bell recast and bell frames repaired for £11 10*s* 1*d*
1588 A bell recast by Newcombe of Leicester for £10 17*s* 6*d*
1589 pd for Ringing the Lord Bishopp into the Citty – ij^d
1595 pd M Newcom' of Leices' for casting of the bell and for his new mettle he put in besides the mettell of the little Bell . vj^{li} xvj^s
Pd for chargis of iij men & ix horses at Leicester iij dayes and iiij nights liij^s iiij^d
Pd for Carriadge of the bell to Leic v^s
Total of expenses £16 13*s* 7*d*
1613 A bell recast by Newcombe for £12 12*s* 6*d*
Rec^d for the Lord Barkley[1] x peales . iij^s iiij^d
1614 paid for ringing when the Bishopp came ij^s
1616 A bell recast by Watts of Leicester for £14 7*s* 5*d*
1617 The fourth bell recast by Watts for £10, with carriage etc, £17 0*s* 2*d*
paid for ringing when the King came to Coventrey v^s
1620 paid for ringing upon the day of Gouri's[2] conspiracy ij^s vj^d
1623 New bell frames
1625 Watts contracts with the parish to recast the 5th or tenor bell, and to warrant it for a twelve month and a day, receiving 15*s* per cwt for recasting and 1*s* per lb for new metal If obliged to cast it twice he is to receive 20*s* per cwt
1626 paid to Mr. Watts for casting the great Bell xviij^{li} v^s
1638 An order made for a bell to be regularly rung at 5 a m
1642 On the appointment of a new Sexton, order is made for a bell to be rung at 5 a m, 6 a m and 6, 7 and 8 p m
1644 pd for ringing the 8th of July when Prince Robert (*sic*) was routed 2*s*
pd for ringing for the taking of Shrewsbury 2*s* 6*d*
1654 Given to the Ringers on the thanksgiven daie, when the peace was concluded betweene England & Holland . . 1*s* 6*d*
On the 18th July a new bell frame was agreed for, the charge for workmanship being £18, for timber etc, £13 16*s* 8*d*
On the 13th July Mr Watts[3] being informed that the Vestry intended selling the great bell, applied for the refusal, which was promised him, but no further account can be traced
1658 The Mayor bought and presented to the church a treble bell, making six
1659 Putting the 6th Bell into the chymes & altering the tune . 3*l* 11*s*
[The chimes were set up in 1623, see Sharp, p 115]

---

[1] At his funeral The usual number is five peals See Introduction, p 91

[2] The Earl of Gowrie's conspiracy against James VI of Scotland in 1600 must be meant, but it is not easy to see why it should be celebrated in Coventry twenty years later

[3] There must be some mistake here Watts died in 1645

1660	pd for ringing all night when the King came to London	12s
1662	pd for ringing when the Bishop came first to this Citie, 3 days	10s
	for ringing the Bishop in and out the second time	6s
	for the like the third time	5s
	pd for ringing at Mr Wanley's induction[1]	4s
1687	pd for ringing when the King was here	6s 8d
1688	pd for ringing for the Prince of Wales	2s. 6d.
	when the Princess Ann was in Towne	5s
	when the B'ps came out of the Tower	2s 6d
1709	Bells rehung	
1711	pd to the Ringers when Dr Sacheverell came to Town	5s
1717	pd the Ringers at the acquitting the Lord Mortimer	5s
1776	29 July A new peal of bells ordered to be cast by Pack and Chapman the tenor to weigh 20 cwt The founders received £284 4s	
1801	Bell frame repaired by H [J?] Over at a cost of £26 15s 6d	

Four of the bells having been cracked were removed from the tower, and in 1855 seven were recast by Mears at a cost of £162 16s the whole ring being hung in a timber campanile where they still are

Browne Willis' list (c 1750) gives '6 Bells'

See also *Notes and Queries* 3rd Ser x (1866), p 143

CUSTOMS —

On Sundays bells chimed for services at 8, 11, 3 and 6-30, 'sermon bell' for last five minutes before Morning and Evening Prayer, on the tenor.

Ringing on Christmas and New Years Eve, practice for six weeks before Christmas

Ringing on King's Birthday, for visit of Bishop, Blue Coat School sermons, and for weddings by request, also on proclamation of peace (? in 1902)

Death knell immediately after death, bells tolled singly and doubly, with usual tellers at beginning and end Muffled peals rung sometimes after Funerals

Curfew on 3rd bell at 8 p m

Pancake Bell on Shrove Tuesday, 4th bell, at 11-30 a m

A bell tolled before Vestry Meetings

An endowment of £100 exists, the interest of which is given to the ringers for a muffled peal on January 24th in memory of one Thomas Smith

Very many thanks to Rev Canon Beaumont, Vicar

H T T, 21 July, 1891

COVENTRY ST JOHN BAPTIST Five bells.

1 HENRICVS ⁂ BAGLEY ⁂ ME ⁂ FECIT ⁂ 1676 ⁂ (27 in

2 RICHARD EATON CH WARDEN 1778 PACK & CHAPMAN OF LONDON FECIT (29½ in

3 *On the crown* – Ꝗ SCI IOHIS

HENRIC DODENHALE ME FIERI FECIT (31½ in

[1] The Rev Nathaniel Wanley was Vicar of Holy Trinity 1662–1680 He must not be confounded with Humphrey Wanley the antiquary

4 ✠ IOHES MALLERI AND ALISANDER YO VICA OF KYRKBY (33½ in

5. I RING ✠ AT ✠ SIX ✠ TO LET MNE KNOW WHEN ✠ TOO AND FROM ✠ THEAIR ✠ WORKE TO GO G R 1675 (38 in

Border on 1st Fig 9

3rd Probably by a Leicester founder (see p 13), cross, stop, and letters, Plate VIII We have a clue to the date of this bell in the name of the donor, Henricus Dodenhale, as one Henry Dodenhale was Mayor of Coventry in 1355 (Dugdale, i, p 147) He came from Doddenhall, in Polesworth parish, the nuns of which place celebrated solemn Masses for his soul (*Ibid* ii, p 1119) The stamps were afterwards in the hands of the Newcombes (see p. 34) This church was dedicated in 1350[1]

4th By Johannes de Stafford (p 15, Plate VII, 16-19) I have not been able to discover anything about Alexander Yo (? Yeo),[2] but John Mallery lived about 1360—1400, which fact may bear on the date of this bell

5th By Henry Bagley, from the old ring at St Michael's, where it was used, as the inscription shews, as the daily bell for workers (see what is said under that head, p 150, it is also there noted that the old cracked treble was recast in 1675 for the St Michael's ring, and probably its place was supplied here by the present treble of 1676) Its weight is 9cwt 3qrs 21lbs (Sharp, *History and Antiquities of Coventry*, p 66)

Sharp, *op cit p* 151 (Fretton's edition of 1871), gives some account of these bells, with sundry extracts from records here quoted He notes that while the church was the chapel of the Trinity Guild there were at least three bells, one known as the Trinity Bell, as chimes are mentioned in 1461

1457	It' p' una corde p' campana misse matutinat' infra Babl' pond' xij *lb* pric' .	xviij^{d}
1459	It'm p' faccone unius clap' campane apud babl' pond xxiij *lb*	xvj^{d}
	It' p' j corda p le wyndyng up de la peyce orilagii[3] apud bablake	viij^{d}
1461	It' sol' Will' o Melody p' uno Gojeon[4] p' le chyme ap'd Babl'	j^{d}
1463	It' sol' p' ij bawdrykes p' ij campanis apud bablake	xvj^{d}
	It' sol' p' belropes usq' ad bablake	xvj^{d}
	It' p' j belrope p' le Trynite bells apud bablake pond' x *lb*	xij^{d} ob
1466	It p' a roppe weyng xiiij *lb* to the chyme at bablake . . .	xvj^{d}
1466	5 July It' p ij p'ms ca pa'is p' le churche mynday & Bablake	v^{d}

[Sharp has come to grief over this entry, which I quote as he gives, but I think 'p'ms' should obviously read 'p'uis,' *i e* 'parvis,' 'mynday,' which he interprets as Monday, is clearly 'mind-day,' or 'memorial day']

1467	It' p' a gogyn & ij stapelys for the bellys at bablake . . .	x^{d}
1468	It' sol' p' grese ad ca'panas de bablake .	j^{d} ob
1519	It' pd for the mendyng of the whele at the bell for the Rodemasse	xij^{d}
	It' pd for a horsse hyde to make Bawdrikks for bablake .	ij^{s} iiij^{d}

In 1633 Richard Barratt was appointed to ring at 5 a m and 7 p m Down to 1834 the 4th bell was rung at 4 a m every morning, this was known as the 'Dyers' Bell'

Browne Willis (*c* 1750) gives 'Bablack 4 or 5 Bells'

---

[1] Brayley and Britton, *Beauties of England and Wales* xv, pt 2 p 131

[2] It is tempting to suppose that he was Vicar of Kirkby Mallory, in Leicestershire Unfortunately the list of vicars of the parish about 1350—1400 is defective (cf Nichols, *Leicestershire*, iv, p 761)

[3] Clock weight

[4] Gudgeon

CUSTOMS —

On Sundays bells rung to within five minutes of service-time, when the tenor is tolled

The bells are rung for first Evensong, Holy Communion, and second Evensong on al Festivals, after midnight on Christmas Eve, and on New Year's Eve after midnight (tolling up to twelve), for one hour on six Saturday evenings before Christmas, and for Weddings, if paid for

Death-knell 12 hours after death, bells tolled successively and afterwards in pairs, with usual tellers at beginning and end.

Tolling on tenor at Funerals, followed by tellers as before

Best thanks to the Rector, Rev A G Robinson

H T T. 21 July, 1891

COVENTRY. ST MICHAEL Ten bells

1 ALTHOUGH I AM BOTH LIGHT & SMALL I WILL BE HEARD ABOVE YOU ALL
PACK & CHAPMAN OF LONDON FECIT 1774 (33 in

2 IF YOU HAVE A JUDICIOUS EAR YOULL OWN MY VOICE IS SWEET & CLEAR
PACK, *etc*, *as last* (34 in

3 SUCH WONDROUS POWR TO MUSICS GIVEN IT ELEVATES THE SOUL TO HEAVEN
2nd line —PACK, *etc* (36 in.

4 WHILST THUS WE JOIN IN CHEARFULL SOUND MAY LOVE AND LOYALTY ABOUND
PACK *etc* (37 in

5 TO HONOUR BOTH OF GOD AND KING OUR VOICES SHALL IN CONSERT RING
PACK, *etc* (38 in

6 MUSICK IS MEDICINE TO THE MIND THOMAS MEARS OF LONDON
FECIT 1799 (40¼ in

7 YE RINGERS ALL THAT PRIZE YOUR HEALTH AND HAPPINESS BE SOBER MERRY WISE AND YOULL THE SAME POSSESS
PACK, *etc*, *as 1st* (42½ in

8 YE PEOPLE ALL WHO HEAR ME RING BE FAITHFULL TO YOUR GOD & KING
PACK & CHAPMAN OF LONDON FECIT 1774 (46 in.

9 IN WEDLOCK BANDS ALL YE WHO JOIN; WITH HANDS YOUR HEARTS UNITE SO SHALL OUR TUNEFULL TONGUES COMBINE TO LAUD THE NUPTIAL RITE
PACK, *etc* (50½ in

10 STEPHEN CORBET ACT C WARDEN 1805 I AM AND HAVE BEEN CALLD THE COMMON BELL TO RING, WHEN FIRE BREAKS OUT TO TELL ✝✝✝✝✝✝
JOHN RIANT HERTFORD FECIT AN DOM MDCCCV ✝ GLORIA DEO IN EXCELSIS ✝✝✝✝✝✝✝ (56½ in

The bells now hang in the octagon (see below)

Weights

	cwts	qrs	lbs		cwts	qrs	lbs
1)	6	3	2	6)	11	2	16
2)	7	0	8	7)	14	0	26
3)	8	1	13	8)	17	1	23
4)	9	0	0	9)	23	0	20
5)	9	2	21	10)	31	1	14

Total 6 tons 18 cwts 3 qrs 3 lbs

On the 4th bell the last three letters of WHITST are incised The cross on the 10th is Pl XXIII 7

The history of these bells has been fully dealt with in Sharp's *Coventry Antiquities*, p 65 (ed Fretton, 1871), from which the following information is taken, with some later additions from Mr. A J Brookes *St Michael, Coventry*, p 27 [1]

The tower was completed in 1395, but the bells do not appear to have been hung before 1429 In 1488 we read, 'This year was great peace throughout the realm, and for joy the Churchwardens of St Michael's, and other well-disposed people, brought to St Michael's a great Bell and called it *Jesus' Bell*, this motto was written about it —

'Jesus Nazarenus Rex Judeorum in me miserecordia'"

[The last three words are probably an error for the familiar 'miserere mei.']

There do not appear to be any Inventories of the year 1552 extant, and the next entry is in 1607, when the third and fourth bells, being cracked were recast, the fourth being cast three times before it was in tune

On March 18, 1674, 'The Vestry agreed with Henry Bagley sen, and H B. jun, of Chacomb in Co Northampton, that they shall have 55*l* for casting the 6 Bells into 8 tuneable ones, of as deep a tone and sound as they now are, to be recast by 24 June next'

The old six were accordingly taken down, as H Wanley tells us, on May 26, 1675, broken up, and cast into eight on May 29th. Their weights were as follows —

	cwts	qrs	lbs		cwts	qrs	lbs
1)	10	3	9	4)	17	3	14
2)	11	1	0	5)	23	1	2
3)	13	2	6	6)	30	1	5

Total 5 tons 7 cwts 8 lbs

The new ring was 6 cwts 3 qrs 8 lbs lighter, the weights being —

	cwts	qrs.	lbs	diam		cwts	qrs	lbs	diam
1)	6	1	11	diam 31 in	5)	12	1	7	diam $40\frac{3}{4}$ in
2)	6	2	26	32 in	6)	14	0	14	43 in
3)	8	0	9	35 in	7)	17	2	12	47 in
4)	9	3	21	$37\frac{1}{2}$ in.	8)	25	0	12	$52\frac{1}{2}$ in

Total 5 tons 1 qr

The inscriptions on these were copied by Wanley, 17 Jan, 1691, [2] as follows —

1 CANTATE DOMINO CANTICVM NOVVM 1675 H B

2 HENRY BAGLEY MADE MEE 1675

3 T E T GEORG DOWNING A D V S M 1675

4 I RING AT SIX TO LET MNE KNOW
WHEN TOO AND FROM THEAIR WORK TO GO 1675

---

[1] See also *Church Bells*, 9 and 16 June, 1883 *Notes and Queries*, 3rd Ser, ix, p 427, 4th Ser, vi, p 524, vii, p 45

[2] Harl MSS 6,030, fol 26 He also gives the weight of both rings, as above

5 RICHARD COLINC IOHN REMINCTON THOMAS REDHAED HUMPHVEY THACKER IOHN LILLEY RALPH PHILLIPS CHURCHWARDENS 1675

6 HENRY BAGLEY MADE MEE 1675

7 I RING TO SERMON WITH A LVSTY BOME
THAT ALL MAY COME AND NONE MAY STAY AT HOME 1675

8 I AM AND HAVE BEEN CALLED THE COMMON BELL
TO RINC WHEN FIER BREAKS OUT TO TELL 1675

(Reproduced on present tenor).

Besides giving the weights and sizes of these two rings, Wanley further states that "the old Tenor, formerly called Jesus Bell, was (as tis said) 3,000[li] weight" The diameters of the bells were taken by him and J H, 3 Jan, 1690-1 He continues — "I have been told by severall eminent Ringers that the old 5th Bell for sound was one of the best if not the very best bell in England, whereof he y[t] broke these 6 was one, he said he thought that he should never have broke it & that it was of the basest metall of any bel that ever he saw The Churchwardens would fain have saved it, to have been the Tenor for the new set, but the ffounder would not undertake to caast a new ring to it As for the old Tenor it must have been taken down presently or else it would have fell down of itself for the cannons of it were so rotten within by Age that the founder wondered that it hung in the steeple so long & that it did not fall when it was lett down by ropes Note that the 3rd bell of this present ring hath no cannons for they are broke, so that there is holes bored through the top of the bel, & irons put on them, & so fastened to the stok w[c] nevertheless hinders not the sound

The 4th bell of the new ring, it will be observed, is now at St John's Church, where it forms the tenor of five and it is interesting to note that in the City Annals there is an entry dated 28 April, 1675 —

Ordered that the treble bell of Babiake, now cracked shall be delivered to Bagley the bellfounder to be new cast and made tuneable to the bells in St Michael's Steeple, and placed there to make those bells more weighty —C C B

Browne Willis (*c* 1750) gives '8 Bells'

In 1770 a new peal of bells was contracted for with Pack and Chapman, of London their proposals being —

To recast the 8 present Bells into a peal of 8 musical ones, both in tone and tune, to weigh 5 tons a little more or less, at 28s per cwt recasting	£140 0 0
8 new Clappers, weight 2 cwt at 9*d*. per lb.	8 8 0
Two new Trebles to make a complete peal of 10, to weigh 12 cwt a little more or less, at £6 per cwt	72 0 0
Two new Clappers, 50 lb at 9*d*	1 17 6
	£222 5 6

The fabric shortly before this had been thought to be in danger from the heavy ring of bells, and from a new weathercock in the form of a dragon and a local humourist observed that the good people of St Michael's were sacrificing their church to "Bell and the Dragon!" When the new ring of ten was hung, this apprehension was so much increased that in 1793 a Committee was appointed to enquire into the state of the tower The bells were taken down, sundry repairs executed, and a new frame (unconnected with the tower and rising from the ground) erected at a cost of £507, and the bells were rehung in December, 1794, where they remained until the restoration of the church They were disposed in two tiers at first but in 1804, when the tenor was recast by Briant of Hertford (having been cracked in 1802) they were rehung and all brought down to the same level

Mr Brookes says —"At the restoration of the church in 1885 it was decided that the tower was not strong enough for the bells to be rung again in full peal, and an effort was made to erect a grand campanile in the churchyard on the north side That scheme failing, and the citizens getting impatient at the loss of the bells, they were again placed in the steeple, but in the octagon, where they are now chimed"

Sharp also gives sundry items relating to ringing and the chimes, which may be here quoted

1467 Also y^{t} ye Clerks of both Churches ryng both day bell & curfew in dve tyme & y^{t} ye clok be duly kept up ye peyn of ij^{d} at every default

1496[2] Hit is ordeyned at y^{is} p'sent lete that all man' p sones that hereaftur woll have the belles to ryng aft'r ye decesse of eny their frends, they shall pay for a pell ryngyng w^{t} all ye belles ij^{s}, xx^{d} y^{ere} of to ye Chircheward' & iiij^{d} to ye clerks And yf he woll have but iiij belles, xvj^{d}, xij^{d} to ye church & iiij^{d} to ye clerks And as for iij belles, ev'r' p'sone y^{t} woll have theym, to paye but iiij^{d} to ye clerks

1586	Pd for Ringing against the quen of Skots	xij^{d}
1587	Pd to ringers at M^{r} maiors Comaundement at death of the Scottishe Quene	xvj^{d}
1588	Payd the Ryngers at the rejoicinge of the overthrowe of the Spanishe flette .	v^{s}
1590	Pd for ryngynge my L byshop twice into the Cittie & furthe of the Cyttie	viij^{d}
1629	Pd the Lord Bishop's man because the Bells did not ring when his Ldship was in Town	6^{s} 8^{d}
1642	Pd for ringing when the Lo' Brooke came in with his army	3^{s} 6^{d}
1654	Pd for ringing May 23, being a day of thanksgiv'g	2^{s}
1656	Pd for ringing Feb 20, being a day of thanksgiv'g	2^{s} 6^{d}
1662	Pd for ringing when ye L Bishop (Dr Hackett of Lichfield) came first	7^{s}
1665	Pd the Ringers at the overthrough of the Dutch	5^{s}

We hear of chimes as early as 1465, when the Mayor and Council granted 40^{s} annually for their keeping up, together with the clock, and in succeeding years payments for repairs are numerous In 1778 a new set of chimes and clock were put up by Worton, of Birmingham, the former costing £277 In 1818 the tunes played were.—

Sunday, 104th Psalm Transferred to Friday and replaced by the Easter Hymn
Monday, Sir C Sedley s Minuet Subsequently The Bells of Meriden
Tuesday, Mudge's Air (by Rev F Mudge, of Little Packington)
Wednesday, Shady Bowers, Subsequently The Heavens are Telling
Thursday, Highland Laddie
Friday, Step In Transferred to Thursday
Saturday Lass of Patie's Mill

Mr Brookes says —"The old clock made in 1778 still keeps faithful time, and the chimes, which have been lately restored by public subscription, play the following tunes —

Sunday, Easter Hymn
Monday, Home, Sweet Home
Tuesday The Minstrel Boy
Wednesday, Aurelia (215 A and M)
Thursday, Ye Banks and Braes
Friday, The Heavens are Telling
Saturday, Hanover (431 A and M)

CUSTOMS —

Bells chimed for Sunday services, the 8th being used as 'Sermon Bell' in the morning and the tenor in the evening, one bell for 8 a m Celebrations A bell used to be rung between 1 and 2 p m when there was an afternoon service

---

1 Leet Book 202 b

2 *Ibid* 279 b This entry seems to indicate that there were then six bells

Bells rung in full peal on Christmas Eve and New Year's Eve, sometimes also on Anniversaries and Royal Birthdays, or on the Election of the Mayor or on November 9th also for Weddings by request

Death-knell Three strokes on tenor, then sixty on first and second alternately 'Ding-dong' ending with twelve on tenor, usual tellers

Bells rung partly or wholly muffled at Funerals

Formerly three bells were rung daily, at 6 a m, 6 p m, and 9 p m The first was to call men to work, the second for them to cease (see the tenor at St John s Church), and the third was the Curfew The 7th bell is used for daily services

Pancake Bell formerly also a bell for Vestry Meetings

There is an endowment for the ringing of a farewell peal to the memory of a former citizen named Edwards, on January 13th, the day of his death

Sundry peal-boards are said to be now in the crypt For an account of the peals commemorated thereon, see *Church Bells*, 25 Apr, 5 Dec, 1874, 1 and 22 July, 1876

Many thanks to Mr A J Brookes Vestryman

H T T, 14 June, 1878

COVENTRY — ALL SAINTS — One bell

Church built 1869

ST MARK — One bell

Church built 1869

ST NICHOLAS — One bell

Church built 1874

ST PETER — One bell

One bell of 1853, by C and G Mears, weighing 7cwt 1qr 7lbs

ST THOMAS — One bell

Church built 1844

CUBBINGTON — ST MARY — Four bells

1  **GOD** *(border)* **SAVE THE** *(border* **KING** *(border)* **1646** (29½ in

2  **IHS NAZARENVS** *(border)* **REX IVDEORVM** *(border)* **FILI DEI** *(border)* **MISERERE MEI** *(border)* **1646** *(border)* (32 in

3 *As the last, dated* **1626** (35 in

4 *As before, dated* **1640,** *with arabesques between the pairs of words and below all round* (38½ in

All by Hugh Watts, with shield, borders between words, the usual 'acorn' type on 1st to 3rd and arabesques on 4th, HE conjoined on 1st The date on 1st and 2nd must be an error, seeing that Watts died in 1643 probably we should read 1640 as on the 4th See p 43

1552 COBYNGTON iij belles a saunce belle'

'Md that ou' and besyde the forsaid p'c'lls the p'ishe sythens the last s'vey have sold to the rep'ac'on of their churche theis p'cells folowing ij hand bells ij lytle belles'

1750 '3 bells' (*sic*).

CUSTOMS —

On Sundays 2nd bell rung at 8 a m and treble after morning service Bells chimed for services, tenor as Sermon Bell for last five minutes

Ringing on Christmas Day and New Year's Eve (11-30—12-30), also twice weekly November 5th to Christmas

Death-knell on morning after at 8 a m, usual tellers

Gleaning bell formerly at 8 a m (tenor)

An endowment for supply of bell ropes

Best thanks to Rev B M Bean, Vicar

H T T, 9 Oct, 1878 H B W, Sept, 1907

CURDWORTH SS NICHOLAS AND PETER Three bells

1 THOMAS ⁂ WILCOX ⁂ EDWARD ⁂ ASTLEY ⁂ 1668 I M

Below, border all round (29⅝ in.

2 + VOX MEA EST DULCIS MEA SCINTLLANS VULTUS THO[S] EAYRE DE KETTERING = FECIT 1756 (30½ in.

3 ✠ SANCTA MARIA VIRGO INTERCEDE PRO TOTO MUNDO (34½ in

1st By John Martin of Worcester, palmettes between words (Pl XXI, Fig 6), and large shield after date (Plate XXI., Fig 10)

2nd The cross fitchee at the beginning (Pl XXIII 7) was also used by Briant, of Hertford.

3rd By an unknown founder, perhaps of Wolverhampton (see p 12), cross and letters Plate VII, Figs 10-15 The cross is also found at Bearley

Bells rehung by Barwell 1905 Clock strikes on tenor

1552 'iij belles in the steple'

1750 '5 Bells

There is a tradition that the tenor was given in gratitude for his preservation by a traveller who was lost in the Forest of Arden, and was guided to Curdworth by the sound of a bell

CUSTOMS —

On Sundays two bells chimed for early celebration, followed by one peal, all three bells chimed, followed by single bell at later services

For daily services the bell is tolled 33 times (representing the years of our Lord's life) the treble is used ordinarily, the 2nd on Festivals, and the 3rd for Celebrations

Ringing on New Year's Eve, for Weddings, by request formerly also on Christmas Day, 29 May 5 November, and King's Birthday

Death-knell at 7 a m on day of Funeral usual tellers, followed by tolling, tolling also before the ceremony, formerly chiming before and after

Curfew Bell revived in 1905, after some years' disuse, rung at 8 p m on week-days (Saturday 7 p m), tenor used, with day of month on treble (formerly also on tenor) H T T noted in 1876 that the Curfew was rung Jan—March

Many thanks to Rev L Mitchell Rector, who also kindly sends the following extracts from the Churchwardens Accounts —

1755	Feb 15 Paid bargaining with Mr Eayre for casting the bell		2	6
	Spent taking the bell down			5
	Carrying it to Birmingham		2	6
	Spent unloading & weighing it			6
	May 2 Expenses at Birmingham loading ye new bell		1.	0
	Carrying the bell from B ham		2	6
	Unloading it			6
	3 new bell ropes		3	0
1756	Paid Mr Thos Eayre for the new bell and for new hanging 3 bells	14	3	6

DERITEND and DUDDESTON. See BIRMINGHAM

DUNCHURCH ST PETER Six bells

1 ● PRAISE ● GOD ● IN ● HIS HOLYNES ● 1724 ● ●
(Running border above and below) (32 in

2 PRAISE ● HIM ● IN ● THE ● FIRMAMENT ● OF ● HIS ● POWER ● 1724 ●
(Running border below) ($33\frac{1}{2}$ in

3 ● PRAISE ● HIM ● IN ● HIS ● NOBLE ● ACTS ● 1724 ● ●
Below —BE IT KNOWN TO ALL THAT DOTH ME SEE THAT IOSEPH SMITH IN EDGBASTON MADE ALL THE
REST AND MEE 1724 (35 in

4 PRAISE HIM ● ACCORDING ● TO ● SIH ● EXCELLENT ● GREATNES ● 1724
(Running border below) (37 in

5 PRAISE HIM ● VPON THE ● WELL ● TVNED CYMBALS ● 1724
Below —MR EDWARD ● DAVIS ● VICAR ● IONATHON WORCESTER ● IOHN BASSET IOHN LVCAS IOHN GVPWELL CHVRCH WARDENS (41 in

6 I TO THE CHURCH THE LIVING CALL AND TO THE GRAVE DO SUMMON ALL W^M^ SMITH T SUTTON J & W^M^ BARNWELL C WARDENS HENRY BROMFIELD VICAR JOHN BRIANT HERTFORD FECIT AN DOM 1792 (46 in

The first five by Joseph Smith, with running scroll-border Plate XXIII, Fig 2 I do not know if the tenor was originally his or an addition

1552 iiij or belles a clock and a saunce belle'
1750 '6 Bells'

Wait, *Rugby Past and Present*, p. 254

On Sundays a peal rung before morning and evening services, a bell at 7-45 a m
Ringing on New Year's Eve muffled peal at 11-30 and open peal at midnight
Thanks to Rev C T B McNulty, Vicar
H T. T, 18 May 1887

EASTERN GREEN St Andrew One bell

Church built 1875 parish formed out of Allesley

EDGBASTON St Bartholomew Six bells

1 *On waist*—(*a*) TO . THE CREATER . CLORY . OF . COD.
CRESSWELL . STRANCE . VICAR.
JOHN . CHARLES . HOLDER . BART. } CHURCH
ELKANAH . MACKINTOSH . SHARP. } WARDENS.
CEORCE . STREET . SEXTON.
(*b*) CAST . BY . CHARLES . CARR . LIM^D
SMETHWICK.
OCT^R 1898 (27¼ in

2 CAST. BY. T. PYKE. BRIDGWATER 1781. (27¾ in.

3 MATHEW (*border*) BACLE MADE MEE 1685. (28¼ in

4 HENRY BAGLEY MADE MEE 1685 (29¾ in

5 MATHEW BAGELY MADE MEE 1685 (31½ in

6 FEARE GOD AND (*border Fig 12*) HONOVR THE (*Fig 12*) KING ⁂ 1685 ⁂ (35 in

Formerly five bells only, in 1898 the 1st was recast by Carr (though the fact is not stated thereon), with old inscription reproduced, and a new treble added

For Thomas Pyke, of Bridgwater see p 77

Weights of new bells 4 cwt 1 qr 10 lbs and 4 cwt [illegible] qrs 32 lbs Tenor 9¾ cwt

H T T noted in 1876 that the old treble was slightly chipped at the lip and the crown of the tenor hollow (?)

Borders on 3rd 4th, and 6th, Fig 11 on 5th and twice on 6th Fig 12 On all four the A form of A is used (see p 70)

1552 'iij belles and ij sacring or small bellks and a handbell'

Ringing for Sunday services, at Christmas and on New Year's Eve and for Weddings

In the ringing chamber is a peal-board dated 17 Dec 1900 recording the first full peal on the bells, when 5 040 minors were rung in different methods by the St Martin's Guild (2 hours 42 mins)

Thanks to the Rev Canon Mansfield Owen, Vicar

H T T 24 July 1891 H B W March 1908

EDGBASTON St Augustine One bell (?)

Church built 1868

St George One bell (?)

Church built 1838

St James One bell

Church built 1852

SS MARY AND AMBROSE One bell (?)

Church built 1897

ELMDON ST NICHOLAS Two bells

1. IESVS BE OVR SPED 1681

(23½ in

2 HENRICVS BAGLEY ME FECIT 1676 (25½ in

1st By Thomas Hancox (p 52), three types of running border between the words (floral, vine, and medallions, see pp 52, 54, and Pl XX 1-3, 5), after OVR an irregular bit of ornament, date in small figures with 3 reversed, and a crown beneath at the end fleur-de-lys and two figures from the middle part of a seal which he uses at Droitwich St Andrew and elsewhere (the seal of Bishop Scambler, of Norwich see p 55 and Pl XIX 7)

2nd Borders between the words Fig 9 p 68

1552 'Itm there two belles'

'M^d that the p she owethe for oon of their saide belles a iiij^s iiij^d'

H T T, 26 June, 1876, H B W, Sept, 1907

EMSCOTE See WARWICK

ERDINGTON ST BARNABAS Eight bells

There is a ring of eight bells here, by Taylor, of Loughborough, cast in 1904 The inscriptions on them, for a copy of which I am indebted to the kindness of that firm, are as follows —

1 RING ON, JOYOUS BELLS; NEVER SLUMBER,

2 LET US HEAR EACH MESSAGE YOU BRING,

3 AND OUR HEARTS, O'ERFLOWING WITH GLADNESS,

4 MUST BREAK INTO MUSIC AND SING;

5 SING PRAISES TO GOD, OUR CREATOR,

6 SING PRAISES TO JESUS, OUR KING,

7 SING PRAISES TO THEE, HOLY SPIRIT;

8 RING ON, BLESSED BELLS, EVER RING!

MARY PROCTOR RYLAND.

THIS PEAL OF EIGHT BELLS
PRESENTED TO ERDINGTON CHURCH
BY THOMAS RYLAND
OF THE REDLANDS, ERDINGTON,
IN MEMORY OF HIS DAUGHTER,
MARY PROCTOR RYLAND,
WHO DIED 2 NOV. 1903.

Weights and diameters —

		cwt	qrs	lbs			cwt	qrs	lbs
1)	26¾ in	4	3	12	5)	31¾ in	7	1	27
2)	27¼ in	5	0	8	6)	35½ in	7	3	17
3)	29¾ in	5	2	22	7)	39½ in	11	0	9
4)	31½ in	6	0	6	8)	44½ in	15	1	15

Church built 1822 parish formed out of Aston

ETTINGTON   St Thomas-a-Becket   Four bells

1 ✠ M[R] GEORG VNDEREHILL 1595 

2 ✠ M[R] VMPHERY VNDEREHILL 1595 

3 ✠ ANNO ◆ DO MI ◆ NI ◆ 1624 ◆ R P

On the waist —*Prince of Wales Arms, with motto*

4. J WATERS KING SUTTON BELL HANGER W HARRIS & E ARCH C WARDENS IOHN BRIANT HERTFORD FECIT 1803

Bells removed from the old church at Lower Ettington (now in ruins) when a new one was built at Upper Ettington, in 1803 They have now been placed in the new Church of the Holy Trinity, built in 1907

1st and 2nd by Edward Newcombe, of Leicester (see p 32) plain initial cross The founder s stamp does not occur elsewhere, but that he used a similar seal in his business we know from an existing document (see under Stratford-on-Avon, and Halliwell *Descriptive Calendar of Stratford Records*, p 387)

3rd By Roger (or Richard) Purdue, of Bristol, the N s of ANNO conjoined, 6 of date reversed On the waist, the Prince of Wales' feathers, as at Brailes See p 124 for the difficulty in connection with this R Purdue's Christian name

The Underhill family settled at Ettington about 1510 and became extinct in 1784 George and Humphrey were two of the numerous sons of its best known member Thomas Underhill, they died in 1650 and 1613 respectively, the former being then Vicar of Oxhill See Dugdale, i p 625 Colvile *Worthies of Warwicksh*, p 767, *Collect Topogr et Geneal*, vi p 383, Brit Mus Add MSS, 29 264 fol 187

1552 'ETYNGTON iij belles, one saunce bell   1750 'Eatington 3 Bells

CUSTOMS —

On Sundays, peals at 10 a m and 5-30 p m (or in morning, single bell for a few minutes), tenor at 10-30, and chiming 10-45 to 10-55 (evening 5-45 to 6 0) 'surplice bell' rung on treble for last four minutes

Ringing on New Year's Eve 11-30—12-30, with pause at midnight at 6 a m on St Thomas Day, and for Weddings, by request

Death-Knell as soon as possible, with usual tellers before and after At Funerals tolling before the service bells 'rung up and down' (as in Death-Knell) at its conclusion

Gleaning Bell formerly at 8 a m, discontinued in 1865

The following extracts from the Churchwardens' Accounts have been kindly communicated by the Vicar —

			s	d
1769	Apr 23	A pulley for a bell	1	0
		[For bell ropes at various times 5s, 14s 3d, 15s]		

1803	For Fetching the bells from the Old Church to the New	1	1	0
	Pd Jno Walker for helping to loae the Bels		1	6
	Pd Willm Baron for the Bel ropes	1	2	0
1804	Pd Willm Hall for fetching the Frames from Banbury	1	3	0

[As the tenor shews, the hanging of the new bell was the work of J Waters of King's Sutton, near Banbury]

Recasting 10¼ cwt of Bell-mettal at 30s pr hundred	15	7	6
Carriage of the old bell to Banbury	1	0	0
,, ,, ,, from Banbury to London	1	1	0
Carriage of the new Bell from London to Banbury	2	11	7
, , , from Banbury to Eatington	1	0	0

[The bell was recast at Hertford, whither it must have gone *via* London unless John Briant was in London at the time]

Many thanks to Rev T H Parker, Vicar

H T T, 16 June, 1887

EXHALL (BY ALCESTER) ST GILES One bell

1 G MEARS & CO FOUNDERS LONDON 1861

The bell hangs in an open stone turret, at a considerable height H T T was unable to discover the date but Mr Falkner's perseverance has surmounted the difficulties of the ascent, and made it finally certain

1552 'ij belles one saunce bell 1750 '2 Bells'

Death-knell tolled for a hour, on receipt of notice

Thanks to Rev A W Sheard, Rector and to Mr Falkner

Previously to 1861, there were two bells here, both Pre-Reformation Drawings of the inscriptions were carefully made by Mr H Kimber while the bells were at the Whitechapel foundry, and these have been, fortunately, preserved I am indebted to Mr Hughes, of that foundry for access to the volume in which they are contained, and from which they are reproduced on pp 27, 28 (Figs 2, 3) The smaller bell was inscribed

✠ AVE MARIA GRACIA

in fine ornate lettering of Midland type, dating about 1400, the larger

✠ SANCTE EGIDI ORA PRO POPVLO

the lettering and cross also occurring at Iwerne Minster, in Dorset, and Magdalen Laver, Essex, the founder is probably a Londoner of about 1320 See above, p 27 and Walters and Deedes, *Ch Bells of Essex*, p 6

H T T, 29 Jan, 1878

EXHALL (BY COVENTRY) ST GILES Three bells

1 BARWELL FOUNDER BIRMINGHAM RECAST 21 DECR A.D. 1900

On waist —(*a*) CHAS SIMMONDS M.A. VICAR

FRANCIS DUCK }
JOSEPH FLETCHER } CHURCHWARDENS

(*b*) IOSEPH SMITH IN EDGBASTON

MADE MEE 1706 27 in

2 *As No 1*

On waist —(a) as No 1 (b) Mr RICHARD SMITH & RICHARD RANDAL CHURCH WARDENS (28½ in

3 *As No 1*

On waist — (a) as No 1 (b) I WILL SOUND & CALL THE CONGREGATION (30½ in

Pits for six, with a view to a future increase in the ring The former three bells were by Joseph Smith, the inscriptions being reproduced on the new bells, with the omission of the dates on the 2nd and 3rd H T T 's notes give IOHN for IOSEPH on the treble (probably a clerical error and WARDINGS for WARDINS on the 2nd the word is also so spelled at Stretton-on-Dunsmore The inscription on the old 3rd also occurs at Water Orton

The restoration and re-dedication of the bells is recorded on a tablet in the lower part of the tower (with names of Vicar and Churchwardens as above)

		cwt	qrs	lbs
Weights —	1)	4	1	14
	2)	4	2	20
	3)	5	2	14

The Vicar says — In A D 1900 the belfry was fitted with new frames and appliances for six bells A chiming apparatus (for six bells) was fitted in the belfry and a brass inscription placed on the belfry wall The dedication was performed by the Bishop of Coventry (Dr Knox), 21 Dec , 1900 "

CUSTOMS —

On Sundays bells chimed at 8-30 a m (at 8 a m on 1st Sunday in month, April Oct), and at all services rung on Festivals before services and after Evensong

Ringing on New Year s Eve, on St Giles' Day (Sept 1st, Patronal Festival, or nearest Sunday in Octave), and for Weddings when desired

Two bells rung singly every day at 9-30 a m

Death-knell on notification of death tellers 3×3 followed by tolling on tenor at intervals fo an hour , age of deceased tolled after Funerals

Best thanks to Rev C Simmonds Vicar

H T T , 2 Oct , 1876, H B W Sept , 1907

FARNBOROUGH St BOTOLPH. 5+1 bells

1 CAST BY JOHN WARNER & SONS LONDON 1875

On waist —PREPARE TO MEET THY GOD.

2 Glory to GOD in the highest ✠

3 ✠ Ano Dni MDCCCXLIIII ✠ On Earth Peace ✠

4 ✠ ✠ Good will toward Man

On waist —W Taylor Fecit Oxon Ano Dni MDCCCXLIIII

5 *As No 1*

On waist ,—SING UNTO THE LORD A NEW SONG

S *No inscription*

2nd, 3rd, and 4th by Taylor of Oxford 1844

1552 'FFARNBURGH. ij belles one saunce bell'
1750 '3 Bells

CUSTOMS —

On Sundays bells chimed at 8 a m, and before other services, followed by ringing the fourth bell, and the smallest for the last two or three minutes

Ringing on Greater Festivals, muffled peal on New Year's Eve, followed by an open one after midnight also on November 5th and King's Birthday, and for Weddings, by request

Death-knell about an hour after death if possible, on tenor tellers 3 for woman, 2 for man, 1 for child Tenor rung up and down for Funerals

Gleaning bell formerly

Thanks to Rev H Holbech Vicar

H T T 14 June, 1887

FENNY COMPTON ST PETER Three bells

1 ✤ CANTATE DOMINO CANTICVM NOVVM ✤ HENRY BAGLE MADE MEE 

Below —1636

28 in

2  F G ~ M I Z (31 in.

3 H E N R Y ✤ B A G L E Y ✤ M A D E M E E ✤✤✤✤✤ ✤ 1 6 3 6 ✤ ✤✤✤✤ (34 in

The treble has a new wheel and stock by Barwell

2nd Cross, Plate XVII, Fig 1 supposed to be by John Appowell, of Buckingham about 1560-70, see p 46

3rd Border, Fig 9; letters wide apart, as at Long Itchington

1552 'FFENNY COMPTON iij belles a little bell

1750 '3 Bells

CUSTOMS —

On Sundays treble rung at 8 a m, second bell at 9 a m (old Mattins and Mass Bells)

Bells chimed for twenty minutes before services, followed by tenor for five minutes when there is a sermon Treble rung immediately after morning service

On the three Mondays before Christmas and on St Thomas' Day the bells are rung at 6 a m, on Christmas Eve from 11-30 till past midnight, on New Year's Eve the old year is rung out and the new in Ringing also on November 5th about 7 p m, and for Weddings, by request

Death-knell rung as soon as death is reported, but not after sunset, usual tellers, followed by tolling at intervals of a minute for half an hour Before Funerals, tolling at minute intervals, afterwards the bell is rung up and down, with tellers as before

A bell rung for Vestry Meetings

Best thanks to the Rector, Rev G S Streatfeild, and to the Rev Preb Deedes, of Chichester To the latter I am indebted for rubbings, and also for the following extracts from the Churchwardens' Accounts —

1729 Pd Joseph Ward for mending the bel whele and Church vats 10d
1731 Pd for Bell ropes 8d

	pd Joseph Warde for mendg yt Church gates and ye Bel whels	5s
	pd Tho Cook for menden the bels	3s
1733	pd Joseph Ward mending ye Great Bell	3s
1734	pd Richard Ducket for mending ye Bell Wheele	6d
1738	pd Mr Cook for mending bell	1s
1739	pd to Joseph Ward for mending ye Bell whele and putting a board in the Steeple window	4s
1740	pd for Bell Ropes	5s
	pd Richd Tims for work done to ye bells	3s 6d

[Payment for bell ropes repeated in most succeeding years]

1746—1750	Several payments for mending wheels	
1749 50	pd for the bells brasses costin	9s 6d
	pd Thomas Ducket for mending the bels & hanning (?) the bels in the new brases	3s
	pd Richard Knight for mending the bels and lcks and cees	1s 8d
1751	pd for a new beel wheel	£1 3s 0d
1752	For getting the First bell up and mending the Wheal and setting 6 plats on the jogings[1]	2s 6d
	Pd Henry Chater for 6 plate and nayls and a stayle and a Cotor and 2 Rings for ye bells	2s 6d
1753	pd Henry Chater for Keying ye Bell	1s 6d
1754—1768	Numerous repairs, but no items of interest	
1769	pd Richard Ducket for a new Stock for the Seckent Bell Claper and Mending the whealle	4s 6d
1770—1781	Sundry repairs as before	
1782	A Bill to ye Church Worden for a Clasp & Caging ye great Bell	1s
1783	for 2 Doble Cags for ye secon Bell	2d
	for Bosing 2 Rolers & 2 pins & 2 Cags	2s 2d
	Etc Etc [Total of bill, 7s]	

[H T T 17 Sept, 1875]

FILLONGLEY. St Mary and All Saints — Six bells

1 ✠ TO THE GLORY OF GOD

Below, vine-wreath and Taylor's trade-mark

GIVEN BY FRANCES HOLLICK
IN MEMORY OF HER HUSBAND
RICHARD HOLLICK
1896. (30 in

2 BRYANVS ELDRIDGE ME FECIT 1653 (31½ in

3 SOLI ♆ DEO ♆ GLORIA ♆ PAX ♆ HOMINIBVS ♆ ♆ EDWARD ♆ HOLBACH ♆ THOMAS ♆ BREARLE ♆ 1654

Below, vine-wreath and Taylor's trade-mark (33½ in

4 I LOVETT AND J WHITE CHURCHWARDENS EDW^D ARNOLD LEICESTER FECIT 1795 (35 in

5  **IHS NAZARENVS** *(border)* **REX IVDEORVM** *(border)* **FILI : DEI** *(border)* **MISERERE : MEI** *(border)* 1628 *(border)* (38 in

[1] Gudgeons

6 JOHN FLETCHER VICAR THOMAS LOVETT AND WILLIAM LAKINS CHURCHWARDENS
 EDW^D ARNOLD LEICESTER FECIT ● 1791 ● (42 in

Down to 1896 there were only five bells in that year a new treble was added, and the old 2nd recast the latter was inscribed —

✤ SOLI ✤ DEO ✤ GLORIA ✤ PAX ✤ HOMINIBVS ✤ EDWARD ✤

✤ HOLBACH ✤ THOMAS ✤ BREARLE *On waist* —  1654

Weight of new treble, 6 cwt 1 lb , of new 3rd, 6 cwt 3 qrs 15 lbs
Borders on 5th the usual 'acorn' pattern
H T. T. notes Clock strikes quarters on 1st and 3rd, hour on 5th'

1522 'FEYI LONGLEY Itm there iiij ^or^ belles a handbell and a sacring bell
1750 6 Bells

CUSTOMS —

Peals rung for Sunday services, a single bell at 8 a m
Ringing at 7 a m on Easter Sunday and Christmas Day, on New Year s Eve a muffled peal at 11-30 followed by an open one at midnight
Death-knell as soon as information is received
Thanks to Rev A B Stevenson, formerly Vicar
H T T, 18 June 1881 H B W Sept, 1907

FOLESHILL. ST LAWRENCE Three bells

1  IHS NAZARENVS (*border*) REX IVDEORVM (*border*) FILI. DEI (*border*) MISERERE (*border*) MEI (*border*) 1635 (*border*) (29 in

2  GOD (*border*) SAUE (*border*) THE (*border*) KINGE (*border*) IL (*border*) UH (*border*) MB (*border*) SW (*border*) 1616 (32 in

3  CELORVM CHRSTE PLATIAT TIBI REX SONVS ISTE 1616 (35 in

The first and second have the clappers tied and are chimed with hammers
All three by Hugh Watts, the 2nd having the Brasyer lettering, borders between words on 1st and 2nd. Plate XXII, Fig 7 See p 42
H T T April 1875 H B W Sept 1907

FOLESHILL ST PAUL One bell

Church built 1842

FOLESHILL ST THOMAS (LONGFORD)

A chime of eight small bells without inscriptions, supplied recently by Taylor, of Loughborough Weights and diameters

		cwt	qrs	lbs			cwt	qrs	lbs
1)	15¼ in	0	3	13	5)	21 in	1	3	6
2)	16 in	0	3	24	6)	22 in	2	0	23
3)	16¾ in	1	0	4	7)	25 in	3	0	11
4)	19 in	1	12	3	8)	28 in	4	1	8

Church built 1874

FRANKTON — ST NICHOLAS — Four bells

1 **IHS NAZARENVS REX IVDEORVM FILI DEI MISERERE MEI 1636**

2 ✠ **BE YT KNOWNE TO ALL THAT DOTH ME SEE THAT NEWCOMBE OF LEICESTER MADE MEE 1607**

3 *As No 1, with date* **1623**

4. **CELORVM CHRSTE PLATIAT TIBI REX SONVS ISTE 1616**

1st, 3rd, and 4th by Hugh Watts, of the usual type
2nd and 4th much flattened

1552 'FFRANCTON iij belles and a saunce belle'
Md that the pishe have sold sithence the last surveye oon of the forsaid bells to the rep'ac on of their churche'

1750 '4 Bells'

CUSTOMS

On Sundays bells chimed for services a bell rung at 8 a m and after Morning Service
Ringing on Christmas Eve and Day, Easter Sunday, New Year's Eve, November 5th, and St Thomas' Day, when a local charity is distributed, also for Weddings
Death Knell at 9 a m on day after death (on receipt of medical certificate), no tellers
Pancake Bell rung until 20 years ago, 3rd bell at 11 a m
Gleaning Bell until 25 years ago, 3rd bell at 8 a m and 6 p m

Thanks to Rev J H Blunt Rector
H T T, 10 Oct, 1878

GAYDON — ST GILES — One bell

1 *No inscription*

The bell is undoubtedly ancient and hung in a turret in the old church
Customs (if any) as at Chadshunt
H T T 19 Sept, 1875

GRANDBOROUGH — ST PETER — Five bells

1 *Above running border*

CANTATE DOMINO CANTICVM NOVVM 1641

2 ● IOSEPH ● SMITH ● IN ● EDGBASTON ● MADE ● MEE 1706 ●

(Running border below)

3 HENRY BAGLE MADE MEE 1641 
(Above pieces of running border)

4 MR CHRISTEFER ● TILLE ●● MINISTER ● *(border)* MR PHILEMON CLARKE AND MR IOHN GOODE CHVRCH ● WARDENS ● 1706

IOSEPH SMITH ● MADE ME ●  ● *(border continuous)*

5 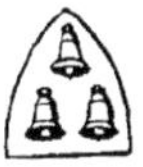 BY MY VOYCE THE PEOPLE MAY KNOWE TO COME TO HEARE THE WORDE OF GOD HENRY ✠ BAGLY 1639 MADE MEE

1st, 3rd, and 5th are examples of the earlier work of Henry Bagley I with the three-bell shield which he afterwards discarded, see p 67 The inscription on the tenor also occurs at Ilmington and at Feckenham, Worcs

2nd and 4th Joseph Smith's trade mark and usual border (Plate XXIII, Figs 1, 2)

1552 'iiij^or^ belles wth a lytle belle'

1750 'Granborough 5 Bells'

CUSTOMS:

On Sundays the tenor is rung for five or ten minutes at 9 a m Bells chimed for half an-hour before services

Ringing on Easter Sunday, Whit-Sunday, Christmas Day, New Year's Eve and Day also practising for six weeks before Christmas

When the bells are rung for a wedding there is also a peal rung at 5 a m on the following morning

Death-Knell rung before noon, tolling for an hour, with usual tellers

Tolling at Funerals for half-an-hour before and afterwards

Pancake Bell rung on tenor from 11 to 12 on Shrove Tuesday

Best thanks to Rev W B Williams, the late Vicar

H T T 21 Jan, 1892

GRENDON ALL SAINTS Six bells.

1 HENRY BAGLEY MADE MEE 1699 WALTER CHETWYND ES^P^

On waist —  (28½ in

2 ✠ GLORIA IN EXCELSVS DEO 1615 (30 in

3 *On waist — (a)* RECAST 1906 *(b) Taylor's trade-mark*

A B D G F E (32 in

4 ♕ ✠ MELEDE GERIT (34 in

5  IHS NAZARENVS REX IVDEORVM FILI DEI MISERERE MEI 1623 (36¾ in

6 *On waist* —(*a*) TO THE GLORY OF GOD (*b*) *Taylor's trade-mark*
AND IN LOVING MEMORY
OF HENRY HANMER
RECTOR OF GRENDON FROM 1844 TO 1904
AND OF SYBELLA ELIZABETH HIS WIFE
THIS BELL WAS GIVEN
BY THEIR SONS AND DAUGHTERS
JULY 1906 (41 in

1st Cast at Ecton (see p 71), the arms are those of Chetwynd *Az.* a chevron between three mullets *or*

2nd By William Clibury of Wellington, Salop (p 50) cross and border, Plate XXI Figs 8, 11 This founder always makes the ablative plural EXCELSVS A similar bell at Wolston

3rd The original bell, the inscription of which is reproduced on the new, was, like the 4th, from the Newcombes' foundry (see p 35) It was inscribed

✠ A B ⁘ D C F E

the cross being Pl XVII 2, as at Berkswell, the crown on the 4th is Pl XVII 3, as at Wroxhall, the fleur-de-lys, *Northants*, 86 Lettering on both as Pl XVI

5th By Hugh Watts without the usual borders

The tenor is an addition to the ring

		cwt	qrs	lbs		cwt	qrs	lbs	
Weights of bells —	(1)	4	3	7	(4)	6	3	8	
	(2)	4	3	10	(5)	8	1	23	
	(3)	6	0	4	(6)	11	2	14	Note F to F sharp.

Walter Chetwynd whose arms are on the 1st, was Lord of the Manor and patron of the living, and M P for Lichfield 1714, he died in 1731, just after being appointed Governor of Barbadoes For the history of the family see Dugdale, *s v* Grendon, p 1101 and Chetwynd-Stapylton, *The Chetwynds of Ingestre*, p 171

1552 'iij belles and a saunce belle
†1760 '5 Bells

CUSTOMS

On Sundays, bell at 8 a m for Holy Communion at 9 a m the 1st and 2nd bells are rung if a sermon is to be preached at Mattins, the 1st only when no sermon Two bells are also rung after Morning Service Before Mattins and Evensong the bells are rung for twenty minutes, followed by chiming for five and tolling for five

Ringing one evening a week November 5th to New Year's Day, also on November 5th for Weddings when desired

Death-Knell rung when notice is given, tolling for 15 minutes with usual tellers at beginning and end. Bell tolled for half-an-hour before funerals, with tellers immediately after the ceremony Muffled peals are rung when desired (three instances of this 1905—1907)

Pancake Bell on Shrove Tuesday (2nd and 5th bells) at 11 15 a m

Many thanks to Rev H Hanmer Rector

H T T 3 Oct 1876

HALFORD ST MARY Three bells

1 ✠ AGIOS IN HONORE SANCTI IOHANNIS BAPTISTE SUM RENOVATA

2 Sancta Katerina Ora Pro Nobis

On waist —Recast by John Taylor & Co, Loughborough 1883

On shoulder (incised) A LAURIE M A, RECTOR

3 PRAYSE THE LORD YE PEOPLE ✤✤✤ H B ✤✤✤ 1639

Below —*Shield with three bells*

Treble by an unknown founder but dating early in the fourteenth century see p 3 and Plate I AGIOS is, of course the Greek ἅγιος=*sanctus* The A is larger than the other letters, and the N s are reversed A cylindrical bell (H T T) Cannons broken off hung above the other two

2nd The old bell was cracked on Sunday, October 29th, 1876, while ringing the 9 a m bell It was by John Walgrave of London c 1430 (p 24), and the inscription has been reproduced on the present one with the exception of the initial cross (Pl XIII 1) and the founder's trade-mark with initials I W (Pl XIII 10)

3rd By Henry Bagley of Barford 2nd, and see p 67 Fleur-de-lys and scroll borders (Fig 9 and *Bucks*, Pl XXXII 2), shield as at Barford etc

Weight of new 2nd 7 cwt 23 lbs, diam 32 in

1552 'HAWFORDE iij belles a saunce belle

1750 5 Bells' (*sic*)

There was formerly a small uninscribed sanctus bell here, about 10 inches in diameter, which hung in a cot at the east end of the nave without cannons I owe to Mr W E Falkner some interesting notes as to its history It was taken down during the incumbency of Mr Simons (1859—1873), who removed it successively to Saintbury, near Chipping Campden, and to Leamington, where he died The bell subsequently came into the possession of Mr F S Potter of Halford in whose garden it now is, but it is hoped that it may be eventually restored to the church

The Rev J H Bloom contributed the following note to the *Stratford Herald*, 5 June, 1908 (from a document found at Worcester) —

To ye Worll Mr Doctor Littleton, Chancellour of Worcester, etc

These are to certify your Worship of a truth, that whereas we lately have had a bell broaken in or p'ish of Halford, it is now new cast and all ye repaires thereunto belonging are pformed accord to yr Worps Appointment In witnesse whereof ye mur Churchwardens of Halford doe heere to subscribe or names

John Horton mr ibdem

John Rose } Churchwardens
Robert Asson }

Thomas Cambden late of Samburne was the werpuler

The paper is undated, but all others in the bundle were of the year 1640 so the document clearly refers to the bell recast by Bagley in 1639 and confirms my reading of the date, which Mr Tilley took to be 1659 (as at Idlicote, the third figure is not very clear) Mr Bloom interprets 'werpuler' as caster' (*werpen*, to cast, Germ *werfen*), but I am not sure certainly the bell is by Bagley The word rather suggests the modern wire puller,' but even if Thomas Cambden was responsible for the re-casting, we can hardly accept this explanation!

H T T, 31 Jan, 1877

HAMPTON-IN-ARDEN SS MARY AND BARTHOLOMEW Six bells

1 ● COME ● LET US SING ● UNTO THE LORD ● 1725

Above and below, arabesques

2 ● GOD SAVE SIR ● CHURCH ● 1725 (scrolls)
Below, arabesques all round

3. IOSEPH ● SMITH ● IN ● EDGBASTON ● MADE MEE ○ 1725 *(scrolls)*
Below, arabesques

4 ● THOMAS ARDEN OF HAMPTON ● AND CLEMENT ISHE. *(scroll)* IOHN TALII AND *2nd line)* —WILLIAM LOWES OF BALSALL CHURCH WARDENS 1725 *(scrolls)*

5 ● SAMUELL LYDIATT D D VICAR ● LINGEN UNITT ● CURATE ● 1725 *(scrolls)*
Below, arabesques.

6 ● I TO THE CHURCH THE ● LIVEING CALL ● AND TO THE GRAVE DOE SUMON ALL 1725
Above and below arabesques (39 in

All by Joseph Smith, the third has ornamented cannons Borders Pl XXIII 2 and Fig 11

Bells undergoing re-hanging (by Barwell) Sept, 1907, they were then examined under difficulties, and diameters could not be obtained (H B W)

1552 'iij belles in the steple'
1750 '4 Bells' *(sic)*.

CUSTOMS —

On Sundays chiming for services, one bell rung at 8 a m and two at 9 a m (the old Matins and Mass bells)

Ringing on Christmas Eve and Day, Easter Sunday Ascension Day, Whit-Sunday, Trinity Sunday, and New Year's Eve, also on King's Birthday and Coronation Day, 29 May and 5 November, and for Weddings

Death-knell with tellers one stroke on *each* bell once round for child two similarly for a woman and three for a man, followed by tolling

Pancake Bell on Shrove Tuesday at 11 a m (5th bell tolled)

A bell rung for Vestry Meetings

Best thanks to Rev T J Morris formerly Rector

HAMPTON LUCY ST PETER One bell

1 REV^D J. LUCY RECTOR 1826 T MEARS OF LONDON FECIT

The Rev J Lucy was appointed in 1815 his father was Vicar of Charlcote

1552 'Itm there iij belles one sance bell
'M^d that the p'ishe have sold sithe the Last S^r vey one bell to the mayntenance of there bridge & to make a Comen Jack for the towne

1750 'Hampton Episcopi 6 Bells (sic)

See *Notes and Queries*, 3rd Ser, x (1866) p 143

H. I T, 3 Aug 1881

HARBOROUGH MAGNA ALL SAINTS Three bells

1 I NORMAN T STEANE C WARDENS GLORIA IN EXCELSIS DEO
Below, a border of ornament

On waist —(a) scroll with I TAYLOR & SON FOUNDERS *(b)*
LOUGHBORO' 1850 

2. BRYANVS ELDRIDGE ME FECIT 1657 R C H S
Below —R W

3 *The same (in one line)*

For Bryan Eldridge, see p 58

1552 'iij belles and a hand belle
1750 '6 Bells'

CUSTOMS —

On Sundays bells chimed for two periods of ten minutes each, with 'come' bell for last five minutes on treble, before services
Death-Knell for half an hour tellers, 3 for man, two for woman, one for child
Ringing after Weddings
Curfew and Gleaning Bell formerly
Thanks to Rev B G Boughton-Leigh, Rector
H T T 15 Oct. 1897

HARBURY ALL SAINTS Five bells

1 T. MEARS OF LONDON FECIT 1811 (31½ in

2 *The same* (34 in

3 *The same* (36 in

4 *The same* (38 in

5 REV^D G NEWSAM VICAR R GARDENER E SABIN CHURCH WARDENS 1811
T MEARS OF LONDON FECIT 1811 (41 in.

		cwt	qrs	lbs		cwt	qrs	lbs
Weights —	1)	6	1	7	4)	9	2	27
	2)	7	0	24	5)	13	0	8
	3)	8	1	0				

The Rev G Newsam was instituted Vicar 1806

1552 'HARBURY iij bells a saunce bell a hand belle and a small bell'
1750 'Heburbury 5 Bells

CUSTOMS —

Bells chimed for Sunday services occasionally rung
Ringing on Christmas Eve and New Year's Eve, and at 6 a m on St Thomas' Day
Death-knell tolling (for half an hour with usual tellers at beginning and end tolling at Funerals
Thanks to Rev J F Beardsworth Vicar
H T T, 19 Sept, 1875

HARTSHILL HOLY TRINITY One bell

Church built 1848, parish formed out of Mancetter
There was formerly an old chapel here

HASELEY St Mary Three bells

1 *No inscription* (20⅝ in

2 ✠ *(dog)* W 3 5 *(dog)* R I *(dog)* H G *(dog)* I *(dog)* E *(dog)* C C B A (24⅝ in

3 **EDWERD : HOP : EDWERD : WINTER : CHURCH : WARDENS :**

Below —**MATTHEW BAGLEY MADE MEE · 1778** (27¼ in

1st 'Undoubtedly a very ancient bell, judging from shape and cannons' (H T T)

2nd Probably by Thomas Newcombe, about 1565 (see p 33), cross Pl XVI 2, lettering also found on Little Packington 2nd (*q v*) See Plate XV, Fig 9 (cross and dog) The reading of the W 3 5 is somewhat doubtful

3rd Small type like Henry Bagley III 's at Barton-on-Heath stops as at Long Compton.

1552. 'Itm there a iij belles 1750 5 Bells' (*sic*)

In *Notices of Warwickshire Churches* i p 99, the 2nd bell is said to be dedicated to the B V M!

CUSTOMS.—

On Sundays bells chimed for half an hour before services, with a single bell for the last five minutes, a bell is also rung for five minutes after the services, morning and afternoon

Ringing on Christmas Day and New Year's Eve for Weddings by request

One bell tolled for about five minutes at 8 a m on the morning following a death tolling at Funerals

A bell rung for Easter Vestry Meetings

Thanks to Rev E Muckleston, Rector and to Mr W E Falkner

H T T 5 Oct, 1874 13 July, 1881

HASELOR St Mary and All Saints Two bells

1 + **H B 1662 + CANTATE DOMINO CANTICVM NOVVM**

On waist — **'VOCO' 'AUDITE' 'VENITE'**

RECAST 1902

JOHN HEATH SYKES VICAR

THEO BOMFORD }
JOSEPH MORRIS } **CHURCHWARDENS** (30½ in

2 ✠ **BE · YT KNOWNE · TO · ALL THAT DOTH · ME SEE · THAT NEWCOMBE OF LEICESTER MADE MEE 1610** *(plait-band)*

The old 1st was inscribed as reproduced on the present one (with the exception of the two crosses), between the words were bits of arabesque ornament, as at Whitnash, and a band of border above the inscription The modern bell is by Barwell of Birmingham, weight, 5 cwt 26 lbs

On the 2nd, after date, plait-band (Pl XX 4) as at Bulkington

1552 iij bells, one sance bell

1750 Hasler 1 Bell' (*sic*)

H T T 27 July, 1881

HATTON — HOLY TRINITY — 6+1 bells

1 **JAMES. BARWELL. FOUNDER. BIRMINGHAM. 1885.** (30 in

2 *The same* (31½ in

3 *The same* (33 in

4 *The same* (34½ in

5 *The same* (37½ in

6 *The same* (42½ in

S IOHN RUDHALL GLOCESTER FECT 1809.

The 5th has a piece chipped out of the rim, caused by the clapper flying out and breaking the bell, but the clerk states that its tone has not been affected Clock strikes on 4th The little bell is hung above the treble, but is not now used, it has no wheel, but a lever It formerly hung on the top of the tower

		cwt	qrs	lbs		cwt	qrs	lbs	
Weights —	1)	5	3	25	4)	6	3	22	
	2)	6	1	17	5)	9	2	27	
	3)	6	2	12	6)	13	2	18	Note said to be F sharp

There were formerly eight bells here, six having been given by the well-known Vicar of Hatton, Dr Parr in 1809, together with the little bell, and two trebles added by him in 1817 The tenor of this ring was cracked in 1874 (H T T), and the whole ring was stated to be unsafe by Taylor, of Loughborough The final result was a reduction to six which, from the ringer's point of view if from no other, seems a pity The old ring was by John Rudhall, of Gloucester, and the inscriptions were as follows (copied in 1881 by H. T T) —

1 GIVEN BY THE REVD DR PARR A D 1817 I RUDHALL FEC
Below — PHILIP 5c 2q 17lb

2. *As No 1*
Below — JAMES 5c 3q 5lb

3 RECAST AND ENLARGED BY THE REVD DR PARR
HIS PUPILS & FRIENDS J809
I RUDHALL FECIT MATTHEW

4 RECAST AND ENLARGED BY THE PARISHIONERS OF HATTON J809
IOHN RUDHALL FECIT MARK

5 RECAST AND ENLARGED BY MRS THROCKMORTON'S TRUSTEES 1089 (*sic*)
I RUDHALL FECIT LUKE

6 RECAST AND ENLARGED BY MRS THROCKMORTONS TRUSTEES & THE PARISHIONERS OF HATTON J809
I RUDHALL FECIT IOHN

7 RECAST AND ENLARGED BY MRS THROCKMORTONS & MRS NORCLIFES TRUSTEES 'THE PARISHONERS
PROPRIETORS & DR PARR J809 I RUDHALL FECT PETER

8 THE GIFT OF THE REV^D^ DR SAMUEL PARR MINISTER HIS PUPILS & FRIENDS 1809 REV^D^ N. BRIDGES B D CURATE

E MARSHALL T MORRIS CHURCHWARDENS I RUDHALL FECT **PAUL**

A copy is also given in *Notices of Warwickshire Churches* ii, p 63

The Rev N Bridges, curate in 1809 was appointed to the living of Henstridge, Somerset, in 1813

1552 'Itm there a iij bells

Dugdale has preserved for us the interesting information that in his time there were no less than three foreign bells in the tower, all from the Low Countries Two of these were there in 1552, but the third was added shortly after, and as he calls these 1st, 3rd, and 5th, it may be assumed that the ring was increased early in Elizabeth's reign The inscriptions as given by Dugdale (ii, 651) are —

'On the I bell is this inscription int jaer ons Heren MCCCCIII maria Is (In the year of our Lord 1403 Maria Is ')

'3 bell THOMAS BOT ET WILHELMVS DE ALTEN ME FECIT 1560

'5 bell ICK GOEBEL ZAEL HEEFT MIN GHEGOTEN INT JAER ONS HEREN MCCCCCXLII ' (I Goebel Zael hath cast me in the year of our Lord 1542)

Foreign bells in England are very rare but most of those now in existence belong to the 16th century See Eeles *Church Bells of Kincardineshire*, p 5

It is said that the sound holes in the belfry storey were made by Dr Parr that the sound of his new peal of bells might be better heard He was passionately fond of the music of bells and by his exertions and mainly at his expense, the bells at Hatton were increased to their recent size and number (*Warwickshire Churches*, ii, p 58) He was Vicar for thirty-nine years, and died 6 March, 1825, aged 78 His monument is in the church He is also said to have given a clock (*Memoirs*, ii, p 313), though not the present one "But of all his improvements none gave him a higher degree of satisfaction than the recasting of the parish bells, with the addition of a new one, and these were so well tuned that he often boasted they were the most musical peal in Warwickshire" (*Ibid*)

In his own words we read "Now I am preparing to close my labours, by assisting to get a new and enlarged set of bells It so happens that from my youth upwards, even to this hour [1807], I have been a distinguished adept in the noble art of ringing that I have equal delight with Milton in the sound of bells that I have far superior knowledge in the science of casting them and that my zeal for accomplishing my favourite project is very great ' (*Op cit* ii p 315) And again (p 316) My peal of bells is come It cost a great sum of money I believe that my Norwich friends would have honoured me, as a country parson if they had seen the harmless but animated festivity of my village on Friday last A new tenor bell had been given them by my pupils my friends, and myself and we have no inconsiderable share in the charges of some of the old bells, which have been recast and enlarged My orthodoxy has endowed all of them with Scriptural appellations The great bell has inscribed upon it the name of Paul, and it is now lying upon our green. It holds more than seventy-three gallons It was filled with good ale, and was emptied too on Friday last[1] More than three hundred of my parishioners young and old, rich and poor, assembled, and their joy was beyond description S Parr, Hatton, July 3rd 1809"

---

[1] This method of inaugurating new bells was only too prevalent in the Georgian period We read of similar performances at Canewdon, Essex, in 1791 (Benton, *Hist of Rochford Hundred*, i, p 12.)

For further details of Dr Parr see Johnstone's *Life* esp pp 81, 816, Colvile, *Worthies of Warwickshire* p 564, and *Dict of Nat Biog*

Bells chimed for services on Sundays

Ringing on Christmas Eve, New Year's Eve and occasionally at other times

Very many thanks to Mr W E Falkner

H T T, 13 July, 1881

HENLEY-IN-ARDEN ST JOHN BAPTIST Six bells

1 GLORIA ● IN ~ EXCELCIS ● DEO ● 1727 ● ~ ● ● ●

Below arabesques all round

2 IOHN ✠ WEVER ✠ CHAPEL ✠ WARDEN ✠ 1707 

3  

4 1707

On waist, a coat of arms 

5 *As No 1*

6 *Above, scroll-border all round*

● THOMAS ● BAKER ● AND ● ROBERT ● MORRELL ● CHURCH ● WARDENS ● 1727 ●

(border of scrolls continuous)

Below, border of arabesques with cable-moulding above

Treble and tenor by Joseph Smith, the latter about 15 cwt Borders Pl XXIII 2 and Fig 11

2nd—5th by Clark and Bushell of Evesham (see p 76), the coat of arms on the 4th and 5th is fully discussed below

The church was formerly a chapel to Wootton Wawen, hence the 'chapel warden' on the 2nd

The clock which strikes the hours and quarters, was made by a native of Henley

1750 '6 bells'

See *Notices of Warwickshire Churches*, i p 137

Hannett, *Forest of Arden*, p 45, states that on the old Town House, taken down in 1793 there was a bell removed from the Chapel in 1693-4 by the Bishop of Worcester's license, for the convenience of the school

The coat-of-arms which appears on the 4th and 5th bells is that of Sir Ralph Boteler, Lord Sudeley, owner of the town and manor of Henley in the reign of Henry VI He founded a guild in the chapel for four priests belonging thereto to pray for his soul (Hannett, *Forest of Arden*, p 41) The same arms were formerly in the east window of the chancel, according to Dugdale (ii, p 807), and are described by him as follows —"Quarterly 1 and 4 gules, a fess counter-compony arg and sa, between six crosses pattées or, 2 and 3 or, two bends gules" It will be noted that on the bell these arms are reversed, from which we may gather that the founders found them on the old bell then being recast and wished to preserve them, but failed to impress them the right way The original bell bearing these arms was doubtless presented by their owner, the founder of the guild

This Sir Ralph Boteler was descended from Ralph le Boteler, who bore the office of butler to Robert, Earl of Mellent and Leicester, in the reign of Henry I In 1369 William de Boteler, of Wem, Shropshire, married Joan, the eldest sister of John de Sudeley, and thus came into possession of the Sudeley estates His grandson and heir, John de Boteler, died without issue, and the latter's younger brother, Ralph, succeeded, being created Baron of Sudeley in 1442 He was Lord Treasurer of England, and built Sudeley Castle

The shield shows the family connections, the fess being derived from Robert, Earl of Mellent and Leicester, the two bends from the ancient Sudeley bearings (through Joan de Sudeley)

[For most of the above information I am indebted to the kindness of Mr W Salt Brassington, F S A , and Mr W E Falkner, of Stratford-on-Avon]

CUSTOMS —

A bell rung at 8 a m on Sundays

Death knell at 9 a m , tenor tolled for two or three minutes, tellers 3 × 3 for man 3 × 2 for woman, 3 × 1 for child At funerals bell tolled for one hour at intervals of four minutes.

Ringing in Advent, at Christmas, and on New Year's Eve , also for Weddings

A bell rung for Vestry Meetings

Best thanks to Rev G. E Bell, Vicar, and to Mr W E Falkner

H T T 11 June, 1883

HILLMORTON   ST JOHN BAPTIST   Five bells

1 THOMAS RVSSELL OF WOOTTON NEAR BEDFORD CAST THIS RING 1781 (32 in

2 ✲ THOMAS RVSSELL OF WOOTTON NEAR BEDFORD ✲ CAST THIS RING IN 1781 (33½ in

3. ✲ RICHARD HVRST AND THOMAS ATKINS CHURCHWARDENS IN THE YEAR 1731 (35½ in

4 MRS COOKE MRS ELIZABETH BRYON WILLIAM EDWARDES EDWARD BODDINGTON ROBERT DAULTON MRS ANN SAWBRIDGE THOMAS ATKINS ROBERT DAULTON WILLIAM IONSON AN PETTEDER WILLIAM MOSES WILSON IOHN CAVE RICHARD COLLINGS IOHN WOOD GAVE £ S D 0 - 5 - 0 BONNER WILLIAM GREEN THOMAS SEDGELEY MARY CROOKE EACH OF THEM 1731 (41 in

5 MR WILLIAM STARESMORE VICAR L S D 4 - 4 - 0 MR EDMVND BROMVICH GENT L S D 2 - 2 - 0 MR IAMES MR HENRY PARKINS L S D 2 - 2 - 0 MR THOMAS BROMWICH L S D 0 - 10 - 6 MR WILLIAM ELMES L S D 0 10 - 6 ELKINTON L S D 0 - 10 - 6 GIVEN TOWARDS THE CASTING OF THIS RING IN THE YEAR OF OUR LORD MRS MARGARET CLARKE L S D 0 10 - 6 THOMAS RVSSELL OF WOOTTON CAST THIS RING

1731 ● ○ (44 in

For Thomas Russell see p 76. Type on the 4th and 5th very small, inscription in a double line

1552 ' iiij^or belles and a saunce bell

1750 ' 5 Bells '

See Wait, *Rugby Past and Present*, p 272

H T. T, 20 Jan , 1892

HOCKLEY HEATH. See NUTHURST

HONILY — St John Baptist — Five bells

1 IOHANNES SANDERS ARM HUJUS ECCL FUNDAT ME PIE VOVIT ANNO DOM QUI OBIT 1727

Below —FUDIT T EAYRE KETTERING 1731

2 *The same*

3 *The same*

4 *The same in one line*

5 *As No 4*

All by Thomas Eayre of Kettering (see p 80)

The church was rebuilt in 1723 by John Sanders, who gave, or rather bequeathed, this ring He purchased the estate in 1708 (See Thomas Dugdale, ii p 643)

H T T, 18 March, 1876

HONINGTON — All Saints — Six bells

1 THIS BELL THE GIFT OF GEORGE & SARAH MARTIN 1810 (29 in

2 *Above, border of scrolls* (Fig 10)

FEARE GOD AND HONOR THE KING 1687 (29⅞ in

3 WEE LIKE MVSICK MAKE A PLEASENT SOVND 1687 (31¾ in

4 PROSPERITY TO THIS PARISH 1726 (33⅛ in

5 MATTHEW BACLY MADE MEE 1687 (37 in.

6 MATTHEW BAGLEY OF CHACOMB MADE MEE 1687

Below, border of arabesques all round (40¼ in

1st By John Rudhall of Gloucester

4th by Abraham Rudhall Borders on 1st and 4th, fig 15

The rest by Matthew Bagley, borders on 2nd, Fig 10, on 3rd, bits of Fig 11 on 5th, Figs 10, 12, on 6th, Fig 10, and 11 below

1552 'HONNYNGTON iiij belles one litle bell'

1760 'Hunnington 5 Bells'

CUSTOMS.

On Sundays a bell at 9 a m (old Mass Bell), also after Morning Service, said to have been originally to denote an afternoon service

Ringing at Christmas, on New Year's Eve, and occassionally at other times, for Weddings by request

Death-Knell as soon as may be usual tellers

Practice ringing for Christmas begins November 5th

A peal of 5,040 changes was rung 2 May, 1908

Best thanks to Rev E H Boddington Vicar, and to Mr W E Falkner

H T T, 20 April, 1887

HUNNINGHAM — St Margaret — Two bells

1 ✠ In ✠ Nomine ✠ Ihesu ✠ Vocor ✠ Sancte ✠ Margareta

2 ✠ AVE MARIA GRACIA PLENA DOMINVS TECVM

1st Probably by Thomas Bullisdon of London c 1510 (see p 26), his trade-mark is wanting, but the stop (Pl XIII 13) is found on other bells by him, the cross is Pl XIII 1

2nd, Similar bells at Ullenhall, and Willoughby Waterless, Leics, founder unknown See p 4 and Pl II 14–18

1552 'Two belles and a saunce belle two handbells' (The two still existing

1750 'Hamingham 2 Bells'

H. T T, 9 Oct., 1878

IDLICOTE — St James — One bell

1 I IOHN RVDD ✠ WILLIAM MARTIN CHVRCHWARDENS ✠ 1636 25½ in

By Henry Bagley there is some uncertainty about the date which may be 1636 or 1656 Scroll border, *Bucks*, pl xxxii, 2

1552 'iij belles and little bell'

1750 'Uthcote 5 Bells' (*sic*).

One or more of the previous bells are said to have been stolen

Many thanks to Mr W E Falkner

H T T, 29 May, 1888

ILMINGTON — St Mary — Five bells

1. *Above, border*

SOLI DEO (*border*) SOLA GLORIA (*border*) H (*ornament*) B (*border*) 1641 (*border*)

On waist, Royal arms, with HONI SOIT QVI MAL Y PENSE

2. *Above, border*

HENRY (*ornament*) BAGLEE MADE MEE (*ornament*) 1641 (*two bits of ornament*) (*border*) 

3 *Above, border*

THOMAS (*border*) KINGE (*border*) RECTOR OF ILMINGTON (*border*) 1641 H  B (*border*)

4. *Above, border*

NATHANIEL EDEN (*border*) AND RICHARD ROSE CHURCHWARDENES (*border*) 1641 (*ornament*) H  B (*border*)

5 *Above, border*

BY MY VOICE THE PEOPLE MAY KNOW TO COME TO HEAR THE WORD OF GOD (*ornament*) 1641 H 

An early ring by Henry Bagley, of Chacombe (see p 67) The inscription on the tenor also occurs at Grandborough

The Rev T King (see 3rd bell) was Rector 1635—1669

The condition of the bell-chamber is very unsatisfactory, and Mr Falkner states that it is impossible to take rubbings or diameters, owing to the absence of any flooring

1552 ‘ iiij belles ij little belles
1750 ‘ 6 Bells.’

CUSTOMS

On Sundays one bell rung at 8 a m two or more at 9 a m , except on first Sunday in month, when bells are chimed , one bell at 10 a m , and one at close of Morning Service, chiming before services at 11 a m and 6 p m

On New Years Eve the old year is rung out and the new in with what is known as a "Devil s peal ' Ringing on November 5th, and for Weddings on Royal Birthdays formerly

Death-Knell one hour after death , usual tellers Chiming at Funerals, especially in the case of a ringer, who is "chimed to church,' and a muffled peal is rung afterwards

Gleaning Bell discontinued 30 or 40 years ago

Fourth bell rung in case of an outbreak of fire

Best thanks to Rev J H Warner, Rector, and to Mr W E Falkner
H T T, 15 June, 1887

IPSLEY ST PETER Three bells

1. ✠ DVM TONAT HOC SIGNVM PRECE PELLE ROBERTE MALIGNVM (31¾ in

2 ✽✽ ALL ✽✽ PRAYSE ✽✽ AND ✽✽ GLORY ✽ BE ✽✽ TO ✽✽ GOD ✽✽ FOR ✽✽ EVER ✽✽✽✽✽✽ 1664

Below, border of arabesques and John Martin's large shield with three bells (34¾ in.

3 ✽ SOLI ✽✽ DEO ✽✽ GLORIA ✽✽ PAX ✽✽ HOMINIBVS ✽✽✽ IOHN HEWSTER ✽✽ WILLIAM ✽✽ OKES ✽✽✽ 1664

Below, cable-border arabesques, and shield as last (38½ in

1st . By the same founder as Aston Cantlow 4th , see p. 9 and Plate V , Figs 12—24. The dedication to St. Robert seems to be unique Cf the bell formerly at Hallow, Worcs , dedicated to St Anne

2nd and 3rd by John Martin of Worcester Shield and ornaments Pl XXI , Figs 1, 6, 10

1552. ‘ IPISLEY Itm there . iij belles ’ 1750 ‘ Ippesley 3 Bells
See *Notices of Warwickshire Churches*, ii , p 1 8

On Sundays bells chimed for services with tolling for last five minutes

Ringing on Christmas Day and New Year's Eve, for Weddings by request , formerly on November 5th.

Death-Knell with usual tellers

Thanks to Rev. H J Newton, Rector
H T T , 29 Nov , 1881

ITCHINGTON, BISHOP'S ALL SAINTS Five bells.

1 **J: TAYLOR & C° FOUNDERS LOUGHBOROUGH.**
On waist – **GLORY TO GOD IN THE HIGHEST.** (28¼ in

2 *As No 1*
On waist —**CUM SONO SI NON VIS VENIRE**
NUNQUAM AD PRECES CUPIES IRE (30¼ in

3 *As No 1*
On waist —**GOOD WILL TOWARDS MEN** (31½ in

4 **J. TAYLOR & C° BELLFOUNDERS LOUGHBOROUGH.**
On waist – **OUR VOICES SHALL WITH JOYFUL SOUND**
MAKE HILLS AND VALLEYS ECHO ROUND (34½ in.

5 *As No 4*
On waist —
I TOLL THE FUNERAL KNELL
I RING THE FESTAL DAY
I MARK THE FLEETING HOURS
AND CHIME THE CHURCH TO PRAY. (38¼ in

		cwt	qrs	lbs		cwt	qrs	lbs
Weights	1)	4	3	10	4)	8	0	7
	2)	5	2	18	5)	11	0	19
	3)	6	0	19				

Total, 35 cwt. 3 qrs 17 lbs

The date of the erection of the ring is 1874 (see *Church Bells* 27 June) To judge by the inscriptions the predecessors of the 2nd and 4th were by Watts of Leicester and Pack and Chapman of London respectively

1552 'ICHYNGTON EP'I iij belles a saunce bell, a hand belle, and a small bell'
1750 'Over Itchington 1 Bell'
H T T, 3 May, 1884

ITCHINGTON, LONG HOLY TRINITY Four bells

1 *Above, cable-moulding*
HENRY (*scroll*) BAGLEY (*scroll*) MADE (*scroll*) MEE (*scroll*) 1670 (*scroll*) (28 in

2 **CVM . SONO SI NON VIS VENIRE NVNQVAM AD PRECES CVPIES RE 1623** (29½ in

3 *Above, border all round, of alternating fleurs de-lys (Fig 9), with cable-moulding above*
HENRY BAGLEY MADE MEE 1649 (32 in.

4. **IHS : NAZARENVS** (*border*) **DEORVM REXIV** (*border*) **FILI : DEI** (*border*) **MISERERE : MEI** (*border*) **1636** (*border*) (35 in

1st The border is *Bucks* pl XXXII, No 2 that after date on 3rd *Bucks*, fig 71

2nd and 4th by Hugh Watts, border on 2nd, Plate XXI, Fig 8 (afterwards used by Clibury and John Martin), on 4th, usual 'acorn'

Bells hung diagonally to the tower

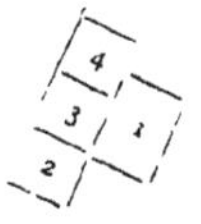

1552 'ICHYNGTON LONGA iij bells a saunce bell and ij handbells'
1750 '6 Bells'

CUSTOMS —

On Sundays bells chimed for services, single bell for last five minutes
A bell rung after Morning Service
Ringing during Advent, on Christmas Eve and New Year's Eve at midnight, and for Weddings with the Incumbent s consent
Death-knell on receipt of notice, usual tellers

Thanks to Rev W E Ellis Vicar
H T T, 1 May 1884 H B W June, 1908

KENILWORTH St Nicholas Six bells

1	**J : TAYLOR & C° FOUNDERS LOUGHBOROUGH 1875**	(30 in.
2	*The same*	(31½ in.
3	*The same*	(34½ in.
4	*The same*	(36¾ in
5	*The same*	(39½ in
6	BRYANVS ELDRIDGE ME FECIT 1656 OP ID	(43 in

Bryan Eldridge, of Chertsey, Surrey cast a ring of five, of which the tenor alone survives, when on a temporary visit to Coventry, 1656 58 (see below and p 58) Of the five bells here at H T T s visit in 1874 the treble was by John Briant inscribed

SAM BUTLER R RUSSELL C W JOHN BRIANT HERTFORD FECIT 1793

the 2nd by Abraham Rudhall or Thomas Eayre, inscribed

MR WILLIAM BEST VICAR JOHN PARKER AND THOMAS GARLIC CHURCHWARDENS 1734

and the 3rd and 4th inscribed like the present tenor See also *Notes and Queries*, 3rd Ser, x (1866), p 143, Tyssen *Church Bells of Sussex*, p 22

Weights of present ring —		cwt	qrs	lbs		cwt	qrs	lbs
	1)	5	2	24	4)	8	3	18
	2)	5	3	23	5)	11	0	17
	3)	7	2	20	6)	14	2	0

1552 'iiij^or belles and a saunce bell' 1750 '5 Bells'

Dugdale (*Antiqs of Warwickshire*, i p 241) says of the Monastery here 'there is nothing now remayning but a very great Bell yet hanging in the Parish Church, made, it seems, by Prior Kederminster, who lived *temp H 4 H 5* and beginning of *H 6* time [*c* 1410—1430], about which there is an Inscription in large characters' On p 252 he gives this inscription in Gothic letters as follows

'Inscribed upon the great Bell

G KEDERMYNSTRE P DE K

MENTEM SANCTAM SPONTANEAM HONOREM DEO PATRIE LIBERATIONEM

ANGELUM PACIS MICHAEL IN ISTAM CELITUS MITTI ROGITAMUS AULAM

This bell must have been the old 2nd, recast in 1734, shortly after Dr Thomas' revision of the work in 1730 (see above) The first line of the inscription is also found on a bell at Bex, in Switzerland, and was formerly on one at Prees, Shropshire It is supposed to have been a kind of talisman against fire (see Ellacombe, *Bells of the Church*, p 440, and Parker's *Glossary*, 1850 edn, i, p 471) but it comes originally from the Acts of St Agatha, being her last prayer at her martyrdom, and is found in the Dominican and Sarum breviaries

The following extracts from the Churchwardens' Accounts are given in *Kenilworth Illustrated* (1821), p 47 —

1618	Item p^d to the Ringers when the Kinge was at Kenellworth	ij^s	viij^d
1622	Item paid for ringing when the prince came	v^s	
1625	Item to the ringers for the princes highnes when he was last at Kenellworth	vj^s	
	Item payd for Ringing for Kinge Charles	ij^s	
1631	An order made May 8 that no parishioners shall have more than 3 peals after their decease, viz one at departure, one before and one after burial with the great bell the peals not to exceed an hour, and if more than 3 peals to pay		12^d
1640	Item spent upon the ringers at the Earl of Monmouth his coming to Kennellworth	ij^s	
1643	Spent on ye ringers to drinke when the Kinge was here and on his holy day	5^s	0^d
1655	Item spent upon the Captaines,[2] at Hancoxes & at Cannings when wee went to move them to give some timber towards the making of a frame for ye bells	1^s	
1657	[Various entries about new casting the Bells and an agreement with the Bell founder, the old bells being broken Also charges for timber for the new bell frame and items concerning the new bells Bryan Eldridge was paid "for castinge ye 5 bells" £8, having previously received £36 10*s*]		

M^d that in 1656 ye old bells being four in number and containing in weight all of them one & fifty hundred, were cast into five bells as followes vizt —

The 1st bell 6 hundred & 16 li ye clapper y^r of 25 li
The 2nd bell 9 hundred & 2 li ye clapper y^r of 27 li
The 3rd bell 8 hundred & an half & 13 li ye clapper y^r of 30 li
The 4th bell 11 hundred & 10 li ye clapper y^r of 36 li
The 5th bell 15 hundred & 13 li ye clapper y^r of 42 li

CUSTOMS —

On Sundays bells chimed for services, with Sermon Bell on tenor for first five minutes followed by treble for last five minutes

Ringing on Easter Sunday Christmas Eve, and New Year's Eve (11-30—12-30) also once a week for six weeks before Christmas, for Weddings by request on King's Birthday and Empire Day

Death-knell only when specially ordered, then as soon after death as possible Tenor tolled at Funerals, muffled peals occasionally

---

[1] It is also to be found on an Italian bell now in a church at Hendon, Middlesex (*Notes and Queries*, 9th Ser, ix, p 406), and on a tile from Great Malvern Priory, now in the Wallace collection

[2] See *op cit* p 41 They were appointed to administer the affairs of the manor under the Protectorate

Curfew at 8 p m on 5th bell
Tenor and treble rung in case of Fires
Many thanks to Rev R F Hanning, Vicar
H T T, 19 Sept, 1874, H B W, Sept, 1907

KENILWORTH — St John Evangelist — One bell

One bell by C and G Mears, 1852, weight 4 cwt 1 qr 6 lbs
Church built 1852

KERESLEY AND COUNDON — St Thomas — Five bells

Church built 1847, a ring of five bells by C and G Mears put up in 1848 Weights and diameters —

		cwt	qrs	lbs
1)	$24\frac{1}{2}$ in.	3	1	21
2)	25 in	3	2	3
3)	27 in.	4	1	14
4)	29 in	4	1	24
5)	32 in	6	1	0

Parish formed from St Michael and Holy Trinity, Coventry

KINETON — St Peter. — Six bells

1 WHEN WE RING I SWEETLY SING A R 1716 ($29\frac{3}{4}$ in.

2 COME AWAY MAKE NO DELAY 1703 A R ($28\frac{3}{4}$ in

3 ABRA RUDHALL OF · GLOUCESTER CAST VS ALL 1708 ($30\frac{5}{8}$ in.

4 GOD SAVE THE QUEEN AND CHURCH A · R 1703 ($32\frac{1}{4}$ in

5 IOHN CHANDLER EDWARD SMITH ✠ CHURCH W^R 1703 A R ($34\frac{7}{8}$ in

6 PROSPERITY TO THIS TOWNE & ALL OUR BENEFACTORS A R 1717 ($40\frac{1}{2}$ in.

All by Abraham Rudhall Borders on 1st, 4th and 6th, Fig 15, on 2nd, Fig 16 on 3rd and 6th Fig 18 5th cracked, and about to be recast, there is at present a clamp over the HA of CHANDLER

Chandlers occur in the Registers as early as 1599

1552 'KYNGTON iij belles one little bell'
'M^d that the p'yshe is in dett Sithe the last S^rvey for the great belle a v^li'
1750 '6 Bells'

CUSTOMS —

On Sundays a bell at 8 a m when no service, bells rung or chimed for 20 minutes before morning and evening service, followed by tenor for ten minutes and treble for thirty seconds, 'Pudding bell' after morning service

Ringing at 9 p m on Christmas Eve and New Year's Eve and 6 a m the following mornings; also at 6 a m on St Thomas' Day (when a charity is distributed), for Weddings when paid for Practice from Nov 5 to Christmas

Death-knell on receipt of notice, usual tellers, tenor then rung up and tolled every minute

For Funerals the tenor is rung up for a few minutes, two hours before, the bells are chimed for fifteen minutes immediately before, and a bell is rung for about thirty seconds afterwards

A bell is rung at 6 a m all the year round, except on Sundays, and for a few days at Christmas In the evening Curfew is rung at 8 p m on week-days (7 p m on Saturdays) from Old Michaelmas Day (Oct 11 to New Lady Day (March 25) The fourth bell is used

The tenor is rung for Vestry Meetings

Many thanks to Rev L Goodenough, Vicar, and to Mr W E Falkner

H T T., 18 Sept, 1875

KINGSBURY. SS PETER AND PAUL Five bells

1 I Taylor & So Bellfounders *(border)* 1849 *(border)*

2 ✠ I T *(border)* 1849 *(border)*

3 ✠ John Taylor and Son Bellfounders loughborough *(border)* 1849 *(border)*

4 *As the last*, & for and

5 THE OLD FOUR BELLS RECAST INTO FIVE 1849 R GLOVER & J CLARKSON C WARDENS

On scroll on waist — I Taylor Fecit loughborough

The bells are very large for a village church (H T. T) They are an early example of the Taylors' work at Loughborough

The old ring, as I learn from a note of the late Dr Raven's, was inscribed as follows —

1 Sanctum Sanctum

2 EDWARDE NEWCOMBE MADE ME 1602

3. IHESVS NAZARENUS REX IVDEORUM

4 BE YT KNOWNE TO ALL THAT DOTH ME SEE THAT NEWCOMBE OF LEICESTER MADE ME 1612

1552 'KYNSBERY iiij ^{or} great bells in the steple a handbell'
1750 · '4 Bells'

CUSTOMS —

Bells chimed for services on Sundays, a single bell for early celebration

Death-knell as soon as notice has been given

Curfew rung from October 11th to March

In 1610 additions were made to the tower to accommodate a new ring of five bells, according to an inscription on the west face on which the names of the then churchwardens and others

The inscriptions on the four old bells (which are partially reproduced on the new) have been also preserved in a careful copy made by the Rev W D Sweeting (Brit Mus Add MSS 37180) He gives them as follows —

1. ✠ I H S Sancta Katerina Ora Pro Nobis

2 HENRY BAGLEE MADE MEE 1656

3 CANTATE DOMINO CANTICVM NOVVM H ✤ B 1656

4 I DO CALL THE PEOPLE ALL 1656 H B

It is clear that the order does not correspond his 1st and 3rd answer to the present 2nd and 1st. Nor is his description of the 1st quite complete, as he omits the important detail of the lozenge over the coin which shews the bell to have been the work of Johanna Sturdy of London (see p 22) The 'ring' from the old bell containing the inscription was cut out and preserved by Canon Ellacombe, and a rubbing from it is in his collection in the British Museum (Add MSS 33203) It is amusing to note how the old inscription has been carefully modified on the new bell to avoid giving any offence

The stamps on the old mediaeval bell were cross Pl XI 2, capital letters Plate XI, Figs 9—14, as at Wolfhamcote, but uncrowned

1552 'LODBROOKE iij belles a saunce bell a sacring belle'
1750 Ladbrook 5 Bells'

H. T T, 3 May, 1884

LADYWOOD. See BIRMINGHAM

LAPWORTH. ST MARY THE VIRGIN Five bells

1 Wᴹ MEARS LATE LESTER PACK & CHAPMAN FECIT 1786

2 BRYANVS ELDRIDGE ME FECIT 1656

3 SANCTA KATERINA ORA PRO NOBIS

4 PRAISE THE LORDE 1600

5 *As No 1*

Pits for six bells, treble hung above the rest The tenor is a square-shouldered bell, weight said to be 18 cwt

2nd Bryan Eldridge of Chertsey was at Coventry in 1656-58, see above, p 58

3rd By a Worcester fifteenth-century founder cf. the old 2nd at Allesley, and see p 10, Pl VII, 5—9

4th By Hugh Watts of Leicester cross, Fig 5 = Pl XV 8, see p 41

1552 'iiij belles a saunce bell 1750 '5 Bells'
See *Notices of Warwickshire Churches*, ii p 26

CUSTOMS —

On Sundays bells chimed for services tenor rung at 10 a m

Ringing on Christmas Eve, midnight muffled peal on New Year's Eve, also on November 5th, and for Weddings by request

Death knell as soon as requested, 3 for man, 2 for woman, one for child, on *each* bell, age rung on tenor.

An endowment of £50 per annum from the Lapworth Charity for the maintenance of Divine Service covers the supply of Bell Ropes (but not ringers' payments)

Best thanks to Rev F L Bell, Rector

H T T 9 Feb 1876

LEA MARSTON — ST JOHN BAPTIST — Three bells

1 **J. TAYLOR & C° FOUNDERS LOUGHBOROUGH 1873.**

2 **I. RUDHALL GLOCESTER FECIT 1791**

3 ✠ **JOHN TAYLOR & SON FACERUNT LOUGHBOROUGH 1855**

Treble weighs 5 cwt 1 qr 13 lbs, diam, 29½ in

1552 'Two bells and a saunce beile a han l belle'

LEAMINGTON. — ALL SAINTS. — 8 + 1 bells

1 MEARS & STAINBANK, FOUNDERS, LONDON

On waist—PRAISE TO THE HOLIEST IN THE HEIGHT (26 in

2 T. MEARS OF LONDON FECIT 1826 (27 in

3. *The same* (28½ in

4 *The same* (31 in

5 MEARS & STAINBANK, FOUNDERS, LONDON

On waist.—RECAST 1901 (34 in

6 *As No 2 (longer ornament)* (35 in

7. *The same* (38½ in

8 *As No 5*

"IN THE DEPTH BE PRAISE"

On waist—THE GIFT OF RICHARD BADGER

IN MEMORY OF HIS WIFE, ELLEN BADGER

A D 1901 (40½ in

Clock C & G MEARS FOUNDERS LONDON 1818

Weights —	cwt	qrs	lbs		cwt	qrs	lbs
1)	4	0	10	5)	7	0	14
2)	4	1	17	6)	7	2	14
3)	4	3	15	7)	9	2	9
4)	5	2	21	8)	12	3	16

Formerly six bells, hanging in a wooden belfry before the erection of the present tower, the old 4th was inscribed like the rest

The clock bell hangs in a separate tower or turret at the N E angle of the church

1552 'LEMYNGTON PRIOR iij belles, a saunce belle and a hand belle'

1750 '5 Bells'

H T. T, 3 June 1884, H B W, June, 1908

LEAMINGTON. CHRIST CHURCH. One bell

1  **IHS NAZARENVS** *(border)* **REX IVDEORVM** *(border)* **FILI : DEI** *(border)* **MISERERE : MEI** *(border)* 1628 (34⅞ in

By Hugh Watts, 'acorn' borders

Church built 1825 as a proprietary chapel, which it still is, the bell is an old one from the parish church, dispossessed when the new ring was put up there in 1826 I am much indebted to Mr Falkner for a description of it, and for his pertinacity in unearthing the sexton, who on the occasion of my visit in June, 1908, could not be traced

LEAMINGTON HOLY TRINITY One bell

One bell by Taylor of Loughborough inscribed

16 FEBRUARY 1895

Diam 45 in, weight 16 cwt 7 lbs
Church built 1847

ST JOHN

Church built 1875, a tower added quite recently Number of bells unknown

ST MARY One bell

Church built 1838

ST PAUL Three bells

Church built 1874

LEAMINGTON HASTINGS ALL SAINTS 5 + 1 bells

1 **C & G MEARS FOUNDERS LONDON 1851** (36 in

2 *The same* (38 in

3  **IHS NAZARENVS** *(border)* **REX · IVDEORVM** *(border)* **FILI : DEI** *(border)* **MISERERE : MEI** *(border)* 1620 *(border)* (39 in

4  **CVM SONO SI NON VIS** *(border)* **VENIRE** *(border)* **NVNQVAM AD · PRECES** *(border)* **CVPIES IRE** *(border)* 1631 *(border)* (41 in

5  GOD *(double border)* SAUE *(double border)* THE *double border)* KINGE *(double border)* 1615 *(double border continuous)* 45 in.

S **ABRAHAM DRACY 1677** (13 in

The three largest bells by Hugh Watts, tenor (see p 42) in Brasyer capitals, as at Coleshill All fine bells, especially the tenor which has an iron band round the crown. Borders on 3rd and 4th, 'acorn' throughout, on tenor, the same with a band of small scrolls (Pl XVII 8) above

Sanctus bell by Richard Keene now unused hung with lever in window

Weight of 1st and second, 8 cwt 2 qrs 15 lbs and 10 cwt 1 qr 20 lbs

1552 'iij belles and a saunce belle'

'M^d that ou' and besyds the forsaid p'cells theis things folowing be solde sythe the last survey . a two handbells'

1750 '6 Bells'

Ringing for Weddings by request
Death-knell with tellers, one for man, two for woman, three for child.
Gleaning Bell formerly
Bells not regularly rung, chiming apparatus in use
Thanks to Rev D. W Sitwell, formerly Vicar

H T T, 10 Oct, 1878, H B W, June, 1908

LEEK WOOTTON — ALL SAINTS — Five bells

1 THE GIFT OF THE HON^BLE MARY LEIGH J BRIANT HERTFORD FECIT 1793

2 *The same*

3 PROSPERITY TO ALL OVR BENEFACTORS *(border)* 1703 A R
2nd line.—MR WINTER CHVRCH W^d

4. GOD SAVE THE QVEEN & CHVRCH A R 1703

5 ✠ IHS NAZARINUS REX IUDEORUM

3rd and 4th by Abraham Rudhall
5th by Johannes de Stafford, S and Z reversed See p 15 and Pl VII Figs 16—19

1552 'iij belles and a saunce bell'
1750 'Lekewotton 5 Bells'

See *Notes and Queries*, 3rd Ser, x (1866), p 143

H T T, 8 Oct, 1878

LIGHTHORNE. — ST LAWRENCE — Four bells

1 *On waist*—*(a)* LAUS DEO
W. R. VERNEY RECTOR
W. LATTIMER } CHURCHWARDENS 1890
W. WILKINS }
(b) LLEWELLINS AND JAMES, BRISTOL

2 *On waist*—*(a)* M. BAGLEY MADE ME 1774
I WAS RECAST IN MEMORIE
OF THE QUEEN'S JUBILEE
1890.
(b) as No 1

3 *Above, scroll-border all round*
THOMAS GREEN AND WILLIAM TOWNSIND CHVRCHWARDENS H B
✠ 1679

4 ✠ IOHANNIS PRECE DVLCE SONET ET AMENE

Formerly three bells, the treble is an addition The 2nd replaces the old 1st, the inscription on which is here repeated, it was cracked in 1875 (H T T)

3rd by Henry Bagley border, Pl XXII, Fig 10, with bits of the same between the words Mr Falkner reports this bell as 'dissonant' in tone

4th by a Worcester founder *c* 1410, see p 9 and Plate V, Figs 12—24 The S is reversed in each case

1552 'iij belles a litle bell' 1750 'Leithorne 6 Bells (*sic*)

See *Church Bells*, 5 Sept 1890, and *Bell News*, 13 Sept, for an account of the new bells

Thanks to Mr W E Falkner

H. T. T., 19 Sept, 1875

LILLINGTON ST MARY Three bells.

1 ✠ Sancta Katerina Ora Pro Nobis ⊕ T H (33 in.

2 **CVM SONO SI NON VIS ⚬⚬⚬⚬ VENIRE NVNQVAM AD PRECES ⚬⚬⚬⚬ CVPIES IRE ⚬⚬⚬⚬ 1625 ⚬⚬⚬⚬** (36 in.

3 ✤ HENREY ✤ BAGLEY ✤✤ MADE ✤ MEE ✤✤✤✤ 1675 (*broad scrolls*) (38½ in

Primitive iron repairs to wheels, cannons of treble broken

1st by Thomas Harrys of London, *c* 1480 (see p 26), the capitals are originally John Barber's (of Salisbury), used by a Worcester founder at Lapworth, see Pl VII, Figs 5—9, XIII, Figs 15 16

2nd by Hugh Watts, a plait-band (Pl XX 4) as stop no shield

3rd cross Plate XXII, Fig 7 Fig 9 between words, and a bold scroll after the date Tenor popularly supposed to weigh one ton!

1552 'LELYNGTON iij belles and a saunce belle

1750 '3 Bells'

CUSTOMS —

Bells chimed for services on Sundays

Ringing occasionally for Weddings, formerly on Christmas Eve and New Year's Eve at 11-30 p m, with peals twice weekly from November 5th previously, this has been discontinued

Death-knell as soon as notice is given tenor rung up, with tellers before and after (three strokes on *each* bell for man, two for woman) Tenor tolled for twenty minutes before and after Funerals

Many thanks to Rev C C Brookes, Vicar

H T T 9 Oct, 1878, H B W, Sept 1907

LONGFORD See FOLESHILL

LOXLEY ST NICHOLAS Two bells

1 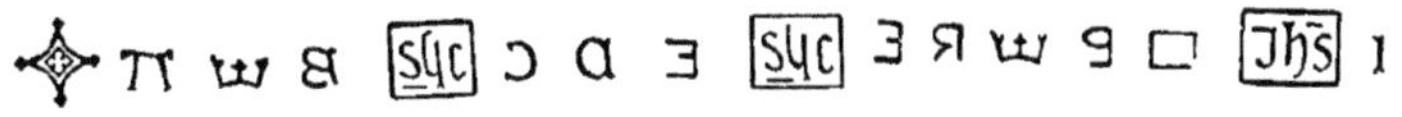 (30 in.

2  **HS NAZARENVS** (*border*) **REX IVDEORVM** (*border*) **FILI DEI** (*border*) **MISERERE MEI** (*border*) **1632** (*border*) (31¼ in.

1st By the same founder as Fenny Compton 2nd (probably Appowell, of Buckingham, see p 46) Cross Plate XVII, Fig 1, the letter and stamp after the second crown are uncertain

2nd By Hugh Watts 'acorn' border

Pits for three bells The 3rd is said to have been sent to the founder to be recast, but he failed and the bell never came back

1552 'ij belles one broken bell'
1750 '3 Bells

Many thanks to Mr W E Falkner, who notes, *inter alia*, that the belfry is 'very old-fashioned' and the floor out of repair, the stocks and wheels are connected by horizontal strips of wood, and the latter strengthened by iron clamps

H T T, 16 May, 1889

LOZELLS See BIRMINGHAM

LUDDINGTON ALL SAINTS Three bells

There was an ancient chapel-of-ease to Stratford-on-Avon here, which is famous as having witnessed the marriage of Shakespeare, and in the time of Edward VI had one bell (Inventory of 1552 'Itm there . j bell') It fell into ruins and a new church, technically a chapel-of-case to Stratford parish church, was erected in 1872

The present church contains three small bells, each inscribed

W BLEWS AND SONS 1871

the respective diameters being 18, 19½, and 21 in They hang in a hexagonal wooden turret and are very difficult of access, they can only be chimed, owing to the way in which they are hung.

Many thanks to Mr W E Falkner for help and information

MANCETTER ST PETER Five bells

1 *Above, border of arabesques*

SOLI DEO GLORIA PAX
O HOMINIBVS 1633 C V

Below, border of arabesques all round, with founder's mark T H *on waist* (34¾ in

2 G A B R I E L (36 in

3 IHS : NAZARENVS (*border*) REX · IVDEORVM (*border*) FILI : DEI (*border*)
MISERERE : MEI (*border*) 1641 (*border continuous*)

Above and below, borders of arabesques (39½ in.

4 HEC IN HONORE PIE
CONSTAT CAMPANA MARIE

(44 in

5 | my | roaringe sound | doth . warninge | give . that | men . cannot | heare alwayſ | live |

R^T GOVLD W GOODWEINE R · BENTLEY 1647 (48½ in

1st By Thomas Hancox, for the various ornaments used see pp 53, 54, and Pl XIX 2 3, 7, Pl XX. 1—3, 7, 8 The ornament before the date is used by Grene at Bulkington The N of HOMINIBVS is reversed, and the last two letters in the inscription are in Gothic capitals. The medallion before HOMINIBVS is fully discussed on p 54

2nd See p 17 and Plate IX

3rd By Hugh Watts, arabesques between the words.

4th Cf St John's, Coventry; date about 1350, see Plate VIII and p 13

5th By George Oldfield, of Nottingham see p. 62, words and letters on *paterae*

1552 'MANCYTOR iiij or belles in the steple'

1750 '5 Bells.'

An annual sum used to be charged out of certain closes adjoining Atherstone for the finding of bell-ropes for the largest bells (see Bartlet's *Manduessedum* in B Nichols' *Bibl Topogr Brit*, ix, p 111) In reference to this Bartlet says —"In or about 16 Isaac Cook, then owner of lands in Manceter, charged two closes lying there (which, in 1782, were occupied by Cass), with the perpetual expense of finding bell-ropes for the three largest bells, which is punctually observed This donation is said to have been occasioned by the following accident Isaac Cook being out one winter evening missed his way, and wandered so near the banks of the river as to have been in the greatest danger, when the curfew bell, beginning to ring directed him to that village, the next day, discovering the great danger he had been in he immediately made the settlement"

H T T, 21 March, 1893, H B W, May, 1908

MARTON. ST ESPRIT Three bells

1  IHS NAZARENVS REX IVDEORVM FILI DEI MISERERE MEI 1624

2 *The same, with date* 1623

3  CELORVM CHRSTE PLATIAT TIBI REX SONVS ISTE 1616

All three by Hugh Watts

1552 'iij belles a saunce bell and ij handbells

1750 '6 Bells

No customs, except that a bell has been rung every Sunday morning at 7 a m. from time immemorial Bells chimed for services

Thanks to Rev P N Bisson Vicar

H T T, 10 Oct, 1878

MAXSTOKE — St Michael and All Angels — Two bells

1 GLORIA DEO IN EXCELSIS 1681

On waist — TH O O (23½ in

2 GOD SAVE THE KING 1641 (25½ in

1st By Thomas Hancox (p 52), small letters On the waist trade mark, as at Bickenhill (Pl XIX, Fig 2), and a twice-repeated impression of the seal of Langdon Abbey Kent, which is fully discussed on page 54 (Pl XIX, Fig 1)

2nd · By Hugh Watts, similar to Corley 1st, cross, Fig 5 (Brasyer), arabesques between words

Bells somewhat cramped, the tower being very small, belfry dark and dirty

1552 'Two small belles in the steple'

Thanks to Rev S Back, Vicar

H. T T, 18 June, 1881, H B W, Sept, 1907

MEREVALE. — St Mary-the-Virgin. — Two bells

"Both bells devoid of inscription, but evidently ancient, they hang in a small turret in the centre of the building" (H T T, 9 Sept. 1876)

MERIDEN — St Laurence — Five bells

1. THE REU^D MR SAMMVELL IONES UICAR 1740 W B (25½ in

2 WHEN MY FIRST AND THIRD BEGIN TO RING

2nd line—THEN I WAS BROKE BEFORE WE ALL DID SING W^M BROOKE CAST ME 1740 (27 in

3. HUMPHRY HAWKSFORD AND EDWARD BECK CHURCH WARDENS 1740 W B (29 in

4 CAST BY JOHN WARNER & SONS L^TD LONDON 1897

On waist —I WAS CAST IN THE 60TH YEAR
OF QUEEN VICTORIA'S REIGN
AND HUNG IN CELEBRATION OF
HER DIAMOND JUBILEE
ALBERT LEWIS WILLETT—VICAR.
CHARLES WRIOTHESLEY DIGBY } CHURCHWARDENS
GEORGE FREDERICK BURR }
1897. (31 in

HUNG BY G DAY & SON—EYE

5 *No inscription, but coins impressed on inscription-band, waist, and sound-bow* (33¾ in

A very light ring, hung left-handed The first three are by William Brooke of Bromsgrove (see p 75), arabesques like Sanders' on 1st and 2nd The 4th replaces a bell lost or stolen many years ago, said to have been the largest The tenor appears to be a mediaeval bell, there are two coins on the shoulder, eight on the waist, and eight on the sound-bow, they are mediaeval groats and half-groats (said to be of Richard II), and on the waist is a French counter of the fourteenth century inscribed IHS, but all are very indistinct

Weights and notes —1) $3\frac{3}{4}$ cwt F sharp; 2) 4 cwt E; 3) $4\frac{1}{2}$ cwt D sharp; 4) $5\frac{3}{4}$ cwt C sharp; 5) 7 cwt B

The clappers of the four old bells hang in the lower part of the tower

1552 'iij belles in the steple
'Note that the p'ishe owithe iiij^li for oon of their aforsaid belles'

1750 '4 Bells

In the ringing-chamber are the following old rules —

"A Reminder
Who rings a Bell let him look well
To Hand and Head and Heart
The Hand for work, the Head for skill
The Heart for worship's part"

H B W, Sept, 1907

MIDDLETON St John Baptist Three bells

1 T. MEARS OF LONDON FECIT 1826 ✦◇◇◇✦ (33 in

2 *The same* (34 in

3 HENRY RUSHWORTH WOOLLEY VICAR ✦◇◇◇✦ T. MEARS OF LONDON FECIT 1826 ✦◇◇◇✦

On waist —JOHN LEES / JOHN GILLMAN } CHURCH WARDENS (39 in

Old bell-frames

The Rev H R Woolley also held the livings of Shillingstone, Dorset (1813) and Shenstone, Staffordshire (1835)

1552 'iij belles and a hand bell'

1750 '5 bells (in a later list 3)

In the belfry is a set of old ringing rules, as follows —

"ALL YOU who are RINGERS
THIS DO YE MARK
HE WHO THROWS O'ER A BELL
PAYS A GROAT TO THE CLERK
IF WITH HAT ON OR SPUR YOU
PERCHANCE SHOULD RING
YOU MUST PAY TWO PENCE
FOR THAT VERY SAME THING
& FOR EVERY OATH TAKEN
YOU ONE SHILLING DO PAY
OR BE EXPELL'D FROM THE BELFRY
WITHOUT AND DELAY"

J HALL
CLERK
1782.

CUSTOMS:

On Sundays the treble rung at 8 a m and two bells at 9 a m, tenor rung up at 10-30 and 6-0, the three chimed for last five minutes before services

Ringing on Christmas Eve and at midnight, New Year's Eve at midnight, St George's Day, May 29th, and November 5th, for Weddings occasionally.

Death-Knell with tolling for an hour on receipt of notice, no tellers. Formerly chiming at Funerals, now only one bell tolled for an hour

Best thanks to Rev R V Hodge, Vicar

H T T, 13 May, 1891.

MILVERTON — ST. JAMES — Three bells

1 **J WARNER & SONS LONDON 1863**

On waist —Royal Arms and PATENT

2 **CAST BY JOHN WARNER & SONS LONDON 1863**

On waist as last

3 Sancta Katerina Ora Pro Nobis   

3rd, by Henry Jordan (p 25, Pl XI, 15—17, Pl XIII, 7—9), cf Brailes 2nd

1552. 'MYLVERTON iij belles and a sacring belle'

H T T, 16 June, 1882

MILVERTON, NEW — ST MARK — Five bells

Church built 1879, and provided with one bell In 1883 four more were added, cast by Taylor of Loughborough, forming 2nd, 3rd, 4th, and 8th of a ring of eight, of which the older bell is the 7th They are used for striking the quarters and hour

		cwt	qrs	lbs			cwt	qrs	lbs	
Weights	1)	3	0	12	23¼ in	4)	9	3	15	38 in
	2)	3	3	24	26⅛ in	5)	14	2	11	42½ in
	3)	5	2	18	29½ in					

MONKS KIRBY — ST EDITH — Six bells

1 *Above, cable-moulding*

SOLI DEO SOLA GLORIA ✤ ~~~ [+++] ✤ [+++] ✤ 1640 ~~~ ✤

MY NOBLE FOUNDERS THEY HAVE BENE SO MANY BECAUSE NOT AL I WILL NOT HERE ✤ ✤

3rd line —NAME ANY ✤ (35 in

2 IOSEPH ● SMITH ● IN ● EDGBASTON ● MADE ● MEE ● 1711 ~~~

Border of scrolls below all round (36½ in

3 **ECCE AGNVS CII ET PVRE PROFETA** (41 in

4  **IHS NAZARENVS** *(border)* **REX IVDEORVM** *(border)* **FILI DEI** *(border)* **MISERERE . MEI** *(border)* **1623** (44¼ in

5 OMNIA FIANT AD GLORIAM DEI ♔♔♔ GLORIA PATRI FILIO ET SPIRITUI SANOTO ♔♔♔ THO EAYRE KETT 1741

Below, a border of elegant arabesques (47 in

6  **IHS NAZARENVS** *(border)* **REX IVDEORVM** *(border)* **FILI DEI MISERERE** *(border)* **MEI** *(border)* **1618** (53 in

1st by Henry Bagley (see p 67), first two lines of inscription on one broad band, as Radford Semele 3rd the ornaments are Pl XXII, Fig 10, and a shield with three swords in pale, points upwards, not found elsewhere

2nd the coins are half-pence, border, Plate XXIII, Fig 2

3rd Cross, Plate V, Fig 12, stop (Pl VII 2) not found elsewhere, lettering, Pl VII 1 See for this bell p 8 The cross and three following letters are nearly obliterated The bell is said to have come from the destroyed church of Stretton Cannons off, edges much chipped CII seems to be meant for DEI, and the inscription is apparently an adaptation of *John* 1 29

6th A very fine bell, weighing about 23 cwt On the stock is cut "John Over Rugby fecit 1795" For John Over see p 80

Acorn borders on 4th and 6th

The tower, bells, and frames are all on a very massive scale

1552 'MONKEST KIRBY CUM MEMBRIS vj belles and a saunce belle

1750 '6 Bells'

H. T T 16 Sept, 1876, H B W, June, 1908

MORTON BAGOT HOLY TRINITY Two bells

1 ✠ S n J t a c t r i n i t a S

2 ✠ K ⚜ maria ✠ K maria K ⚜ maria ⚜ ✠ maria

Both bells probably date from the first half of the sixteenth century The smaller is by an unknown founder, the cross and lettering (Pl VI, 3-5) differing from those on the other The first word is, of course, a blunder for 'sancte Each letter is on a well-marked 'patera,' the S reversed

The larger bell is probably by Nicholas Grene of Worcester (*ob* 1541), as I have endeavoured to show (p 12) The fleur-de-lys occurs at St Martin, Worcester, on a bell by another founder, the cross (Pl VII 4) does not occur elsewhere, but the other stamp K is the well-known head of Edward III as at Aston Cantlow, etc The word 'maria' is all on one 'patera' The old bell at Bearley (p 109) appears to have been similar See Pl VI, Figs 1, 2.

1552 'Itm there one belle' This does not agree with the fact that there are two similar pre-Reformation bells here

H T T, 9 Feb, 1876

MORTON MORRELL. HOLY CROSS Three bells

1. PRASE THE LORGE 1616

2 *The same*

3 ✠ NEWCOMBE OF LEICESTER MADE MEE . 1609

1st and 2nd probably by a Newcombe (see p 37) The D is inverted Note the shortened formula on the 3rd (see p 38)

1552 'MORTONE iij belles a litle bell
H T. T, 30 Jan, 1877

NAPTON — ST LAWRENCE — Five bells

1 ✠ THOMAS RUSSELL MADE ME *(scroll)* WILLIAM RENOLDS AND JOHN MARKHOM ✲ CHURCH WARDENS

2 THOMAS *(scroll)* RUSSELL *(scroll)* OF *(scroll)* WOOTTON *(scroll)* MADE *(scroll)* ME *(scroll)* 1731

3 *The same*

4 *The same*

5 CAST BY JOHN WARNER & SONS LONDON 1874
On waist.— THIS BELL WAS RECAST
AT THE EXPENSE OF EDWARD BEERE ESQ[R]
WHO WAS VICAR'S CHURCHWARDEN
1874

1st—4th for types of Hillmorton scrolls between words See p 76

1552 'iij belles, a saunce belle, a hand bell, a small bell'
1750 '5 Bells
H T T, 1 May, 1884

NEWBOLD-ON-AVON — ST BOTOLPH — Six bells

1 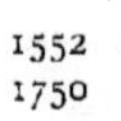 EX DONO REV J O GLORY TO GOD IN THE HIGHEST J BRIANT HERTFORD FECIT 1792

2 J BRIANT HERTFORD FECIT 1792

3 JOHN BRIANT HERTFORD FECIT 1782

4 *As No 2*

5 J BRIANT HERTFORD FECIT 1792 GLORIA DEO IN EXCELSIS

6 J PARKER VICAR T COMPTON J NORMAN & R WEBB C WARDENS VIVOS AD CÆLUM MORTUOS AD SOLUM PULSATA VOCO J BRIANT HERTFORD FECIT 1792

The date on the 3rd is probably an error for 1792 The theology of the inscription on the tenor is not very correct for if the first use of the bell refers to the Church militant the second ignores the existence of a Church triumphant if the only future remaining for the dead is the soil! Or are we to understand *vivos* as equivalent to *animos*, *mortuos* as *corpora*?

The Rev J O on the 1st refers to the Rev J Onley, member of a family long connected with the parish

Weight of tenor said to be 19½ cwt

1552 'NEWBOLDE PAUNTON' 'iij belles a saunce bell and ij hand belles'
1750 '4 Bells'
See Wait *Rugby Past and Present* p 213
The bell-founder's receipt for casting four bells into five in 1792 is extant, the treble being an additional gift

On Sundays a bell is rung at 7 and 8 a m Sermon bell on tenor and 'parson's bell' for last five minutes before services.
Ringing at Christmas, Easter and Whitsuntide, and on New Year's Eve, also on November 5th
Death-Knell at noon on following day tellers 3 × 3 for man 2 × 2 for woman
Thanks to Rev J B Hewitt, Vicar
H T T 8 March, 1887

NEWBOLD PACEY — ST GEORGE — Four bells

1 1707 *On waist*  
2 *The same*
3 ✠ SAMVEL ✠ HOBINS ✠ IO ✠ CVRTIS ✠ CH WAR 1707
4  ✠ 1707  ✠ 

All four by Clark and Bushell of Evesham (p 76) cf Henley-in-Arden They hang in a wooden turret

1552 'NOWBOLDE PACYE' iij bells a sance bell a hande belle
1750 '5 Bells'

CUSTOMS

Bells chimed or rung for Sunday services
Ringing on Christmas Eve and New Year's Eve practice begins on first Tuesday in November Bells also rung before the annual Choir Supper!
Death-Knell with tellers and age tolled
At Funerals the tenor is rung up and down at 9 a m tolling before service and bell rung up and down after it
Bell rung for Vestry Meetings
Thanks to Rev H J Adams Vicar
H T T 30 Jan, 1877

NEWNHAM REGIS. — ST LAWRENCE

Church now in ruins, though the tower still remains benefice united with Church Lawford

1552 'iij belles and a saunce bell' 1750 '1 Bell'

NEWTON REGIS — ST MARY — Two bells

1 *Above, border of arabesques*

✠ RAPHE WOOLLEY CHAROLES HOLDEN HARRE SPENCER CHVRCH WARDENSE 1602

Below, border of acorn-pattern, with scrolls above

On waist—crowned rose four times (34 in

2 *Above and below, borders of arabesques*

FEDCBA (border) MLKIHG (border) XWVTS (border) ROPON (border) FEDCBA (border) MLKIHG (border) 1642 (border) XWI (37 in

1st by one of the later Newcombes (p 38) the ornamental patterns are those used by Hugh Watts (Pl XVII 8, 9) for the lower one of Leamington Hastings tenor For the crowned rose see Plate XVI Fig 1 and cf Offchurch 2nd

2nd by Hugh Watts similar bells at Clifton and Seckington see p 44 Arabesque borders between words, N reversed

Pits for three bells, there seems to have been a treble formerly

1750 '3 Bells'

H T T, 3 Oct, 1876, H B W, May 1908

NORTON LINDSEY   Holy Trinity   Two bells

Two small bells in a turret both without inscription, the smaller appears to be modern, the larger ancient Both are without cannons The clerk in 1882 stated that the smaller bell was recast at the restoration of the church, before which time the bells were in a closed turret

1760 'Norton Linsey 2 Bells

H T T, 24 Jan, 1882

NUNEATON   St Nicholas   Eight bells

1 CAST BY JOHN WARNER & SONS LONDON 1873

On waist—THIS AND THE 2ND BELL WERE SUBSCRIBED FOR BY THE PARISH 1873
H W BELLAIRS VICAR
J H CLAY, } CHURCHWARDENS
J HALL } (28½ in.

2 CAST BY JOHN WARNER & SONS LONDON 1873 (30 in

3 ABRA RVDHALL OF GLOCESTER BELL FOVNDER AN D^O 1703 (31½ in

4. J HUSKINSON & J GEARY C W J BRIANT OF HERTFORD FECIT 1809 J OVER B H (34 in

5 *As No 2* (36 in

6 WILHELMO SMITH ✠ IOH WATTS ✠ RIC WISE ✠ ECCLESIÆ GVARDIANIS 1708 (37½ in.

7 *As No 2* (40 in

8 CAST BY JOHN WARNER & SONS LONDON 1873

On waist—THIS AND THE 3RD AND 5TH BELLS WERE RECAST AT THE EXPENSE OF THE PARISH 1873

(*Vicar and Churchwardens as on 1st*) (44½ in

Formerly six bells by Rudhall of 1703, the tenor was recast in 1725 and the 2nd (now the 4th) in 1809 the tenor again with the 3rd and 5th in 1873, when two trebles were added The cost of the five new bells was £301 10s

On the 4th B H stands for 'bell-hanger' Over acted in this capacity elsewhere for Briant he lived at Rugby See p 80

The 3rd 4th, and 6th have been quarter-turned and the cannons removed

Mr Chapman Head Ringer, notes that the tenor is a good bell for her weight, which is 14 cwt 1 qr 5 lbs, key of E 7th and tenor rehung about 1892 by Warner

Chimes formerly

The Rev H W Bellairs (see treble) was Vicar of Nuneaton 1872 91, Rural Dean and Hon Canon of Worcester 1882-96

1552 'Itm there . iij belles 1750 Nun-Eaton 6 Bells

In *Notitia Parochialis* in the Lambeth Palace Library (1705) is the following —' The steeple of the said Church (Nuneaton) lately containing Five heavy Bells the Tenor whereof being Broke and another of the said Bells Faulty They were by Agreement of the Parishioners, a gift of the Honourable Sr Thomas Acton Baronet, one of the Lords of the Manor, and a Levy granted to the Church Wardens, new Founded or cast into a very Tuneable Peal of Six Bells By Mr Abraham Rudhall Bell Founder in Gloucester, A D 1703"

The old tenor, a good bell (15 cwt), was cracked while being rung for service on Sunday, 3 Nov 1872 The clapper, being broken was repaired by a local blacksmith and was said to have been made too heavy for the weight of the bell

CUSTOMS

On Sundays peals are rung before services

Ringing on Festivals, Anniversaries, and at midnight on New Year's Eve, for Weddings by request, muffled peals on the death of Royal personages

Death-knell with tellers, each bell being struck three times for a man, twice for a woman, the tenor is then rung up and tolled two or three times a minute, for 15 or 20 minutes, for a child the 6th or 7th bell is used

The 2nd bell is rung daily for two or three minutes at 5 a m from March 25th to September 25th, at 6 a m the rest of the year (Sundays excepted)

Curfew rung at 8 p m on 7th bell, Saturday and Sunday excepted

Upwards of forty peals of 5 000 changes have been rung on these bells Four of these are recorded on boards —

13 April, 1889 5,040 Grandsire Triples (the first by local ringers)
24 Oct, 1890 Do do
1 Feb, 1890 5,040 Bob Major
2 Oct, 1890 5,056 Treble Bob Major

The first peal rung on the eight bells was one of Stedman's Triples of 5,040 changes by members of St Martin's Guild, Birmingham 19 April 1873 See also *Church Bells* 12 July, 1889.

Many thanks to Rev Dr J G Deed, Vicar and to Mr Thomas Chapman Head Ringer

H T T, 7 Sept, 1876

NUNEATON St Mary One bell (?)

Church built 1878.

See also ATTLEBOROUGH, STOCKINGFORD

NUTHURST — St Thomas — One bell

There was formerly an ancient chapel here, in connexion with the parish church of Hampton-in-Arden, which appears to have been in ruins in Dugdale's time The present church was erected in 1880, and contains one bell by Barwell of Birmingham, put up in that year, diam 26 in, weight 4 cwt 14 lbs Hannett, *Forest of Arden* p 132, seems to imply that the old chapel or a successor was standing in his time, and gives a view of it

OFFCHURCH — St Gregory — Four bells

1 ✠ SANCTE . MICHAEL ORA PRO NOBIS (32 in

2 ✠ BE YT KNOWNE . TO ALL THAT . DOTH ME SEE THAT . NEWCOMBE OF LEICESTER MADE ME 1605 *(border)*

On the waist —large rose and crown (Pl XVI 1) *above and below the inscription arabesques* (35½ in

3 ✠ VIRGINIS ♔ EGREGIE ♔ VOCOR ♔ CAMPANA ♔ MARIE (39 in

4 ● THOMAS ⁂⁂ SMITH ⁂⁂ AND ⁂⁂ THOMAS ⁂ PAGE ⁂ ● CHVRCHWARDENS ⁂ M *(rosette)* B ● 1681 (43 in

1st and 3rd by Robert Hendley of Gloucester (p 7) cf Butlers Marston Cross and letters, Plate V, Figs 1—9; crown on 3rd, Plate V, Fig 10

2nd On the waist a large crowned rose as at Newton Regis (Plate XVI, Fig 1) 'acorn' border (Pl XVII 7) after date

4th By Matthew Bagley, popularly said to weigh 18 cwt, but obviously less ornamented cannons Over the initials M B are stamped parts of three coins Between the words arabesques (Fig 11)

1552 'OFCHURCHE. iij^or belles in the steple
'Note that their is vj^li to be paid yet by the p'ishe for the forsaid great bell'
'Itm vj^li is owing yet for the p'chase of thother'

1750 '4 Bells.'

CUSTOMS

On Sundays bells chimed for services, with treble for last five minutes, a few strokes on tenor after Morning Service A bell every Sunday at 8 a m and also on Good Friday

Death-Knell on tenor as soon as possible, usual tellers with tolling afterwards, tolling in minute strokes before funerals

Curfew rung at 8 p m, Michaelmas Day to old Lady Day (April 6th) on tenor

Gleaning bell rung until about 1900, at 8 a m and 7 p m, on the tenor discontinued because farmers refused to pay for it when gleaning became obsolete

The Vicar notes —'The few strokes rung after Morning Service are variously explained by old inhabitants, as (1) to give notice of another service later, (2) to warn those who are responsible for cooking dinners, (3) to enable parents and masters to know of any loitering on the way home from church The custom is, of course known elsewhere e g at Tysoe

From the Churchwardens Accounts, which begin in 1617, the Vicar kindly sends the following extracts —

1664	Item paid to Tho Rawbond for his work about the bells	8^s 9^d
	Item for 2 bell ropes one at 2^s 6^d the other at 1^s 8^d	4^s 8^d
1665	Item for a bell rope to Townesend at Warwick	2^s 0

Many thanks to Rev J J Agar-Ellis, Vicar

H T T 11 Oct, 1878 H B W, June, 1908

OLTON. St Margaret One bell

Church built 1884, parish formed from Bickenhill The bell hangs in an open turret

OXHILL St Lawrence 5 + 1 bells

1 WILLIAM BAGLEY MADE MEE 1701 25 in

2 **J. TAYLOR & C° FOUNDERS LOUGHBOROUGH 1878**

On waist — **LAUS DEO** (27½ in

3 WILLIAM BAGLEY MADE MEE 1701 (28 in

4 *As No 2* (33¼ in

5 *The same* (37¼ in

S *No inscription*

Formerly three bells by William Bagley the old tenor was inscribed

IOHN WARD IOHN BLACKFORD CH WA 1701

It was cracked in 1877 (H T T) The sanctus bell is probably modern, it is not now used

		cwt	qrs	lbs		cwt	qrs	lbs	
Weights —	1)	3	2	0	4)	7	0	7	
	2)	4	1	14	5)	8	3	13	Total 27 cwt 3 qrs 20 lbs
	3)	4	0	11					

1552 'Oxhull iij^or bells & ij litle bells'

1750 '3 Bells'

Customs

On Sundays bells chimed for services, one bell for service at 8 a m A bell is rung after Morning Service when there is to be one in the evening

Ringing at Christmas (midnight peal), Easter, Ascension, Whitsuntide and Sunday after St Lawrence's Day (10 August, Patronal Festival) on New Year's Eve a muffled peal followed by an open one after midnight Also on King's Birthday, November 5th and for Weddings by request.

Death-Knell one hour after death tellers 3 for man 2 for woman, 1 for child At Funerals tolling at 8 a m, and before and immediately after the ceremony

Priest's bell, now disused, formerly rung as 'call bell' before services.

Best thanks to Rev J Carter, Rector, to whom I am also indebted for the following extracts from the Churchwardens' Accounts (1729—1840) —

1729	Paid for a rope for the Saints bel		1	6
1731	Paid for three bell Ropes		8	0
	Paid to William hiron (?) for to new Bell wheles and other woork	2	3	0
	Ale for do		1	6
1735—1750	Frequent payments for bell ropes			
1741	Gave to the Ringers at Cristmus		2	0
1746	Paid for ye ringers ye midnite peal [i.e. at Christmas]		2	6

[This entry repeated in most successive years]

1758 Repairing ye frames of the bels and for wood & nails & woorkmanship and for a lether for the First bell ... 4 0

1761 p^d the Ringers at the Kings Coronation . 3 0

[Miscellaneous entries down to 1840 referring to Christmas ringing, new bell ropes and small repairs the payment for the midnight peal occurs continuously from 1775 onwards]

H T T, 31 Jan 1877, 29 May, 1888

PACKINGTON, GREAT St James 1+1 bells

1 ✠ TRES OLIM CAMPANÆ E QUIBUS RUPTÂ QUÂDAM VICTORIAM AD TRAFALGAR RESONANDO A{D} MDCCCV IN UNAM FUSÆ A{D MDCCCVIII ✲ O
JOHN BRIANT HERTFORD FECIT 1808 ✲ GLORIA DEO IN EXCELSIS ✲ ✠ ✠ ✠

S + AVE MARIA GRACIA PLENA S I D

The bells hang in a small pepper-box turret at the N W angle of the church which bears the palm in the county for ugliness re-built 1789) they are somewhat difficult of access

The large bell, though modern, is not without interest as recording (1) that there were formerly three bells, (2) that one was broken in ringing to celebrate the victory of Trafalgar It seems a pity, however, that the injury done to one should have entailed the recasting of the other two The marks in the inscription are a cross *fitchée*, double triangle, bell and calvary cross (Plate XXIII, Figs 4, 6 7) as at Shotteswell, and a sort of large comma

Sanctus bell by a Worcester founder *c* 1480, see p 11 and Plate VI 6-7, also H T T in *Trans Birm Mid Inst* 1892, p 24 The meaning of S I D is not clear

1552 'PAKYNGTON MAGNA iij belles and a saunce belle
H T T, 19 May, 1883

PACKINGTON, LITTLE St Bartholomew Three bells

1 S A N N A (22 in

2 DOG RO Eman EHc In (24½ in

3 K Y E I H ✥ D A E T D S A [illegible] (28¾ in

Bells clocked awkward to reach and belfry very dark The stamps are very much worn on all especially on the 1st and 3rd All three are from the Newcombes foundry at Leicester but probably not all of the same date

1st By Thomas Newcombe, see p 34 Cross stop and lettering as on Mancetter 4th, also occurring at Budbrooke (Plate VIII) shield Plate XXI Fig 3 It is just possible that this bell is by the earlier Thomas (see p 17)

2nd Probably by Edward Newcombe and Hugh Watts I in partnership, see p 34 The lettering is mixed, the E, H I as on Haseley 2nd, the others as Olney, Bucks (Fig 6 p 33), and South Luffenham Rutland The date of this bell is about 1595

3rd By one of the Newcombes see p 36 Crosses Pl XXII 2 and Plate XV Fig 2, stop *Leics* 43 as on 1st Braser shield and head of King as at Stoneleigh (Pl X Fig 3), lettering, Pl XV 3-7 Similar bells at Higham Ferrers (old 4th) Overbury, Worcs and Old Weston, Hunts

1552 'PAKYNGTON P'I'S thre belles in the steple.'
1750 'Packington p'ish 3 Bells'

No customs
Many thanks to Rev. Canon Waller Vicar
H T T 4 March, 1876, H B W May, 1908

PACKWOOD — ST GILES — SIX BELLS

1 **BARWELL FOUNDER BIRMINGHAM**
On waist—(*a*) **TE DEUM LAUDAMUS** (*b*) *Barwell's trade-mark*
IN MEMORY OF
THOMAS SAVAGE M.D.
1907 (22⅞ in.

2 CANTATE (*scroll*) DOMINO (*scroll*) CANTICVM ● NOVVM ● 1686 ● (*scroll*)
On waist—*coat of arms of Featherston*, *on sound-bow, six coins* (25¼ in

3 HENRY BAGLY MADE MEE 1686
On waist shield as last (26¾ in

4 *Above, scroll-border as 2nd all round*
MATHEW BAGLY MADE ● ● ● MEE 1686 (*scroll*)
On waist, shield as before (29 in

5 HENRY ● ● BAGLY MADE MEE (*scroll-border*) 1686
On waist, shield as before (30⅜ in

6 FEAR GOD AND HONNOR THE KING (*scrolls continuous*)
2nd line—THOMAS (*scroll*) FETHIRSTON (*scroll*) ES[q] (*scroll*) 1686 (*scroll continuous*)
On the waist within a circle of coins, a garter with motto enclosing the Royal Arms (33¼ in

Originally a light ring of five the joint production of Henry II and Matthew Bagley The treble is an addition actually put up in 1908 weight 2 cwt 3 qrs 14 lbs The ornament on the 2nd, 4th and 6th is Pl XXII 10 on the 5th a narrow scroll between cable-mouldings The N s are reversed throughout The 4th is hung above the rest

The arms on the tenor are the Royal Arms of James II s time, but omitting those of France which appear on the coins ornamenting the 3rd, 4th, and 5th bells, where they quarter England The garter has the motto HONI SOIT, etc, and is surmounted by a crown and surrounded by mantling In the circle are 28 impressions of coins and there are small ornaments (described by Mr Falkner as flags) between the garter and the shield

The shield on the waist of the four middle bells bears the arms of Featherstone *gules*, on a chevron between three ostrich feathers *argent*, as many annulets *sable* This family lived at Packwood, but is now extinct in the male line (see *Warw Ant Mag.* part 2 (for pedigree), and Grazebrook, *Heraldry of Worc*, I, p 199) The name was revived by Royal licence in 1833 and a Mr John Featherston was a contributor to the *Warwickshire Antiquarian Magazine*, started in 1859

1552 'iij belles a hande bell'
1750 'Pacwood Cap 5 Bells'

Many thanks to Mr W E Falkner, and to Mr Salt Brassington for heraldic notes *per* the former

H T T 9 Feb 1876

PILLERTON HERSEY St Mary Three bells

1 HENRY ✤✤✤✤ BAGLEY ✤✤✤✤✤ MADE ✤✤✤✤ MEE ✤✤✤✤ 1668 ✤✤✤ ✤✤ (29½ in

2 ✤ HENRICVS ✤ BAGLEY ✤ ME ✤ FECIT 16L2 ✤✤✤ ✤ (32¼ in

3 ✠ **BE YT KNOWNE TO ALL THAT DOTH ME SEE THAT NEWCOMBE OF LEICESTER MADE ME 1602** *(acorn border inserted)*

Above, arabesques (Watts) below acorn-border (35⅝ in

1st Border of fleurs-de-lys (Fig 9) ornament at end doubtful

2nd Cross before date is at Lillington (Plate XXII, Fig 7) stamps at end see Pl XXII, Figs 6, 9

3rd The borders here are those usually employed by Hugh Watts II (Plate XVII, Figs 7, 9)

Bells re-hung by Bond of Burford 1901 the old frame made into altar rails All cannons removed

1552 Pillerton Hersey iij belles a saunce belle
1750 4 Bells

Ringing practised from November 5th to Christmas
The Vicar refused to give any information as to Customs, etc
Many thanks to Mr W E Falkner

H T T, 17 Sept, 1875

PILLERTON PRIORS

This church was destroyed by fire in 1666 and was never re built
The Inventory of Church Goods, *temp* Edward VI, gives
'Oue Pillardington Priors iij belles one litle bell

POLESWORTH St Edith Six bells

1 ERECTED BY PUBLIC SUBSCRIPTION 1896 *(vine-border)*

On waist—(a) J G TROTTER VICAR (b) *Taylor's trade-mark*

F TIBBITS } CHURCHWARDENS
J G DAVIES

FOR THE GLORY OF GOD (30½ in

2 THE GIFT OF Mr EDWD TOON BORN AT DORNDON IN THE PARISH OF POLESWORTH A R 1740 (32¼ in

3 **To Honour Both of God & King Our Voices shall in Consort Ring**

Below—**Pack & Chapman of London Fecit 1776**

Incised—Wm KETCH WARDEN (33½ in

4 *Above border of arabesques*

FEARE *(border)* **GOD** *(border)* **HONOR** *(border)* **THE** *(border)* **KING** *(border)*
1667 *(border)* (36 in

5. *Above and below borders of arabesques*

IOHN *(border)* **YOUNG** *(border)* **THO** *(border)* **LACKIN** *(border)* **IOHN**
(border) **HOLLMES** *(border)* **DAVID** *(border)* **CORBESON** *(border)*
WARDENS  **1654** *(border)* (39½ in

6 *Border above as 4th*

ALL *(border)* **GLORI** *(border)* **BEE** *(border)* **TO** *(border)* **GOD** *(border)*
ON *(border)* **HIGH** **1664**  *(border)* (43⅝ in

Formerly five bells only treble by Taylor 2nd by Abel Rudhall

The three largest by George Oldfield, of Nottingham see p 62 Foundry stamp Plate XXII Fig 1[1] borders Pl XXII Figs 3, 4

		cwt	qrs	lbs		cwt	qrs	lbs
Weights —	1)	6	1	14	4)	7	1	14
	2)	6	1	3	5)	10	0	15
	3)	6	1	0	6)	11	2	11

1552 POLLESWORTH Itm there iiij^or^ bells and a saunce belle
1750 5 Bells'

In the ringing chamber are some old Belfry Rules —

Who will divert themselves with ringing here
Must nicely mind to Ring with Hand and Ear
And if he gives his Bell an Overthrow
Pay Sixpence a forfeit for doing so
He who in Ringing wears Spurs Gloves or Hat
Pay Sixpence as a forfeit for that
All persons that disturbance here create
Forfeit one Shilling towards the Ringers treat
Those that to our easy laws consent
May Join and Ring with us we are content
Now in love and unity Join a pleasant peal to Ring
Heavens bless the Church and George our Gracious King Amen

H T T 25 July 1876 H B W May 1908

See also WARTON

PRESTON BAGOT ALL SAINTS Two bells

1 G BLEWS & SONS 1879
LAUS DEO (17 in

---

[1] The stamp illustrated is that of his predecessor Henry Oldfield, which George used but placed a G over the H partly concealing it

2 W BLEWS & SONS 1879
GLORIA DEO IN EXCELSIS (19 in

Formerly two bells the smaller 'inscribed with the name of a Bromsgrove founder' (Sanders or Brooke), the larger, GOD SAVE THE KING 1663 In 1879 when the church was being restored, one of these was recast being cracked, and as the other one sounded inharmoniously with it, it was also recast (H T T)

1552 Item there j bell one han bell
1750 '2 Bells

Many thanks to Mr W L Falkner

H T T, 20 July 1891

PRIORS HARDWICK. St Mary Three bells

1 CANTATE DOMINO CANTICVM NOVVM H B 1670

2 SANCTA MAREA

3 HENRICVS (border) BAGLEY (border) FECIT (border) 16L0

1st and 3rd by Henry Bagley
2nd by Thomas Newcombe stamps, Pl XVI 2 3

1552 'iij belles a sance belle
1750 Hardwick 3 Bells'

H T T, 2 May, 1884

PRIORS MARSTON St Leonard Six bells

Above, border of arabesques

1 **CANTATE DOMINO CANTICVM NOVVM H B 172J**

Below scroll-border (Pl XXII 10)

2 (*Above arabesques all round*)

HENREY BAGLEY OF BVCKINGHAM MDAE MEE J72J (*border*)

3 **IOHN BRADSHOW GEORE ELWARD CHVRCH WARDENS J72J**

4 *Above, arabesques all round*

IOHN BRADSHOW GEORGE ELWARD C WARDENS H BAGLEY MA ME J72J

5 **IOHN BRADSHOW GEORG ELWARD CHVRCH WARDENS H B J72J**

6 AHOLIAB WEST GAVE $\overset{L}{100}$ TOWARDS THE CASTING OF THESE SIX BELLS 1721
(*border of oak-leaves as below, and stamp of ox to left*)

On waist —(*a*) (*eagle*) (*b*) J JOHNSON

(*acorns*) JOHN TAYLOR & SON (*acorns*)
(*eagle*) LOUGHBOROUGH (*eagle*)
(*acorns*) (*acorns*)

FOUNDERS
1845
(*oak leaves*)

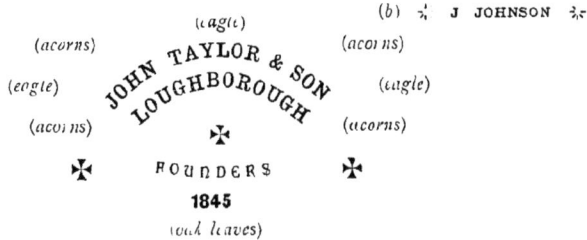

On sound bow — OS MEUM ANNUNCIABIT LAUDEM TUAM

An original ring of six by Henry Bagley III cast at Buckingham (see p 71), there is no other evidence of his working there but it must have been a temporary visit

H T T says the clerk remembered the old tenor being removed from the belfry and falling down owing to the chains giving way but no one was hurt

The present tenor is one of the earliest bells cast by Taylor at Loughborough (see p 82), the ornaments on the waist, a figure of an eagle and an oak pattern, occur also on the treble and 3rd at Elvaston Derbyshire (1847),[1] as does the inscription on the sound-bow The ox stamp also occurs at Christ Church, Coventry

1552 'iij belles a litle belle

CUSTOMS

Bells chimed for services on Sundays
Death-knell as soon as possible no tellers
Many thanks to Rev E E T Candler Vicar
H T T 2 May, 1884

RADFORD SEMELE St NICHOLAS Four bells

1 GOD (*border*) SAVE (*border*) THE (*border*) KING (*border*) 1636 (*border*) (30½ in

2 T. MEARS OF LONDON FECIT 1818 (32½ in

3 *Above cable-moulding, on a broad band with double line of inscription* —
(*scroll border* Pl XXII 10) (*scroll as before*) 1641 HENRY BAGLEE MADE MEE (35 in

4 CVM SONO · SI NON VIS (*border*) VENIRE (*border*) NVNQVAM AD PRECES (*border*) CVPIES IRE (*border*) 1636 (*border continuous*) (38½ in

[1] See *Reliquary* xix p 242 pls 22, 23

1st and 4th by Hugh Watts: acorn borders.

3rd. The inscription and ornament above are all on the same band, with no beading between (cf. Monk's Kirby 1st): the upper borders are *Buds*, fig. 71 and Pl. XXII. 10, the former repeated before HENRY. For the three bells (not here on a shield), cf. Barford.

Bells very dirty.

1552. 'iij belles, a saunce belle, a hand-bell, a sacring bell.'

1750. 'Radford Comitis 3 bells.'

See *Notes and Queries*, 4th Ser. iii. (1869), p. 501.

H. T. T., 11 Oct. 1878; H. B. W., June, 1908.

RADWAY. St. Peter. Five bells.

1–5. ROBERT STAINBANK FOUNDER LONDON 1868

Weights and diameters:

		cwt.	qrs.	lbs.	
	(1)	3	0	8	21 in.
	(2)	2	1	8	24½ in.
	(3)	3	2	22	25 in.
	(4)	4	1	2	27 in.
	(5)	5	0	26	29½ in.

Bell given by the executors of the late Mrs. Magan of Cheltenham, at a cost of £280.

1552. 'ij belles ij hand-bells.'

1750. '1 Bell.'

H. T. T., 21 April, 1887.

RATLEY. St. Peter. Three bells.

1. G MEARS FOUNDER LONDON 1859

2. HENRY (*border*) BADLEY MADE MEE (*border*) 1677 (*border*)

3. **IOHN HITCHCOCKS · CHURCH WARDEN : MATTHEW B . MADE M J763**

Weight of treble, 3 cwt. 2 qrs. 2 lbs.

3rd by Matthew Bagley.

1552. 'Rotteley iij belles one litle belle.'

1750. 'Rottley 3 Bells.'

Customs:—

A bell formerly rung every Sunday at 8 and 9 a.m. (Mattins and Mass Bells), the former now only rung when there is Holy Communion). A bell was also rung at noon when there was afternoon service.

Ringing at midnight on Christmas Eve and New Year's Eve; also for Weddings if paid for.

Death-knell as soon as possible, but not after sunset: tellers, three for man, two for woman, one for a child. Tolling before and after Funerals.

Gleaning bell until recently: two fields being available a bell was rung at 8 a.m. for entry into one field, at 1 p.m. for the other.

Thanks to Rev. J. A. Mason, Vicar.

H. T. T., 21 April, 1887.

ROWINGTON St Laurence Five bells

1 WILLIAM COWPER THOMAS *(border)* TIBBATS *(border)* C 1633 

On waist —**CARR OF SMETHWICK REMADE ME 1887**

P. B. BRODIE M.A. VICAR

W. DRAPER

J. CLARKSON CHURCHWARDENS 1887 (31½ in

2  CREDE RESIPISCE *(double border)* MORI *(double border)* MEMENTO *(double border)* 1633 *(double border)* (33¼ in

3 ✠ NEWCOMBE OF LEICESTER MADE MEE 1609 (35⅛ in

4  **IHS NAZARENVS** *(border)* **REX · IVDEORVM** *(border)* **FILI : DEI** *(border)* **MISERERE MEI** *(border)* **1620** (38¼ in

5  CUM SONO SI NON UIS UENIRE NUNQUAM AD PRECES CUPIES 1633

2nd line — IRE *(arabesques continuous)* (43 in

Treble hung in middle above the others and slantwise. old inscription (by Hugh Watts) reproduced in facsimile Weight 9 cwt 1 qr 6 lbs

2nd, 4th, and 5th also by Watts, the use of the Brasyer capitals after 1615 is unusual, especially for one of his stock inscriptions as on the 5th. see pp 42 45 Border on 2nd Pl XXII 8 as on Leamington Hastings 5th, on 4th 'acorn', on 5th arabesques

3rd Border as at Allesley (Pl XXII 3)

1552 'iij bells oon litle sance bell' 1750 'Rowington 5 Bells

Notices of Warwickshire Churches ii p 74

Customs —

On Sundays a bell rung at 8 a m chiming for services, followed by tenor as Sermon Bell

Ringing on Christmas Day, New Years Eve, and special occasions, such as Harvest Festival (after Evensong) for Weddings by request

Death-knell on receipt of notice no tellers toll for a few minutes for a child, and age in case of adults Tolling before Funerals

The bells are rung from the body of the church

A brass tablet records the restoration of the ring in 1887, in commemoration of the Jubilee

Many thanks to Mr W E Falkner also to Rev A Pritchard, Vicar, and to Mr W. Ryland, F S A

H T T 13 July 1881

RUGBY ST ANDREW 5+8 bells

IN THE OLD (WEST) TOWER —

1 VNVS ● DEUS, VNVS ● DOMIN, VNA ● FIDES, VNA ● SPES VNA ● ECCLESIA

2nd line —MR LOV SMITH AND ● MR ● WILLIAM ● BETTS ● CHVRCH ● WARDENS 1711 ● (30 in

2. SI DVO EX VOBIS CONSENSERINT, QVOD PETIERINT, FIET 1711 (30½ in
Below scrolls all round

3 TIES SVNT QVI TESTIFICANTVR IN CALO, PAT FIL ET SP SANCT 1711 (32½ in
Below, scrolls all round

4 SVPER HANC PETRAM VIZ PAT FIL ET SP SANC ECCLESIAM ÆDIFICABO 1711
Below, scroll, not continued all round (35½ in

5 GLORIA PATRI ET FIL ET SPIRIT SANCTO, AMEN FR BVRDEN RECTR 1711 (39½ in
Below, scrolls all round

This ring is by Joseph Smith, of Edgbaston and was put up in October, 1711 The inscriptions are taken with more or less exactness from the Vulgate of the N T —(1) *Eph* iv, 4, 5, (2) *Matt* xviii, 19, (3) 1 *John* v 7, (4) *Matt* xvi, 18, on the 3rd TIES should be TRES, and CALO should be CAELO On the 1st MR LOV SMITH is incised All the bells are somewhat square-shouldered

IN THE NEW (NORTH-EAST) TOWER —

1—8 MEARS & STAINBANK, FOUNDERS, LONDON, 1895

On waist —1 ✠ WE GIVE THANKS TO THEE
FOR THY GREAT GLORY,
O LORD GOD HEAVENLY KING
GOD THE FATHER ALMIGHTY

2 ✠ WE GLORIFY THEE

3. ✠ WE WORSHIP THEE

4 ✠ WE BLESS THEE

5. ✠ WE PRAISE THEE

6 ✠ GLORY BE TO GOD ON HIGH,
AND IN EARTH PEACE
GOODWILL TOWARDS MEN

7 ✠ O COME LET US SING UNTO THE LORD

8 ✠ TO THE GLORY OF GOD
THIS PEAL OF EIGHT BELLS
FOR THE PARISH CHURCH OF RUGBY
IS THE HUMBLE OFFERING OF
GEORGE CHARLES BENN
1896

This additional ring was cast by Mears and Stainbank in 1896

The inscriptions on the first six are of course from the Gloria in the Liturgy but in reversed order

Rugby is probably unique among English parish churches in possessing two distinct rings of bells, each in a separate tower

Weights notes, and diameters —

			cwt	qrs	lbs		
Old Bells	1)	30 in	4	2	2	D	
	2)	30½ in	4	1	20	C	
	3)	32½ in	5	2	3	B	
	4)	35½ in	6	2	22	A	
	5)	39½ in	9	0	9	G	
			30	1	0		
			cwt	qrs	lbs		
New Bells	1)	31¼ in	6	3	2	D	
	2)	32¾ in	7	0	25	C	sharp
	3)	35¼ in	8	0	27	B	
	4)	37¼ in	9	1	19	A	
	5)	41 in	11	2	22	G	
	6)	42 in	12	2	8	F	sharp
	7)	47¼ in	17	0	11	E	
	8)	53 in	24	3	8	D	
			97	3	10		

1552 ' ROOKBY iij belles a clock a sacring belle ij hand belles

It is stated that at a subsequent period there were four bells in the tower heavier than the present five, the tenor of which was cracked in 1711 In 1721 a set of chimes was put up which do not now exist, but in the new tower Ellacombe s chiming apparatus has been fixed

1750 6 Bells (*sic*)

Many useful and interesting notes about the bells in Wait s *Rugby Past and Present*, p 26

CUSTOMS —

The old ring of five is used for chiming for Daily Services, and also rung on Christmas Eve at midnight till 12 30 a m and on October 20th at 6 a m , 1 p m , and 7 p m in commemoration of Lawrence Sheriff the founder of Rugby School

The new ring is used for peals before services on Sundays and all great Festivals also after Evensong on Festivals, formerly the bells were only chimed

The 4th and 5th bells of the old ring were formerly rung at 9 a m on Sundays, and again at 2 p m The treble was also rung at the conclusion of morning service (said to be for the distribution of a dole of bread) When there was a sermon the tenor was rung for the last few minutes before services as Sermon Bell, when no sermon the 2nd Bell instead

Ringing on Christmas Day from 12 to 1 p m and on New Year's Eve from 11 30 to 12 30 (first half-muffled, then open), also on King's Birthday and Accession Day and for Weddings by request

Death-knell with usual tellers at beginning and end tenor for adults, treble for child under eleven years

Curfew formerly, on 3rd bell, at 8 p m, also Pancake Bell (4th) at noon on Shrove Tuesday, and 4th bell tolled for Vestry meetings

The first peal on the new bells was rung on April 3rd 1899, by the Midlands Counties Association (5,040 Grandsire Triples in 3 hrs 25 min), as recorded on a peal board. There is now an energetic society of local ringers, with sixteen active members

Very many thanks to Mr Arthur L Coleman

H B W, June, 1908

RUGBY

ST MATTHEW — One bell

Church built 1841

HOLY TRINITY is a chapel-of-ease to the Parish Church, and has one bell in the central tower

RYTON-ON-DUNSMORE.

ST. LEONARD — Three bells

1 G MEARS & Co, FOUNDERS, LONDON 1864
On waist —RICHARD LICKORISH INCUMBENT,
THOMAS CONEY BODDINGTON CHURCHWARDEN (33 in

2  wILLAM wATTES aabcdefghiklmnopqr yvzaqzqrr klmnopq vusttbsrip (35¼ in

3  SOLI ✤✤✤✤ DEO ✤✤✤✤ GLORIA ✤✤✤✤✤ PAX ✤✤✤ HOMI-NIBVS ✤✤✤✤✤✤✤✤✤✤✤✤✤✤✤ 1653 ✤✤✤✤✤✤✤✤✤✤ I ✤✤ M ✤ (39 in

The treble weighs 6 cwt. 3 qrs 11 lbs Its predecessor was from the Nottingham foundry, dating from the fifteenth century (see p 20), and was inscribed

Sca maria mater dei ☐

At the end of the inscription was a figure of the Virgin and Child, as at Stanion Northants (North Northants, fig 92) and below, an incuse diagonal cross in a shield  the same as on Stoneleigh 2nd (Pl X 2) A drawing of the inscription by Mr Kimber is preserved at Mears and Stainbank's foundry

2nd By William Watts, of Leicester or Bedford, c 1595 (see p 40), the base of the shield is cut off, as at Weston A similar bell at Sherington Bucks (see Cocks p 149) In the alphabet a and r occur twice in different forms, the ten letters at the end are somewhat uncertain

3rd By John Martin, of Worcester, cross and ornament Plate XXI, Figs 6, 7, the N is reversed.

The Rev Richard Lickorish was instituted in 1821

1552 'RUYTON SUP' DUNFSMORE iij belles a saunce bell ij hand belles,
1750 'Ritton 4 Bells
H T T, 18 May 1887, H B W, June, 1908

SALFORD PRIORS — ST MATTHEW — Eight bells

1. T MEARS FECIT THE GIFT OF MR IOHN SLATTER OF THIS PARISH 1826 (29½ in

2. *As No 1*

3. ✠ IF WEL YOU RING WEEL SWEETLY SING ✠ 1735 R S (29¾ in

4. ✠ GOD PROSPER THIS PARISH R S 1735 O oOOO *(scrolls)* (32 in.

5. IOHN HARRIS PEACE AND GOOD NEIGHBOURHOOD R S 1735 (33⅜ in

6. ✠ RICHARD SANDERS MADE US ALL 6 ●●● 1735 ✠ ●● (35½ in

7. ✠ IAMES HARRIS ✠ IOHN HAYWOOD C H WARDENS 1735 ✠ ●●● ●●●● (38½ in

8. MEARS & STAINBANK FOUNDERS LONDON

On waist —

RECAST A D 1867
SAMUEL GARRARD VICAR
THOMAS SHAILER } CHURCHWARDENS
JOHN SLATTER } (43 in

1st and 2nd Probably recast by Mears at Gloucester where he occupied John Rudhall's foundry for a year or two after winding up the latter's business the type is Rudhall's, not Mears These two bells were additions made in 1836 to the ring of six cast by Richard Sanders just 100 years before Since then Sanders tenor has been recast it weighs 15 cwt 1 qr 2 lbs

4th After the date is an impression of a medal inscribed ' FOR EVER' (first word indistinct), followed by a farthing and three halfpence of George II and a scroll border Similar impressions on 6th and 7th There is also a doubtful ornament after the date on 5th

The two smallest bells are hung above the rest

Clock by Gillett and Bland, striking the quarters

Mr Falkner gives the diameter of the tenor as 44½ in but the above is Mears and Stainbank's estimate (weight 15 cwt 1 qr – lbs)

The Rev S Garrard (see tenor) was Vicar from 1860 to 1901

1552 'iij belles one litle bell
1750 '1 Bell (*sic*)

CUSTOMS —

On Sundays the tenor is rung for half-an hour followed by chiming for half-an-hour before services

Ringing on Christmas Eve, New Year's Eve, and occasionally at other times; practice twice a week from November to Christmas

It is said that when the ring was increased to eight, the Bidford people thought of having eight also, but Salford replied that if Bidford had eight, they would have ten

In the tower are two boards on which are five four-line stanzas extolling "the fame of Salford bells;" but they are hardly worth quoting *in extenso*

Many thanks to Mr W E Falkner

H T T, 29 Jan, 1878

SALTER STREET St Patrick Five bells

Church built 1843 parish formed from Tanworth

SALTLEY See Birmingham

SECKINGTON All Saints Four bells

1. ✠ **I E S V S** (26¼ in

2 **J : TAYLOR & C° FOUNDERS LOUGHBOROUGH 1886**

On waist — **LAUS DEO**

GIVEN BY T. H. FREER.

1886. (28¼ in

3  MLKIHG (*border*) FEDCBA (*border*) XWVTS (*border*)

RQPON 1640 (*border*) (32 in

4 **: TAYLOR & C° BELLFOUNDERS LOUGHBOROUGH 1886**

On waist — **1886**

W. H. FREER, RECTOR.

R. THIRLBY, CHURCHWARDEN (32¼ in

Formerly two bells only of the two added by Taylor the larger is almost the same size as the old 2nd, though nearly 1 cwt heavier

1st from the Nottingham foundry see p 22 Plate X 9-11 It is a square-shouldered bell and looks early

3rd By Hugh Watts of Clifton and Newton Regis acorn borders N reversed

Bells in good order, but dirty cannons off 3rd bell

	cwt	qrs	lbs		cwt	qrs	lbs
Weights —1)	3	1	22	3)	5	3	24
2)	4	2	24	4)	6	2	27

1552 'iij belles in the steple'

1750 '2 Bells

H T T 3 Oct, 1876, H B W May 1908.

SHELDON St Giles Four bells

1 ICHN ● RICHARDS CHVRCHWARDENS ● 1723 ●

On waist — ●  ● *and border as before all round*

2 *No inscription*

3 ✠ S MARIA 

4 SOLI DEO GLORIA PAX HOMINIBVS IO WO 1650 *(border)*  *(border)*

1st By Joseph Smith, border and trade-mark, Plate XXIII Figs 1 2

2nd 'plain band, as Over Whitacre, etc, it is perhaps therefore the oldest bell in the tower (H T T).

3rd By Thomas Newcombe, see p 30

4th By John Martin, large heart-mark (Pl XXI, Fig 3)

1552 'iiij^or belles and ij lytle belles'

On the base of the tower is an inscription recording the building of it in 1461

Bells chimed for Sunday services, tolling at Funerals
H T T, 23 Aug, 1874 9 Dec, 1881

SHERBORNE ALL SAINTS Six bells

1—3 G MEARS & CO FOUNDERS LONDON 1863

1 *On waist*.—BE WITH YOU ALL AMEN (27 in

2 *On waist* —AND THE COMMUNION OF THE HOLY GHOST (28½ in

3 *On waist* —THE GRACE OF THE LORDE JESUS CHRIST & THE LOVE OF GOD (30½ in

4  CVM SONO · SI · NON VIS *(border)* VENIRE *(border)* NVNQVAM AD · PRECES *(border)* CVPIES · IRE *(border)* 1632 *(border)*

Incised on waist —GOOD WILL TOWARDS MEN (33 in

5 *As 1—3*

On waist —ON EARTH PEACE (36 in.

6 *As 1—3*

On waist — GLORY TO GOD IN THE HIGHEST (40 in

4th by Hugh Watts

		cwt	qrs	lbs			cwt	qrs	lbs	
Weights —	1)	4	1	25	D sharp	4)	6,	2	0 (approx)	A sharp
	2)	4	3	26	C sharp	5)	8	0	26	G sharp
	3)	5	2	13	B	6)	11	1	17	F sharp

1552 'SHERBURNE Itm ij belles

Formerly (down to 1863) two bells only,[1] though there were pits for three, there is a

[1] Cf *Notices of Warwickshire Churches*, ii, p 95 (inscriptions not given)

tradition that the third bell was seized by the people of Budbrooke in payment of a debt (but see another tradition under Barford)

CUSTOMS

On Sundays bells chimed for services, peals before Mattins on Festivals, tenor bell rung up after chiming when there is a Sermon

Ringing on Christmas Eve, Christmas Day, New Year's Eve, on September 29th (Dedication Festival), for Weddings by request

Death Knell rung about one hour after death, tellers 3×3 for man, 3×2 for woman, two strokes for child on tenor, age of deceased tolled when requested Tolling before and after Funerals

Bell-ropes are paid for out of the endowment of the church

In the parish accounts about 1765 and succeeding years occurs the entry

P[d] for Ringing the Bells at times for the poor people that be not able to pay 5s

Many thanks to Rev G Sedgwick, Vicar

H T T, 3 Aug, 1881

SHILTON ST ANDREW Four bells

1 EDW[D] ARNOLD LEICESTER FECIT 1795 RICH[D] WAKELIN CHURCH WARDEN

2 *The same*

3 ✠ BE YT KNOWNE TO ALL THAT DOTH ME SEE THAT NEWCOMBE OF LEICESTER MADE MEE 1603

4 ✠ IESVS BE OVR SPEED 1614 R W 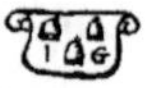

4th by John Greene of Worcester cf Bulkington treble Shield Plate XXI, Fig 4

1552 'iiij[or] belles'
1750 '4 Bells'

See W C Adams, *Ansty and Shilton*, p. 32

Customs as at Anstey with which this benefice is united
Thanks to Rev T C P. Pyemont of Anstey

H T T, 26 Aug, 1876

SHIRLEY STREET ST JAMES Five bells

Church built 1832 the parish being formed out of Solihull Four bells by C and G Mears put up in 1855 Weights and diameters

		cwt	qrs	lbs
1)	27 in	4	1	17
2)	28 in	4	2	9
3)	29½ in	5	0	24
4)	32 in	6	2	2

Mr W E Falkner informs me that there are now five bells

SHOTTERY ST ANDREW One bell

Church built 1870, strictly a chapel of ease to Stratford on-Avon

The bell hangs in a small wooden turret at the junction of chancel and nave, and being closely netted round is quite inaccessible (letter from Mr Falkner, 27 July 1908)

SHOTTESWELL St Lawrence 5 + 1 bells

1 E. G WALFORD VICAR J ABBATS C W (ornaments) JOHN BRIANT HERTFORD 1808 (28 in

2 CANTATE DOMINO CANTICVM NOVVM 1674 (ornaments) (30 in

3 T H C W M B MADE MEE 1774 (32 in

4 H. BOND & SON FOUNDERS BURFORD OXON 1888
On waist —C J READ VICAR
G H BULL G BUSBY CHURCHWARDENS
On sound-bow —RECAST TO COMMEMORATE THE
JUBILEE YEAR OF THE REIGN OF QUEEN VICTORIA (34 in

5  IHS NAZARENVS *(arabesques)* REX IVDEORVM *(arabesques)* FILI DEI *(arabesques)* MISERERE MEI *(arabesques)* 1625 *(arabesques)* (38 in

S 1634 (ornaments) *(continuous)* (14 in

The old 4th was inscribed

THOMAS HUNT CHURCH WARDEN M BAGLEY MADE MEE 1774

H T. T notes that it was cracked in 1875

Treble hung above the rest, after C W are a double triangle, two small bells and a Calvary cross, as at Great Packington (Plate XXXIII, Figs 4, 6)

2nd by Henry Bagley, as is also the small bell, border the same on each (Pl XXII 10)

3rd by Matthew Bagley.

5th by Hugh Watts arabesque borders

The Rev C J Reade, of St John's Oxford was Vicar 1872 88 the Rev E G Walford 1805-32, holding also the living of Frieston Lincolnshire and subsequently that of Chipping Warden, Northants

1552 'iiij belles a litle bell'
1750 '4 Bells'

Customs

- On Sundays bells chimed for services followed by "Priest's bell", 4th bell rung before Holy Communion, a single bell at 8 a m
- Ringing on Festivals and New Year's Eve also on November 5th and for Weddings by request
- Death-Knell on same day or next day if death occurs after mid-day, tellers, 3 for man 2 for woman, 1 for child before tolling At Funerals, tolling before the arrival of the corpse and for two or three minutes after the service
- The treble is rung for Vestry Meetings and also for the "dole" on Good Friday

In the ringing chamber is the rule

He that rings and breaks a stay
Half-a-crown he must pay

Best thanks to Rev R C Wyatt, Vicar and to Rev Preb Deedes for rubbings

H T T, 18 Sept, 1875

SHUCKBURGH, Lower St. John Baptist Three bells

1  **IHS NAZARENVS** *(border)* **REX IVDEORVM** *(border)* **FILI DEI MISERERE MEI 1628**

2 ✠ A B C D E F G H I

3  PRAISE THE LORDE 1601

1st By Hugh Watts
2nd By Thomas Newcombe, but no shield cross Pl XVI 2
3rd By Hugh Watts, resembling the 4th at Lapworth, cross, Fig 5 See p 41
H T T 2 May, 1884

SHUCKBURGH, Upper St John Baptist Four bells

1 **THE GIFT OF SIR RICHARD SHVKBVRGY KNIGHT 1651**
Below —**RECAST BY J TAYLOR & C° 1864** (28¼ in

2 **F S. BARONETTUS FIERI FECIT**
Below —**JOHN TAYLOR & C° FOUNDERS 1864** (29¼ in

3 HENRY *(border)* BAGLEE *(border)* MADE MEE 1640 *(two bits of border)*

4 HENRY *(border)* BAGLEE *(border)* MADE MEE 1651 *(border)*

The old treble was by Bagley, like the present tenor
Weights of new bells 4 cwt 24 lbs and 4½ cwt

1552 'Over Shukborough iij belles a saunce bell and ij hand belles
'Note that for the greatest of the forsaid three belles the p'ishe oweth ph (*sic*) to Mr Shukborough'

Sir Richard Shuckburgh who gave the original treble was Knight of the Shire in 1641 was wounded and taken prisoner at the Battle of Edgehill and died in 1656 His descendant Sir Francis, 8th Baronet who gave the 2nd bell was born in 1789 succeeded in 1809 and died 29 Oct, 1876

H T T 2 May, 1884

SHUSTOKE St Cuthbert Five bells

1 *On waist* —*(a)* **UNTUNED BY LIGHTNING FLAMES & FIRE 1886** *(b) Taylor's trade-mark*
AGAIN I LEAD THE STEEPLE CHOIR 1887 (27¾ in

2 OF FORE HE CAST VS INTO FIVE 1698

3 REPAIRD OVR CHVRCH AND BELLFREE HERE 1698

4 **Lester & Pack of London Fecit 1768**

5 **Jo^s Gibson C^h Warden Lester,** *&c as last*

The treble by Taylor of Loughborough, weighs 4 cwt 2 lbs Its predecessor was inscribed

✠ M[R] ROBERT MALLERON VICAR AS I DO TELL AND JOSIAS ALLEN CHURCH WARDEN WHEN I WAS MADE A BELL W B : BROMSGROVE 1736

the founder being William Brooke (p 75) The re-casting was necessitated by damage done to the tower and bells by lightning in 1886, as the inscription implies

2nd and 3rd by William Bagley evidently recording a donation of the whole ring It is a pity that the name of the donor[1] is lost as well as the rhymes which were probably on the other bells (*i e* the donor s name on the treble and a couplet on the tenor) Between the words on each are bits of scroll-pattern (Fig 10) the P on the 3rd is reversed and the A s have hooked tops (see p 70)

On a beam in the belfry is carved Ios GIBSON C W 1769

1552 : 'SAUSTOCKE v belles' 1750 'Shustock 5 Bells'

Bells chimed for services on Sundays ringing at Christmas and on New Year s Eve

Very many thanks to Rev W R Finch, Vicar

At BENTLEY in this parish is a chapel-of-ease (ST JOHN) built in 1837, with one bell There was formerly a chapel of the Holy Trinity there, ruined in Dugdale's time

SHUTTINGTON ST MATTHEW One bell

1 IESVS (*border*) BEE (*border*) OVR (*border*) SPEED (*border*) 1664 (*border*)

By George Oldfield of Nottingham cf Polesworth, border between words Pl XXII 3 foundry stamp below inscription *inverted* Plate XXII, Fig 1, with a G for b

1552 'SHOTTINGTON Itm there two belles in the Steple'
1750 '1 Bell'

H T T 3 Oct 1876

SMALL HEATH. See BIRMINGHAM

SNITTERFIELD ST JAMES Six bells

1	J. TAYLOR & C[O] FOUNDERS LOUGHBOROUGH 1887	(29 in
2	*The same*	(31 in
3	CAST AT GLOCESTER BY ABEL RUDHALL 1708 (*ornaments*)	(31½ in
4	*On waist*—(*a*) V R JUBILEE 1887 (*b*) (*Taylor s medallion*) 1887	(35½ in
5	J : TAYLOR & C[O] BELLFOUNDERS LOUGHBOROUGH 1874	(39 in
6	*Same as No 4*	(41 in

[1] Possibly he was John Dugdale of Blythe Hall son of the famous antiquary, who died in 1700 or else Thomas Huntbach, who endowed schools and almshouses at his death in 1712

Formerly three bells of which the present 3rd formed the treble The old 2nd, recast into the present 4th in 1887, was inscribed

WILLIAM (*border*) BAGLEY (*border*) MADE (*border*) MEE (*border*) H ✣ B (*border*) 1703 (*border*)

the old 3rd, recast in 1874, and now the 5th

• HENRY BAYLEY MADE MEE 1663 IOHN HARBICE AND THOMAS MEEDES CHVRCH WARDENS

In 1887 the ring was increased to six by the addition of a tenor and two trebles, the old 2nd being recast at the same time

The old 2nd was one of the latest bells in Warwickshire by William Bagley It is uncertain whether the initials H B stand for Henry Bagley of Ecton (who died in that year), or Henry Bagley III, son of William (see p 71)

Border on 3rd, Fig 15

		cwt	qrs	lbs		cwt	qrs	lbs
Weights of bells—	1)	5	0	23	4)	8	3	11
	2)	6	0	24	5)	12 cwt (approx)		
	3)	7 cwt (approx)			6)	16	1	13 note 1

1552 SHYSTERFORD iij belles one sance bell' 1750 3 Bells

See also *Notices of Warwickshire Churches*, ii, p 92

CUSTOMS —

A bell rung at 8 a m. on Sundays

Ringing on Church Festivals and New Year's Eve for Weddings by request

Death-knell on notification of death tenor tolled Tolling before and after Funerals

Thanks to Rev E R Gayer, Vicar, and Mr W E Falkner

H T T 24 Jan 1882

SOLIHULL ST ALPHEGE Ten bells

1 BARWELL FOUNDER BIRMINGHAM

On waist—(*a*) **RING OUT THE FALSE** (*b*)  (27 in

2 *As No 1*

On waist—(*a*) **RING IN THE TRUE 1894** (*b*) *Barwell's mark* (28½ in

3 HENRICVS (*arabesques*) GRESWOLD RECTOR (*arabesques*) DONO DEDIT (*arabesques*) 1683 (*arabesques*) (30 in

4 CANTATE (*arabesques*) DOMINO (*arabesques*) CANTICVM (*arabesques*) NOVVM (*arabesques*) 1683 (30⅞ in

5 *As No 1*

On waist—(*a*) **GLORIA IN EXCELSIS DEO 1894** (*b*) *Barwell's mark* (32¾ in

6 HENRY (*arabesques*) BAGLEY (*arabesques*) MADE (*arabesques*) MEE (*arabesques*) 1685 (*arabesques*) (35½ in.

7 *As No 1*

On waist —**SANCTE SANCTE SANCTE**
D'ME DEUS SABAOTH 1894 (28 in)

8 HENRY *(scroll)* BAGLEY *(scroll)* MADE *(scroll)* ME *(scroll)* 1686 *(scrolls)* (39½ in)

9 FEARE GOD AND HONOR THE KING 1685
On waist —Royal Arms above the inscription, broad band of arabesques all round (42⅝ in)

10 I § T § R § C § C § W 1685 THE FORMOR TENOR WAS MADE MR WILLIAM BAINTON AND THOMAS HAW *(arabesques)* C W 1659
Below, arabesques as on last all round (48½ in)

New frames and hangings by Barwell 1894
Clock strikes hour on tenor, quarters on two other bells

	cwt	qrs	lbs		cwt	qrs	lbs
Weights —1)	5	2	1	6)	8	3	0
2)	5	3	0	7)	9	3	2
3)	6	0	2	8)	11	0	12
4)	6	2	25	9)	12	2	21
5)	7	2	4	10)	19	1	21

Formerly eight bells cast by H Bagley in 1683 86 Of these the 3rd (re-cast in 1894 and now the 5th) was inscribed merely (without date)

HENRICVS BAGLEY ME FECIT

The old 5th was re-cast in 1753 by Lester and Pack of London with the inscription

THO^S LESTER & T PACK OF LONDON FECIT *(stamp of head)* **EDWARD SMITH & BENIAMIN HEDGES CH: WARDENS 1753**

This was cracked in 1874 (H T T), a large piece being broken out of the sound-bow and one cannon gone it was recast in 1894, when the two trebles were added

On the 1st, 2nd and 5th is Barwell's trade-mark (Fig 20)

The 3rd, 4th, and 6th have arabesque borders (Fig 11) between the words, or bits of the same ornament the 8th has scrolls (Pl XXII 10), the 9th arabesques all round above the inscription and the tenor the same below on the waist of the 9th, the Royal Arms on the tenor before C W, a border of arabesques The latter bell was originally cast by John Martin of Worcester (see below), the initials I T R C indicate John Tandy and Richard Cole the churchwardens of 1685 All the N s on Bagley s bells are reversed, and the A s have a hook at the top (see p 70)

The Rev Henry Greswold, D D (see 3rd bell) was rector 1660—1700 Born in 1628 the son of Humphry Greswold of Greet, he was educated at Trinity College, Cambridge (1645-48) and became in turn Minor Fellow (1649) sublector tertius (1652) and Lector Graecae linguae ' (1653) of his College In 1660 he came to Solihull and there he soon brought order out of chaos, his forty years incumbency leaving a healthier tone in the parish than it had known for many a long day the Registers and Accounts bearing eloquent testimony to his great diligence and exactitude ' He was also Sub-Dean of Ripon and Precentor of Lichfield "a man of great ability and energy, and was respected no less for his piety than for his learning" (Pemberton *Solihull and its Church* p 74, the pedigree of his family is given on p 43 of the same work)

1552 'SOLYHULL iij belles and clock and ij sacring belles 1750 Solyhull 8 Bells.'

A writer in the *Warwickshire Antiquarian Magazine* (i, 1860 p 3), gives the following account of the bells The third bell was recast [about 1600] by Gawin Baker, of Henley who agreed to do it and warrant it tunable for one year for the sum of vj^{li} 13^{s} 4*d*, and if any of the metal was lost in the casting he was to restore it again: for this he received in earnest sixpence and above. In 1618 this bell was again recast by Paul Hutton, of Nottingham, who delivered it to the churchwardens the 28th of August in that year; it then weighed 15 cwt and 34 pounds; he found metal, warranted it tunable and from breaking for a year and a day, and received for it and his workmanship ten pounds; he was likewise presented with twenty shillings for his well doinge thereof."

The Gawin Baker mentioned above is probably identical with Godwin Baker, of Worcester (see p. 56), who must have come to Henley to cast this bell; his earliest date known is 1615, so that his bell cannot have lasted long. For Paul Hutton see p. 61.

The above account is probably taken from the Churchwardens' Accounts, which are of early date and considerable interest. From the same source Pemberton (p. 118) gathers that a bell was recast in 1581; and by the kindness of the Rector I am able to give other extracts here relating to the bells:

1533-4	Rec de diversis personis pro sans bell		xj^{s}	j^{d}
	vj^{d} Solut' Rob^{to} Payne pro Mendyng of the Cloke and clyppur for the sans bell			
	viij^{d} solut' Will^{o} Herewell p' custod' campanor			
	xvj^{d} solut' Will^{o} Hatton p' the clapur of the lytill bell			
1544-45	Item paid for cordds for ye saunce bell & for ye lamppe			viij^{d}
			s	d
1650	For ringing on the 5th of November		4	0
1660	To Ringers for ringing on Thanksgiving Day for the Kinge's returne to his Kingdome and Crowne		4	0
	My expenses with the bell founder when he came to hang the bell			4
	Bestowed upon the men in beare that came to hange the great bell			6
	To Busby for hanging the great bell	1	5	0
	To John Martin for casting the greet bell	13	0	0
1713	Gave ringers for ringing on the Peace [of Utrecht]		10	0
1753	Mr Lester for recasting the 5th bell	18	2	0
1754	Thomas Sarsons for altering the gallery fronting the Chancel & for hanging the 5th bell		12	2
1759	To Ringers when the Bishop came to the Town		5	0

In 1673 a resolution was passed at a Vestry Meeting that the Churchwardens were not to appropriate the old bell ropes.

In 1757 a hurricane did much damage to the spire, but "the 8 bells accapt well but all the wheels and guggins was broke to peses," and the great bell fell or had to be rehung, as there is an entry:

		£	s	d
For	raising up the greet bell into its place ..	1	7	6

The bells were re-tuned in 1858, and the belfry repaired in 1867.

The following testimonial to Bagley's work when he cast the new ring, in 1685, is given by the writer already quoted (*Warw. Ant. Mag.*, i, p. 5):—

27th Aug. 1686.

These are to certify whom it may concern that I Samuel Scattergood ministre of Blockley in the County of Worcester, having severall times viewed and tryed ye sound of ye 8 New Bells lately cast by Mr Henry Bagley Bellfounder for ye Parish Church of Solihull in ye county of Warw. & now hung in ye s^{d} Church, especially at ye Ringing thereof ye day & yeare above s^{d} by myself & about 20 other skilful p'sons accompanying me from Leicester to that purepose doe (with ye gen^{ll} approbation and consent of ye s^{d} Parsons) judg all ye s^{d} 8 Bells to be well & workmanlike made, every way right for tone & mettall, ye chearfullest & best Ring of Bells for their weight that I ever heard. And also that ye Clappers & other

Iron work & tackle with which ye afores^d 8 Bells are hung are now made good, so as to need no further alteracon that I know of

In witness whereof I have hereunto sett my hand this afores^d 27th day of August ano dni 1686

CUSTOMS

On Sundays bells rung for morning and evening services, then tolling and treble tolled about twelve times just at the last formerly the 3rd bell was rung at 6 a m the 4th at 7, and the 6th at 8 but this was discontinued about 1874

Ringing on Christmas Eve at midnight, and on Christmas Day for service, on New Year s Eve at 11-45 and after midnight, with a pause while that hour strikes Also for Weddings by request

Bells formerly rung at 6 a m on Birthday of Queen Victoria discontinued since her death

Death-Knell on tenor, age indicated and bell then rung up and down

Bell chimed at the Funeral of a Ringer, and sometimes for their near relatives

Pancake Bell on Shrove Tuesday on 8th bell (formerly 6th) at 11 a m

Curfew rung on 6th (formerly 4th) at 8 p m from Michaelmas to Lady Day (Saturdays 7 p m) day of month tolled afterwards

Formerly a bell was rung when doles were given out in the Churchyard on All Saints' Day discontinued since 1876

In the ringing chamber are various peal boards --

8 Oct 1786 Complete peal of 5 184 by St Martin s Youths (copied from the peal book of St Martin s Birmingham)

3 Dec, 1894 First peal on the ten bells

6 Oct, 1906 First local peal of Grandsire Triples (8 bells)

Others dated 29 Dec, 1894, 15 and 25 Feb 1897 10 Dec, 1904

Very many thanks to Rev T B Harvey Brooks Rector

H T T 8 April 1881 H B W Sept, 1907

SOUTHAM ST JAMES Six bells

1—3 G MEARS & CO FOUNDERS LONDON

1 *On waist* — A D 1596
MAY OUR TONE SO SOUND ON THE EAR OF MAN ON EARTH
AS TO BRING HIM TO HIS FATHER IN HEAVEN
RECAST MARCH 10, 1863 (30 in

2 *On waist* —(*a*) ALBERT EDWARD PRINCE OF WALES AND
ALEXANDRA PRINCESS OF DENMARK
MARRIED MARCH 10, 1863
(*b*) ADDED MARCH 10, 1863 (32 in

3 *On waist (incised)* —IHS NAZARENUS REX JUDEORUM MISERE MEI 1613
RECAST MAR 10 1863
THE LORD BLESS US AND KEEP US (35 in

4  CELORVM CHRSTE PLATIAT TIBI REX SONVS ISTE 1615

5  SOLI DEO GLORIA PAX HOMINIBVS ROBERT SPICER IOHN BRAYFEILD 1650

Below C W 

6 RICHARD BVDD AND THOMAS ASKEW CHVRCH WARDENS
HENRICVS BAGLEY ME FECIT 1676 *(ornament)*

4th by Watts of Leicester as was also the old 3rd

5th by John Martin of Worcester, cross Plate XXI Fig 7 trade-mark, Plate XXI Fig , N reversed

6th ornaments between words and at end

Weights of the three smallest bells 5 cwt 1 qr 10 lbs, 6 cwt 4 lbs, 7 cwt 2 qrs 14 lbs

1552 'SOWLHAM iiij[or] belles and a saunce belle

1750 '5 Bells

CUSTOMS —

On Sundays a bell tolled at 9 a m (old Mass Bell), also at 7 a m from Easter to Michaelmas one bell for Celebration at 8 a m bells chimed for other services with tolling for last five minutes

Ringing at Christmas and Easter, on St Thomas Day and New Year's Eve also for King's Birthday and for Weddings by arrangement

Death-knell on receipt of news of death tolling once a minute with usual tellers at beginning

Curfew daily at 8 p m (4th or 5th bell) also the 1st or 2nd tolled daily at 1 p m

A bell tolled for Vestry Meetings

Best thanks to Rev J Hart-Davies, Rector, and to Mr Falkner

In the Churchwardens Accounts for 1641 is the entry

Paid to the King's footmen who sealed up the Church doors for not ringing when the King came to Town . . . 6s 8d

Paid also to them for not ringing when the King went out of the town ... 5s

In 1556-57 John Walter, Yeoman, bequeathed 12d to the reparation of the bells (Bloom, *Topog Notes, Stratford* p 13)

H T T 3 May 1884

SPARKBROOK See BIRMINGHAM

SPERNALL St LEONARD One bell

1 *No inscription*

About fifty years ago there were two bells in a wooden turret similar to that at Morton Bagot one being cracked they were recast into one and the present open turret of stone was built shortly afterwards this bell was cracked and a large piece of the metal fell out of it It was then sent to Birmingham and the present bell cast from it by Messrs Blews (Mr Farmborough to H T T)

1552 Itm there ij belles ' 1750 '3 Bells

See also *Notices of Warwickshire Churches* ii p 127

H T T, 2 Sept 1891

STIVICHALL St JAMES One bell

1 1778

Probably by Pack and Chapman

H T T 21 July, 1891

STOCKINGFORD St Paul One bell

Church built 1824 There was formerly a chapel here which in the 18th century was in ruins

STOCKTON St. Michael Three bells

1 ✠ BE YT KNOWNE TO ALL THAT DOTH ME SEE THAT NEWCOMBE OF LEICESTER MADE MEE 1608

2  IHS NAZARENVS *(border)* REXIV DEORVM *(border)* FILI DEI *(border)* MISERERE MEI *(border)* 1622 *(border)*

3  IHS NAZARENVS *(border)* REX IVDEORVM *(border)* FILI DEI *(border)* MISERERE MEI *(border)* 1620

2nd and 3rd by Hugh Watts

1552 'Stocton iij belles and a saunce belle
1750 '5 Bells'

H T T 1 May, 1884

STOKE-BY-COVENTRY St Michael Eight bells

1 JOHN TAYLOR & C° FOUNDERS LOUGHBOROUGH

On waist — JOSHUA PERKINS DONOR

1905 (25½ in

2 *As No 1*

On waist — PRESENTED BY

JOSHUA PERKINS

1902 (28 in

3 *The same* (30 in

4  IHS NAZARENVS *(border)* REX IVDEORVM *(border)* FILI DEI MISERERE MEI *(border)* 1624 (31½ in.

5 *As No 1*

On waist —SIT NOMEN DOMINI BENEDICTVM (32½ in.

6 ✠ sit nomen domini benedictum (34¾ in

7 *As No 2* (38½ in

8 *As No 1*

On waist — JOSHUA PERKINS DONOR

1905

REV CANON T A BLYTH D.D VICAR

WILLIAM PRIDMORE }
JOSHUA PERKINS } CHURCHWARDENS (42½ in

Up to 1902 there were only three bells the present 4th and 6th, and an intermediate bell inscribed exactly like the 6th The 4th is, of course, by Hugh Watts with shield and the usual borders the 6th and former 2nd by Johannes de Colsale, c 1410 (cross and letters Pl IX Figs 6-8 cf Corley and p 19) In 1902 the 2nd was recast and three more added, the ring being increased to eight by a treble and tenor in 1905

		cwt	qrs	lbs		cwt	qrs	lbs	
Weights -	1)	4	0	12	5)	6	1	16	
	2)	4	0	5	6)	7	1	15	
	3)	4	2	3	7)	9	3	26	
	4)	5	0	8	8)	13	1	9	Total, 54 cwt 3 qrs 10 lbs

H T T has given a graphic account of his difficulties in reaching the old bells in 1891 (*Trans Birm and Mid Inst*, 1892, p 21) The bells are now approached by a very lengthy vertical ladder, there is not too much room for them in the tower

No Edwardian Inventories

CUSTOMS

On Sundays bells rung or chimed before services, with tenor tolled for last five minutes

Ringing at Christmas and other Festivals, on New Year's Eve, National Anniversaries (not specified), and for Weddings by request, also muffled peals when desired

In the ringing chamber is a peal-board recording a peal of 5,040 Grandsire Doubles rung on the six bells November 5th, 1904 in 2 hrs 45 min

Many thanks to Mr A W Flowers, Head Ringer

H T T 21 July 1891

STONELEIGH St Mary Five bells

1 EX DONO IOHANES HUDSON GENEROSI DE STONELEIGH A-D ✤ ● ✤ 1782 +
T · EAYRE · FECIT (30 in

Below, arabesques all round

2  MICHAELE TE PULSANTE WYNCHELCUMBAM A HETENTE DEMONE TU LIBRA IQIK

On waist — R  K (31 in

3  IHS NAZARENVS *(border)* REX IVDEORVM *(border)* FILI DEI *(border)*
MISERERE MEI 1632 *(border)* (32 in

4 J JUDD & J SIMPSON C WARDENS J BRIANT HARTFORD FECIT 1792 (35 in

5 *As No 3, a long bit of border before date arabesques all round below* (38 in

These bells are fixed dead, with hammers and are never rung The treble has a curiously moulded top

1st by T Eayre of St Neots the cross crosslet was also used by Briant of Hertford, who may have inherited Eayre's "plant" Acorn borders on 3rd The old 4th was inscribed [1]

O KENELME NOS DEFENDE NE MALIGNI SENTIAMVS POCVLA

and was by the same founder as the 2nd which is fully discussed in the Introduction (p 19) The initial mark is Plate X Fig 2 at the end of the inscription are the second (B)

[1] Ellacombe *Church Bells of Glouc*, p 132 see above, p 10

set of Royal Heads (Pl X Fig 3) the crowned shield below is Pl X 7=Fig 137 in North's *Lincs* For the lettering see Pl X, Figs 4 5 This bell was probably cast at Nottingham about 1400, if not later and in all probability both came hither from Winchcombe at the Dissolution

Colvile *Stoneleigh Abbey* p 39 gives the inscriptions and says there were four bells down to 1752 Eayre's treble being an addition (but see the 1552 Inventory)

1552 'v belles and ij sacring bells'
'Itm they owe ytt for their bells viij^{li} vj^{s} viij^{d}'

In 1507 John Rayes bequeathed 13s 4*d* to the church bells and 16*d* to the ringers (Bloom, *Topog Notes*, *Stratford*, p 12)

1750 Stoneley 3 Bells (obviously wrong)

H T T, 15 May, 1889 H B W Sept, 1907

STRATFORD-ON-AVON Holy Trinity Eight bells

1 *On waist* —(*a*) QVEEN VICTORIA'S JUBILEE 1887 (*b*) *Taylor's trade-mark* (27½ in.

2 *On waist* —(*a*) GOD SAVE THE QUEEN 1887 (*b*) *As No 1* (28 in

3 **WILLIAM DYDE THOMAS BADGER CHURCH WARDENS H BAGLEY MADE M 1742**
Below border all round (arabesques) (30¼ in

4 MATHEW (*arabesques*) BAGLEY (*arabesques*) MADE (*arabesques*) MEE (*arabesques*) 1683 (*arabesques*) (32 in.

5 *On waist* —(*a*) MIKELL EVITT SAM TOMBS (*b*) *As No 1*
CHURCHWDS R S 1733
RECAST 1887 (33¾ in

6 *On waist* —(*a*) JOHN WAKEFIELD AND THOMAS SPIERS (*b*) *as No 1*
CHURCHWARDENS 1683
RECAST 1887 (35¾ in.

7 IOHN ✿ TAYLOR ✿✿ AND ✿✿✿ IOHN ✿✿ HVNT ✿ CHVRCHWARDENS ✿ 1683 ✿ (*On waist, three coins*) (39½ in

8 *Above, arabesques all round*
✠ IOHN COOKS RICHARD GOODE AVERY EDWARDES RICHARD SPIRES C W 1717
Below, founder's mark (Pl XVIII, Fig 9) and arabesques continuous (44 in

Formerly six bells, of which the 3rd was by Richard Sanders, inscribed

✠ ●●● MIKELL EVITT ✠ SAM TOMBS CHURCH WDS ✠ R S 1733

The 4th by Matthew Bagley

IOHN WAKEFIELD THOMAS SPIERS CHVRCHWARDENS 1683 ✿

with borders between the words is on the present 4th and 7th In 1887 two trebles were added by Taylor of Loughborough (whose trade-mark is on the waist) and the 3rd and 4th were recast The inscription on these four are incised The whole ring was originally by Matthew Bagley

(1683), but the treble was recast by Henry Bagley in 1742 and the 3rd and 6th by Richard Sanders in 1733 and 1717 respectively, on the latter, the present tenor, is the founder's mark (Plate XXIII, Fig 9) For the arabesques on the 3rd, cf Tysoe 5th, they are not the same as those used by Matthew Bagley on the 4th (Fig 11), yet another type is used by Sanders on the tenor

The old inscriptions are given in *Notes and Queries*, 3rd Ser x, 1866, p 143, the new ones inaccurately in Bloom's *Shakespeare's Church*, p 104

		cwt	qrs	lbs		cwt	qrs	lbs
Weights —	1)	5	0	8	5)	0	3	22
	2)	5	0	27	6)	8	2	6
	3)	6	0	7	7)	12 cwt approx		
	4)	6	0	26	8)	18 cwt approx		

1552 STRATFORD-SUP-AVON Itm there ij belles

'M^d that the p'ishe have solde sithe the Last Survey two broken bells to the mayntenn'nce of theire bridge the pavem^{ts} of the towne & the relief of the poore"

In 1502-03 John Bedill, alias Sclatter, bequeathed 6s 8*d* to the reparation of the bells (Bloom, *Topog Notes, Stratford* 1903, pp 6 10)

1750 6 Bells

The following extracts from the Vestry Books are given by Halliwell in his book with that title —

24 Oct 1617 Item we were scited to Worcester because the Church and Belles were out of order

29 Oct Item payd Thomas Hornbye for making the Greate Bell Claper and irones to hang the Bell viij^s iiij^d

Item payd Carpenter for trussinge the Bell . xx^d

Item payd for trussinge of another Bell . ij^s

Item payd Richard Rodes for a Baleringe[1] for the Great Bell . ij^s

15 Dec Item payd for castinge the Bell . iij^l xij

Item for takeinge downe the Bell and carringe and bringinge yt home and our charges about the casting of yt xxx^s

Item payd for a Nett to keepe the brides of[2] of the Belfry . iij^s vj^d

Item for keping the leades and the Belles iij^s iiij^d

23 Apr 1622 An order given to cast 2 Bells

24 Feb 1741 The treble bell directed to be recast

CUSTOMS —

On Sundays bells rung for half-an-hour before services, chimed with Ellacombe's apparatus for early Celebrations and Children's Services

Ringing at midnight on Christmas Eve, and on Christmas Day, at 6 a m on Easter Sunday, on Ascension Day after Evensong or Harvest Festivals, on New Year's Eve from 10 to 11 p m and again (after service) at midnight

On Good Friday the tenor only is used

Ringing also for Weddings, Mayor's Day (9 Nov), and Shakespeare's Birthday (23 April) at cost of Memorial Association Muffled peals rung for Royal Family and local notabilities

Tolling at Funerals

There is a peal-board recording a peal of 5,040 Grandsire Triples by the St Martin's Society, Birmingham

Many thanks to Mr W E Falkner

H T T 15 Nov, 1881

1 Baldrick 2 Sc 'The birds off'

St James Chapel of Ease, built 1855 has one bell of that date by C and G Mears

See also Luddington Shottery

STRATFORD-ON-AVON

GUILD CHAPEL Holy Cross 1 + 1 bells

1  D ꝯ B — H ꝯ W — H ꝯ S — I ꝯ W — R ꝯ B — [F ꝯ] A — A ꝯ C — R ꝯ H — T ꝯ C — W ꝯ S — R ꝯ T — H ꝯ N — R ꝯ W — A ꝯ L — T ꝯ O — U — I ꝯ B — RICHARD WALFORD

(2nd line) — STRATFORD — BURGES — 1633 RICHARD — CASTELL — B — ANTHONNEI — SMITH — A — HENRI ꝯ NORMAN C

Below, a border of arabesques (52½ in

Fire Bell *On sound-bow* —ROB^T^ WELLS ALBOURNE FECIT 1782 (*scrolls*) (24 in

Large bell by Hugh Watts, inscription partly concealed by an iron band The initials in the first line are those of Stratford burgesses at the time, on the second, those of principal officials, the letters in each pair are separated by small floral ornaments, and between each pair are bits of "acorn" border, indicated by ▭, the same ornament in second line throughout The reading of the first line is somewhat uncertain, for the reason above stated, as is also part of the second, Mr Falkner reads in the first T Q . . O IG for TO . . U IB, and in the second BURGUS. He further says "All the aldermen of the time are represented with the exception of Aynge, and either Shaw or Smith Henry Norman, a burgess appears to have been Chamberlain, and was succeeded in the office by Richard Walford The single letters B A, C, in the second line perhaps denote 'Bailiff,' 'Alderman,' and 'Chamberlain'" (*Stratford Herald* 18 Nov 1904) The latter interpretation seems undoubtedly correct, and Richard Castell was therefore Bailiff, Anthony Smith Capital Alderman The same gentleman kindly informs me by letter that the following names occur in the list of the governing body of Stratford for that year, corresponding to the initials on the bell —

D B	Daniel Baker	R H	Richard Hathaway
H W	Henry Walker	T G	Thomas Greene
H S	Henry Smith	W S	William Smith or Shaw
I W	John Woolner	R T	Richard Tyler
R B	Robert Butler	H N	Henry Norman
F A	Francis Aynge	R W	Richard Walford
A C	Arthur Cawdrye		

The last four pairs of initials do not occur in the list and the doubtful reading cannot therefore be verified Mr Falkner seems to be incorrect in his statement quoted above that Aynge does not appear

The two bells weigh respectively 29 cwt and 3 cwt Of the larger Mr Falkner says "The edge is a little jagged[1] the cannons are decorated the crown of the bell is raised, as is usual in most old bells The note is somewhat between D and E flat Therefore it is not in accord with concert pitch, but as the bell is rung by itself this is of no consequence" (*Stratford Herald loc cit*) He points out that the bell is in need of a few small repairs, and notes that the bell-chamber compares well for cleanliness with others in the district

The capitals used are mostly from the smaller Brasyer alphabet (Pl XVIII 7-10 *i e* Watts usual set) but some, *e g* A, H, F may be from the larger set (Pl XVIII, 1-5), as at Wootton Wawen

The great bell is rung daily at 6 a m and 8 p m, being always raised in the evening but only occasionally in the morning It is also rung, with the smaller one, in case of fires

The records of the Guild Chapel bells go back as far as the beginning of the fifteenth century, the earliest of the Guild itself date from 1353 Mr Falkner kindly communicates the following extracts from the Accounts in the Corporation Records —

1402-3	For a cord for the Sanctus Belle		4^d
1410-11	making le clappus for the Bell of the Holy Cross		2^d
	Cord for the said bell		3^d
1430-1	for a cord for the bell (in the chapel)		1^d
1442-3	paid Robert Carpenter for hanging the bell of Sir William Bysschopiston Knight in the belfry in the Chapel and for mending forms etc	2^s	1^d
	nails and bordys for the said bell		9^d
1471-2	for an iron wheel for the bell in the Chapel called Le clock	6^s	8^d
	1 Stobull wheel for the said bell	3^s	4^d
1481-2	for a rope for the bell in the Chapel		5^d
	for 2 cords for the bell in the Chapel		7^d
	1 bauderyke for the bell hanging in the Chapel		3^d

Thus we see that the great bell was in existence at least as far back as 1442, the Sir William Bishopston who gave it was alive in 1418, but his gift may be of a date nearer this first record In 1591 it was recast at Leicester, and there exists "a bond of obligation by Edward Newcombe and Francis Wattes, of the town and county of Leicester, bellfounders,[2] to William Wilson of Stratford, woollen draper, and William Wilson of the same, whyttthawer, in 200 marks"[3] It is sealed with the seal of Edward Newcombe, a bell between the letters E N (cf Ettington) On January 24th, 1597-8, in a letter from Abraham Sturley to Richard Quiney, it is mentioned that this bell was broken, and the extracts given below imply that it was recast in 1606 by Richard Daukes and again in 1616 In 1633 the present bell was made by Hugh Watts

On July 10th of that year a note is made in the Council books that "Mr John Woolmer and Rich Robins have promised to ride to Leacester to see the bell cast" Their expenses are given with much detail, as follows —

Paid for eight horsses to nights att grase	viij^s	
Paid for our to horssese three nightes and provender	iiij^s	x^d
Paid for beare to the workmen when the bell was a vuing and dresinge and our owne men	v^s	ij^d
For wacthinge the bell to nightes		xij^d
Paid for wine w'ch wee dranke with Master Wats and othoer	iiij^s	viij^d
Gave to hed workman and the other workmen and the people in the house	iiij^s	x^d

---

1 He attributes this to a defect in casting But I imagine it has merely been chipped for tuning

2 For this evidence of partnership see above, p 34

3 See Halliwell, *Descriptive Calendar of Stratford Records*, p 387

There are also entries for a lobster a crab and other fresh fisch and for other refreshments by the way the total expenses amounting to £3 8s 8d The bell was duly paid for that year —
'It receued of Mr Richard Wallford, chamberlin of the burrough of Stratford, the som of eight poundes in parte of payement for castinge the grete bell the 23 of Octob 1633 — Hu Wattes

There are also numerous entries in the Council books relating to the ringing of the bell

18 Jan 1572 No person to have the great bell rung except he pay to the use of the chamber for each time 4d and to the bellringers 8d

27 Apr 1623 Thomas Tybetts and Edward Heming chosen bellringers for the great bell in the chapel

23 Feb 1654 'It is ordered at this hall that the bellringers shall ring the great bell at the decease of any person but four peales, that is to say, one peale at the departure and three more, and not to exceede halt an hour at each peale, and they are not to ring the bell so hie as to sett it a end"

Mr Falkner points out that the meaning of the last clause is that the bell was not to be actually raised and rung in the modern method

On May 24th 1731 it was enacted that a tax of 6s 8d be laid on all who desired the great bell to be rung at funerals, and if they refused, they should have the little bell after the sex had been denoted on the great one

Further information may be derived from Halliwell's *Stratford Accounts* (1589—1597) and *Chamberlain's Accounts* (1585—1619) all the entries in which appear to relate to the Guild Chapel bells

From the *Stratford Accounts* —

1590	Paid for amending the Claper of the bell		x^s	viij^d
1591	Paid to Thomas Godwine for the bell claper		vj^s	viij^d
	Paid to the roper for two short ropes for the greate bell			vj^d
	Paid to a workeman that holpe Toole about the bell			vj^d
	Paid for the bell which was borowed of the maisters	vj^{li}		

[Apparently the money to pay Watts and Newcombe (see above), not the bell that was borrowed]

	Paid for the charges of the bell	iiij^{li}	xi^s	v^d
1592	Receaved of Mr Parsons at a court holden the 19 January of money gathered for the bell		x^s	vj^d
	Rec of Mr Barber of the same money		iij^s	vi^d
	Payd to Abell the joiner the first day of Aprill for mending the wheels of the litle bell at they chappell			viij^d
	Payd to Clemson and another to help hym aboute the great belle			xij^d
	Payd to goodman Godden for makeinge the buckelle to the baldrike for trussinge up the belle		ij^s	viij^d
	Paid to John Knight for a bauldricke			viij^d
	Item Sir Higges had trayne to use aboute the belle			j^d
1593	Paid for two small quordes for the great bell			iiij^d
1594	Item for trussinge the greate belle		iiij^s	
1595	It for trussinge up the greate belle like to have fallen out of the frame		x^s	
1596	Item paid the 11 of Marche for a corde to eiche the greate bell rope			iij^d

[8 Oct A similar entry]

	Paid more the 21 of October to John Knight for mending the bauleridge[1] of the greate bell			vj^d

[In most years there are receipts for death-knells on the great bell.]

[1] Baldrick

From the *Chamberlain's Accounts*

1589	Paid to Peter joyner for mendinge the bell whell			vd
	Paid to Prisse for a cord to pese the bellroppe			iijd
1600	Paid Robert Roades for mendinge the bell rope			vjd
1601	Paid for ij small roppes that the ryngers do rynge by to the great bell			viijd
1602	Paid for mending the Chappell bell rope			iiijd
1604	(10 May similar entry, vd)			
1606	Paid to Spenser for trussinge up the Chappell bels		vij	iiijd
	Item to the bellfounder of Evsham[1] for his paines			xijd
	Item for a rope for the Chappell litle bell			vjd
	Paimentes and charges about the bell[2]			
	Imprimis for the taking down of the bell		iijs	
	Item for drinke and victualls upon Daukes and his people that did helpe him that day that the bell was caste on			xviijd
	Item to Richard Greene and Harrington for watchinge the night after the bell was caste			xijd
	Item to Spenser and others for helpinge us out of the pit with the bell, and for gettinge her into the Chappell, in money and drinke		ijs	viijd
	Item for hempe that he did use about the bemould		ijs	viijd
	Item for wax and rosen and tallow when he did caste the bell		ijs	
	Item to Richard Daukes for mettall and his charges goinge to Warwicke about the bell		vijs	ijd
	Item to goodwife Tomlins for mettall		iiijs	viijd
	Item for five loades of clay that he did use about the mound and the furnace		iijs	iiijd
	Item for two loades of stoun		vs	
	Item to Mr Waterman for ston		iiijs	vjd
	Item for four score and seven poundes of morter mettall		xliijs	vjd
	Item for three hundred of mettall and the cariage of hit from London	ixli	xs	
	Item to Daukes for castinge of the bell	viijli		
	Item to Mrs Smithe for a pott		xxs	
	Item for two bagges of coles to dry the mouldes		ijs	
	Item for wood for to melte the bell withall		xs	
	Item to Thomas Hornebee for iron woorke for the bell		ixs	
	Item for iron that we bought		vjs	vjd
	Item to Watton the smithe for iron woorke about the hanginge of the bell		xs	
	Item for nailes about the bell			vjd
	Item to Spenser for timber for the bell frame, and for plankes for the steple floore, and his woorke, and the bell stocke	iijli	xvjs	vjd
	Item for nailes for the steeple floore			xijd
	Item for cariage for the bell stocke and other timber to the Chappell			xijd
	Item for a bell rope for the great bell		iijs	
1607	Item 1080 brick for the bell	jli	xijs	
1608	Paid for the baldridge of the Chappels great bell		iiijs	iiijd
	Paid for the logar of the Chappells bell			viijd
	Paid the first of December for ij smale roopes for the great bell			vjd
	Paid for mending the great bels rope			viijd
1609	Paied for to ropes for the gret bell			vjd
	Paied Spencer for mendinge the Chapell belle			xijd
1610	Paid to Williams for mending the wheele and stocke of the great bell in the Chappell		ijs	iiijd

[1] Probably the Richard Daukes mentioned below He was a Worcester man, but may have been temporarily at Evesham (see p 56))

[2] Also quoted by Walter, *Shakespeare's True Life* p 229

	Item for two cordes for the great bell			vjd
1611	Paid to George Sneath for mending the wheele of the littill bell at the Chappell			vd
	Paid to Watton for trussing up the littill bell with new plates and nailes			vd
	Paid to the roper for making new the gable of the great bell from the floore downeward			xxd
1612	Payd for the mending the ropp of the greete bell .	0	0	vjd
1613	Inprimis paid Januarie the xviijth for a roope for the Chappels great bell			xd
	Paid Septemb xx° for a baldryke for the littill bell of the Chappell			vjd
	Paid Novemb xxv° for a corde to peece the bell roope of the Chappell .			viijd
1614	Item for ij cordes for the great bell			vjd
	Item for lycker for the bell			ijd
	Item payed to Richard Roodes for the balrige			xviijd
	Item for the bockell to hit .			iiijd
1615	Paide to Mr Wolmore for xlv pounde of iron for the bel .		viijs	vjd
1616	Paid in yearnest for casting the great bell		ijs	
	Paid for wax and rasin that he yoused about the bell			xviijd
	Paid to Richard Cowell and his men for helping downe with the great bell .		vjs	iiijd
	Paid in charges when the great bell was a casting			xviijd
	Paid for waching the mettell when the bell was cast			xviijd
	Paid for diging the bell out of the groung		ijs	vjd
	Paid for having up the bell in the bellfree		iiijs	
	Paid for stoking the bell and hanging and laying the floise		vijs	xd
	Paid for a bawdrig and mending the roope		vs	iiijd
	Paid to the bellfounder for casting the bell	vjli	xvjs	
	Paid for making two bandes for the bellfounder			viijd
	Paid for beare when the bell wase draud up .			vjd
	Paid for trussing the bell last .		ijs	xd
1617	Payde for tachinges to the Chaple bell rop			ixd
1619	Paid for a small rope for the bell	0	1	2

In Halliwell's *Descriptive Calendar of Stratford Records*, p 74, is the following —

> That the Great Bell shall be new cast and make six bells about forty hundred waite with chymes provided we can raise subscriptions to pay for the same 12 Jan, 1721

Evidently the subscriptions were not forthcoming, an event perhaps hardly to be regretted! Browne Willis, in 1750, notes 'Holy Cross 1 Bell.'

See also *Notes and Queries*, 3rd Ser, x (1866), p 143

Many thanks to Mr W E Falkner for much of the above information (see *Stratford Herald*, 16 Nov, 1904)

H T T, 15 Nov, 1881

STRETTON-ON-DUNSMORE

ALL SAINTS Three bells

1 IOSEPH ∙ SMIIH ● IN ∙ EDGBASTON ● MADE ● MEE ● 1705

(*Coins on sound-bow*)

2 ● IAMES ● ELKINTON ● AND ● THOM S ● BROMAGE ● CHVRCH ● WARDINGS 1705

3  **IHS . NAZARENVS REX IVDEORVM FILI DEI MISERERE MEI 1620**

1st and 2nd by Joseph Smith, scroll-border (Pl XXIII 2) on 1st The Vicar gives the date on the 2nd as 1703

3rd by Hugh Watts

Weights given as 6, 9, and 18½ cwt, which if correct, imply the 2nd, 5th, and tenor of a ring of eight in the key of E

1552 'STRETTON SUP' DUNESMORE iij great belles, a saunce bell, iij small belles and two handbells'

There is a tradition that the bells came from Wolston

CUSTOMS —

A bell rung every Sunday at 9 a m (formerly 7 a m)

Death-knell on receipt of notice, no particular method Tolling at Funerals as the procession approaches

Ringing on New Year's Eve and for Weddings

Best thanks to Rev S G Collier Vicar

H T T, 18 May, 1887

STRETTON-ON-FOSSE. ST PETER One bell

1 *On the sound-bow* —T MEARS FECIT 1841

1552 'STRATTON-UPON-FFOSSE ij bells a litle belle

H T T, 8 Aug, 1888

STUDLEY ST MARY Five bells

1 IOSEPH POTTER MINISTER 1688
Below, arabesques all round (29⅝ in

2 MATTHEW BAGLEY MADE MEE 1688 (31½ in

3 EDWARD BENTON AND THOMAS SMITH C W 1688 (32½ in

4 CHARLES RVSSELL AND WILLIAM PARR C W 1688
On sound-bow —THOMAS PERKINS GEORG ROBINS COLECTOR
(with three coins below) (35 in

5 FEARE *(arabesques)* GOD *(arabesques)* AND *(arabesques)* HONOR *(arabesques)* THE KING *(arabesques)* 1688 *(arabesques)*
(Three coins on waist) (38⅞ in

All by Matthew Bagley probably cast at Evesham (see p 70)

1552 'Itm there . iij belles

1750 '6 Bells'

Notices of Warwickshire Churches, ii, p 127

Best thanks to Mr Falkner

H T T., 19 Oct, 1881

SUTTON COLDFIELD. HOLY TRINITY — Eight bells

1 **J. TAYLOR AND C° FOUNDERS LOUGHBOROUGH 1884** (29½ in

2 *The same* (30 in

3 THO^S MEARS OF LONDON FECIT 1795 (34⅛ in.

4 *The same* (36¾ in

5 *As No 1*

Below —**GIVEN BY THE CORPORATION 1795**

RECAST 1884 (38⅞ in

6 *As No 1* (41¾ in.

7 *As No 5, with* **LEICESTERSHIRE** *before the date* (45 in.

8 *As No 7* (51 in

		cwt	qrs	lbs		cwt	qrs	lbs
Weights —	1)	5	2	18	5)	10	3	12
	2)	6	0	14	6)	13	1	25
	3)	7	2	0	7)	16	2	17
	4)	9	0	0	1)	23	1	17

Formerly a ring of six by T Mears, dated 1795, of which the old 1st and 2nd remain The old tenor weighed 22 cwt

1552 'SUTTON-IN-COLFILDE iiij^or belles and a saunce belle
1750 'Sutton-in-Colfield 6 Bells'

Additions to Dugdale (Brit Mus Add MSS, 29,264, fol. 53) 'a deep peal of 6 BELLS

In 1556 Richard Veisey, Yeoman bequeathed 3s 4d 'towards the castyng of the fyrste bell and making it consonant with other bells

In 1784 the Corporation voted 100 guineas towards a new ring, which was apparently obtained and shortly afterwards superseded, for we read in the Registers that in 1786 one William Hughes was killed by a piece of timber which fell while the workmen were preparing to put up the bells

CUSTOMS —

Bells rung or chimed for Sunday Services
Ringing on Christmas Day, New Year's Eve, and Trinity Monday (the local feast day), also for Weddings and on Mayor's Day (9 Nov)
Muffled peals for Royalty, clergy of the parish, or prominent Churchmen
Pancake Bell formerly (discontinued about 1870)
A bell rung for Vestry Meetings down to about 1902

In the ringing-chamber is a peal-board recording two peals of 5,040 Stedman Triples, rung by the St Martin's Guild, Birmingham, on October 3rd, 1891, and November 27th, 1897

On June 8th, 1891, a muffled peal of 1,260 changes was rung for Mr Preston, Head Master of the Town School A muffled peal was also rung at the death of Queen Victoria (22 Jan, 1907)

See *Bell News*, 16 Aug, 1884

Many thanks to Mr G. Sidwell

SUTTON COLDFIELD St. James Hill One bell

Church built 1834

St. John, Walmley One bell

Church built 1845

St. Michael, Boldmere. Eight bells

Church built 1857. A ring of eight bells by Barwell of Birmingham put up in 1906. All bear the founder's name and date, the tenor having in addition this inscription —

TO THE GLORY OF GOD
AND IN MEMORY OF THEIR FATHER
THOMAS INSTON
THIS RING OF BELLS WAS GIVEN
BY HARRIET AND CHARLOTTE INSTON
A.D. 1906.

Weights and diameters

		cwt	qrs	lbs			cwt	qrs	lbs
1)	27⅜ in	4	1	9	5)	33¼ in	6	3	6
2)	27⅝ in	4	1	11	6)	35 in	7	2	3
3)	28¼ in	4	2	0	7)	39½ in	9	3	3
4)	30¼ in	5	0	24	8)	43¾ in	13	3	14

SUTTON-UNDER-BRAILES St. Thomas-à-Becket 5+1 bells

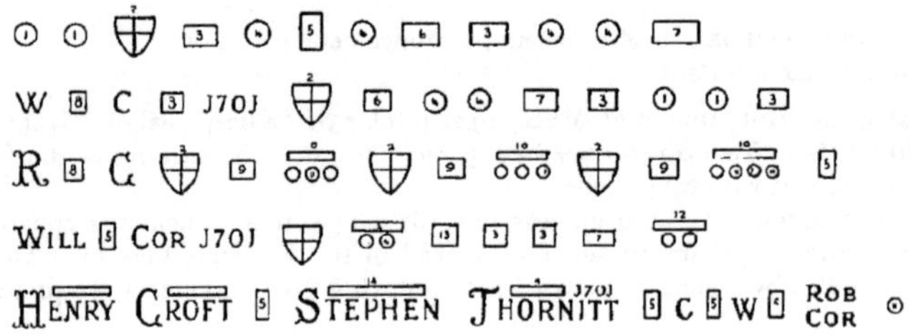

1 (27 in.
2 (28½ in
3 (30½ in
4 (32½ in
5 (36¾ in

S. *No inscription, may be ancient*

A remarkable ring by William and Robert Cor of Aldbourne, Wilts, whose bells are not usually found so far from home; see page 77. The 1st and 2nd are very ugly bells, with curious high crowns. All are very richly ornamented, but the variety and elaborateness of the stamps is so great that it is impossible to reproduce them in type. As indicated by the numbers they are as follows —

(1) Medallion of the Adoration of the Magi (Pl XXV 6). (2) The Royal Arms (Pl XXVI 4). (3) Head in foliage (Pl XXIV 3). (4) Wheel (Pl XXV 2). (5) Plant (Pl XXV 4, XXVI 2). (6) Two figures holding up mask (Pl XXV 5). (7) Cherub (Pl XXV 3). (8) Floral ornament. (9) Monogram (CC ?) (Pl XXVI 3). (10) Border of Cupids and floral patterns (Pl XXIV 1). (11) Coin of William III. (12) Head in foliage (Pl XXV 1). (13) Grotesque face (Pl XXIV 2). (14) Arabesque or floral border (Pl XXVI 1).[1]

[1] On the 1st bell the last mark but two should be (12) not (4); on the 2nd the mark (5) should be inserted after (2); on the 4th for (12) read (14) in each case, and in place of (3) (3) read (6) (12). The long border on the 5th is (14) in each case.

The parish of Sutton was formerly in Gloucestershire, and is still in Gloucester diocese, but it is now in the administrative county of Warwick As Ellacombe omits it, I make no apology for including it here

H B W Apr 1907

TACHBROOK, BISHOPS ST CHAD 3+1 bells.

1 IESVS ✿✿✿✿✿✿ BEE ✿✿✿✿✿✿ OVR ✿✿✿✿✿✿✿✿ GOOD ✿✿✿ ✿✿✿✿✿ SPEED ✿ I ✿ M 1653 ✿ (28½ in

2 JOHN SAVAGE C W 1719 *(border of arabesques, continuous)* (30½ in

3 ✿ WHEN FOR DEAD I RING OR TOLE ✿ THE LORD IN HEAVEN RECEVE THEIR SOLE ✿ ~~~ W^M BROOKE 1740 (34 in

Clock THOMAS MEARS FOUNDER LONDON 1842 (23¼ in

1st By John Martin, of Worcester border (Plate XXI, Fig 6), between words thick letters

2nd By Richard Sanders of Bromsgrove with his foundry stamp (Plate XXIII Fig 9)
3rd By William Brooke, of Bromsgrove cf Meriden

All cannons off Clock bell hung dead, without clapper, above the others
Weights 4¾, 5½, and 7 cwt, notes, D, C and B flat

1552 TACHBROOK BUSSHOPPE iij belles a litle bell'
1750 Tachbrook Ep 1 4 Bells'

CUSTOMS —

On Sundays bells chimed for services, *preceded* by single bell as 'Sermon Bell A bell rung at 8 a m and 9 a m (old Mattins and Mass Bells)
Ringing after Sunday evening service in Advent, on Christmas Eve, and New Year's Eve, for Weddings by request also on November 5th and St Thomas' Day
Tolling at Funerals before and after the service
Pancake Bell on Shrove Tuesday at noon
Gleaning Bell discontinued only a few years since

In the Churchwardens Accounts for 1740 there appears the following —

	£	s	d
The Wate of the great bell is 6^cwt 1^qr 14^lbs when taken down and casting at 20 shilling the hundredweight	6	7	6
The new bell at 6^cwt 3^qrs there is 52 lbs of new Methell at 13^d per pound added to it	2	16	4
For making the claper 7 lbs heavier than the old one and new working of it		5	6
For time in coming over of Wm Brookes	1	0	0
Paid caring of new claper from Birmingham			6
To Warwick carrier for bringing great bell from Birmingham		6	3

Many thanks to Rev J T Hallett, Vicar

H T T, 30 Jan, 1877, H B W, June, 1908

TANWORTH ST MARY MAGDALENE Six bells

1 PROSPERITY TO THE CHURCH 1707

2 **RICHARD SANDERS OF BROMSGROVE CAST US ALL**

On waist — **1707**

3 **HENRY HARIS IOHN SALLTOR C W 1707**

4 **H H I S C W 1707** *(border)*

5 **GOD SAVE QVEEN ANN 1707**

6 Mᴿ IOHN WELCHMAN VICAR WILLIAM CHAMBERS THOMAS PARSONS WILLIAM HYATT RICHARD INSULL CHURCH

Below — WARDENS 1788 *(and scrolls continuous)*

All by Richard Sanders, of Bromsgrove, except the tenor, which is by Joseph Smith

The arms on the tenor are those of Archer of Umberslade *azure* three arrows in pale, *or* with a dragon's head issuing from a mural coronet as crest (see Dugdale, ii, pp 777 781)[1] The Archer of the time, Thomas, who re-built Umberslade House, and died in 1743, may have given this bell

Bells re-hung 1894

1552 'TONWORTH iiij belles a saunce bell 1750 'Tamworth 6 Bells'

See also *Notices of Warwickshire Churches*, ii, p 13

The Vicar kindly sends the following extracts from a paper in Sir Simon Archer's collections 'to preists the clerk ryngars & light at an yearly obit ij^s viij^d and in breade & ale at the sayde obit viij^d

There is a tradition that the Curfew Bell here (see below) was often of assistance to people lost on dark nights, but that once a man lost on the heath hearing it ring, made straight for the church and was drowned! (From the Registers)

CUSTOMS —

Bells chimed or tolled on Sundays at 8 a m, 10 a m, 10-50 to 11-0, 5 p m, 6 p m and 6-20 to 6-30 (chiming for 13 minutes before services, tolling at other times)[2]

Ringing on Christmas Eve and Christmas Day, Easter Eve and Easter Sunday, Whitsuntide, Harvest Thanksgiving and New Year's Eve, for Weddings by request

At Funerals bells chimed, rung, or tolled as requested, the bell used being regulated by age of deceased

Curfew rung at 8 p m on tenor (Saturdays 7 p m) from 25 September to 13 March for this there is an endowment of 30s per annum

Pancake Bell formerly

Hannett, in his *Forest of Arden*, p 116, remarks on the singular custom of ringing a bell at 9 a m, 1 p m, and 8 p m here in his day (1863) The daily bells at 9 and 1 were only discontinued about 1879. (H T T)

Best thanks to the Hon and Rev R C Moncrieff, Vicar

H T T, 29 Nov, 1881

---

[1] The history and pedigree of the family is given in Brit Mus Add MSS, 20,264, fol 140

[2] H T T notes (1881) 'Bells 1 and 2 rung at 8 a m and 2 p m'

TEMPLE BALSALL St Mary One bell

1 WILLIAM ELDRIDGE MADE MEE 1670 ◆ ◆ ◆ ◆ ◆

In a turret at the S W corner of the church, one cannon broken

William Eldridge of Chertsey, was a son of the Brian Eldridge who cast several Warwickshire bells in 1657-58 He is not usually found far away from home See p 58

H T T 1 July, 1876

TEMPLE GRAFTON St Andrew One bell

1 WILLIAM ~~~ WALKER ~~~ IOHN ~~~ HEMING ~~~ 1661 ~~~

Below — Border of arabesques and

By John Martin, of Worcester, borders Plate XXI Fig 8, trade mark, Pl XXI, 2

1552 Itm there ij belles

H T T 15 Nov, 1881

TYSOE St Mary 6 + 1 bells

1 (arabesques) ✠ 1719 (arabesques) ⚜ (arabesques) ⊕ (arabesques)

Below — *Arabesques all round* (29⅝ in

2 ✠ 1719 (*long band of arabesques*) 56789 ABCDEFGHIKLMNOPQRSTUVWXYZ 1234 ABCDEFGHIKLMNOPQRSTUVWXYZ 1234 (32⅛ in

3. ✠ 1719 (*arabesques*) (*arabesques*) (34⅛ in

4. THOS CLARKE WILLM GREENWAY CH-WARDENS A R 1750 (36¼ in

5 SIMON . HEWENS RICHARD GREENAWAY CHURCH WARDENS :

2nd line — MATTHEW ⁖BAGLEY MADE . MEE 1782 . (38¼ in

6 ✠ VALENTINE WIGGINS LAMPEART MANDERS CHURCH WARDENS 1719 ⚜

Below — *Trade mark,* Pl XXIII *9, as on first three, and continuous arabesques* (43⅜ in

S SANCTUS SANCTUS SANCTUS

1715

RCGASG

1886

The first three and the tenor by Richard Sanders, with his large trade-mark (Plate XXIII, Fig 9), arabesque ornaments, etc The alphabetical and numerical filling up of the line on the 2nd seems to be unique 4th By Abel Rudhall

5th Ornament at end also found at Ufton, this is Matthew Bagley's latest bell Tenor rehung by Bond without cannons its wheel is disproportionately small

Sanctus bell in original cot, now inaccessible probably by Blews its predecessor was probably by Sanders

1552 'iij belles a saunce bell a hand bell

1750 '6 Bells'

CUSTOMS —

On Sundays a bell rung at 8 a m for Services, and formerly also on week-days, when there was any service during the day A bell is rung after morning service, which is variously explained as 'driving the Devil away' and warning housewives to prepare dinner!

'Midnight Peals' rung on Christmas and New Year's Eves (paid for out of the Churchwardens' Accounts), ringing for Weddings by request, and sometimes on secular occasions

Death-knell on tenor, as soon as notice is received (but not after sunset), tellers 3 for male, 2 for female, 1 for child At Funerals a bell is tolled at 8 a m on the morning of the day, 'Bearers' Bell' rung two hours before the ceremony, and the tenor is tolled for a short time afterwards

Until 1871 a bell was rung daily at six, originally at four but whether A M or P M is not stated the sum of £2 used to be paid for this from a farm at Lower Tysoe, but was then refused owing to the alteration in time of ringing A similar arrangement used to prevail at Brailes

Pancake Bell on Shrove Tuesday at noon (5th bell)

Gleaning Bell formerly

A bell rung for Vestry Meetings, and before the Parish Councils Act, also for election of Parish Officers

The 1st and 5th bells are rung in case of Fire, formerly the sanctus bell was used for this purpose, but this bell is now only used for Week-day Services and Choir Practices

About forty years ago all the ringers bore the name Hancox

Best thanks to Rev F V Dodgson, formerly Vicar, and Mr W E Falkner

H T T, 19 April 1887

UFTON ST MICHAEL Three bells

1 I ALDER ✤✤ T PRATT ✤✤ C ✤✤ W ✤✤ M ✤✤ B ✤✤ MADE ✤✤ WE ✤✤ THREE ✤✤✤ J779

2 TIMOTHY ✤✤ PRATT ✤✤ IEREMIAH ✤✤ ALDER ✤✤ CHURCH WARDENS M ✤✤ B J779

3 **IEREMIAH ✿✿ ALDER ✿✿ TIMOTHY ✿✿ PRATT ✿✿ C ✿✿ W M ✿✿ B J779**

All three by Matthew Bagley II *arabesques* between the words, the same as on the 5th at Tysoe

1552 'iij belles, a saunce bell and ij hand belles'

CUSTOMS —

A bell rung on Sundays after Morning Prayer also at 8 a m for Holy Communion
Death-knell on receipt of notice, usual tellers

Thanks to Rev J Barker, Rector
H T T, 3 May, 1884

ULLENHALL (OLD CHURCH) ST MARY THE VIRGIN One bell

1 ✠ AVE MARIA GRACIA PLENA

Cross and lettering as on the larger bell at Hunningham, see p 5 and Pl II Figs 14—18 Probably by a local founder (John Kingston, of Warwick?) about the latter half of the fourteenth century

The bell hangs in an open cot on the W gable of the church, and is best reached by climbing along the comb of the roof The church is now only used as a mortuary chapel Before the new church was erected in the village there were two bells here, the other (smaller than the present one), had no inscription but is noted by H T T as long-waisted and "a very ancient cylindrical bell It is now at Emmanuel Mission Church, in the parish of Christ Church, Sparkbrook, Birmingham (see p 1)
H T T, 9 Feb, 1876, H B W Aug 1894

1552 OWNALL-IN-WOTTON Itm there j bell' (Clearly an error, as there must have been two there at the time)

1750 Outenhall 2 Bells See also *Notices of Warwickshire Churches*, 1, p 145

There is a local tradition that the old bells were brought from Studley by a Mr Knight, and it is said that this can be verified But in view of the date of the Studley ring it must have been over two hundred years ago

ULLENHALL (NEW CHURCH) Eight bells

1—7 **J. WARNER & SONS LONDON 1874**

On waist —
1 **NOISE**
2 **JOYFUL**
3 **A**
4 **MAKE**
5 **US**
6 **LET**
7 **COME**

8 CAST BY JOHN WARNER & SONS LONDON 1874

On waist EN ◇ MRN (20 in

The shield on the tenor has three battle-axes, the arms of the Newton family, of Barrells; it is lozenge-shaped, to indicate a female owner of the property. The initials are those of Elizabeth and Mary Rose Newton, the donors. It will be seen that the text on the first seven reads upwards; also that the bells are exceedingly small. They are very oddly hung, in four apertures in the sides of the tower, in pairs one above the other. Mr Falkner, who kindly examined them for me, says: "The bells can be rung, but the only musical ones are 4, 5, 6, 7, 8; the addition even of 3 spoils the others. When chiming the whole peal may be used without offending the ears."

Church built in 1875.

WALSGRAVE-ON-SOWE St Mary Five bells.

1. W & J TAYLOR FOUNDERS OXFORD 1843 (24 in.

2. *The same* (25 in.

3. J: TAYLOR & C^O FOUNDERS LOUGHBOROUGH 1872

On waist —REV^D R: ARROWSMITH VICAR

I: B: IZON W: WATSON

CHURCH WARDENS 1872 (29 in.

4. RICHARD ADRIAN VICAR IOHN BOWLES THOMAS HARRIS CHVRCHWARDENS 1702

(*2nd line*) —HARKEN DO YE HEARE OVR CLAPERES WANT BEERE ● ● ● ● ● ● ●
(30¾ in.

5. QVANTVM SVFFIIFIT BIBIERE MOLO CLANCVLA VOS MVSICA TONE 1702 (34 in.

4th and 5th by William Bagley; on the 4th, in the second line, 'claperes' appears to be a euphemism for 'ringers.' The inscription on the 5th is in somewhat cryptic Latin, but I suspect the sentiment to be the same as on the other. N reversed on 4th and 5th throughout.

A beam in the belfry is dated 1673.

1552. 'Sowe. ij belles and a lytle sacring belle.'
'm^d that ou' and besyds the forsaid p'cells the pishe have solde sythens the last survey oon bell the greatest of three for the rep ac'ons of their churche.'

H. T. T., April 1875; H. B. W., Sept., 1907.

WALTON D'EIVILE St James. One bell.

1. • • MEARS FOUNDER LONDON • • • •

The bell hangs in an open turret, and is very difficult of access. The Vicar kindly examined it with glasses and was able to read the above, but not to see the date. As, however, the church was enlarged in 1842 when Walton was reconstituted as a parish, it may fairly be assumed that the bell was put up then. It is not likely that there was one while it was a private chapel. We may then read the inscription as (THOMAS) MEARS FOUNDER LONDON (1842), the type being the same as at Wilmcote.

1552. 'Itm there ... ij belles.' 1750. Walton 5 Bells (*sic*).

CUSTOMS —

Bell tolled for fifteen minutes before Services on Sundays
Death-knell as soon as notice is given, tellers 3×3 for man, 3×2 for woman 2×2 for child
Tolling at funerals

Many thanks to Rev H G Elton Vicar

WAPPENBURY ST JOHN BAPTIST Three bells

1 BRYANVS ELDRIDE ME FECIT 1657

2 ✠ S GEORGE

3  **IHS NAZARENVS REX IVDEORUM FILI DEI MISERERE MEI 1629**

1st ELDRIDE should be ELDRIDGE, see p 58
2nd: By one of the Newcombes. cross Plate XVI, Fig 2, see p. 30
3rd By Hugh Watts
Bells and belfry in bad order

1552. 'WATTONBURY iij belles and a saunce belle two pression [? procession] bells a sacring Bell

CUSTOMS —

'Ting-tang' (? treble) rung on Sundays at twenty minutes before Services, and 'Sermon Bell (? tenor) five minutes before
Death-knell at 8 a m on morning following death
A bell rung for Vestry Meetings.

H T T. noted in 1878 'When there is a morning service a bell is rung at 7 and 9, when in the afternoon, at 9 and 12.'

Thanks to Rev E L Wise Vicar
H. T T, 9 Oct, 1878

WARD END (LITTLE BROMWICH) ST MARGARET 2+2 bells

1 THE ✲ ROYAL ✲ HOSPITAL ✲ AT ✲ GREENWICH ✲ 1716 (21½ in

2 THOMAS MEARS OF LONDON FOUNDER 1834 (26 in

There are also two very diminutive bells without inscriptions, on which the clock strikes the quarters

The smaller bell is by James Bagley, of London (see p 72) It is obviously a second-hand bell, and it would be interesting to know how and when it came to Birmingham[1] It is said that William Hutton, the historian, presented or bequeathed bells to this church about 1815, and possibly the Greenwich bell was his gift

The present church dates from 1835,[2] but is the successor of an older church or chapel

[1] The chapel of Greenwich Hospital was destroyed by fire in 1770 and rebuilt in 1789, possibly the bell was sold about that time

[2] According to Thomas' edition of Dugdale the church was re-erected about 1750 but it is described as being in ruins in Hutton's time In any case, the present church is not of so early a date

founded in 1512 in the parish of Aston The larger bell was either put up or recast when this one was built

H B W, March, 1908

WARMINGTON St Michael Three bells

1 T ROBINSON H B HARRISON VICAR J BRIANT HERTFORD FECIT 1811

2. PRAISE THE LORGE 1616 (36 in.

3 EDWARDE NEWCOMBE MADE MEE 1602 (39 in

New wheels stocks, and fittings by F White, of Appleton

2nd bell from the Leicester foundry, with Newcombe's cross and lettering but the date is unusually late for these stamps, it may be one of Edward Newcombe's latest cf Morton Morrell and Birdingbury, and see p 37

3rd by Edward Newcombe, but in Watts (se Brasyer s) alphabet the cross is the Brasyer cross (Fig 5), which was Watts property and the bell was clearly cast while the two were in partnership (see p 32)

The Rev R B Harrison was appointed Vicar in 1802

1552 ' iij bells A sance bell '
1750 ' 3 Bells

Thanks to Rev Preb Deedes

H T T 18 Sept 1875

WARTON Holy Trinity One bell

Church built 1849, parish formed out of Polesworth

WARWICK St Mary 10 + 1 bells.

1. PROSPERITY TO ALL OVR BENEFACTORS A R 1703

Below, vine-border *On waist* — (*a*) REGAST A D 1901 (*b*) *Taylor s trade-mark*

CANON RIVINGTON M A VICAR

T KEMP } CHURCHWARDENS
S W COOKE } (27 in

2 PROSPERITY TO ALL OVR BENEFACTORS I B ESQ[R] (28½ in

3 GOD SAVE THE QUEEN PROSPERITY TO THIS PLACE (*arabesques*) A R

Below as No 1 (30 in

4 PEACE & GOOD NEIGHBOVRHOOD 1710 A R ++++++++++++++++

Below as No 1 (31¼ in

5 ABRA RVDHALL OF GLOVCESTER CAST VS ALL ANNO 1702 (33¾ in

6 A R (*Border Fig 14 continuous*) (37⅞ in

7 GOD PROSPER THIS PLACE AND ALL THAT BELONG TO IT A R 1702
Below as No 1 40⅛ in

8 PEACE AND GOOD NEIGHBOVRHOOD A R 1702
Below as No 1 (42½ in

9 GOD PRESERVE THE CHURCH AND KINGDOM AND GRANT VS PEACE
1702 (48 in

10 **PROSPERITY TO THIS TOWN THE REV^D R P PACKWOOD VICAR I. ARKESDEN I ALLEN CH WARDENS 1814** (*chain-pattern*)
2nd line —**T. MEARS OF LONDON FECIT** (*chain-pattern*) (54⅜ in

Fire Bell (Unhung) 1670

Bells rehung in steel frames by Taylor 1901

The Rev Canon Thurston Rivington, of Trin Coll Camb was Vicar of St Nicholas 1884 99 and of St Mary 1899—1906 He was made Hon Canon of Worcester in 1897 and became Vicar of Putney in 1906

Weights and notes —		cwt	qrs	lbs			cwt	qrs	lbs	
	1)	4	2	10	F sharp	6)	9	2	2	A
	2)	5	0	7	E	7)	11	1	11	G
	3)	5	3	4	D	8)	13	1	11	F sharp
	4)	6	1	14	C sharp	9)	18	0	21	E
	5)	7	1	20	B	10)	24	3	20	D

The Fire Bell is now in the crypt it is by Henry Bagley and is the only one which escaped the fire of 1694

The previous history of the bells, so far as is known is as follows —

In 1552 Warwicke the p'ishe of Saynt Mary Itm there x belles

In the course of the next hundred years another appears to have been added, as Dugdale (i p 439), gives six bells previous to 1656 of which three at least were of pre-Reformation date the additional treble apparently had no inscription The others he gives as follows —

2 Vox Domini Jesu Christi vox exaltationis
3 Aeternis annis resonat campana Johannis
4 Isabel Beauchamp first founded me (this may be a later recast bell)
5 Trinitati sacra fiat haec campana beata
6 Det sonitum plenum Ihesus et modulamen amenum
Ihesu have merci on me Isabell

About the skirt thereof' —

"Ἅγιος ὁ Θεὸς ἅγιος ἰσχυρὸς ἅγιος ἀθάνατος ἐλέησον ἡμᾶς

The 2nd was probably by Newcombe (cf Bulkington), the 3rd from the Worcester foundry (of the same type as at Aston Cantlow), the 5th from that at Nottingham which is the only foundry employing that inscription The donor of the original 4th and of the tenor was

Isabella Despenser, Countess of Warwick, who died in 1439; she was the wife of Richard, Earl of Warwick, and foundress of the Beauchamp Chapel, in which her monument stands (Dugdale, i. p. 413).

In the Corporation Accounts of 1564-65 occurs the entry:—

The Steple in Saint Marys Churche	Rycherde Tuckott Carpynter for making twoo floures in the Churche overthrowen wth the falle of the great bell as well as for his workmanship as for the Tymber going to the same floures xli xiij iiijd

In 1656 three new bells were cast by Eldridge at Coventry (see p. 58), apparently the old tenor was melted down and two additional ones supplied, making a ring of eight. In 1694 occurred the disastrous fire, which completely destroyed the bells and necessitated a new ring of ten, cast by Abraham Rudhall in 1702. Of these the tenor was recast in 1814 and the 1st, 2nd, 3rd, 4th, 7th and 8th in 1901, by Taylor of Loughborough. The old inscriptions have been exactly reproduced from Rudhall's bells but not in the same lettering.

See *Notices of Warwickshire Churches*, i. pp. 29, 84; *Notes and Queries*, 3rd Ser. x. (1866) p. 143. Browne Willis in 1750 gives "10 Bells."

CUSTOMS.—

Bells rung on Sundays for morning and evening Services; chimed for Celebration at 8 a.m.

Ringing at midnight on Christmas and New Year's Eves; for Weddings by request; for King's Birthday, Election of Mayor (9 Nov.), on arrival of Judges to hold Assizes, and for the Sunday School Feast at midsummer.

At Funerals a bell is tolled for twenty minutes at 8 a.m. and before and after the service, followed at the end by the usual tellers.

Pancake Bell on Shrove Tuesday (6th bell) from 11.30 to 12.30.

The 3rd bell is rung daily at 1 p.m. and the 8th for Curfew at 8 p.m.

On Statute Fair Days people were, until recently, allowed to "make as much row as they could by pulling the ropes, on payment of sixpence to the Sexton. It is a wonder that the bells survived it!"

In the ringing chamber are three peal-boards:—

28 Dec., 1786. 5,040 Grandsire Caters in 3 hrs. 35 min. (St. Martin's Guild, Birmingham).

23 Sept., 1869. 5,021 Stedman Caters in 3 hrs. 30 min.

26 May, 1900. 5,173 changes in 3 hrs. 24 min., by the St. Martin's Guild, Birmingham.

See also *Church Bells*, 11 April, 1874.

In the Churchwardens' Accounts are some interesting entries relating to the bells, some of which have been printed in *Notices of Warwickshire Churches*, i. p. 29. They do not go back further than 1656, but in the will of Thomas Okens, dated 24 Nov., 1570, we read that he wills "that the viijt ringers shall have for their paynes viijs." As we know from Dugdale that there were only five bells, it must be supposed that the larger bells required an extra man, or that the whole company of ringers numbered eight. The ringing was presumably John Okens's funeral peal.

The entries in the Accounts are as follows:—

1656. Recd in Bell metteil (viz. of the Great Bell and the chippings of the other Bells) thirty nyne hundred and one half hundred and eight pounds which was disposed of as followeth that is to day delivered backe againe three new Bells with new Brasses to them weighing five & twenty hundred forty & foure pounds weight.

	£	s	d
Paid to John Wyse for making new Chimes on the eight Bells	5	1	0
Paid to Mr Eldridge for casting three new Bells and making the rest tunable	28	0	0
Paid for going to Coventry to seal the articles with the bellfounder	0	3	0

		£	s	d
1665	Paid to the Ringers for ringing the Bells at the Coming of the Duke[1] and his Duches to the Towne	0	16	0
	Paid to the Ringers for ringing for the victorys against y Duch	0	9	4
1670	Paid for casting the fire bell	1	8	0
	Paid for making the chimes (Severall entries, in all about)	40	0	0
1671	Paid for removing the Fire Bell and frame to hang it in	0	4	0
1680	Great Bell money Rec for M[r] Dewett a highwayman hanged .	0	[illegible]	6
1685	At the parish meeting it was ordered that for the future any person who will have the Great Bell rung for any person dec[d] shall pay 4s 6*d* and it was ordered that every poore person that dyeth having not money to pay for the ringing of the 5th Bell may have the liberty to send (*sic*) any person to ring that Bell without paying for y[e] same And if the party dec[d] hath none to ring the Bell for him nor money to pay for the same that the clarke shall ring the said Bell without receiving any pay for ringing the said Bell			
1688	Paid to the ringers for ringing on y[e] day the King was proclaimed	0	5	0
1690	Given to the ringers when the King got the victory in Ireland	0	5	0

The Accounts do not go further than the end of this century In 1694 we find an entry

Paid for Horse hire and two days charges going to Towcester to look after Pickford that stole y[e] Bell Metal . ..		0[s]	0[d]

This was, of course, the metal of the bells melted in the Fire

From the Corporation Accounts the following items are taken —

		£	s	d
1704 5	Paid to the Ringers upon the News of the Duke of Marlborough forcing the French lines		15[s]	0[d]
	to the Ringers on thanksgiving day		15	0
	for Ringing on the News of the Victory of Ramilies		15	0
1706	Paid to Mr James Prescott being towards making two Trebbles for the Ring of 10 Bells for the Church of St Marys	£5	0	0
1708	To the Ringers upon the News of the Victory in Flanders		15	0
	" " , Raising the Siege of Brussels		15	0
	" , , taking Tournay .		15	0
	, , " the French being beaten		15	0
1709	Ringing upon the News of King Charles beating the Spaniards		15	0
	, , the 2nd Victory in Spain		15	0
1711	, on news of taking possession of Dunkirk		15	0
Nov 1712	To Ringers on Peace being concluded	1	0	0
	[And other similar entries, 1708 1712]			
1713	for Ringing the Day King George entered London		15	0
	Coronation Day	1	2	6
1714 (?), Sep 20	Tolling Bell the Night the Queen was interred		3	0
1720	Gave to encourage young Ringers		2	6
1802-3	Nov 7 Gave the Ringers for Ringing for Lord Nelson at Warwick by order of the Mayor	1	1	0
1805	(in Churchwardens' Accounts) Gave the Ringers for Nelson's Victory	1	1	0
Nov 23	Gave the Ringers for tolling and muffling[2] the bells an hour for Lord Nelson's burial	1	1	0
1815	Paid to the Ringers for the News of the Battle of Waterloo	2	2	0
	Ditto for taking of Bonaparte	1	11	6

Very many thanks to Mr E Adams Sexton for much of the above information also to Mr Falkner

H T T, 15 May, 1889

[1] *I e* The Duke of York, afterwards James II

[2] *Sic* Muffling

WARWICK — St Nicholas — Eight bells

1 MEARS & STAINBANK FOUNDERS LONDON

On waist THE VICARS BELL

THIS BELL WAS PRESENTED TO THE PARISH CHURCH
OF ST NICHOLAS WARWICK IN COMMEMORATION
OF THE JUBILEE OF THE REIGN OF HER MAJESTY
QUEEN VICTORIA JUNE 20TH A.D 1887
BY THE REVD THURSTON RIVINGTON M A VICAR
S HARWOOD } CHURCHWARDENS
W GLOVER }
"O LORD ACCEPT THIS BELL OF ME
TO CALL THY PEOPLE UNTO THEE" (28 in.

2 *As No 1 to seventh line* (JUBILE *for* JUBILEE, *after* 1887 BY A FRIEND THE REVD *etc*)

Below —SACRED TO GOD ON HIGH AND IN THE TEMPLE RAISED
MAY HOLY SOUNDS FROM ME BE HEARD AND HE BE PRAISED (29 in

3 *As No 1* *On waist* —

VERE BROUGHTON SMITH M A VICAR
GEORGE MOORE } CHURCHWARDENS 1877
THOMAS BELLAMY DALE } (30 in

4 **LAVDATE DOMINVM IN EXCELSIS M D CXCV** (32 in

5 C. & G MEARS FOUNDERS LONDON

On waist —REVD JOSHUA R WATSON VICAR
THOMAS TURNER } CHURCHWARDENS 1849 (34½ in
GEORGE JAKEMAN }

6 **RICHARD KEENE CAST THIS RING M D CXCV** (37 in

7 ROBERT MILLER VICAR EDWD WILLIAMS EDWD WHEELER CHURCHWARDENS EDWD ARNOLD LEICESTER FECIT 1798 (40 in.

8 **I TO THE CHURCH THE LIVING CALL & TO THE GRAVE . DO SOMMONS ALL** (*border*)
IOHN BIRD AND IOHN READING CHURCH WARDENS MATTHEW BAGLEY MADE ME J773 (43½ in.

Weights	cwt	qrs	lbs		
1)	4	1	20	5)	8 cwt
2)	4	3	22	6)	9 cwt
3)	5	2	0	7)	12 cwt
4)	6	0	0	8)	16 cwt

Formerly six bells, cast by Richard Keene in 1695 (see p 60), of which the 3rd had merely the date MDCXCV, of this ring the 2nd and 4th form the present 4th and 6th Keene's treble and tenor were recast in 1770 and 1773 by Matthew Bagley, the 3rd (present 5th) in 1849, the treble inscribed

MATTHEW BAGLEY MADE MEE J770

was recast in 1877, and in 1887 the two trebles were added In 1798 the 5th was recast by Arnold, of Leicester, and now forms the 7th What is known of the earlier history of the bells may be summarised as follows —

In 1552 "WARR THE P'ISHE OF SEYNT NICHOLAS v bells a sance bell ij hand b' "

"M^d^ that the belles afforrehersyd ar gevyn to the burgesses of War as dothe appere by the Kings l'res patents Henry the viij^th^ whose dat' is the xv^th^ day of May in xxxvij^th^ yere of his reign"

There were then five bells in 1552 Of these the 3rd and 4th were recast in 1554-59 by Newcombe of Leicester We hear of other recastings by Newcombe in 1561, 1562 and 1565, but the number of the bell in the ring is not given Those of 1561-2 may all refer to the same transaction or to the repetition of an unsuccessful casting but probably the 1st and 2nd are the bells then recast In 1571 another bell was recast by Newcombe, and as the weight is 16 cwt, we may infer that it was the 5th or tenor Thus in 1571 there were five bells by Newcombe, dated (probably) 1561—1565—1554—1559—1571 The 4th was again recast by Daukes and Baker in 1619 (see below, under that year) and we do not hear of any other alteration until 1695 Browne Willis, about 1750, gives '6 Bells' See also *Notices of Warwickshire Churches*, i, p 92, for inscriptions in 1849

CUSTOMS —

On Sundays before Services the 7th bell is rung 3×3 strokes, followed by chiming for ten minutes, and then the tenor is tolled for ten minutes as 'Sermon Bell Before the 8 a m Celebration was introduced (about 1885) each bell was tolled eight times, and then the 7th bell 3×3 strokes

Ringing on Christmas Eve Ascension Day, St Nicholas Day New Year's Eve and Easter Tuesday ("Churchwardens' Day") on King's Birthday Mayor's Day, and Arrival of Judges for Assizes for Weddings by request

A bell rung for all Vestry Meetings and Annual Meeting of the Chamberlains of St Nicholas' Meadow

Pancake Bell on Shrove Tuesday 4th bell, at 11 a m

Curfew at 8 p m on 7th bell, formerly also the 6th was rung at 5 a m (up to 1870)

Death-knell at 8 a m on morning of Funeral on 6th 7th or 8th bell and the same at the time of the Funeral, with usual tellers in each case, and age tolled at the end

Muffled peals for Royalty, family of Earl of Warwick and Bell-ringers

Bells re-hung by Barwell 1909

Very many thanks to Rev F H Lawson, Vicar

H T T 1 May 1889

The very interesting Churchwardens Accounts of this parish, which begin in 1547, have been partly transcribed and edited by Mr Richard Savage in the local *Parish Magazine* (Warwick, Cooke, 1890), and from them we can quote many entries of interest relating to the bells, which appears to have undergone numerous alterations in the period covered down to 1621 These are given below —

1547-48	Item p^d^ to henri pors[1] for ix*li* of Iron & workemanship to the iiij^th^ bell stoke	ij
	Item payd to John abbott for kepyng the belles	xx^d^
	Item payd for licur[2] for the belles	iiij^d^
	Item payd for whitledur[3] for the belles	viij^d^

[1] Powers [2] Liquor, i e, oil [3] White leather, i e, for the baldricks of the clappers

Item payd for ij belropes ij^s ij^d
It'm payd for ij bell roppys ye p sc[1] ij^s viij^d
It'm payd to Henry porse for the exchange of vij pond of Irone y^t mad a color[2] to the gret belle iiij^d
It'm for the workemanschyp of ye same Irone and i days worke at the same bell viij^d
It'm for a belle rope xx^d
It m payde to John bothe for kepyng of the bellys xx^d
1550 51 It' payd to harry porse for trussyng ye second bell iij
It John a both a the same worke ij^d
It' for a bell rope ij^s ij^d
It to thom' brey for Irone & workema'shype to ye forthe bell ij^s
It to Jhon bothe for kepyng ye belles xx^d
It to henry porse for keyvse & naylys to ye belles ij^d
1551 52 It'm payd ffor ij bawdedrykes ij^s
It'm to Jhone a bothe ffor makyng a bawdrike iiij^d
1552 It'm payd to Harry porres ffor mendynge the ffyrst bell wheel iij^d
It'm payd to Harry porres ffor nalles to the same whele j^d
It'm payd ffor lycur ffor the beeles ii^d
It'm payd to Jhon a bowthe ffor whytelether & ffor kepynge off the beelles xvj^d
1553 It'm payd ffor iij bele ropes v^s
It'm payd to Edward Knythe ffor mendyng the gret bell wheylle iiij^d
It'm nalles bestoyd A bowtne the beelles at the same tyme vj^d
It'm payd to Harry pores ffor trusshyng off the beeles & lerne worke abowt the same xx^d
It'm payd to Harri pores agayne ffor trusshyng off the beeles & to Jhon a bothe ffor helpyng to the same xiij^d
It'm payd to Jhon a bothe ffor kepyng off the beeles xx^d
1554 It'm reseuvd off m^r Thom s ffysher to the castyng off our herede bell newly cast at lecitur off late iij^s iiij^d
[And sundry smaller contributions to the same]
It'm payd ffor a roppe ffor the sances belle & a nother ffor the lampe vj^d
It'm payd to Thom s browne ffor helpyng to hange vp the lampe & helpyng aboothe the sances belle ij^d
It'm payd to Thom's bre ffor workema shype belonggyng to the trushyng off the sances bell & ffor Iorne to the same woorke xiiij^d
It'm to colles off snyte ffylde[3] ffor hys paynes takyng to cu' in to the parishe to geve co'sell to the ffylynge off the the ede q^r bell & spente on hym & upo one y^t dyd ffetche hym viij^d
It'm payd to Thom s Leede ffor ffylyng off the same bell ii^s
It'm bestoyd off William s'hepherd & other co pany at the stokekyng off the same bell at y^t tyme vj^d
It'm a litull bell bowgt off Thom's genenes the pryse ij^d
It'm payd for a hande belle ij^s vj^d
It'm payd to Thom's payne ffor ryngyng off eght i cloke & v a cloke iiij^s
It'm payd to Thom's bre for makyng a eye to the iiij^th bell claper & mendynge the balle off the same claper xvj^d
It m payd to Robart newcu' bellfounder off lecetur ffor the castyng off a belle callyd the iij bell in parte off paiment vj^s
It'm payd ffor all charges & expenses bothe ffor horsmet & mans mett carrygge and recarrygge belongyng to the same belle sense the tyme y^t the belle founders servant ca' hether to ffetche the tyme off the belle xiiij^s
It'm payd to John a brothe ffor kypyng off the beells xx^d
It'm ffor mendyng off the belle whelles iiij^d

[1] Piece [2] Collar [3] Snitterfield

		s.	d.
1555	PAMENTES FFOR THYS YERE REPARACIONS OFF THE BELLES		
	It'm payd ffor ij bell roopes	iijs	iiijd
	It'm payd ffor workemā'shyppe a bowte the grett bell		iijd
	It'm payd for candell to lyght them yt dyd ryng corvarde[1] in cristemas wyke		jd
	It'm payd to Thomas mades ffor whitlether at ij sundry tymes	ijs	iijd
	It'm payd to John a boothe ffor whiteletner at ij sundry tymes		viijd
	It'm payd to Harry porris ffor nalles & Iorne worke a bootte the iiijth bell		vijd
	It'm John a bothe ffor helpyng to the same worke		iijd
	It'm a bell agayne the prise	ijs	
	It'm payd to William sheperd & harri porris & John a bothe on all hallen evyn ffor mendyng off the beell		vjd
	It'm payd to shurwode ffor mendyng off a bell wheyle		ijd
	It'm for nalles to the same worke		jd
	It'm payd agayne for the a bell rope		xxd
	It'm for nalles to the belles		iijd
	It'm to Thomas wayne ffor lycur ffor the beelles		ijd
	It'm payd ffor Iorne & workemā'shype abowte the iiijth bell claper		xd
	It'm payd agayne ffor lycur ffor the beelles		ijd
	It'm ffor mendyng off the sance belle		ijd
	It'm to Jhon a boothe for kepyng off the belles	ijs	
	It'm payd to Robart newcum belffounder off lecetur the whyche was dwe to hym at the assuncion of our lady to be bro'ght to hym by the handes off Thomas pornes & Thomas bre or there assynes ffor the later pament ffor castyng off the iij belle	xls	
	It'm payd ffor horse mett & manse mett to leceter & ffro leceter ffor to cairy the last pament off our money ffor the belle	iijs	
	Sm belongyng to the stypull of beelles	lviijs	viijd
1556	PAMENTES BELONGYNG TO THE BEELLES		
	[Sundry small payments for repairs as in preceding year.]		
	S'm off the reparacion off the belles	xxijs	vdob
1557	It'm paid to Henry Poores for ernys to dyght the belles for one hoole yere		ijd
	It' p'd for grece for the belles all thys yere		jd
	It p'd for a Bell Rope bought at the ffeare	ijs	iiijd
	It'm p'd to Henry Poores for iij dayes in takynge vpp the belles & Trussyng them & for nalys & other stuff	ijs	iijd
	It'm paid to the Ryngers on Corpus Xp's Day & Holy Thuresday [This entry erased.]		vjd
1558	It'm in brede & aylle to the ryngeres at the generalle prosessyon ffor quyne Elsabethe		viijd
	It'm payd ffor mendyng off the therde bell claper to Harry pornes		viijd
1559	PAMENTES FFOR THE BELLE		
	It'm payd to the bellfounder upon parte off pament	xlvjs	viijd
	It'm payd ffor caryegge & recaryege & ffor meat & drynke horsse meat & ffor helppe at sundry tymes to loode ffrom lecetur & to lecetur	xxvjs	iiijd
	Item payd to blyke ffor makyng off the claper	iijs	iiijd
	It'm payd to the bellefounder at the last beyng here	vj	viijd
	It'm payd to hym ffor iiij brasses	ijs	xd
	It'm payd ffor takynge downe off the belle the ffyrst tyme & drawyng vp off the belle ageyne the ffyrst tyme & ffor stokyng off the belle & ffor meat & drynke ffor them yt dyde hepe about the belle	vs	iiijd
	It'm payd ffor stokenge off the belle the last tyme	ij	
	It'm payd ffor a belle roppe		xviijd

[1] Curfew

It'm payd ffor whithelether . . xx[1]

Su' — iiij[li] xxij[s] iiij

1560 PAMENTES FFOR THYS YERE FFOR THE BELLES OR STYPULLE

It'm payd to Jeorge tatam[1] the belleffunder ffor the iiij[th] beelle . xl[s]

It'm payd ffor Costes & Charges off horse meat & manes meat & all other Charges when the belffunder was here . vj[s] ij[d]

It'm ffor the Claper for the fforthe belle iij[s] vij

It'm ffor the hangyng off the grett belle . xx[d]

It'm payd to Thomis payne ffor kypyng off the beelles . iij[s] iiij

It'm payd ffor a belle rooppe . xviij[d]

S'm—lvj[s] ij[d]

1561 CHARGES BELONGING TO THE STIPULLE

It'm payd ffor Caryyng off the beelle to lecester a bowt mydsomer & ffor horsse meate & manse meat at the same tyme viij[s]

It'm payd ffor expensyes off twane off the churche wardens rydyng to lecetur to se whate Casse the beelle was in . iij[s] ij[d]

It'm payd for expenssyes and Charges Callyd Custum at the Castyng off the beelle xiij[s] iiij[d]

It'm payd ffor takyng downe the beelle at the same tyme . ij[s] viij[d]

It'm payd For lycur ffor the beellyes iij[d]

It'm payd ffor horsemeat & mansmeat ffor Rycharde bykar rydyng to lecetur xviij

It' payd ffor Chargys & expenses & ffor the ffeciyng hom off the belle at thys last tyme . xv[s] viij[d]

It'm payd to Harry porries ffor hangyng off the belle & ffor makyng off nallyes viij[d]

It'm payd ffor lycur ffor the beellyes iiij[d]

It'm payd ffor Castyng off the beelle . xi[li]

It'm payd to Thomis payne ffor kypyng off the beellyes iij[s] iiij[d]

It'm payd to Thomis payne ffor ryngyng off v a Clocke beelle vj[s] viij[d]

It'm payd ffor brede & ale at the hangynge vp off the beelle . viij ob

S'm—v[li] ij[s] j[d]ob

1562 PAMENTS FOR THYS YERE & FFYRST OFF ALLE FFOR THE STYPULLE

It'm expenses goynge to lecetur Thomis Alyn & Jhon Coocke horsse mett manse mett . . . iij[s] v[d]

It'm Jhon Coocke hym selfte goynge to lecetur xxj[d]

It'm ffor Wnytelether payd xvj[d]

It'm ffor bayllynge the grett belle Claper to oleycke vj[s]

It'm ffor takynge downe the belle good manne Shepherd & other Company iiij[s]

It'm a belle roppe .. xvij[d]

It'm hangynge vp the belle another tyme ij[s] iiij[d]

It'm a nother tyme goynge to lecetur Rychard bykar xx[d]

It'm payd ffor the belle ffounderes manse soper & ffor the bylle makyng to sende to lecetur . . v[d]

It'm ffor lycur ffor the bellyes j[d]

It'm payd ffor the Castyng off the belle & beynge ffurthe iij dayes vj[s]

It'm payd ffor hyre off ij horses to helpe to bryng the belle whom iij[s] iiij[d]

It'm payd ffor goynge to lecetur Ryc bykar ij[s]

It'm payd ffor goynge to lecetur Ryc bykar & Thomis Alyn iij[s]

It'm at hangyng the belle last off alle iij[s] v[d]

It'm payd to Thomis Tede ffor sutyng off Irons ij[s]

It'm payd to the belle founder ffor hyes last pament & ffor metalle xxxj[s] viij[d]

It'm payd to Harry porries ffor hangynge the belle vj[d]

It'm payd to Harry porries ffor makynge off the fforthe belle Claper viij[d]

It'm payd Harry Porres A nother tyme ffor vntrussynge off the belle viij[d]

[1] Probably Newcombe's foreman

It'm payd to Thomis payne ffor helpynge to make the iiijth belle Claper — iiijd
S'm—iijli xiijs xd

1563 It'm payd at the bargenyng off the fforthe belle Claper — vjd

1564 It m payd to William Shepard ffor trussynge off the grett belle & Kerynge off the brasses — iiijs
It'm ffor makynge off the Claper — vd
It m payd to Thomis Leede ffor the grett belle Claper — ijs ixd

1565 It'm Receuyd over & Above ffor sertene metylle lafte at the Castynge off the belle — ijs
It'm payd ffor Expenses apon the belfunder at hys ffyrst Comynge — ijs
It'm ffor breade & aylle takynge downe off ye belle — viijd
It m to John grosse goynge to leceter — ijs viijd
It m to Thomis Howe ffor carynge the belle to lesseter — xiijs iiijd
It'm bestoyd agayne on ye belffunder when he was here — ixd
It m payde ffor Chargys ffor horse meate & mannes meate at the Carynge off the belle to leceter — xxixs vjd
It m payde ffor Carte Clottes shoynge & such other lyke at ye Carynge off ye belle — xvd
It m payd to ye belffunder in parte off pamente off ye belle — ls
It m payd to Robarte Wryght & Thomis payne ffor stockynge off ye belle — vijd
It m payde ffor trusshynge off ye iiijth belle & seconde belle — ijs
It m lykur ffor the beellys — vjd
It m to Thomis payne ffor kypynge off ye clocke & the beellyes — vs

1566 It m payd to the belffunder ffor the latter payment of the belle — ls
It m spente vpon the bellefunders man — iiijd
It m pd to the Ryngers when the Quine was here — ijs
It m pd ffor kypyng off the clocke & the beellys — vs
It'm payd to Thomus Payne ffor mendyng off the guogyns off the fryrst bele & for lycur for the same beelles & for pavynge in the churche — xxjd
It'm ffor mendynge off the ffourthe belle clapper — vijd

1569 It'm payde ffor ij beelle Roppes — ijs viijd
It m paid to Thomus lee ffor mendyng the ffourthe belle whelle — vjd
It'm payde to Thomus lee ffor mendynge off the fframe off the belles — iiijd ob
It m payde to Raffe marten ffor a pece off Tymber ffor the fframe off the belles — ij
It m payde ffor sawynge off thre Kersses off the same — iiijd
It m payde to Robarte Wryght and Thomus payne for trussynge off iij off the belles — ijs
It m payde to John mydelltun ffor Mendynge the fframe belongynge to the belles in the stypulle — xviijd

1570 It'm payde to Thomus Anderson and Rycharde Porse for turnynge the greate belle Claper — xd
It m payde to Robarte Wryght and Thomus Payne ffor trussynge the greate belle & mendynge the treble belle whelle — vijd
It m payde to Thomus sherwode ffor a hoope to ye same whelle — ijd
It'm payde to John Aven ffor bossynge off the therde belle Clapper & mendynge off a locke off the greate Coffer — iijs vjd

1571 It'm payde ffor Ryngynge to the Ryngers at the day off the entrance off our soueranie ladie the Quene — vijd

CHARGES BELONGING TO THE STIPLE

It'm payde ffor wyne & sugar at the Cummynge off master newcum the belffunder at Whitsuntyde — xiiijd
It m payde ffor our charges at coventre when we bargenyd wt hym for the belle — xjd
It m payde to Cristopher Knyght ffor carynge off the beelle to lecetur — vjs viijd
It'm goynge forwarde to leceter payde ffor our breckefaste at bradeforde [Bretford? — viijd
It'm payde ffor our supperes at leceter the same nyght — iis iiijd
It m payde for our dyner & our drinkynge on the thursday — ijs vdob

It'm payd for wyne & sugar that was spente on master newcombe & hys men on thursday at nyght xxij^{d}
It'm payde for a quarte off muscadene gyven to mastres newcome on friday mornynge viij^{d}
It'm payde & that was geven to the workemen off the howse & for other charges in the nowse . . .. . xx^{d}
It'm payde ffor our charges on ffriday & tylle we cam home . .. xviij^{d}
It'm payde for the meate that the cattelle dyde Latte that drew the beelle to leceter iiij^{s} vj^{d}
It'm payde to phylyppe coo for makynge the oblygacion ffor the beelle xij^{d}
It'm payd to Thomas anderson for sutynge off the great belle claper & the baalle off yt & mendynge the fourthe bell claper the iee[1] & the baalle . ij^{s} ij^{d}
It'm payde to Mr Newcum the belfunder ffor metelle belongynge to the belle vij^{li} xj^{s} x^{d}
It'm payde to m^{r} newcum beltfunder in parte off pament off a more sum xlvj^{s} viij^{d}
It'm payde to m^{r} Rycharde brockes ffor serten metalle bought off hym for the belle xlj^{s} viij
It'm ffor trussynge off the fourthe belle viij^{d}
It'm payde to Thomas payne ffor kepynge the clocke & the beelles & Ryngyng eght a clocke & fyve a clocke .. viij^{s} iiij^{d}
It'm gathered in olde metelle iij quarters xx^{li} iij poundes
It'm the olde beelle wayd xij^{c} iij quarters vij poundes
It'm the new beelle waythe xvj hundrethe weght
& so the hoolle charges belongynge to the stypulle thys yere ys
S'm xiiij^{li} iij^{s} xj^{d}

1572 It'm payde to Thomas newcum belfunder for the laste pamente off a more sum xlvj^{s} viij^{d}
It'm payd to Ryngers when the Quene was here & also for Ryngynge at the day off hur graces Entrance[2] of hur yeres . xx^{d}

[Also payments for the clappers of 4th and great bells

1573 Sundry small repairs.
1574 Item payde to the Ryngers for Ryngynge at the day of the entrance of the Quene xx^{d}
1575 Item payde to the Ringers for Ryngyng on the Quines holy day beinge ye xvij day of November ... xx^{d}
1576 Item paide to William marclene for ballynge of iiij Clapers of our belles ix^{s} v^{d}
Item payde to the Ryngers for Ryngynge on the xvijth day of november beinge the fullfyllynge of the xviijth yeres of our Soueraigne ladye our Quene ij^{s}
1577 Item payde to the Ryngers for Ryngynge the xvijth day of November beinge the fulfyllinge of the xix yeres of the Reigne of our moste Dreade soueraigne ladye Elizabethe our Quene . .. ij^{s} ij^{d}
Item paide to the Ryngers to make them to Drinke when my lorde byshoppe was Wronge[3] in to ye towne . . iiij^{d}
1578 Sundry small repairs and payment for ringing on Accession Day.
1579—1583 " "
1584 " "
Item payd for takynge downe of one of the belles .. vj^{d}
Item payd ffor Expenses Rydynge or goynge to barbye to look vppon a belle ij^{s}

[The last two entries seem to suggest a proposed exchange of bells]

1585 As in previous years
1586 Item paide to Edwarde paine ffor bowlinge[4] one off the belle Clapers .. iij^{s} iiij^{d}
1588 Payd vnto the Ringinge on the xvijth daye of November beinge the Entrance of the xxxj yeares of the prosperouse Raynge of our Soveraigne ladye Queene Elyzabethe Long & longe to Endure ij^{s} vj^{d}

---

1 Eye
2 i.e. Accession
3 Rung
4 This would seem to be the same as 'shooting' or 'suting' i.e. casting, recorded in previous years

	Payd for the Ringinge on the xixth daye of the same monthe beinge the worthye Remembraunce of the victorye over our enymves by godes provydence moost prosperouse[1]		xx^{d}
1590	Besides payments for new brasses, stocks, etc, the following entries may be noted as of interest —		
	Also p^{d} to Edward Payne for makinge of iiij^{or} newe gudgins iiij^{or} great boltes viij great Cotters, ij great staples, peircinge viij stirroppes, makinge 120 bribbes, nales, one staple for a baldrigge, leyinge xij^{li} of newe Iron of ye great bell claper etc	xx^{s}	
	worke about ye third bell		
	Also p^{d} for makinge a newe bowe & ij newe blades for a peare of sheires & peicing all ye rest of ye stirropes & sheues & xx^{t} nales		xx^{d}
	Also p^{d} for peicinge ye crowne staple		ij^{d}
	Also p^{d} for peicinge ye plaite y^{t} holdethe the wheele		x^{d}
	iron worke about ye fforthe bell		
	Also p^{d} for new bowinge ij peire of sheires & makinge a blayde & peicinge ye rest		vj^{d}
	Also p^{d} for layinge iron vpon the crowne staple & makinge it		ij^{d}
	Also p^{d} iiij^{or} cotters makynge		ij^{d}
	Also p^{d} for makinge of ij newe cotters		ij^{d}
	Also p^{d} for peicinge ye plaite y^{t} holdethe ye wheele		j^{d}
	Also m^{r} Knight bestowed one bell stocke frely		
	S'm vij^{li} x^{s} iiij^{d}		
1592	Also p^{d} to John Tooley for trussing of the belles y^{t} were newe stocked ye last yere & for puttinge in a newe beame vnder the mydle flower of ye steple	xj	xiij^{d}
	Also p^{d} in bred & drinke to those persons as toke paynes in puttinge in of the same beame ij dayes & a halfe		xiiij^{d}
	Also p^{d} to Thomas Owen for iron worke about the belles, & for nales when the were newe trust, xij great nales occupied about the beame	iij	ix
	Also p^{d} to the saide Owen more for newe ballinge the iij^{d} & iiijth bell clapers, & for makinge other thinges newe about the clocke, and mendinge the same clocke in some other thinges	xi^{s}	
1594	Also p^{d} to fraunces the Cloksmyth for Iorne worke as he did about the Cloke & belles		x^{d}
	Also p^{d} to william martlen for worke as he did about the cloke & beles		xxij^{d}
	Also p^{d} for two new bellropes to serve the thirde bell & the forth bell	ij^{s}	xiij^{d}
	Also p^{d} to John towley for all his singlinge the church, & for his peynes all the yere & for to ouer see the cloke & beles, & for a new stoke, as the same John founde, to trysse the seconde bell wth	xi^{s}	
	Also p^{d} in bred & drinke to thowse as did ringe in my lorde byssHep at his comminge to Warr		vj^{d}
	Also p^{d} for A gallan of ale as the wringers had on the quenes hollidaye		iiij^{d}
1596	Also p^{d} to Sturdye of wallswotton for welminge of the forth bell claper	xj^{s}	
1598	Also p^{d} to a chimer, for chiminge of the belles		xxiij^{d}
	Also p^{d} to the Ringers, for Ringinge in the lord Byshop		xiij^{d}
1599	Also p^{d} to John owen for five buckles for the bavdries of the beles, a hinge, & a hocke, to the church	ij^{s}	vj^{d}
1603	Also p^{d} to the Ringers on the Kings holliday	ij^{s}	vj^{d}
1607	Also p^{d} to the Ringers on the Kings crounenacion daye	ij^{s}	vj^{d}
	Also p^{d} to the Ringers on the Kinges hollidaye being the fyvft of August	ij^{s}	
	Also p^{d} for a Thimnell to the bell Claper		vj^{d}

[1] This entry is erased. Why? It refers, of course, to the victory over the Armada.

1608 Also pd to the Ringers on the fyfte of August the Kinge being as that daye preserved from Earle Gowre[1] . . ijs vjd

1610 Also pd more to the Ringers, for Ringing on the fyvfe of Nouember xijd

Also pd to manes the Roper, for a newe Bell Rope . ijs

1611 Also pd to the wringers on the Kinges crounenacion Daye, & the daye of the papes conspiracie . vs

1612 Also Rec for Ringinge of the Bells at sendrie times ijs iijd

Also pd to the Ringers on the Kings hollidayes at two times that is to say on the xxvth[2] of marche & the fyvft of november vs

IRON WORKE

Also pd for two stirrops for the great bell brabbs . viijd

Also pd for two Rodds for the bells wringe (? wenge) 14 pounds at 3 the pound iijs vjd

1615 Also Rec for Ringinge of the bells at pleasure at sertain tymes vs ijd

Also pd to the Ringers, for wringing on the xxiiijth daye of marche laste ijs vjd

Also pd to william pedlye for comming over to look of our bells before the were mended xijd

Also pd to the same william pedlye for xxiij (sic) dayes woorke for him selfe about the bells xxs viijd

[And similar payments]

Also pd to John Wakefield for on pece of Timber, for to stocke two bells, & for on pece to make shrude bordes & for on pece for spokes to the whells . ijs iiijd

[Numerous other repairs]

1616 Pd to John Marrett for Clout Leather for the Eyes of the Bells for the wholle yere js viijd

1619 pd to Robert Newcombe[3] for ij strikes of Lyme mending to of the Church wall that was broken and for mending the Pavement in the Church wch was broken by the Bell .. iiijs

CHARGES AT CASTING OF THE FOURTH BELL

Imprimis pd to Richard Dawkes[4] in Ernest when he undertooke the Casting of the fourth Bell xijd

pd for a quarte of wyne given to Richard Baker when he came over first about taking of the bell . xijd

pd to mr Yardely for making of a Band when mr Wyatt and mr Wast stood Bound vijd

pd for beere for the Belfounders when they came over to seale the Bond vjd

pd to Richard Overton & his men for helping downe wth the Bell the first tyme iijs

pd to oliver Yelson for helping them iiijd

pd for bread and beere for them the same time xvjd

given to others wch helped vs to loade the Bell . vjd

pd for our Charges wth the Teeme at ii severall Tymes going wth the Bell to Stratford xxxiijs vd

pd to Richard Overton & his men for helping to hange the Bell the first Tyme iiijs

pd for bread and beare for them the same tyme xvd

given to Symon Baker at his Coming over in hope he could haue mended the tune of the Bell ijs

pd to Richard Overton & his men for helping downe wth the Bell the second tyme ijs

pd to him and his men for helping vp wth the Bell againe the second tyme iiijs

pd to Roger Ley for lending vs a Beame to way the Bell & helping vs xijd

pd to Richard Ridge and Richard ffletcher fetching waightes and helping vs about the bell xijd

pd to Richard Overtons men for Carryeing home the Rolle the Leavers & the gable Rope wch wee Borrowed about the Bell vjd

[1] The Gowrie conspiracy, a day appointed by order to be observed

[2] I e Coronation Day given as 24th March in following years

[3] A local man, not the bell founder

[4] See p 56 He was probably a Worcester man, but the bell seems to have been cast at Stratford

p^d to m^r Yardley for making a Bond wherein the Belfounders stand bound for a xij monethe & daye — vj^d

p^d to m^r Yardley for making another bond wherein m^r Wyatt stand bound to discharge the parishe of all demandes from the Belfounders — vj^d

p^d to Michael ffarr for a newe Cartroope for William Bolton bycause his was broken about the Bell — iij^s

p^d more to him for a Belrope — iij^s iiij^d

p^d to Thomas Sharley for trussing vp the third Bell — vj^d

given to Thomas Hinde for helping him .. .. — ij^d

p^d to Thomas Hinde for helping about the Bell all the wholle tyme . — iij^s

p^d to William Savage for making a Newe eye to the Little bell clapper — viij^d

p^d to him for peeceing of the great bell clapper & Layeing ij pound & a half of Iron thereon .. .. . — vj^d

p^d for xxx brabbes vj Cotters iiij Ringes and for peecing the stirropes to the Newe Bell . . — xviij^d

p^d for peeceing the stirrops & for nayles to the Third Bell stock — vj^d

p^d to Mr Wyatt & the Belfounders for Casting of the Bell & xiij poundes of newe mettle . ... — ix^{li} ij^s

given to Symon Baker the Belfounder over and above — v^s

Some of the Charges about the Bell amounteth to ... — xiij^{li} iij^s iij^d

1620 Receyved of the Inhabitantes vpon a Levy made towardes the Castinge of the fourth Bell as by the particulers appeareth the some of — vij^{li} iij^d

p^d for Loggers for the Bells . — x^d

[And numerous other repairs]

Item theire is also at this meeting allowed by the Inhabitantes of the said parishe that xiij^s iiij^d shall be yearely paid to Six Ringers & the Clarke to Ring every Sabbath day & hollyeday in the yeare a Sollempne peale before morning & Evening prayer

1621 (Payment to the clerk and ringers in accordance with the above resolution) — xiij^s iiij^d

[It should also be noted that in every year occur receipts of money for ringing the bell at the death of parishioners, the usual charge being fourpence]

The Vicar very kindly sends some additional extracts relating to the recasting of the bells in 1695, which are here appended He notes that they come from different pages of the accounts for the two years 1695-96, but belong to one continuous account The accounts at this time were made up every two years

Memorandum of a meeting held on this day being the 7th day of January 1694 upon due notice given in the Church yesterday by the Churchwardens of this Parish It is agreed by the Feoffees and Inhabitants of this parish, that the Churchwardens for the time being shall upon request pay unto Wm Bolton Esquire Mr Aaron Rogers Mr Wm Tarver Mr Richard Hand Mr Wm Makepeace and Mr Sam Jemmal the sum of (*illegible, but see below*) which is to be employed by them or the major part of them toward the new casting of the 5 bells into 6 bells and for new hanging the same as they shall think fit

Witness our hands

Twenty pounds is the sum agreed upon

(*Five signatures here*)

the mark of

(*Seventeen names here*)

Money gave by severall persons for the casting of the Bells

(*Here follow 73 names, amounts given varying from £5 to 1/-*)

Total money given to cast Bells .. .	£27 .	0	0
Paid to the men in drink y^t helped to weigh the Bells	00	01	00
Paid to men that sat up to watch the Bells when broke	00	01	00

Paid to the Bell founder in drink at several times	00	02	00
Paid to the Bellhangers in drink .	00	01	00
Paid to the men in drink that holp to weigh the bells cost	00	01	00
Paid to John Richardson for shoes for ye Bellfounder	00	08	00
Paid to Tho Williams & John Hope for hanging the Bells as appears by the Articles	11	00	00
Paid to John Williams for Timber & worke used about the steeple as by Bill appear	07	07	04
Paid to Henry Townsend for slow (?) Time & worke used about the steeple as by bill appears	02	06	03
Paid to William Grey for worke done about the steeple as by bill appears	00	06	06
Paid to William Perkes (?) for 22 yards of mating for the Floor in the steeple	00	11	10
Paid Nicholas (*illegible*) for work & materials for the Chimes as by Bill	06	00	00

A FURTHER ACCOUNT OF THE BELLS, ETC

Bells weighed out March 22nd 1694

	c	qr	
I	6	2	11
II	8	1	19
III	10	1	0
4th	14	0	7
5th	18	1	09
Tot	57	3	10

Bells weighed in March 29, 1695

	c	qr	li
1	[illegible]		5
2^{d}	6	0	5
3^{d}	7	1	12
4	8	2	11½
5	10	0	21½
6	15	0	21½
Tot	52	02	20½

Memorand the parish is to allow Keen the Bellfounder 4^{li} wast for every hundred & then Keen must make good the remainder of the weight to the Parish

The weight delivered falls short of that delivered out by 5 hundred 17 pound and a halfe

Deduct = 2 c = 0 qr = 7 li out of 57 c = 3 qr = 10 li for wast at 4^{li} y^e^ hundred

there remaining 55 = 3 = 3 - - the new Bells so that there remains to y^e^ parish

= 3 c = 0 qr 10½ li

Memorand Keen the Bell founder had also 56^{li} of Block (*word illegible*) at 9^{d}

		£	s	d
a pound come to		02	02	00
also he had in chippings	0 = 1 qr = 0			
at 10^{d} a pound come to		01	03	04
He had in shoes of John Richardson .		00	08	00
		03	13	04
The 3 = 0 = 10½ of mettall		14	08	09
So then he has had in y^e^ whole		18	02	01

WARWICK. ALL SAINTS, EMSCOTT Eight bells

Church built 1861 A ring of six bells cast by Taylor of Loughborough in 1876, to which two trebles, presented by Miss Philips, were added by the same firm in 1885 See *Church Bells*, 13 May, 1876 13 Nov 1885

		cwt	qrs	lbs			cwt	qrs	lbs	
Weights and diameters —	1)	4	1	0	26 in	5)	7	3	4	33½ in
	2)	4	3	0	27 in	6)	8	3	14	36 in
	3)	5	2	5	29½ in	7)	10	3	4	39¼ in
	4)	5	3	25	31½ in	8)	16	1	18	44½ in

WARWICK. St Paul One bell

Church built 1844

WARWICK Leycester Hospital Chapel St James One bell

Bell merely dated 1721, probably by Richard Sanders a beam in the belfry is dated 1724 See *Notes and Queries*, 3rd Ser, x (1866), p 143

On a mortar of bell-metal now at the Warwick Arms Hotel is the inscription

Peter Milburn 1706

It is probably the work of Richard Sanders (cf Kinwarton bell)

A rubbing of this, from Rev J H Bloom, is in the Department of MSS British Museum (Add 37180)

WARWICK CASTLE

In the gatehouse is a bell with the inscription

THIS BELL ✤ WAS ✤ FOVNDED ✤ ANNODOMINI ✤ FOR ✤ WEDGNOCK 1605

It is by Henry Farmer of Gloucester (p 47), and is described by Lady Warwick in her *Warwick Castle and its Earls*, i, p 212 It is used as a clock-bell, and is 26 in in diamerer I am much indebted to Mr F H Adams of St Mary's and to Mr W E Falkner for their trouble in examining this bell The inscription seems to show that it was not originally made for the Castle, but Wedgnock Park (in Leek Wootton parish) was then the property of the Greville family (see Dugdale, i, p 272) There was no chapel there in 1605

WASPERTON St John Baptist Two bells

1 1686

2 1817

The smaller bell by Henry Bagley the larger by John Rudhall or Mears They are small bells, hanging in a cot at the west end

1552 'ij belles one litle bell'
1750 'I Bell
H T T, 3 Aug, 1881

WATER ORTON. SS Peter and Paul Two bells

1 ✪ ✠ IOHN BVRTON ● CHVRCH ● WARDEN 1709

2 ✠ I WILL ● SOVND ● AND ● CALL THE CONGREGATION 1709

Both bells very small they are by Joseph Smith The inscription on the 2nd was also on the old 3rd at Exhall by Coventry
H T T, 4 Sept, 1876

WEDDINGTON St James One bell

1 GILBERTVS ADDERLEY ARMIGER HV ECCL · PATRONVS 1703

Founder probably George Oldfield II of Nottingham, see p 63

Trap-door to bell-chamber apparently hermetically sealed up at the time of my visit, so that I regret not having been able to verify this bell

1552 'Itm there oon bell'

The Adderley family purchased the Manor of Weddington about 1570, and it was owned by this Gilbert about 1700—1720 he married Lucy Savage of Elmley Castle (See Dugdale ii, p 1096)

H T T 5 July 1876

WEETHLEY St James One bell

1 WARNER & SONS LONDON 1857

On waist —Royal Arms and PATENT

In an open turret put up when the church was re-built in 1857 The date is a guess both H T T and Mr Falkner failed to verify it with certainty

H T T, 5 Oct 1881

WELLESBOURNE St Peter Six bells

1 CANTATE DOMINO CANTICVM NOVVM 1681

2 HENRY BAGLEY MADE MEE 1681

3 HENRY BAGLEY MADE MEE 1681

4 HENRY BAGLEY MADE MEE 1681
(border of scrolls)

5 ROBERT HOPPER AND RICHARD HOPKINS CHVRCH WARDENS 1681

6 *Above, border all round (arabesques)*

PRO REGE ET *(broad scroll)* ECCLESEA 1681

Below, border all round (arabesques inverted) (36 in

All six by Henry Bagley, treble estimated at 3 cwt, tenor 19½ cwt *(sic)*

Borders on 1st and 3rd Fig 11, on 2nd floral ornament and Fig 11 on 4th, Figs 9, 11, Pl XXII 10, on 5th, cross Pl XXII, Fig 7 floral ornament and Fig 11, on 6th, Fig 11 and *Bucks*, Pl XXVII 5, and a rosette Coins of Charles II apparently farthings

The bells of Thelsford Priory, about 1½ miles away founded by Sir William Lacy temp Henry III, are said to have been given to Wellesbourne at the Dissolution (the Vicar says only the tenor)

1552 'WELSBURNE iiij belles one litle bell'

1750 '6 Bells'

CUSTOMS

Bells chimed on Sundays rung on greater Festivals Ringing on Christmas Eve and New Year s Eve from 11-45 to 12-15, for Weddings by request

Death-Knell on receipt of notice, tellers 3×3 for man 3×2 for woman 3×1 for child Muffled peals rung on eve of funerals of persons of note such as the Bishop

A bell rung for Vestry Meetings

The bells were formerly rung on St Thomas Day at 6 a m for half-an-hour but the Vicar, believing there was no reason for the custom (for which see p 89), has transferred it to the Patronal Festival (St Peter s Day) at a later hour

Best thanks to Rev R W Rudgard Vicar, and to Mr Falkner

H T T 3 Aug 1881

WESTON-UNDER-WEATHERLEY

St MICHAEL Four bells

1  **IHS NAZARENVS** *(border)* **REX IVDEORVM** *(border)* **FILI DEI MISERERE** *(border)* **MEI** *(border)* **162** *(border)* (27½ in

2 **GALFRIDVS ◆ GILES ◆ FECIT ◆ ME ◆ ANNO ◆ DM 1583 ◆**

On waist — ✠ **Cantate Dno Canticum Nouum Laus Eius In Ecclesia Sanctorum**

3 **Morgan** *(coat-of-arms)* **Sanders Anno dni 1585**

On waist — ✠ **Laudate Domn Quia Bonus Donus Psallite Noie Eius quoniam Suaue**

4 **THOMAS**  **MORGAN**  **S** 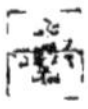 **SQUIER 1592**  (34 in

The 2nd is cracked right down, and the 3rd round the middle, bells dirty and neglected

1st Watts, of the usual type acorn borders

2nd and 3rd For this founder see p 47 the inscription on the waist of the 2nd is from Ps 149, 1 (Vulg) that on the 3rd apparently an adaptation of Ps 147, 1 The capitals are large and coarse, of quasi Roman type very flat and thin and the smalls are of similar character

4th By Hugh Watts I (see p 41) the earliest dated of his bells in the county except Wootton Wawen the bottom of the shield is cut off

1552 'WESTON-UNDER-WETHELEY iij belles and a saunce belle

CUSTOMS as at Wappenbury with which the living is united[1]

The inscriptions on the bells are mentioned in Thomas' Dugdale, i, p 297, where it is also stated that the Manor of Weston was granted in 1557 by Queen Mary to Sir Edward Sanders,

Knt of Newbold chief Baron of the Exchequer and to Thomas Morgan, and their heirs which Thomas married Mary sole daughter and heir to the said Sir Edward Thomas Morgan was patron of the living 1576—1600 he was born in 1533 died at Weston, and was buried at Heyford, Oxon The three larger bells were his gift The Morgan-Sanders arms, which appear on the 3rd bell, are (or were) also to be seen in the chancel In Brit Mus Add MSS, 29264, fol 173, this and other additional information is given supplementing the printed account, with a drawing of the coat-of-arms The latter is not quite explicit but the coat may be roughly described as follows Arms of Morgan Party per pale—(1) Argent, on a bend sable three roses of the field in chief sable, a cross between two fleurs-de-lys argent (2) quarterly (1 and 4) arms of Pemberton (?) (2) [*doubtful*] (3) three animals passant ( ) Impaling the arms of Sanders Party per chevron sa and arg, three elephants' heads erased and counterchanged of the field

From the same MSS we learn that the second bell was cracked by clocking as long ago as 1830 or, as the writer says, by the careless wilfulness of tying a string around the bell when ringing

H T T, 9 Oct, 1878, H B W, Sept, 1907

WESTWOOD. One bell

Church built 1844 Parish formed from Stoneleigh

WHATCOTE St Peter Three bells

1 WILLIAM BLEWS AND SONS BIRMINGHAM 1878

On waist — (*a*) ✠ AD DEI GLORIAM ET IN USUM
ECCLESIAE S PETRI APUD WHATCOTE
D D ERNESTUS THOMAS SACERDOS ✠
✠ TE DEUM LAUDAMUS ✠
(*b*) CANTATE DOMINO CANTICUM NOVUM
H B 1653

2 IOHN ✠ CLARK ✠ MED ME 1711

3 M. BAGLEY MADE MEE 1766 WILLIAM MARSHALL WILLIAM BLAKEMAN CHURCHWARDINS

On waist —RECAST QUEEN VICTORIAS DIAMOND JUBILEE YEAR 1897
WILLIAM SANDERSON MILLER RECTOR
H. BOND & SONS FOUNDERS BURFORD OXON

2nd John Clark must be a successor of the William Clark who cast the bells at Henley and Newbold Pacey (see p 76)

The old treble and tenor were inscribed as indicated on the new bells H T T noted the former as badly cracked in 1876 He also says there has evidently been a fourth bell here (see below) which is said to be the one now at Idlicote

1552 iiij belles a litle belle 1750 4 Bells

Many thanks to Mr W E Falkner
H T T 18 Jan 1876

WHICHFORD St Michael 6+1 bells

1 O sing unto the LORD a new song ✲

Below vine-border all round Taylor's trade-mark and

✲ 1904 ✲ (27¼ in

2 John Taylor & Co ✲ Founders ✲ Loughborough ✲ 1904

Below vine-border and

Ye people all who hear us ring

Be faithful to your GOD and King (29 in

3 Praise GOD in His sanctuary ✲ ✲

Below, as on 1st (31½ in

4 WILLIAM BAGLEY MADE MEE 1695 (31¾ in

5 REV^D R B PINIGER RECTOR W TAYLOR 1848 FECIT J WILKES & R GIBBS CHURCH WARDENS (35 in

6 Behold, how good and how pleasant it is for brethren to dwell together in unity ✲

Below, as on first (41¾ in

S WILLIAM BAGLEY MADE MEE

On waist —1706

On sound-bow —THOMAS HARRASS ROB WALKER IO TAPLIN C W

All re-hung in Taylor's H frames Formerly five bells, the treble inscribed

CANTATE DOMINO CANTICVM NOVVM 1695

the old 2nd and 3rd like the present 4th, with borders between the words, the 3rd having also a border above the inscription The additional bell is therefore the tenor

Borders on 4th, Figs 10, 13 The capital letters on the new bells are copied from the well-known and beautiful letters found at South Somercotes Lincolnshire They have also been used by Taylor at Worcester Cathedral

		cwt	qrs	lbs		cwt	qrs	lbs
Weights —	1)	4	1	1	4)	4	3	26
	2)	5	0	1	5)	6	2	8
	3)	5	3	20	6)	12	3	23

The remarkable lightness of the 4th bell is to be noted

The sanctus bell hangs in a cot over the chancel arch

The Rev R B Piniger (5th bell) was appointed Rector in 1839

1552 iiij belles one sanct bell 1750 5 Bells

' At Whichford there is a pretty ring of bells which rang immediately we came out of church (Diary of Thomas Archer of Merton College, Oxford 1801)

H T T, 20 June 1879 H B W, Sept, 1908

WHITACRE, NETHER, St Giles — Three bells

1 **W^M^ BUTLER C W THO^S^ HEDDERLY OF NOTTINGHAM FECIT 1783**

2 **✠ NEWCOMBE · OF LEICESTER MADE MEE 1612**

3. **THO^S^ HEDDERLY NOTT^M^ FECIT 1785 WILLIAM BVTLER CHVRCH WARDEN**

1552 'iij belles a saunce bell and a hand bell'

Customs

On Sundays a bell rung from 7-45 to 8 a m , for morning and evening Services one bell rung for fifteen minutes then chiming for fifteen

Ringing on Greater Festivals, and on New Year's Eve from 11 30 p m to 12 15 a m for Weddings by request

Death-knell on day of death or following day between 8 a m and 5 p m , tellers 3 × 3 3 × 2, and 3 × 1 (the latter for infants under three), age of deceased tolled Tolling for half-an-hour before Funerals

Thanks to Rev H E Metcalfe, Rector

WHITACRE, OVER St Leonard — Two bells

1 *No inscription*

2.  **CELORVM CHRSTE PLATIAT TIBI REX SONVS · ISTE 1616**

1st Probably mediaeval
2nd By Watts
Bells very difficult to get at
1552 'iij belles in the steple and a hand bell'

Both bells used for Services on Sundays and for 'ringing' at Weddings, chiming immediately after Funerals

Best thanks to Rev J G Lane, Rector

WHITCHURCH St Mary — One bell

1 ✠ I N R I ✠ A E M A G A

Cross and lettering as on 1st and 3rd at Beaudesert see p 4 Plate II 1–9 The inscription is not so difficult to interpret as may seem at first sight, it is in fact an abbreviation of the two at Beaudesert 'I(hs) N(azarenus) R(ex) I(udeorum) A(v)E M(ari)A G(raci)A Probably by a Warwickshire founder of about 1350

1552 'Whitechurche iij belles a hande belle
1750 '1 Bell'

Best thanks to Mr Falkner and Rev J H Bloom

H T T 15 June 1887

WHITNASH St Margaret — Six bells

1 **J TAYLOR & C^O^ FOUNDERS LOUGHBOROUGH ✲ 1896**

On waist THE CHURCHWARDEN

EDWARD CRUMP } WARDENS
EDWARD READING, JUNIOR }

1896 (26¼ in

2 J · TAYLOR & C° FOUNDERS LOUGHBOROUGH MDCCCXCII

On waist — A. H. M. RUSSELL, M.A., RECTOR

J. WOOD, PARISH WARDEN (27½ in

3 MATTHEW BAGLEY MADE MEE 1680 (29¼ in

4 IOHN FREEMAN AND HENRY CHAMBERLAINE CHVRCH WARDENS 1680 (31¼ in

5 *As No 2*

On waist — "THE RECTOR"

IN MEMORY OF CANON YOUNG

RECTOR 1846–1884 (34½ in

6 J : TAYLOR AND C° FOUNDERS LOUGHBOROUGH MDCCCXCII

On waist — TO THE BELOVED MEMORY OF

ELIZABETH WISE OF SHRUBLANDS

LEAMINGTON

H. LEEKE AND E. H. LEEKE

CHRISTMAS 1891 (38½ in

Taylor's H-shaped iron frames.

Borders on 3rd, Pl XXII 10; on 4th Fig 11. The large floral ornament on the 3rd before MATTHEW also occurs at Wormleighton. Type on tenor larger than on the other Taylor bells; it is their more recent variety, as at Allesley and Berkswell.

Formerly two bells only; 2nd, 5th, and 6th added in 1892 (see *Church Bells*, 4 March) and the treble in 1896.

		cwt	qrs	lbs		cwt	qrs	lbs
Weights —	1)	4	0	14	4)	5	1	12
	2)	4	1	11	5)	8	1	2
	3)	4	3	0	6)	10	3	15

1552 'WYTNASHE ij belles a saunce bell and ij small belles.'
1750 '3 Bells.'

CUSTOMS –

On Sundays bells chimed for Services; a bell rung at 8 a.m. and also at 9 a.m. (old Mattins and Mass bells).

Ringing on Christmas Day, Easter Day, New Year's Eve and Day, and for Weddings by request.

Death-knell on receipt of notice, usual tellers, followed by tolling age of deceased and tellers repeated.

Thanks to Rev A H M Russell Rector

H T T 30 Jan, 1877 H B W Sept, 1907

WIBTOFT

One bell by Hedderley, of Nottingham, dated 1758 see North's *Church Bells of Leicestershire*, p 302

The Parish Church was formerly in Leicestershire but the parish is now wholly in Warwickshire

WILLEY.

St Leonard Three bells

1 BRYANVS ELDRIDGE ME FECIT 1658

2 IHS NAZARENE REX IUDEORUM FILI DEI MISERERE MEI ANNO DOM 1730

3  | GOD | SAVE | THE KING | 1617 |

1st See p 58
2nd By Eayre of Kettering
3rd By Watts
The bells are very small

1552 Wylley iij belles and i saunce belle, a hand belle
1750 3 Bells

H T T, 14 Oct, 1897

WILLOUGHBY

St Nicholas Six bells

1 ✠ MR ROBERT WATSON FARMER AND MR WILLIAM CLERKE CHVRCH WARDENS 1713
(Running border below)

2 ✠ ● IOSEPH ● SMITH *(border)* ● IN ● EDGBASTON ● *(border)* ● MADE ● MEE ● 1713 *(border)*

3 ✠ GOD ● *(border)* SAVE *(border)* ● *(border)* ● HIS ● *(border)* ● CHVRCH *(border)* ● 1713 ●
(Running border below)

4 ✠ MR ROBERT WATSON FARMOR AND MR WILLIAM CLERKE ● CHVRCH WARDENS ● 1713 ●

5 ✠ MR WILLIAM ● TVRTON MINESTER MR ROBERT WATSON FARMOR AND MR WILLIAM CLERKE CHVRCH
Below.—WARDENS 1713 *and running border*

6 JOHN MALLING & HENRY MILLS CHURCH WARDENS W^M CHAPMAN OF LONDON FECIT 1781
On waist.—MY MOURNFULL SOUND DOTH WARNING GIVE THAT HERE MEN CANNOT ALLWAYS LIVE

Usual scroll borders on 1st—5th (Pl XXIII 2)

6th Bells by William Chapman alone are very rare (see p 83)

There were formerly chimes here playing at 12, 4, and 8, said to have been brought from Southam, the six tunes played were "Cannon," "Suffolk," "New Court," "Belle Isle March," "Captain Thornton's March," and a French tune

1552 iij belles and a saunce belle'
1750 5 Bells

H T T 20 Jan, 1892

WILMCOTE ST ANDREW One bell

1. THOMAS MEARS FOUNDER LONDON 1841 (23 in

The bell is placed in a small wooden erection in the Churchyard

There was an ancient chapel here, but the present building is entirely modern (built in 1840) see Hannett, *Forest of Arden*, p 70

H T T 15 Nov, 1881

WILNECOTE One Bell

1 **THOMAS HEDDERLY FOUNDER NOTT 1763** (17¾ in

Bell very much corroded NOTT is, of course, Nottingham

Lynam, *Staffordshire*, p 36 gives ANNO DOMINI in place of NOTT

H T T, 3 June, 1891

WINDERTON See BRAILES

WISHAW ST CHAD Two bells

1 THOMAS GOODARD CVRCH WARDIN 1650 T C

(28¾ in

2 MICKEL WALFORD RECTOR 1650 (31½ in

Both by John Martin of Worcester, cross, Plate XXI, Fig 7, small heart-shaped trade-mark (Plate XXI, Fig 2) border Pl XXI 8 The N is reversed The Rev Michael Walford was Rector 1629—1662

Said to have been formerly three bells, but one sold about 70 years ago to raise money, H T T in 1874 noted that the wheel and stock of the third bell still remained

1552 'WYSHAWE iij belles in the steple
1750 '3 Bells'

CUSTOMS

On Sundays a bell always rung at 8 a m, for later services both bells chimed for ten minutes, and then after a five minutes interval for five again followed by a few strokes on one bell as "Sermon Bell"

Ringing for Weddings, Death-Knell, and tolling at Funerals, all by request

Thanks to Rev W B Stanford, Rector, and to Mr Falkner

H T T 25 Sept, 1874

WITHYBROOK ALL SAINTS Four bells

1 **CHRISTOPHER WRGHT OF HAPPISFORD ESQUIER 1582**

On waist —**BARWELL FOUNDER BIRMINGHAM**

RECAST 1907 (28¾ in

2 **BRYANVS ELDRIDGE ME FECIT 1656.**

On waist - as on 1st, in addition

IN MEMORIAM

A. C. DALZIEL ESQ OF IRVINE N.B. (29 in

3 **SOLI DEO GLORIA PAX HOMINIBVS 1654**

On waist as 1st (33 in

4 ✠ **BE YT . KNOWNE TO . ALL THAT DOTH ME SEE THAT NEWCOMBE OF LEICESTER MADE ME 1612** (36 in

The first three bells being cracked (the 2nd and 3rd as long ago as 1876, as noted by H T T) have now been re-cast, with old inscriptions repeated According to H T T's notes they were as follows —

1 ✠ ✠ **CHRISTOPHER** [K] **WRGHT** [K] **OF** [K] **HAPPISFORD** [K] **ESQUIER**

Below —**1585**

2 BRYANVS ELDRIDGE ME FECIT 1656

3 ✠ SOLI ✿✿✿ DEO ✿✿✿ GLORIA ✿✿✿ PAX ✿✿✿ HOMINIBVS 1654

(*with border at end*)

The treble was by Robert (?) Newcombe of Leicester, being the earliest dated bell by that firm in the county (see p 31) If the date given on the new bell is to be trusted it was also the earliest dated bell in the county at the time of its disappearance but H T T gives the date as 1585 and is more likely to be right as it is quite conceivable that a peculiarly formed 5 may have been mistaken for a 2 Unfortunately my predecessor left no rubbing. The cross and letters are Plate XVI, Figs 2 7 10, the stamp used as a stop is the head of King Edward III (Plate X, Fig 3), as found on other Newcombe bells

2nd for Bryan Eldridge, see p 58

3rd by John Martin of Worcester cross, ornament between words, and trade-mark, Plate XXI, Figs 3, 6 7

On the present 4th the N's are reversed

1552, iij belles and a saunce bell

Best thanks to Messrs Barwell for information about the new bells

Christopher Wright of Happisford, J P, the donor of the old treble died 6 Dec, 1602, there is an altar tomb to him in the church with incised effigy and his arms above, also the inscription (remarkable at this date) "whose soule God rest" See Dugdale, i, p 217

H T T, 16 Sept 1876

WIXFORD — St Milburgha — Two bells

1 *No inscription*

2 ALL PRAYSE AND GLORY BE TO GOD FOR EVER 1672

Smaller bell ancient larger by John Martin of Worcester, with running border between words, and small heart-shaped trade-mark (Pl XXI 2 8) In a small wooden western turret originally in an open double cot One of the two is said to be cracked and disused

1552 'WICKILFORD Itm there j bell'

Death-knell tolled for an hour, on receipt of notice

Thanks to Rev A W Sheard, Rector

H T T 29 Jan, 1878

WOLFHAMCOTE — St Peter — Two bells

1 PACK & CHAPMAN OF LONDON FECERUNT 1780

2 ✠ ✠ ✠ In Multis Annis Resonet Campana Iohannis

The larger bell is probably by John Sturdy of London, c 1430 (p 22) the crosses are Plate XI, Figs 2 3 and the crowned capitals are Stephen Norton's (Pl XI 6-8 10) It is unusually large for a small church, weighing 18 or 19 cwt

1552 'WOLHAMCOTE two belles in the steple'

H T T, 21 Jan, 1892

WOLFORD, GREAT — St Michael — Six bells

1 MAIOR THOMAS KYTE CAST MEE LEADER OF THIS RING TO BE 1 6 9 0
Below, arms of Keyte (29 in

2 CAPTAIN THOMAS KEYTE CAST MEE 1 6 8 9 (31 in

3 · W FLETCHER & T FOX WARDENS 1792 I RUDHALL FEC (34 in

4 MAIGOR KEYTE CAST THIS RING 1690
Below arms of Keyte thrice (36 in

5 THO SHEPHARD WM HALL C . W : M B MADE · ME : 1752 (39 in

6 *On waist* — (*a*) RECAST BY G MEARS, & CO, 1864
A WHITE & SONS BELLHANGERS

(b) G D WHELER VICAR
JOHN RAINBOW, }
JOHN FLETCHER, } CHURCHWARDENS, 1864
"I SWEETLY TOLL WHEN MEN DO CALL"
TO TASTE ON FOOD THAT FEEDS THE SOLE' (41 in

All in excellent order and very clean The 3rd has cabled cannons

Weight of tenor 12 cwt 3 qrs 1 lb

The 1st, 2nd, and 4th by Richard Keene (see p 60) small letters on 1st and 2nd inscription on 1st also occurs on the treble at Chipping Campden, Gloucs

5th By Matthew Bagley

1750 'Wolsford 5 Bells

Thomas Keyte, of Wolford, who gave the bells was a younger brother of Sir William Keyte Bart, of Ebrington, Gloucs He died in 1701 The family arms which appear on the 1st and fourth bells are —Azure, a chevron between three kites heads erased or

H B W, Apr. 1907

WOLSTON St Margaret Four bells

1 **J : TAYLOR & C° FOUNDERS LOUGHBOROUGH** *(wine-pattern)*

Below, border of fleur-de-lys pattern, like Fig 18 inverted

On waist **1894**

THE GIFT OF
THE REV JOHN WILCOX
VICAR OF WOLSTON. (29½ in

2 ✠ MARCUS MATHEUS LUCAS IOHES (31½ in

3 ✠ GLORIA ++++++++ DEO +++++++++ IN +++++++ EXCELSVS ++++++++++++++ 1620 +++++++

2nd line) —IOHN WAWLE WILLIAM ROWE CHVRCH WARDENS (34½ in.

4 *Above border of loops* ◇◇◇ *all round*

W & T. MEARS LATE LESTER PACK & CHAPMAN OF LONDON FECIT 1789 ✠◇◇✠ *(continuous)* (37½ in

Formerly three bells, the treble (weight 5 cwt 1 qr 23 lbs) is an addition

2nd By Johannes de Stafford (p 15), cross and letters, Plate VII, Figs 16—19 The inscription is unique, and the order in which the Evangelists are arranged is noteworthy (cf. some old tiles at Malvern Priory, Worcestershire, Brassington, *Historic Worcs*, p 122) [H T T]

3rd By William Clibury of Wellington, Salop (see p 50) cf Grendon 2nd Cross Plate XXI, Fig 11, border Plate XXI, Fig 15

Bells very dirty access to the bell-chamber can only be obtained from outside the tower

1552 'iij belles and a saunce bell'
1750 'Woolston 6 Bells' (sic)

CUSTOMS —

On Sundays bells chimed for Services, bell rung formerly after Morning Service
Ringing at Christmas and on New Year's Eve, for Weddings by request
Death-knell as soon as possible after death
Gleaning Bell formerly

Best thanks to Rev H A M Wilcox, Vicar

H T T, 8 March, 1887 H B W, June 1908

WOLVERTON ST MARY Two bells

1 T RUDHALL FOUNDER 1771

2 *No inscription*

The larger bell appears to be very ancient

1552 'Itm there a ij belles
1750 Wolverdington 2 Bells
Notices of Warwickshire Churches ii, p 81

H T T, 24 Jan, 1882

WOLVEY ST JOHN BAPTIST Three bells

1  **GOD** (*arabesques*) **SAVE** (*arabesques*) **THE** (*arabesques*) **KING** (*arabesques*) **1625**

2 **I ASTLEY ESQ C FITCH GENT T FRASER GENT E PHIPPES GENT**
2nd line — **I TOONE C W TOBY NORRIS CAST ME 1680**

3\. + GLORIA IN EXCELSIS DEO

1st By Hugh Watts

2nd The only bell in the county from this foundry (see p 61) The borders are, on first line, scroll patterns, on second, a narrow plait (Pl XXI 4) the initial cross is Pl XXII Fig 5 All the N's are reversed

3rd By Johannes de Yorke (see p. 17), for lettering see Pl X Fig 1 the only example of his work in the county. Date probably about 1400 It is said to have come from Nuneaton Abbey at the Dissolution

Weights given as 12 15, and 19 cwt respectively (notes C B A) probably 8, 9, and 11 cwt would be nearer the mark

1552 'iij belles a saunce bell and ij sacring belles'
1750 '5 Bells

CUSTOMS

1st and 2nd rung at 8 a.m. every Sunday, bells chimed for half-an-hour before other services
Ringing at midnight on Christmas Eve and New Year's Eve, for Weddings by request
Death-Knell at 9 a.m. after death, with clapper tied, and usual tellers. Tolling for half-an-hour before Funerals

Many thanks to Rev. T. D. Williams, Vicar

H. T. T., 15 July 1891

WOOTTON WAWEN ST. PETER Six bells

1 **IOH[N] MORRIS HEN[R]Y [G]R[EE]N** *(border)* **[C]HVR[C]H** *(border)* **WARDENS** *(border)*
HENRY *(border)* **BAGLEY** *(border)* **[O]F WIT[N]EY** *(border)* **MADE** *(border)* **MEE J742** *(border)* (28½ in.

2 *On crown* —1591 *(border, Pl. XVII, Fig. 8)*

|A|B|C|D|E| |F|G|H|I|K| |L|M|N|O|P|Q|R|S| (30¾ in.

3 **I. RUDHALL GLOCESTER FECIT J803** (32½ in.

4 1784 *(the rest filed away)* (34½ in.

5 THO^S HAYNES & IOHN BUFFERY CHURCH WARDENS ·:· 1761 (37¾ in.

6 **IOHN MOORE RECTOR IOB FISHER IOHN ATTWOOD C W 1719** • *(arabesques)*

Below — (41½ in.

1st. For Bagley at Witney see pp. 65, 71. Cracked and mended with iron rivets, which prevent portions of the inscription from being seen; but the words as they stand are certain.

2nd. An early example of Watts, of Leicester (probably Francis, see p. 40). Cross Plate XVIII, Fig. 6; larger set of Brasyer lettering (Pl. XVIII, 1-5).

4th. Inscription filed away except date and border: probably T. Rudhall (border Fig. 15).

5th. By Thomas Rudhall; border, Fig. 18.

6th. By Richard Sanders: trade-mark Plate XXIII, Fig. 9.

1552 'WOTT'N WAUGHEN. Itm there . . . iij belles'

'Q^e that the p'ishe have solde sithe the Last S^rvey oon bell to the buyldinge of theire churche and a oyle'

1750 'Wotton Waven 6 Bells'

See *Notices of Warwickshire Churches*, i, p. 128; Sweeting MSS., Brit. Mus. Add. 37180.

CUSTOMS —

A bell at 8 a m every Sunday

Ringing on Christmas Eve New Year's Eve, and King's Birthday

Thanks to Rev F T Bramston Vicar, and Mr W E Falkner

H T T 11 June 1883

WORMLEIGHTON ST PETER Three bells

1 *Above border of linked fleurs-de-lys*

CANTATE DOMINO CANTICVM NOVVM 1642 H ✲ B

2 **Celorum xie placeat tibi rex sonus iste**

3 IHS NAZARENVS REX IVDEORVM FILI DEI MISERERE MEI 1617

1st By Henry Bagley, border above, Fig 9, between initials, ornament, as at Whitnash

2nd By Richard or Robert Mellour, of Nottingham, c 1500—1520 (see p 21), on the waist a rose and Mellour's trade-mark (Pl X, Figs 6, 8)

3rd By Hugh Watts, said to weigh about one ton (?)

1552 'iij belles a saunce belle

1750 '3 Bells'

CUSTOMS —

On Sundays bells chimed for Services, the 2nd being rung afterwards as Sermon Bell for five minutes, and the 1st for the last two minutes

Ringing on New Year's Eve, also twice a week before and after Christmas beginning in November, on November 5th, and for Weddings by request

Death-knell on tenor for half-an-hour with usual tellers at beginning and end, tenor tolled before and after Funerals

Best thanks to Rev G P Alford Vicar

H T T, 14 June 1887

WROXHALL ST LEONARD Three bells

1 HENRY BAGLEY MADE MEE IOHN EALES CHVRCH WARDIN (*border*) 1664

2 PRAES THE LORDE ALWAEIS

3 Assit Principio Sca Maria Meo

2nd By one of the Newcombes, c 1600 (see p 57), cf Burton Hastings Cross, Plate XVI, Fig 2, used as stop, the crown is Plate XVII Fig 3

3rd A fine specimen of the work of Thomas Bullisdon, of London (1500—1510 see p 26) initial cross Plate XIII, Fig 14, formerly in hands of William Woodewarde (see p 23) founder's shield Plate XIII, Fig 17 initial capitals Plate XIII The inscription seems to imply that this was the founder's first effort, cf his contemporary, Culverden, at Takeley Essex

John Eales (see 1st bell) died in 1718 His will is given by Ryland, *Records of Wroxhall*, p 227

A legend recorded by Dugdale (*Monasticon*, iv., 88), tells how Hugh of Hatton, Lord and founder of Wroxhall in the 12th century being taken prisoner in the Crusade, was miraculously delivered by St Leonard, to whom in gratitude he founded the Priory here, and the chains of his captivity were partly used as metal for the bells See also Ryland *op cit* p 215

1552 ' WRAXSALL Itm there iij belles '

According to a tradition recorded by Bloxam the Priory had seven bells before the Dissolution, and four were then removed to Baddesley Clinton, but in any case the present tenor must be one of the old ring See also Ryland *op cit*, p lviii, and *Warwickshire Churches*, ii, p 53

Mr Ryland, in his magnificent volume *Records of Wroxall* (1903), gives some additional information relating to the bells It is clear, he says (p li), that there was an important belfry in the mediaeval church, as it is specially mentioned in the original grant to Burgoyne in 1544 (*op cit*, p 186), it appears to have been a central tower, whereas the present western tower only dates from the seventeenth century In 1556 it is reported that two of the bells had been sent to Studley

On one of the beams in the belfry is carved the date 1664, which is that of the treble, and indicates that the bells were re-hung when that was put up There is an entry in the Parish Accounts for that year

' Layd out upon the Church xviij^li vij^s vij^d

which sum may possibly include the re hanging of the bells

In 1631 occurs the entry

Three new bell wheels xxiij^s

There are no ringing customs

Thanks to Rev F W R Mason, Chaplain

H T T, 5 Oct, 1874

WYKEN

ST MARY MAGDALEN — One bell

1 IHC NAZERENUS REX IUDEORU ● 23 in

The cross and lettering (Pl II Figs 10–11) do not seem to occur elsewhere, but the old bell at Baxterley was similar in character (see p. 5) The final M has been obliterated

H T T Apr, 1875 H B W, Sept 1907

APPENDIX

The following extracts relating to Burmington and Coughton appeared in the *Stratford Herald* in December, 1909, after the descriptions of those bells had been passed for press. In printing them here, it is necessary to note that they entail a modification of the statements made under those headings, pp. 128, 131. Obviously two out of the three bells at Burmington were sold in 1692, and at Coughton there were only three previous to 1686.

BURMINGTON

COMMISSION TO INQUIRE INTO THE RUIN OF BURMINGTON CHAPEL

Edward, by divine permission, Lord Bishop of Worcester, to our beloved Christopher Cook, D.D., Rector of Little Compton, Richard Watkins, B.D., Rector of (Which)ford, and Dean Rural of the Deanery of Kington, Samuel Scattergood, B.D., Vicar of Blockley, Henry Hickes, A.M., Rector of Stretton-upon-the-Foss, William Richardson, M.A., Vicar of Brayles, Rowland Aris, A.M., Vicar of Honnington, Richard Croft, A.M., Rector of Barcheston, in the counties of Worcester and Warwick in our diocese of Worcester, greeting.

Whereas wee have received a petition from Charles Stephens, clerk, M. of Arts, and curate of the parochial chapell of Burmington in our said diocese, and from the parishioners there inhabiting, wherein they set forth that the church or chapel of Burmington aforesaid, by reason of great decays, fell down about four yeares sithence, altho they took all the care they could to keep it up and in repair, which still lies in ruine, and that the rebuilding of it in the former dimensions is beyond their ability, the inhabitants being few in number and alleging their poverty. And whereas it is suggested that a much less structure than the old one would be sufficient to receive all the inhabitants, and that one good bell would be enough for the giving notice of the times when they are to assemble for the service of God, and do thereupon pray that they may make use of the rest of the bells and lead as well as the other materials of the old chappell to enable them the better to erect the new one, which yet will at a modest computation cost £100, more than an equal levy of six shillings in the pound.

Wee being willing so far to comply with their petition as is agreed to the conveniency and decent performance of the service of God in the said place, do hereby authorise and require you or any four or more of you to repair to the place aforesaid and seriously to consider and debate the matters contained in the said petition, and after your personal view and conference thereupon within the space of three weeks to return this commission, together with your opinion and report in writing under your handes and seales what you shall find that we may direct which is reasonable to be don herein, and that you certify the dimensions of the ground which you shall think sufficient for the raising the new intended chapel, upon having still a respect to the great use and service for which the said building is designed.

Given at our Palace at Worcester under our Chancellor's seal the 24th day of August, in the year of our Lord God, 1692, and in the third year of our consecration.

Tho. Vernon, Reg.

COUGHTON.

To the Right Reverend father in God, Lord William Bishopp of Worcester. My lord, these are to lett your good lordship understand the agrevances of the inhabytants of Samborne in the p'ish of Coughton and county of Warwicke. Whereas wee had in our p'ish church at Coughton three large able bells keept in as good repaire as any bells in the county untill aboute November 1686, S[r] Robert Throckmorton, S[r] John Yeats, popish recusants, with a crew of evell popishly affected p'sons who thought the bells not musicalle in the night-time, did by the consent of the minister and churchwardens enter into our church with lights and with smith sledges and greate hammars did breake and disable two of the said bells soe that for five monthes wee had no bells to ringe to prayers: and since they have bine cast into six very small bells [*sic*] ading more metall, which metall and charges amounts to eyghty pounds and uppwards, which moneyes the said S[r] Robert, with his vicar and churchwardens, hee overpowering of them, have leaved uppon the inhabytants and tennants of the p'ish, contrary to the lawes of this kingdom, S[r] Robert being in great power then enforced many to pay to the said charges, but other refusinge to pay. By reason the bells are made useless to the one p[t] of the p'ish, namely Samborne, which before they could heare and know what time to go to church to prayer and other dutyes, which since the bells are soe smalle they cannot heare them, but antient men that goe two miles or moore to church in winter-time com sometimes to early and so take colde, and many times to late and loose the benefit of divine service since the bells are soe spoyled. S[r] Robert was before offended at the greatnes of the bells; they made too much noyse in his house standing neare the church and caused the steeple windowes to be stoped upp with bricke untill he caused the bells broken, but since the bells are soe small the windows are laid open so they have the musicke and wee must paye for spoyling our good bells . . . . . . Whearefore wee humbly crave your lordshipp's good faviour that they that destroyed our good bells may paye the charges and make our bells usefull to us againe, etc. etc.

Samborne, Maye the 9th, Anno Dom. 1689

John Chillingworth

Cons. Court, No. 9609.

[There is no comment on the petition, or citation to defend the transaction, and as the "six very small bells" of 1686 (the tenor is about 10 cwt.) still hang in the tower, it is clear that the Sambourne people had to pay up and grin and bear it.]

INDEX

PLATE II

1–9 BEAUDESERT AND WHITCHURCH 10–19 WYKEN AND BAXTERLEY

BELLS RECAST.

BIRMINGHAM M P S AT LONDON FOUNDRY.

9/2/1937

NEW "RING" FOR ST PHILIP'S

To-day, at a Croydon bell foundry, Birmingham M P s saw the recasting of the bells of St Philip's Cathedral Church Birmingham (writes the London representative of the "Mail") Five tons of metal were tapped from the furnace and run into four moulds designed for the group of bells which were taking shape to day

Birmingham is to have a ring of 10 bells, which have to be cast in sections to meet the requirements of the foundry

In front of the furnace there was a roughly constructed platform along which the M P s stood to throw into the moulds the silver coins which had been sent for the occasion by Sir Charles Hyde This perpetuates an old custom but it has no effect on the actual tone of the bells

The Birmingham representatives who attended were Sir Austen Chamberlain, Sir Patrick Hannon Mr Smedley Crooke Mr E W Salt, Mr L S Amery and Wing Commander Wright They were accompanied by one of the members of Parliament for Croydon Mr H G Williams, and the Mayor and Town Clerk of Croydon

The scene in the foundry was impressive as the molten metal came out in a steady stream from the furnaces around which men were busy in the smoke taking precautions that it should not be spilt from the ladle, a giant affair able to hold all the metal necessary for four bells of good size

After the ladle had been filled it was raised on a travelling gantry and carried into position for filling each of the moulds Before the recasting the Birmingham M P s were taken round the foundry to inspect the work that is being carried out in preparation for the Coronation

There were bells for churches in various parts of the country and important contracts for abroad A large peal destined to hang in the tower of Gizeh University, Egypt was struck so that its great booming tones filled the shop

Another interesting peal was a miniature set of five bells for a private estate in Scotland and on this specially arranged chimes were struck by a demonstrator

On No 10 bell there will be the inscription "These bells were recast for the Coronation of King George VI, chiefly through the generosity of Sir Charles Hyde"

The peal, when recast, will weigh 6¼ tons as before and the tenor bell will be 31cwt compared with 29cwt before The frames will weigh ten tons and the fittings four tons

The great frames on which the bells are to hang have already been cast and were pointed out to the visitors They are of metal and will replace the old wooden frames which were in as poor condition as the old bells of St Philip's

ATHERSTONE-ON-STOUR 2nd (Gloucester Foundry).

THE SKIES.

yal Air Force and the Army is in the delivery
. Experiments were recently witnessed in
ice Corps. Supplies are contained in metal
parachutes. The whole is fixed to the under-
'plane). They fly over the troops and drop
linders.

PHYSICAL TRAINING.

MINISTER EXPLAINS NEW SCHEME.

LORD ABERDARE'S POST.

ATHERSTONE-ON-STOUR 2ND AND 1ST (GLOUCESTER FOUNDRY).

1—10. R. HENDLEY OF GLOUCESTER. 11. MORTON BAGOT, ETC.
12—24. ASTON CANTLOW, ETC. (WORCESTER FOUNDRY).

PLATE VI.

1—5. MORTON BAGOT (Nicholas Grene?). 6, 7. GREAT PACKINGTON SANCTUS.

1, 2. MONK'S KIRBY. 3, 5—9. LAPWORTH. 4. MORTON BAGOT.

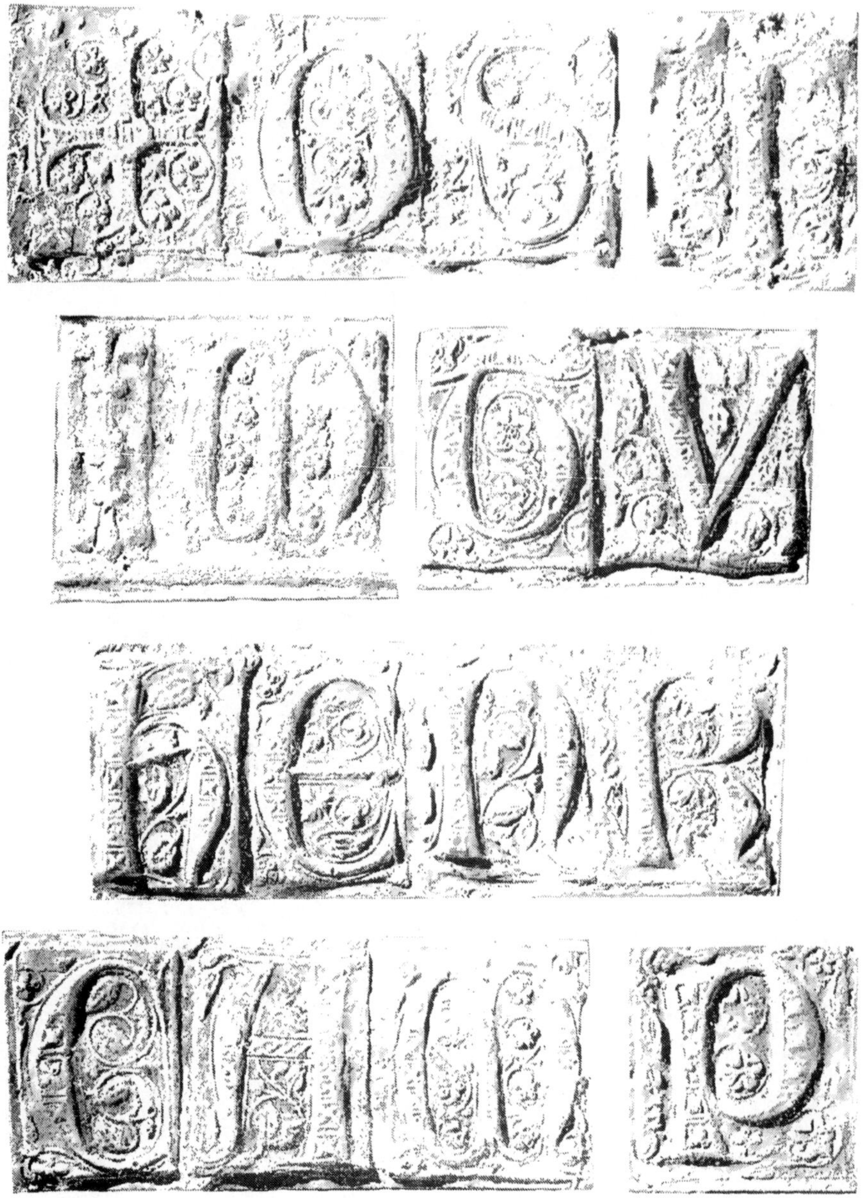

1—5. MANCETTER. 6—8. STOKE AND CORLEY (J. de Colsale).

PLATE X.

1. WOLVEY (J. de Yorke). 2, 3, 7. STONELEIGH (Nottingham Foundry).

1—14. CROSSES AND LETTERING USED BY THE STURDYS OF LONDON (1430-1450).

15—17. STAMPS OF HENRY JORDAN OF LONDON (1450-1470).

BRAILES. Old Tenor by John Bird of London (about 1420)

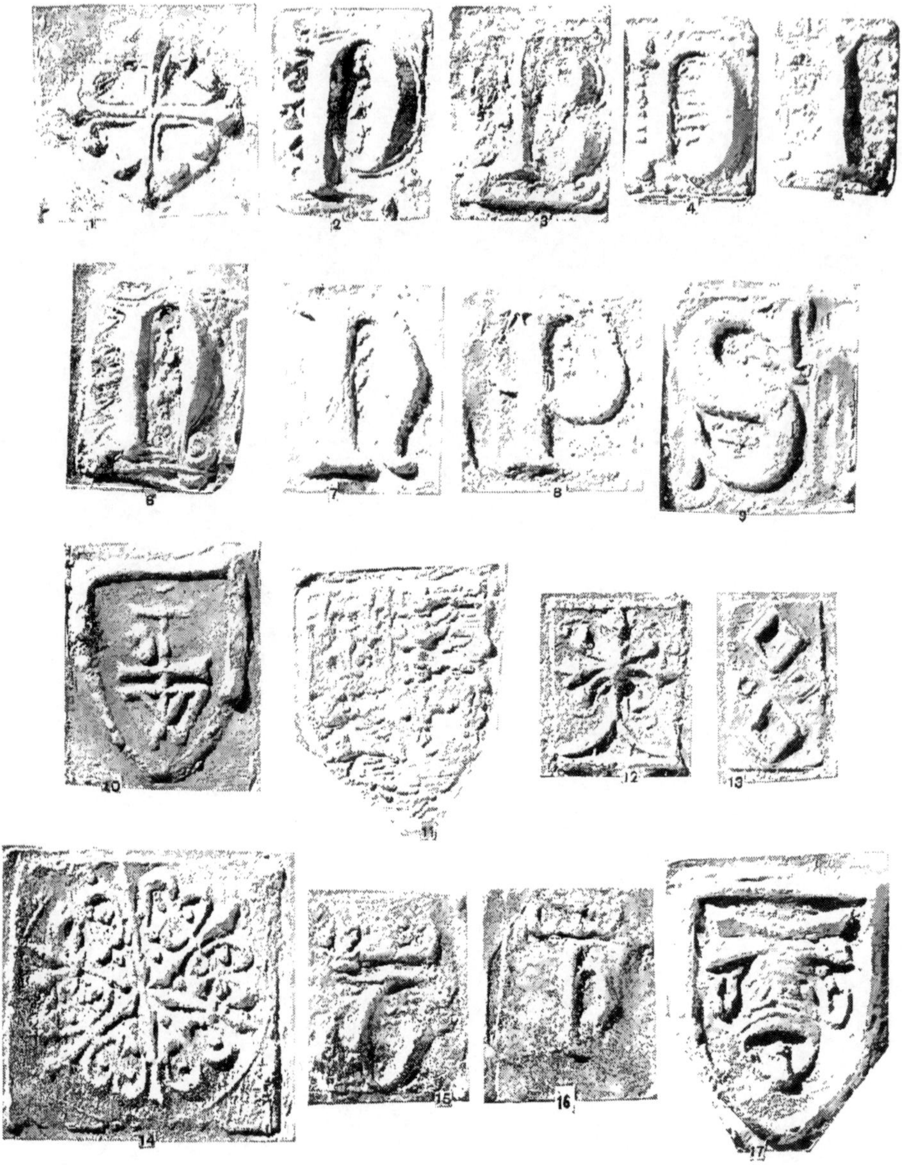

1—17. STAMPS OF LONDON FIFTEENTH CENTURY FOUNDERS.

PLATE XV

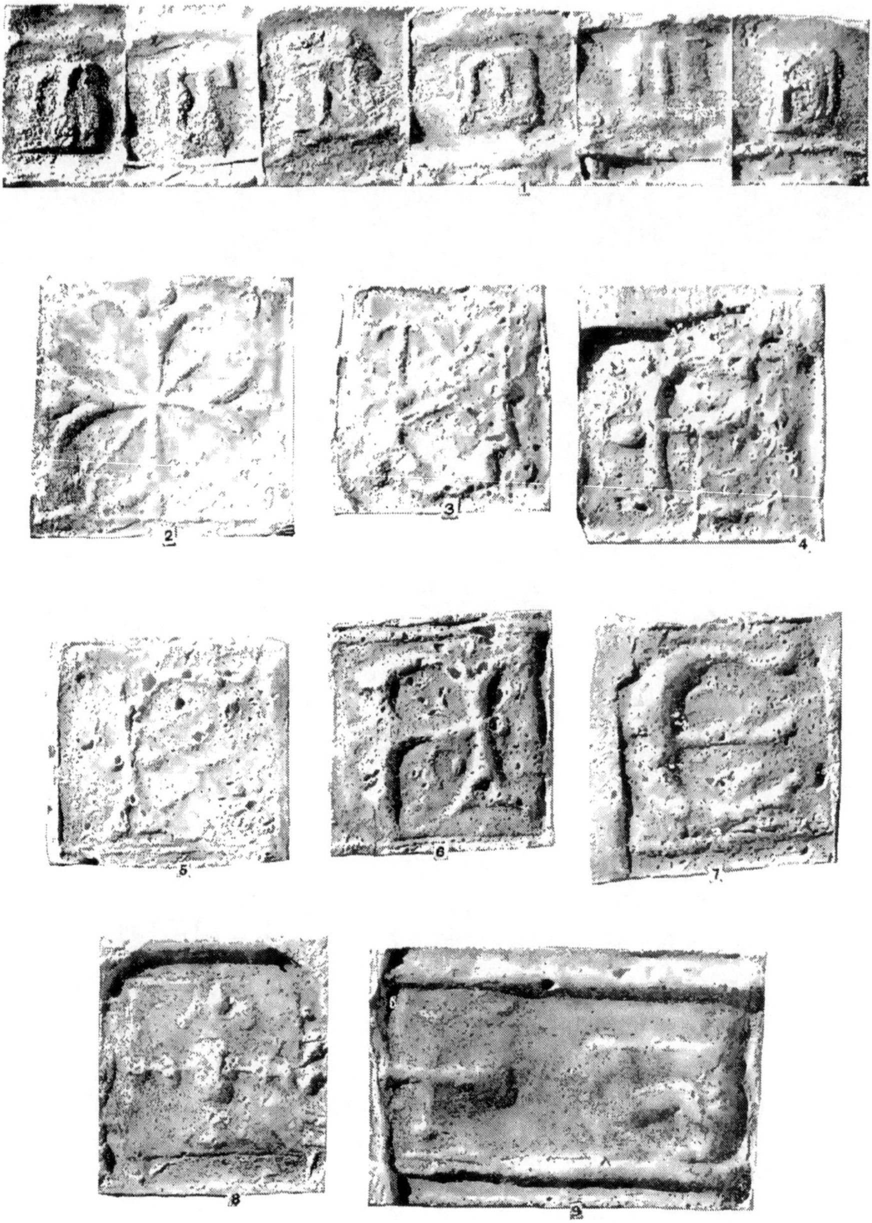

[illegible] USED BY THE NEWCOMBES OF LEICESTER (1560-1610)

1. FENNY COMPTON (Appowell?). 2, 3. NEWCOMBE STAMPS (Berkswell).
4, 5. BUTLER'S MARSTON (Newcombe). 6—9. HUGH WATTS OF LEICESTER.

STAMPS USED BY THOMAS HANCOX OF WALSALL (1622-1640).

ORNAMENTAL BORDERS USED BY THOMAS HANCOX AND OTHERS (17TH CENTURY).

1—8, 10. STAMPS OF JOHN MARTIN OF WORCESTER (1641-1693).

9, 11—13. STAMPS OF WILLIAM CLIBURY OF WELLINGTON (1605-1641).

1–4. THE OLDFIELDS OF NOTTINGHAM (17TH CENT.). 5. TOBIE NORRIS OF STAMFORD.
6–11. THE BAGLEYS OF CHACOMB (1630–1709).

1, 2. JOSEPH SMITH OF EDGBASTON (1700-1730). 3, 9. RICHARD SANDERS OF BROMSGROVE (1760-1
4, 6, 7. BRIANT OF HERTFORD. 5, 8. RICHARD KEENE OF WOODSTOCK.
10. COAT OF ARMS AT HENLEY-IN-ARDEN

THE GODS OF ALDBOURNE ([illegible])

PLATE XXV.

THE CORS OF ALDBOURNE (Sutton-under-Brailes).

PLATE XXVI.

THE CORS OF ALDBOURNE (Sutton under Brailes).

Milton Keynes UK
Ingram Content Group UK Ltd.
UKHW020849041024
449263UK00009B/479

9 781017 041439